D1593649

The Cameroon Federation

The Cameroon Federation

Political Integration in a Fragmentary Society

By Willard R. Johnson

Princeton University Press
Princeton, New Jersey
1970

Publication of this book has been aided by the Whitney Darrow Publication Reserve Fund of Princeton University Press.

This book has been composed in Linofilm Times Roman

Printed in the United States of America

by Vail-Ballou Press, Binghamton, New York

Contents

Foreword

THIS BOOK presents a study of political integration. It centers on a single but exceptionally instructive example, the experience of the Federal Republic of Cameroon. Though it is a study of a single case, the case involved provides us with issues that are relevant to all of Africa, indeed, to most of the new states of the world. This set of issues acquires its widespread relevance from the ubiquitous process with which it is closely associated—the modernization of societies and their political systems. In Africa the issues also derive from the profound challenges of its history of cultural impingement and clash.

Worlds do collide in Africa. The interpenetration of so many different foreign cultures with so many varying indigenous ones makes culture clash a problem for every new African state. The problem is intensified by the rise of an incipient, modern, urban culture which penetrates the hinterland and fragments the traditional societies at their base. Culture complexes, which elsewhere and erstwhile were separate and complete, cleave in the African context of transplantation and competition, and they scatter bits and pieces all about in a kaleidoscopic mélange. This process changes villagers into big city dwellers, who then become the modern urban poor; the children of nonreading folk become *docteurs en science,* or *fonctionnaires,* or simply opinionated boors. The African family has become a kind of cultural crossroads: some of its members have adopted Christianity, while others profess Islam; sons may auto to offices while a sister wants for shoes; the children may laugh incredulously at their conversing elders; brothers may become strangers to each other as they return from their foreign studies, one from Kiev and the other from Kalamazoo.

Every African society is now confronted with a severe problem of cultural and political integration. Cameroon is not alone; indeed, it is a microcosm of almost all of new Africa precisely in this respect. Like all leaders of new states, those of Cameroon must find ways to control if not eliminate ethnic rivalry, regionalism, religious competition, status and even class conflict, and the disruptions occasioned by starkly uneven rates and levels of social mobilization and modernization. Cameroon stands apart, however, inasmuch as, to the myriad other internal discontinuities just mentioned, it adds one between British and French colonial legacies. Much of the interest in the integration problems and progress of Cameroon stems from this fact. Perhaps part of the interest derives from the probably false assumption that it is just as difficult to build a political community made up of Englishmen and Frenchmen who are black as it is to build one among those who are white. Interest also comes from the fact that Cameroon has, for the first six years of its life as a bilingual, multicultural federation, achieved steady progress in this direction, while many other African states, even unitary states with single colonial legacies, have barely held together if not actually lost ground to centrifugal forces.

Cameroon has been a meeting ground of diverse cultures throughout recorded history. Its more than 150 distinct peoples make it one of the most pluralistic of indigenous African societies. All the European influences Africa has known have affected these traditional cultures, some of them profoundly. Portuguese, Spanish, and Dutch trading companies operated important stations in the area 250 years before the missionaries set up permanent posts in the mid-19th century. The only previous experience these peoples had had with common political rule was that provided by the Germans which began in 1884 and lasted until French and British military forces began to drive the Germans out in 1914. The old German colony of Kamerun was later divided between the invaders along a line running roughly from the outskirts of Douala northeast to the Lake Chad basin. This line was the border of effective military occupation achieved by the two armies. France and Britain gained international recognition of authority over their respective portions of Kamerun when the territories were formally taken from German jurisdiction by the provisions of the Treaty of Versailles in 1919 and made a part of the mandate system of the League of Nations. As Class C mandates, the two territories were subject to minimal League supervision, but later, when they were made part of the trusteeship system of the United Nations, international supervision became more effective. The promise of "self-government or independence . . . [according to] the freely expressed wishes of the peoples concerned" contained in Article 76b of the UN Charter provided the basis for nationalist claims in Cameroon, which were advanced in terms of a strategy of achieving "reunification," that is, the restoration of the political unity which the Kamerun colony represented. After a campaign of nearly 15 years, these claims led the UN to conduct a plebiscite in British Cameroons which offered the choice of achieving independence and a termination of trusteeship status through union with the then independent Federation of Nigeria, with which it had been administered throughout the trusteeship and mandate periods, or union with the then independent Republic of Cameroun, formerly administered by France. It

viii

was as a result of the plebiscite vote, which those in the northern part of the Territory cast differently from those in the Southern Cameroons, that the Federation came into being. Northern British Cameroons was incorporated into the Northern Region of Nigeria as Sardauna Province through a plebiscite. This book is concerned only with the union of the two Territories that retained the name Cameroon—West Cameroon, the former British-ruled Territory, and East Cameroon, formerly under French rule. At the time of union, West Cameroon accounted for about nine percent of the total land area and twenty percent of the population of the new Federation.

In order to appreciate fully the nature and meaning of the Cameroon experience, it is necessary to go into some detail about the general theoretical literature on the processes of political union and integration, along with the details of the Cameroon situation. Readers interested in the theoretical aspects of the subject may not be interested in the in-depth analysis of the Cameroon experience. I hope the reader will bear with me throughout. However, for those whose principal concern is for the more general processes involved, Part I on the theoretical considerations, and Part III on the nature and extent of the integrative advances achieved in Cameroon are the most relevant. Those interested in Cameroon in particular, and the patterns of African politics, will find Part II on the background of the creation of the Federation essential reading, while Part I may be of marginal interest. I attempt to unite the entire analysis in the Conclusions.

Acknowledgments

I GRATEFULLY acknowledge the assistance of the many Cameroonians, from both states, in America, Africa, and Europe who so willingly and conscientiously helped me assemble the information for this book. I hope it is worthy of their efforts in my behalf and of their prodigious efforts to advance their country and all of Africa. I take full responsibility for any errors of fact or distortions of interpretation that may be found.

I am especially grateful to the Foreign Area Training Fellowship Program which provided most of the funds necessary to carry out the research for this book. I also wish to thank the M.I.T. Center for International Studies for the assistance given me in gathering additional materials in the field and in having the manuscript typed and index prepared.

My book could not have been brought to completion without the understanding support and active assistance of Vivian R. Johnson, who still remains the same cheerful, wise, and adventurous woman I married— evidence of a most remarkable strength of character.

W.R.J.

The Cameroon Federation

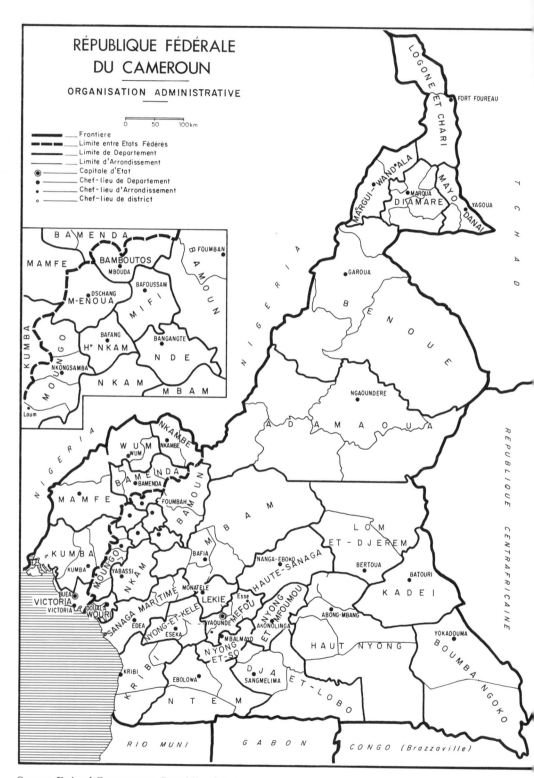

RÉPUBLIQUE FÉDÉRALE DU CAMEROUN

ORGANISATION ADMINISTRATIVE

0   50   100km

Frontiere
Limite entre Etats Fédérés
Limite de Departement
Limite d'Arrondissement
Capitale d'Etat
Chef-lieu de Departement
Chef-lieu d'Arrondissement
Chef-lieu de district

LOGONE ET CHARI
FORT FOUREAU
MARGUI-WANDALA
MAYO DANAI
DIAMARE
MAROUA
YAGOUA
T C H A D

BAMENDA
MAMFE
BAMBOUTOS
MBOUDA
B. FOUMBAN
DSCHANG
BAFOUSSAM
M-ENOUA
MIFI
BAMOUN
KUMBA
MOUNGO
BAFANG
H\t NKAM
BANGANGTE
NKONGSAMBA
NDE
NKAM
MBAM
Loum

GAROUA
B E N O U E
NIGERIA

NKAMBE
NKAMBE
WUM
WUM
ADAMAOUA
NGAOUNDERE

BAMENDA
BAMENDA
NIGERIA
MAMFE
FOUMBAH
BAMOUN
MBAM
LOM ET-DJEREM
BERTOUA
BATOURI
KADEI

KUMBA
KUMBA
MOUNGO
YABASSI
NANGA-EBOKO
HAUTE-SANAGA
ABONG-MBANG
YOKADOUMA
BOUMBA NGOKO

VICTORIA
BUEA
DOUALA
WOURI
VICTORIA
SANAGA MARITIME
MONATELE
LEKIE
Esse
NYONG ET MFOUMOU
HAUT NYONG
REPUBLIQUE CENTRAFRICAINE

EDEA
NYONG-ET-KELE
YAOUNDE
MEFOU
AKONOLINGA
ESEKA
MBALMAYO
NYONG ET-SO
KRIBI
DJA ET-LOBO
SANGMELIMA
EBOLOWA
N T E M

RIO MUNI   G A B O N   CONGO (Brazzaville)

Source: Federal Government, Republic of Cameroon

PART I

Theoretical Considerations

THE WAYS in which separate political systems come together are some-times the same as those that keep them together, and sometimes they are quite different. The process of political integration involves both types of unity. Mixed into this process of political integration are many distinct but related activities, involving many related ideas for the analyst: the idea of system itself, the peculiar features of political systems, the forms of unity and the idea of identity—the pursuit of which usually motivates the quest for unity. Because the coming together of separate things obviously involves change, theories about integration and systems must also relate to the processes of political change generally. A consideration of these issues will permit us to derive more meaning from the subsequent analy-sis of the experience of Cameroonians with political integration.

1

Integrating Political Systems

NATIONALISM and the independence it has won for the new African states has not and cannot satisfy their quest for modernization. Independence has revealed more clearly than anything else the extensive range of aspirations and values that lie beyond nationalism as part of the ideology of modernization.[1] The basic motives remained the same—a desire for self-government, improved material well-being, and greater individual and collective efficacy. But the programmatic themes which supported them have changed. Economic themes have become more important, and with the failure to achieve significant progress in the economic sphere, a concern with achieving order and stability, perhaps for their own sake, has come to preoccupy the leadership.[2]

What were and are the obstacles to achieving modernizing objectives after independence? I cannot examine here the whole range of relevant factors; I wish to concentrate on the most fundamental, the problem of fragmentation in the society—the internal divisions and discontinuities that existed and were being created in the African societies—which generates exceptional problems of integration.

Africa is the continent of diversity par excellence. It has more languages and perhaps less "communication" than any continent; it has

---

[1] Essentially the process of social modernization is the creation of a science-based, infused culture, having an impact on every aspect of society, from the political to the psychological. Through this process, the society and the individuals and groups that make it up are reorganized and reoriented to control and initiate changes within the society and its environment more efficiently. The changes occurring within and being pressed on the modernizing societies stem from many sources: an accelerated accumulation of knowledge, technology, and instrumentation, basically, the impact of which is amplified and diffused through expanding communications patterns and facilities; the imperial expansion of economic and political power; increased physical and social mobility throughout the world; and ideological and psychological clashes. As a conscious policy, modernization is an effort to organize and coordinate the behavior of people, that is, to control them in order to achieve greater and more efficient productivity, higher levels of economic output and welfare, greater security, and a fuller measure of equality in the distribution of knowledge, power, and wealth.

[2] One of the most helpful discussions of the concern with order and the creation of single-party systems and their fusion with the state apparatus into a party-state, is presented by Aristide Zolberg in his *Creating Political Order, The Party-States of West Africa* (Chicago: Rand McNally, 1966).

4

some of the world's densest and most verdant forests and its largest and driest deserts; it harbors some of the world's richest resources and its poorest people, some of its oldest polities and most of its newest. Mere diversity is not Africa's special problem, however. Most states throughout the world harbor disparate ethnic, racial, religious, or other social groups. Nor are sharp class divisions peculiar or even very important in Africa, though its new states contain elite-mass gaps as severe as are to be found anywhere. Many countries, including the United States, wrestle with the difficult problem of creating or permitting a sense of being "in" among all important social groups in the system. Africa's problem of modernization goes beyond the need for nation-building. Not only are the societies of the new African states divided and fragmented in many respects but the divisions tend to reinforce each other.

The lines of tribal, ethnic, regional, and even religious disparities tend to coincide with those of wealth, patterns of social evolution, welfare benefits, and political power. Disparities, tensions, and conflict arising from differences in values and patterns of identity enhance those that arise from the differences between more hardcore economic and political interests. More thoroughgoing Westernization, earlier education, more turbulent and uprooting Christian impingement, denser urban settlement, greater industrialization, more lucrative and expansive cash crop agriculture—all work together to set certain peoples apart in the new African states. Within each of them there are the "up-country cousins" who most often are less well educated, closer to traditional values (often with a richer and more continuous political and religious history), poorer, but, in the modern democratic age, conveniently more numerous. The haughty disdain displayed for them by the *evolués,* the "black Englishmen," the "been-to's," and the racial firsts still piques the memory of many of these unprivileged folk. As the unprivileged also emerge into power, however, or become aware of the possibilities of doing so, they put the universalist and equalitarian tenets of the nationalist and modernizationist credo to their most severe tests. Where national resources are as scarce as they are in Africa, and where avenues of social and economic mobility are so limited, one seldom finds any pervasive sense of equity and munificence.

Thus in the Nigerian Federation not only were the regionally based dominant national groups different in culture and patterns of identification, they were different in the extent of their social evolution toward Western forms, in the levels of their experience with modern science and technology and Western styles of education, and most importantly, in

5

wealth.[3] Similarly, in countries such as Sierra Leone and the Ivory Coast, distinctive tribal groups and cultural regions are differentiated by levels of economic development and patterns of social change and mobilization as well.[4] In Cameroon and many other new states of Africa, the fact that there are rich tribes and poor tribes is certainly as important as the fact that there are many tribes.

Confronted with the realities of this kind of fragmented society— with severely disparate levels and rates of development, and severe competition among the groups within the society for any available increments—tactical elements of the modernization effort such as a demand for sacrifice, discipline, organizational unity, and order came to be elevated to dogmas; as such, they served as ideological rationalizations of the authoritarian party-state. The fact that the rationalizations were created by the few who dominate the political systems and that they therefore often provoked dissent among those who are excluded or made the victims of harsh rule should not obscure the fact that they stemmed from an ideology that was widely shared. In Cameroon, as throughout the newly independent countries of Africa, political factions at the center or on the margins of the power system all pressed for rapid economic growth, wanted most of it in their own areas, distrusted others, and expected to be distrusted in terms of their willingness to cut the cake of wealth evenly. They all believed in unity and a certain amount of discipline, but they also believed the costs of this unity and discipline would be less under their own leadership than under anyone else's. Thus it is not at all evident that those who provided the greatest push in moving the African countries toward the commonly held objectives of the independence campaign (and in Cameroon, of the reunification campaign) would be able, through the same orientation and approach, to move them most effectively toward the achievement of the objectives of economic and political development.

[3] For an understanding of the character and evolution of the Nigerian political system and society, see James S. Coleman, *Nigeria: Background to Nationalism* (Berkeley: University of California Press, 1958); and David Schwartz, *Nigeria: The Tribe, the Nation or the Race* (Cambridge: M.I.T. Press, 1966). For an analysis of the internal disparities contributing to the disintegration of the system see my "Political Disintegration, Political Instability and U.S. Policy Towards Africa," presented to the Center for International Systems Research Symposium on Great World Issues of the Next Decade, May 1966.

[4] For excellent analyses of these factors in the Ivory Coast see Aristide Zolberg, *One-Party Government in the Ivory Coast* (Princeton: Princeton University Press, 1964); and for Sierra Leone, Martin L. Kilson, *Political Change in a West African State* (Cambridge: Harvard University Press, 1966).

Having noted these factors, I may ask: "What then is Africa, with its many Presidents, Prime Ministers, and Kings?" Is it like so many toy soldiers wound up and standing in a row, united solely by the surety of their eventual mutual collision and upending, rather than by the cadence and direction of their march? Is Africa really an awakened giant, perhaps still an ungainly titan, which will pull itself together and take its rightful place among the world's movers and shakers? Or will it remain inchoate in its sense of self-awareness, disparate in its motives, and disjointed in its movement? To answer such questions we must know what is real about the identity of Africa, what is real about its many and diverse parts. We need to know the source and significance of its unities. To know this we need to know the forms and sources of social unity, i.e. what is real about identity.

CREATING THE ONE FROM THE MANY

Identity is a matter of the significance of a thing, a question of purpose and perspective. The achievement of a sense of identity is most significant when it involves acquiring a sense of oneness from many separate distinct events or objects, when it is a question of parts and wholes. In this case it is a product of synergism, in the sense that the meaning of the parts does not give the meaning of the whole, for there inheres in the whole a quality not to be found in the separate parts. Most people can easily understand identities born of homogeneity, or the complete fusion of separate parts. We accept water as something unto itself that hydrogen and oxygen are not when considered apart. We do not search the glass for the visible properties of the sand. Complex identities are more difficult, for things are not always what they seem: "Stone walls do not a prison make, / Nor iron bars a cage." The cloud to one who views it from afar is only so many droplets of water to one immersed in it. Which is the real thing, the aggregation of droplets or the singular cloud? Are the properties of the group any less real than those of its individual components? The concept any less real than the object that manifests it?

Identities born of mere juxtaposition often resist the imagination. Juxtaposition is seldom enough, if it is only a matter of proximity, to generate a coherent and distinctive meaning. Crowds and mobs look different, though some people—the police with increasing frequency—are prone to see a mob in every crowd of people they dislike or fear. Very few people see anything more to sardines in a can, though for those few who do they become a Harlem Steak. Much larger is the group of people who can find something singular in sugar on grapefruit, salt on watermelon, oil on

7

vinegar. These identities preserve the distinctions of the separate parts but add something new in combination.

It can readily be appreciated that complex new identities arise from the integration of separate elements. Integration is a process of interaction of things or events which permits the appreciation of a unique consequence of the interaction, an appreciation that could not be attained through a study of the properties of the separate parts. To study integration one must study not only the character of the parts, but especially the relations between them and the total effect they produce. We can appreciate neither the properties nor the character of a nation, its identity, from knowledge of the individuals in it, nor can we derive it except through a study of the behavior of these individuals. Only as we appreciate the interdependency of their actions and especially of their political loyalties can we identify the nation. And only by bringing the actions of its people into interdependent relationships can the nation come into being.

Dependent relationships between a definite set of actions constitute a system. System is simply a way of conceptualizing the interaction of things. This can be one-way or two-way interaction. If the latter, there is interdependency, a more highly integrated state than dependency, because feedback and thus the potential for coordination is involved. In addition to the idea of interdependency, system includes that of a determinate (a limited and predictable) set of actors, thus the idea of a boundary and an environment. In the real sense a boundary does not exist in a system. We mean by this only that the pattern of interaction is persistent enough to permit a determination of what is within and what is without this pattern. The relationship between the two is what the boundary is, and what is without the pattern of interdependent action is the environment. For all practical purposes we may describe this relationship as a property of the system itself.

Since the idea of system refers, among other things, to the property of interdependency between actors, it refers to integration. Integration may thus be said to be a condition, a property of systems. All interdependent relationships are integrated ones. This is nothing more than saying that the relationship is a deterministic one.

Because the essential feature of system is interdependency, all systems are deterministic at some level, though this determinism may derive from "probabilistic-based" patterns of action. Systems differ with respect to their relations to the environment, however. Some are "closed" or autonomous so that the environment produces no change in the internal pattern of interaction of the system. Others may be "open," so that they interact with the environment. The latter may be said to have incomplete or intermittent boundaries. The environment may cause changes in the internal patterns of the system, or, in other words, may contribute inputs to the system. Where such changes are persistent and patterned, however, so that once known their continuing effects may be predicted, the idea of the determinism of the system is preserved. The system may be momentarily affected by the environment and soon adjust itself to restore the old order, or it may adapt itself to a change in the environment by effecting a new and persisting order, or it may undergo continuous but patterned change and become dynamic. In each case, however, order and pattern remain; interdependency, determinism, and thus integration continue to pertain. Talcott Parsons takes this view of integration when he defines it as "the conditions of internal stability or a relational system shared by actor and object." [5] Nevertheless, systems that are in the "open mode" may experience recurring and variant disruptions from the environment, so that it becomes impossible to predict future patterns or states of the system. Thus it is useful to speak of a "deterministic system" where its future states, in the words of Ernest Nagel, "are *uniquely* determined by its state at some previous time." [6]

In durable deterministic systems, integration is a condition. But integration is also a process. It is of considerable importance in social analysis that integration can be considered both a condition and a process. Were it merely a condition, which either does or does not exist, there would be little value in the present or any other prolonged discussion of this idea with respect to social situations—for two reasons. First, in social relations there are no interactions that are strictly deterministic. Thus, strictly speaking, we would have to say that there are no social systems. Second, even if social systems did exist, strictly defined, integration studies would concern themselves only with the task of noting their presence or absence. In terms of political integration, for example, there would be only two categories of polities—identifiable and unidentifiable. One category remains intact long enough to exhibit a pattern of political life, and one does not. There would be no room for comparison and characterization of polities. There would be little utility in such an approach, since all identifiable polities would look alike according to these

---

[5] Parsons, "The Pattern Variables Revisited," *American Sociological Review* (1960), p. 467.

[6] Nagel, *Logic Without Metaphysics* (New York: Macmillan–Free Press, 1956), p. 248.

criteria, and it would be an enterprise futile in the extreme to look for the unidentifiable ones.

What constitutes the logical basis for considering integration to be a process as well as a condition is the fact that the concept of system arises from action.[7] The concept of system cannot relate to a static situation. Systems exist neither physically nor only momentarily; what exists is a set of *related* actors. Time and change are prerequisites to their interaction.[8] Repeated or persistently determined interaction has order or pattern, and it is this order that permits one to *conceive of* the relations between the actors in question as systemic. System is thus a way of conceptualizing patterned movement. System refers to process, since process is action or change directed toward a particular result. Patterned movement, determinate movement, has direction of this sort. If one act truly determines the next, there is a "built-in" limitation to its consequences; we may thus impute to it a goal, an end toward which action proceeds.

The particular ends toward which the change or movement proceeds may be multi-faceted however, and the patterns may not be absolutely clear. According to Philip Jacobs and Henry Teune, "it might be more useful to envisage a set of relationships which are more or less integrated, or a progression of events leading to an increase or a decrease of integration."[9] I have said that determinate movement proceeds toward a particular end, or "goal." Rather than discard the notion of social system,

[7] A "system" describes behavior. Although it is true that from certain theoretical points of view, each variable in an arbitrary system may be represented by zero degree of quantity or activity, and thus the system may appear inoperative, the very concept of system demands that we preserve the notion of behavior in systems. All systems behave. Where all activity or position is represented in zero degree, we must either consider that the system has disintegrated (died) or is a dormant subsystem of some larger system in which activity or location continues. See W. Ross Ashby, *Design for a Brain,* pp. 18ff; and Paul Berman, "Systems Theory and Political Development," Social Science Research Council paper, typescript, September 1967, M.I.T. Center for International Studies archives.

I reject Berman's argument that systems do not die, that they merely become "inoperable." His paper presents an adequate basis for rejecting this notion. His caveat, derived from Ashby, is useful, however, in that momentarily inoperative systems may well be reanimated by new inputs which change the value of the variables. Such systems should be distinguished from "inoperable" ones, which, I believe, are better referred to as dead, or ex-systems.

[8] Thus a certain amount of durability is also a quality of system. It is usually more convenient to treat time as external to the system. Ashby, Chap. 2.

[9] Philip Jacob and Henry Teune, "The Integrative Process: Guidelines for Analysis of the Bases of Political Community," in Jacob, Teune, and J. V. Toscano, *The Integration of Political Communities* (Philadelphia: Lippincott, 1964), p. 7.

which might require more determinism and singularity of goals than social action ever exhibits, it is useful to consider social system (or integration, as an attribute of system) as being a tendency in various kinds of social situations. To the extent that social interaction becomes determinate, or leads to precisely predictable outcomes, it can be said that this set of social interactions becomes more systemic. The process of political integration would thus rightly be considered the process whereby political interaction becomes more systemic.

This discussion suggests that the problem facing the leadership of the new states is largely to create a political system, to make political life more predictable by organizing it into a pattern with the properties of system. Thus, too, much of the task of analyzing integration is simply to determine if systemic qualities exist in the patterns of political life. But the problem of creating and analyzing integrating political systems is more complicated than this. Important though the ability to create or identify systematic patterns of political life may be, it is even more important to be able to predict their behavior or viability, or to know something about their character and how it may differ from the character of other political systems, what the consequences of the differences may be, and what the sequential pattern of development within such systems are.

Some things about systems that become important to this kind of analysis—in addition to the fact that the system indeed exists—concern the state of the system at any given time, the likely pattern of change under given conditions, the range of variation that is in keeping with the basic character of the system (its field), what the internal changes would be in the system to certain changes in the parameters, and under what conditions and in what manner the system changes its field, its basic character, and becomes a different system.[10]

---

[10] An excellent exposition on the range of considerations of importance in analyzing system behavior is in Ashby's *Design for a Brain,* Chaps. 1–5. The terms used here merit brief definition: *State* of the system refers to the specific values which the variables (action range) have at a given moment of time. All systems may be described in a table of measurements of the variables which make up the system (the specific variables in question are always selected aspects of action in the real world). In every system the states may change to some extent and yet preserve the pattern of interaction. Representation of a succession of behaviors (i.e. changes of state over time), together with the time intervals, constitutes a "line of behavior" and all the lines of behavior the system may assume within a fixed and unchanging environment constitutes its *field;* it is the system's typical way of behaving. Of course, we are not really concerned with all the variables contained in the environment, but rather only those we may truly call *parameters*—variables not part of the system, which nevertheless may affect the system.

The Mechanisms of Integration

I am suggesting that integration is an overall effect of the interaction of separate things—the effect of system, or of interdependency in these interactions and the process whereby interaction becomes more systemic. If the concept of integration is singular, however, the ways in which it can be achieved are multiple. This is often a source of confusion, because the various and variable mechanisms by which political or social integration might be achieved are sometimes considered as representing the whole of the process itself. Deutsch, Jacob, Levine, North, Weiner, and Zolberg have summarized most of these mechanisms.[11]

Weiner's compilation of definitions of political integration in general covers the work of the other scholars. He suggests that the concept is defined in five ways in the literature: (1) the creation of a sense of territorial nationality which overshadows, or eliminates, subordinate parochial loyalties; (2) the establishment of national central authority over subordinate political units; (3) the linking of government with the governed, or overcoming "elite-mass gaps"; (4) the creation of a minimum value consensus necessary to maintain a social order; (5) expansion of the capacity of a people for concerted action. As do many other students of the process, Weiner concludes that each view of the integration process merely reflects some form of an integration problem or crisis a society might confront. They actually refer to the dimensions of the process or the mechanisms which might be involved. The most appropriate single definition of integration, he suggests, is, "what it is which holds a society and a political system together . . . at a level commensurate with what their political leadership needs to carry out their goals." Weiner and several others call the quality of holding together, *cohesiveness*.[12] I wish to emphasize the

[11] K. Deutsch, in a number of works, the most important of which are *The Nerves of Government* (Free Press of Glencoe, 1963); and *Nationalism and Social Communication* (Cambridge: MIT Press, 1953); Jacob et al., *Integration* (Deutsch and W.L.C. Wheaton also contribute to this work); Donald Levine, "Cultural Integration," a draft article for the *International Encyclopedia of the Social Sciences* (forthcoming); and Myron Weiner, "Political Integration and Political Development," *The Annals of the American Academy of Political and Social Science* (Philadelphia, March 1965). See also R. C. North, H. E. Koch, Jr., and D. A. Zinnes, "The Integrative Functions of Conflict," *The Journal of Conflict Resolution* (September 1960), 354–74.

[12] Another student is Roger Williams, *American Society: A Sociological Interpretation* (New York: Knopf, 1960), who discusses the concept of cohesiveness as social interaction without a disabling degree of overt conflict, regardless of the condition on which this state of affairs may depend. For Williams integration is a more

12

singularity of this concept as an overall effect, or consequence, of interaction; but I prefer the term *interdependency* because it permits easier conceptualization in terms of system, and highlights the existence of interaction. Also, the term more readily suggests the possible variations in degrees of integration than does *cohesiveness* (which might imply that a polity either stays together or falls apart).

Jacob and Teune construct a list of 10 factors that seem, on the basis of evidence from previous research, to exert an integrative influence on people; the factors represent the various mechanisms a society may use to achieve higher levels of integration, and as such constitute the main variables one must measure in an analysis of the process of political integration.[13]

A careful consideration of the various definitions suggested by Weiner, or the 10 variables suggested by Jacob, Teune, Deutsch, and others, can be placed along one or the other of two spectra of variations in political action, or lines of behavior of a political system—one a quantitative and the other a qualitative line.[14] The quantitative line denotes variation between conjunctive and disjunctive political action; that is, it concerns the degree of connectiveness in political action. The qualitative line has to do with the amount of mutuality in the consequences of political action, and denotes variation from full complementarity on the positive side, through mere compatibility or neutrality to incompatibility or conflict on the negative side. Let us consider each type of political action.

exacting condition, going beyond causal regularity or coordination to include common value-orientations. This is measured by the degree to which conformity is voluntary (and conscious). Claude Ake shares this view in his *A Theory of Political Integration* (Holmwood, Ill.: Dorsey Press, 1967), p. 4. I use the term *integration* as Williams does that of cohesiveness, and reject his insistence on defining integration in the narrower sense of common values.

[13] The 10 factors are: (1) the proximity of the people; (2) their cultural and social homogeneity; (3) the nature and number of transactions among them; (4) their mutual knowledge; (5) the convergence of functional interests; (6) the basic collective character of the community or communities involved; (7) the political structure of the society; (8) the sovereignty-dependency status of the community; (9) the effectiveness of governmental institutions; (10) the previous integrative experience of the people. Jacob and Toscano, *Integration,* pp. 13–14.

[14] I am restricting myself to political activity, and excluding proclivities or motivational predispositions because political systems are systems of action. The subjective aspects are not unimportant, however, and cannot be ignored by political leaders who desire to achieve greater integration. Subjective factors are much harder to identify, assess, and evaluate than behavioral ones, and over time are subsumed by the behavioral factors (if they become relevant). With enough data I could analyze the subjective problems in the same way I do the objective ones.

13

COMPLEMENTARY POLITICAL ACTION

Complementary political actions are mutually supportive in their effects. Such action represents positive interdependency, and as such is the clearest example and most effective mechanism of political integration.[15] But it is important to realize that it is not the only mechanism. Many students of integration erroneously equate integration with the growth of shared values or "devotion to the claims of the state." [16] My contention here is that complementary actions are but one type of integrative action. They are by definition integrated, but the converse of the proposition is not necessarily true.

To be sure, one central aspect of the integration process is consensus formation. By this, I mean the progressive emergence of a core of values and attitudes held in common by all members of the society, or more practically, among the most important (powerful) individuals and groups within the society. The idea of core values and attitudes is important, for I do not mean to suggest that integration depends on achieving unanimity on every idea, attitude, belief, and value held by members of a society. I am concerned with those values and beliefs that determine one's general outlook, that set the range or limits to the variations tolerated in secondary values and beliefs. For example, a general value that legitimizes the assertion of individual desires against the group may permit a society of patriots to tolerate a pacifist though the country is engaged in a war. Consensus is sometimes erroneously conceived as requiring something approaching unanimity, or agreement on proximate objectives, rather than ultimate ends and the *range* of means to be considered appropriate to their realization. Political life throughout a polity can become systematized—at least among the major elite groups—most easily when a basic agreement emerges on: whether all those living in the territory are to belong to and identify with the same system; whether ultimate or proximate objectives are to guide the systems; the legitimate means of the pursuit of these objectives; and which specific objectives are to be pursued. The more disparate and conflicting the fundamental values and identifications of important political groups are, the more difficult is the task of achieving political integration.

---

[15] This dimension encompasses several of the factors Jacob and Teune list: homogeneity, mutual knowledge, functional interests, communal character, and previous integrative experience.

[16] Cf. Ake, *Theory of Political Integration,* p. 1, and Jacob and Toscano, *Integration,* pp. 4–6.

14

Consensus-formation, in the more rigorous sense I mean to consider it, is then another way of talking about the subjective systemization of social life, or in the present case, of political life. To this extent—but only to this extent—consensus-formation and integration are two names for the same process (another name for the end product is "political culture"). This concept, which derives from the increasing relevance of anthropology and social anthropology to political science, a relevance born with the emergence of non-Western political systems and the consequent need for and interest in truly comparative techniques of analysis, has recently received considerable attention.[17] However, it would seem that much of the literature on political culture deviates from the earlier anthropology-based conceptions of culture, which stressed the idea of coherence as a necessary and fundamental part of the definition of culture.[18] In the incisive and indispensable conclusion to his *Political Culture and Political Development*, Sydney Verba states that his definition of the concept is a very loose one, in that it "refers to orientations to all aspects of politics"; later he says, "Not all political cultures are well integrated and consistent." [19] Although Verba is surely correct, that political cultures may differ in level of integration, he tempts one to consider that integration is not in itself a characteristic of culture. I do not share his view. My argument is that although any study of the cultural dimension of the political system must examine the values and beliefs of all the people in that society, in the final analysis not all of them (the values, beliefs, or the people) may be relevant to *the* political culture of the country. In fact, a country may be without a superlative political culture, and a society may embody a variety of political cultures in juxtaposition, conflict, or competition. According to this view, the cultural integration of the society entails the creation of *a* pervasive culture which overarches the others and ties them all together, at least at the base, around a core of values universally ac-

[17] See Gabriel Almond and Sydney Verba, *The Civic Culture* (Princeton: Princeton University Press, 1963); Pye and Verba, *Political Culture and Political Development* (Princeton: Princeton University Press, 1965).

[18] Ruth Benedict, in *Patterns of Culture* (New York: Penguin Books, 1946), states: "A culture, like an individual, is a more or less consistent pattern of thought and action. Such patterning of culture cannot be ignored as if it were an unimportant detail. The whole, as modern science is insisting in many fields, is not merely the sum of all its parts, but the result of a unique arrangement and interrelations of parts that has brought about a new entity. . . . Cultures, likewise, are more than the sum of their traits."

[19] Pye and Verba, *Political Culture*, pp. 518, 520.

15

cepted, a core that gives singularity of meaning to the existence, if not the substance, of all the subcultures contained in the society.

Complementary action is usually consciously complementary; thus it is usually concertive. Measures of integration which use an index of collaborative action in the pursuit of common goals are too narrow. Actions may be complementary in their meaning to each of the actors without being collaborative, as is the case when popular local and national candidates of different parties or philosophies help each other by producing a larger vote. Actions may also be complementary in their meaning for the larger system of political action without being collaborative or even complementary to each other, as is exemplified in any honestly fought election in which each candidate attempts to identify the faults and beliefs of the other. Dissenters on policy decisions may not collaborate with the supporters of it, either in councils or among the populace; in fact, they may do a number of "disruptive" or annoying things, yet in a democratic system, so long as these actions are legal (and sometimes even when they are not), the whole system benefits from such opposition.

One of the most effective types of complementary behavior needed in the new states is the pursuit of objectives by political groups according to a common set of rules. The political game must be played in a way that does not arbitrarily or artificially bias the chance of any powerful political group to aggregate the interests and marshal the support most consonant with its leaders or program. This is not to say that free rein must be given to the expression of all political claims, for many do conflict with the requisites of national unity or the fundamental rights and requirements of other critically located political groups. Almost everywhere the dominant political forces have sought to create a single framework capable of encompassing or eliminating altogether all other organized political tendencies. In a number of cases such an approach may have served national integration, given the parochial and essentially disruptive potential of the opposition groups. The United Party opposition to the Convention People's Party (CPP) in Ghana, the Conakat opposition to the Movement National du Congo (MNC) in the Congo, the Kabaka Yekka opposition to the UPC in Uganda, may represent this type of opposition.

On the other hand, many of the dissident, parochial forces, including those mentioned above, have been real and strong enough to demand some recognition. Various methods have been attempted in trying to accommodate these forces, most of which reflect communal interests such as tribal, ethnic, or regional associations, or which reflect economic or

16

social interests such as trade unions, student associations, and the bureaucracy. In some cases such as the National Council of Nigerian Citizens (NCNC) of Nigeria, the Parti démocratique de la côte d'ivoire (PDCI) of the Ivory Coast, the UNC of Cameroon, regional or cultural forces operate as subgroups within the dominant or single party. Tanzania African National Union (TANU) in Tanzania, while rigorously screening out the language of communalism and tribalism, nevertheless permits local expression through a system of multiple candidacies, all under the banner of a single party. Much of my analysis of Cameroon concerns the attempt made there to develop a set of commonly accepted ground rules for the game of politics.

CONFLICTFUL (INCOMPATIBLE) POLITICAL ACTION AND INTEGRATION

I will consider two aspects of the relationship between conflict and integration. One concerns the macroanalytic level of social analysis and the other the microanalytic level. On the first level conflict is viewed as compatible or incompatible with integration according to whether one considers that whole societies either can or cannot exist for long where there are conflictful relationships within them. On the second level, one may consider that even if conflict *can* exist in a society, conflictful relationships, per se, might or might not have integrative consequences for those involved in them.

A. *The Macroanalytic Level*

On the macroanalytic level it is usually asserted that integration theory is a way of conceiving of society, that is, as a set of complementary relationships; thus conflict is ignored or considered to be incompatible with integration. It is therefore often argued that the concepts and approach of the "integration" school of social analysis are incompatible with those of the "conflict" school. The integration school supposedly conceives of society as the product of the mechanism of common values, cultural homogeneity, and the working of the "general will," whereas the conflict school sees it in terms of coercion, the manipulation of interests, the effect of law and constraints. For this reason the former is sometimes called a "utopian" and the latter a "rationalist" view of society. These dichotomies are real enough in much of sociological literature; they reflect the dichotomy identified by David Lockwood between influence and reason, values and interests, stability and instability, equilibrium and disequilibrium.[20]

[20] Lockwood, "Some Remarks on the Social System," *British Journal of Sociology*, VII, No. 2 (1956).

Ralph Dahrendorf [21] has reduced the two models of society to seemingly incompatible sets of four principles:

Integration Model	*Conflict Model*
1. Every society is a relatively persistent, stable structure of elements;	1. Every society is at every point subject to processes of change; social change is ubiquitous;
2. Every society is a well-integrated structure of elements;	2. Every society displays at every point dissensus and conflict;
3. Every element in a society has a function, i.e., renders a contribution to its maintenance as a system;	3. Every element in a society renders a contribution to its disintegration and change;
4. Every functioning social structure is based on consensus of values among its members.	4. Every society is based on the coercion of some of its members by others.

Drawn this way, the two models are incompatible. But this view of each model is overdrawn; certainly the integration model is overdrawn, for Dahrendorf attributes to it all the faults to be found in the literature of the functional school of social analysis—faults, however, which have been ably repudiated or answered by Robert Merton.[22] Merton repudiates the exaggerations, and answers the criticisms of functional analysis by revising and restating the functional (system, or integration) model of society in this way:

> . . . the provisional assumption [is] that, although any item of culture or social structure may have functions, it is premature to hold unequivocally that every such item must be functional.

> . . . a theory of functional analysis must call for specification of the social units subserved by given social functions, and that items of culture must be recognized to have multiple consequences, some of them functional and others, perhaps, dysfunctional.

> . . . [another] provisional assumption [is] that persisting cultural forms have a net balance of [eu] functional consequences either for the society considered as a unit or for subgroups sufficiently powerful to retain this item intact, by means of direct coercion or indirect persuasion. . . .

It is assumed that there are certain functions which are indispensable in the sense that, unless they are performed, the society (or group or individual) will not persist. This, then, sets forth a concept of *func-*

---

[21] Dahrendorf, *Class and Class Conflict in Industrial Society* (Stanford: Stanford University Press, 1959).

[22] Merton, *Social Theory and Social Structure* (New York: Macmillan–Free Press, 1957), esp. the chapter, "Latent and Manifest Functions."

18

tional prerequisites, or *preconditions functionally necessary* for a society. . . .

Proceeding further, we must set forth a major theorem of functional analysis; just as the same item may have multiple functions, so may the same function be diversely fulfilled by alternative items. Functional needs are here taken to be permissive, rather than determinant, of specific social structures.[23]

There is no inherent incompatibility between the view of the functionalist or integration model, as presented above, and the conflict model of society, especially if one admits the exaggerations in Dahrendorf's presentation of the latter. Even Dahrendorf does not suggest that every element in a system need provide pressure for change or display conflict at all times, and certainly not that a system needs always to display a net balance of conflict.

There is also no reason why coercion should be excluded from the mechanisms by which societies achieve or raise their levels of integration, unless one arbitrarily defines integration to be based only on common values and motives. Merton argues convincingly that it is not motive but consequence that counts. The functional contribution of an element, and thus its integrative significance, may be latent and not manifest— recognizable to an objective observer while not to the actor. The object of coercive action, even its perpetrator, may be blind to the integrative consequences of such action for the larger group or the whole system.

To say that social systems are never completely deterministic is to suggest the presence of stress and tension, and persistent pressures to change. We might expect not to find conflict in truly deterministic systems, because relationships that constantly produced injury or punishment to one of the parties would either be broken off or lead to the destruction of that party. It is hard to imagine any system of deterministic interaction in which there is for very long a preponderance of negative or destructive interactions, for this would mean that most actions in the system would overcome the resilience of one of the actors, however strong and resistant it may be; yet the interaction would persist. How? It must be that durable systems do endure because their parts are able to absorb the injuries and wear that action causes them, but in such a case there would be no balance of negative consequences. In probabilistic systems, however, it may be that no interaction has a negative product, on balance, every time the action occurs. Rewards may be mixed with punishments, permitting

[23] Merton, *Social Theory,* pp. 33–35 (emphasis mine).

or even stimulating the continuation of the interaction. Even if occasionally there is a preponderance of negative covariance in the system, on other occasions there may not be. Individuals may be inspired to continue injurious relationships out of the "hope" of eventual reward. Thus such a system may continue to function for quite long periods of time despite the sporadic occurrence of a preponderance of negative or conflictful relationships.

B. *The Microanalytic Level*

There is no theoretical necessity, even on the microanalytic level, to consider conflict and integration as incompatible processes or states of a system, certainly not in probabilistic systems. Lewis Coser, organizing and interpreting the works of Georg Simmel, one of the best theorists of the functions of conflict, suggests 16 propositions about the way conflict may contribute to social processes, enhancing integration in many cases.[24] At the base of each of these propositions is Simmel's thesis that no group can be entirely harmonious, for if it was, it would lack structure and process altogether. Conflict groups may enhance general integration by sharpening group boundaries, bolstering fledgling loyalties within them, binding antagonistic groups into a pattern of interaction, generating mutual appreciation of needs and capacities, and perhaps balancing reciprocal enmities in the system. Conflict may offer opportunities for protest and a venting of hostilities on displaced objects, which may make deprivations or irritants more bearable and enhance loyalty to group or even to the whole system and unblock readiness and capacity to participate in it. Even where conflict produces schisms it may promote integration by rationalizing faction-formation and intragroup fragmentation and it may also stimulate counterbalancing alliances and coalitions.

Conflict is necessarily incompatible with integration only where and when action destroys its object. An action may prove injurious but not be destructive; it may be wearing on the part, place it under stress, etc., but perhaps fail to match its resilience, resistance, or enduring power—or the compensatory powers of the system of which it is a part. Unless and until one can be sure there are no potentially compensating or restoring factors in the system, he cannot say such wear will be destructive to the system. If there are such compensating factors which are activated to re-

[24] Coser, *The Functions of Social Conflict* (New York: Free Press of Glencoe, 1964), *passim*, based on Georg Simmel, *Conflict*, tr. Kurt Wolff (Glencoe, 1955). Also see R. C. North, H. E. Kock, Jr., and D. A. Zinnes, "The Integrative Functions of Conflict," *Conflict Resolution*, IV (September 1960).

store or preserve the system, then there is an integrative capacity in the system capable of "handling" the disintegrative strain placed on it.

Even in biological systems, which are highly deterministic, there is constant conflict and destructive wear. Is this necessarily a promise of disintegration? As Anatol Rapoport notes: "During the course of my life every molecule in my body has been replaced several times. Are the cells of which my body was composed several years ago still the same cells? If one argues on the basis of the molecular turn-over that they are not, what has happened to the old cells? Are they all dead? If they are, can I say that I too have "died" several times? It seems, then, that the identity and the viability of an organism (which, upon reflection, turn out to be the same thing) become diffuse concepts, even on the level of clearly identifiable organisms.[25]

CONJUNCTIVE POLITICAL ACTION

The second dimension of the integration process is the need to link in a common web of interaction the isolated individuals and groups that may inhabit the state.[26] It is a matter of creating a society large enough to fill out the national territory, of weaving the behaviors of each citizen into the fabric of national political life, whether that fabric is coherently patterned or not. This need is implied conceptually in the term interdependency, for in order to be so, actions must be connected. So far I have discussed only the qualitative aspect of social connections, surely the more important, but the quantitative aspect is important as well. Indeed, much of the early integrative effort in the new states of Africa is to "mobilize" the people, to get them involved in the activities of political institutions, without much concern for the quality of the involvement.

Almost every new African state contains many, perhaps a majority of the population, who continue to live in a circumscribed area of activity, too parochial to link up effectively with the other members of the national society. Isolated in a rural, illiterate social order, producing only for themselves, trading and communicating only with themselves, such peoples must be considered essentially as being outside the new political systems. The economic growth and political development of the new

[25] Rapoport, "What Is a Viable System?" presidential address delivered to the annual meeting of the Society for General Systems Research, December 29, 1965, at Berkeley, California. Reprinted in *ETC., A Review of General Semantics,* Vol. 23, No. 4 (December 1966), pp. 463–74.

[26] The factors in Jacob and Teune's list encompassed by this dimension (and of course by its counterpart, the disjunctive) are proximity, transactions, political structure, and governmental effectiveness.

states depends ultimately on their becoming participants in a larger order. Even in the towns and cities individuals and groups often pursue their activities apart, without any meaningful relation to the national political effort, although they may do so through apparently modern associations. The approach usually taken in the new African states to the achievement of conjunctive political action, of a connectiveness to political action, has been to seek to affiliate or incorporate such organizations or individuals into a mass national party, perhaps a single party, in an effort to "embody the nation." Thus in Cameroon, as elsewhere, youth organizations, sporting clubs, tribal improvement unions, cultural societies, and women's organizations have all been pressed, at one time or another, to fuse with the dominant political party in order to form a single, closely articulated structure of political action.

The state apparatus itself has been an important instrument for the forging of political connections between people and groups in Africa. In Cameroon, which is faced with the problem of uniting two separate states, this was especially so. The merger of jurisdictional power, the linking of administrative organizations, of legal jurisdictions, and of the police and the armed forces were all involved in the effort.

Transactions among the populace also generally constitute an important aspect of the conjunctivity dimension in political integration.[27] Transaction flows mediate correlated variations in individual behavior; they link them and reveal their interdependence; they are the observable processes of interaction, such as communication, trade, and physical contact. Trade flows (in terms of changes in size, direction, composition, and balance between the trade of the partners), communication patterns, transfer of people (travelers, workers, technicians), the reorganization or reorientation of social and interest groups in order to effectively operate at the national level, in this case the federal level, all figure in my own analysis of Cameroon integration.

[27] Since these are the activities that can be made subject to precise quantitative measurement, social scientists of the Deutsch school tend to focus on this aspect as the principal measure of integration. Deutsch and other theorists who conceive of social systems in probabilistic terms, point out that covariance in social action can produce both positive and negative results. Positive results would be those which each actor considers to be a reward or which reinforces his behavior, as in the case of complementary action already discussed. Negative results would be those that frustrate or penalize the object of the action or threaten to deflect it from its goals. Deutsch considers that only the positive type covariance is integrative, the negative type leads to conflict, a type of interdependency but the opposite of integration. I reject the view that negative interdependency and integration are opposites. See Karl Deutsch, "Power and Communication in International Society," in A. deReuck, ed., *Conflict in Society* (Boston: Little, Brown, 1966).

Conjunctive action is not always directly complementary, however. Thus many integration theorists consider that it is not necessarily integrative. *Mobilization* is certainly not. Familiarity does still sometimes breed contempt. Bringing heretofore isolated groups into contact with each other may result in conflict between them as well. If the conflict is intensive enough it may disrupt the contact and thus become disintegrative. Indeed, much of the violence that has occurred in Africa in recent years between various tribes arose out of the new contexts in which these tribes have been placed through the coming of European power, colonialism, the slave trade, or the rise of cities and the establishment of new territorial units. The violence between these groups may define their interdependency initially but ultimately threatens to lead to the destruction of one or the other side or to the ties between them, even the ties of conflict itself. Thus to be integrative, conjunctive action must either be durable or on the complementary side.

Disjunctive Political Action

Perhaps it is more appropriate to think of the disjunctive political action dimension of the integration problem as being concerned with inaction rather than action. In a mechanical sense interdependency obviously requires some kind of interaction; thus, mechanically, disjunctive trends in political action deny integration. I am only concerned here with strategically located disjunctions, however. The breakup of political connections between actors, or the termination of political action altogether, may curtail the performance of important, even vital activities. People may drop out of the network of political interaction, cease to vote, to communicate or perceive communications in the system, or cease to bestow their loyalty on it. In other words, they may become alienated. If they withdraw from society psychologically and exhibit a high level of ennui, the social nexus could dissolve and the society disintegrate. In a sense, then, Jacob and Teune are correct in taking the level of collaborative effort in the service of common goals as a direct measure of the level of integration.[28] This would not require agreement on values and loyalties.

It is important to keep in mind that integration, as defined above, is primarily a question of significance and meaning, which applies as much to inaction as to action. It is conceivable that inaction may have integrative consequences by isolating potential incompatibilities. In that event, the lack of certain interactions in the system remains consequential to it

---

[28] Jacob and Toscano, *Integration*, pp. 5ff.

and makes a positive "contribution" to it. This situation can be another case of latent functionalism, where the effect of an action (constraint or the refusal to interact is here considered to be a kind of action) is unintended and/or unconscious on the part of the persons involved. It may be that the leadership of a country realizes its objectives because the level of mobilization and political participation is low and the rate of change slow. An example of this situation could be the Ivory Coast where the leadership relegated significant mobilization of the rural populace to a low political priority, in favor of rapid development of an economic infrastructure and prosperity in the cities. Liberia is the outstanding example of a regime that has deliberately restricted the level and pace of social mobilization in the hinterland, initially in the selfish and blind pursuit of "overclass" interests. Recently she has done so in order to attenuate the disintegrative effects of rapidly expanding the network of political life to include those formerly denied the rewards of the modern economy and political system.

My attempt in this book is not to equate opposites: action with inaction, interaction with autonomy, or interdependence with independence. I do not argue that those who are inert or act outside the network of systemic action really contribute directly to the system's integration. Rather I wish to point out the fact that the *meaning* of their exclusion or isolation may be that the level of integration *within* the system is increased or enhanced. In terms of positive action, as opposed merely to inaction, the act of breaking a political connection or of excluding an actor or group of actors from the system may lower the level of incompatible or conflict-producing action and thus increase integration. Those who choose to focus on the coercion or discontinuity that may be involved in actions of this sort, and to consider this to be inherently disintegrative mistake form for the substance of integration.[29] Polities embodying large amounts of either may be potentially unstable but not necessarily so; whatever one may consider ideal, the more plausible historical norm is the polity that successfully makes possibly heavy but judicious use of both coercion and selective exclusion.

In summary, I conceive of political integration as the systemization of political life. This process is to be understood through a determination of the extent and nature of the connections between political actors and the quality of those connections. I refer to the degree of connectiveness as the

---

[29] Many students of politics have postulated "the inherent instability" of any polity that employs a great deal of coercion. An example is A. Kaplan and H. Lasswell in *Power and Society* (New Haven: Yale University Press, 1950), pp. 265ff.

conjunctive aspect of political life; the qualitative dimensions are considered in terms of the mix of *complementarity* and *conflict,* and the meaning these may have to the emergence and preservation of a discernible pattern of political life. It is the pattern of political life that gives to the political system its identity. In this book I attempt to discover the identity of the Cameroon political system, to discuss the process by which it emerged, and to determine the meaning of the various political leaders, organizations, and events in the country in terms of their contribution to this process since World War II.

⚛ 2 ⚛

Integration and System Change

THE TASK of integration theory, or even of conflict theory, is not to predict and describe political systems in creation or expunction, but to do so for the many in change. The greatest challenge to integration theory is to make comprehensible the character and direction of the change. The significance of change in a system relates to its identity, which involves change and constancy.

Identity—the capacity of a system to persist, its viability—is based on the "invariants" of the system. As Anatol Rapoport argues: "My identity as a living organism is a fact because of the aspects of my behavior which remain invariant in spite of the changes constantly occurring in me. . . . To survive is to preserve some invariants of structure and behavior.[1]

Francesca Cancian, calling on the work of Ernest Nagel, postulates that the invariants of the system are one of two fundamental types of variables within the system.[2] The invariant property of the system, which Nagel labels as G, is a function of the interactions of the second type, described by the state coordinates, which are those variable actions and properties that determine the state of the system. Integration is achieved, according to this theory, as a relation between G and the state coordinates, such that G is in fact maintained. The preservation of these patterns, despite conflict or the death and decay of specific components, is termed "structural isomorphism" by the general-systems analysts.[3]

[1] Rapoport, "What Is a Viable System?"

[2] Cancian, "Functional Analysis of Change," in *American Sociological Review*, 25 (1960), 818–27. Cancian draws heavily on Nagel's *Logic Without Metaphysics*, in which Nagel maintains that rather than assume that "G" (certain stable core elements of the state of the system, including a stable rate of change, or moving equilibrium) is stable in a social system, the job of functional analysis is to show that G is or is not maintained because certain state coordinates do or do not compensate for each other's variations.

[3] Rapoport, "What Is a Viable System?", notes: "the epistemological antecedent of isomorphism is analogy," but the latter has been discredited in scientific discourse as inconclusive and misleading. Systems theorists have revived and upgraded the device by making it rigorous and operational, especially through mathematical argument. "For example, two mathematical models isomorphic to each other are structurally identical even though they may refer to phenomena of widely different contents. Therefore, it is legitimate to transfer the mathematical consequences of one model to the other. Such analogy is not 'mere' analogy, disdained by rigorous scientists. It is logically compelling analogy." (p. 464).

26

The duality of stasis and change in systems forces me to return to my earlier assertion that identity is basically a question of purpose and perspective, that is, the *meaning* of a thing. This meaning must be intrinsic and not simply imposed by the observer, though it need not be conscious to the actors involved. Systems are abstractions of reality and invariably represent selection of variables, but the selection cannot be arbitrary. The relationships between the variables must be consequential to their behavior. In terms of viability, what is invariant about a system, that which determines its identity, is not necessarily any particular part or relationship, but rather the meaning of the whole. One component or another may be destroyed or cease to function, but it will be replaced by another which does the same job, or failing this, if it is a critical function, the system will disintegrate, or "die."

There are some postulated critical functions that must be performed in all systems as systems.[4] Since not all systems are political, however, we must concentrate on those prerequisites or critical variables peculiar to political systems. Several of the nine functional prerequisites identified by D. F. Aberle *et al.* for whole societies (social systems at the societal level) are potentially relevant but many are too general.[5] The analytical model of a political system developed by G. A. Almond and G. B. Powell is the most useful among the many developed so far for the purposes of the present study.[6] This model provides for functional analysis on three levels:

[4] The four most widely accepted essential functions of all systems are: (1) latency (replenishing of the components); (2) adaptation (adjusting to changes in the environment); (3) goal attainment (obtaining from the environment certain inputs); and (4) integration (the coordination of all parts in order to preserve the system of action and its particular character or field). Cf. Talcott Parsons, *The Social System* (Glencoe: Free Press, 1951); and Talcott Parsons and Edward A. Shils, *Toward a General Theory of Action* (Cambridge: Harvard University Press, 1951). Also see Robert T. Holt and John E. Turner, *The Political Basis of Economic Development: An Exploration in Comparative Political Analysis* (Princeton: Van Nostrand, 1966), pp. 50–56, who, unlike Parsonians, center the integrative function among the other three because it relates them to each other and is the most fundamental aspect of systematic behavior.

[5] D. F. Aberle, A. K. Cohen, A. K. Davis, M. J. Levy, Jr., and F. X. Sutton, "The Functional Prerequisites of a Society," *Ethics,* 60 (January 1950). Their nine requisites are: (1) provision for adequate relationship to the environment and for sexual recruitment; (2) role differentiation and role assignment; (3) communication; (4) shared cognitive orientations; (5) a shared articulated set of goals; (6) the normative regulation of means; (7) the regulation of affective expression; (8) socialization; and (9) the effective control of disruptive forms of behavior.

[6] Almond and G. Bingham Powell, Jr., *Comparative Politics: A Developmental Approach* (Boston: Little, Brown, 1966), Chap. 2.

27

(a) On the boundaries between the political system and its environment (other social systems of the same society). Analysis at this level considers the parameters and input/out patterns of the system.

(b) At the level of the operation of the system itself. This involves changes in the state of the system, as well as changes in its field.

(c) At the level of the subsystems more specifically devoted to the performance of integrative tasks. This involves characteristic patterns of dominance and emphasis and sequential development in the system.

System change can be described in terms of each of these factors and levels: in terms of the capabilities of and patterns of operation of the system vis-à-vis the environment, of the patterns of operations within the system which convert the inputs into outputs (how rules are made, applied, and adjudicated, how interests are aggregated and articulated, and how political activities, etc., are communicated), and in terms of the changes of the dominant patterns of ways in which the integrative needs of the system are satisfied.

CHANGE INVOLVING THE BOUNDARIES OF THE SYSTEM

Some studies of integration such as that by J. Coleman and C. Rosberg, for example, refer to territorial integration as a "horizontal" dimension to the process of national integration, one which concerns the "boundaries" of the system.[7] This kind of integration problem "arises from the effort to form large-scale federations or unions embracing politico-administrative systems which previously had, or have since acquired, considerable autonomy, or, in some instances, even sovereignty, and it is, of course, but one aspect of the larger problem of territorial integration confronted by all the states of Tropical Africa."[8]

Territorial integration is in my view but one aspect of an integrative task involving the boundaries of the system; it is not limited to a "horizontal" dimension. The problem of bringing into the network of interdependent political action the activites of all the people, especially the powerful groups contained in a specific territory or state-society, is equally if not more important because it is more relevant than expanding those territorial boundaries or even establishing control over distinctive regions by a central government. It may prove more difficult and signifi-

[7] Cf. James S. Coleman and Carl G. Rosberg, Jr., eds., *Political Parties and National Integration in Tropical Africa* (Berkeley: University of California Press, 1964), pp. 8–12.

[8] *Ibid.,* p. 11.

28

cant a task to reintegrate into the pattern of national politics the Ibos of Biafra-Nigeria than it would be to incorporate into Nigeria the Yoruba or the other groups now living in Dahomey or the Hausa-speaking (or other Moslem) peoples of Niger.

If we go beyond a territorial-jurisdiction view of the polity and consider the sociological aspects, we can conceive of boundary problems that have nothing to do with territorial location or "horizontal integration." People living in the capital city of a polity may in effect persistently act outside the system. Bringing them into the system is a boundary problem akin to what Coleman and Rosberg have called the "vertical" dimension of integration, or the more truly political dimension, namely that of overcoming an "elite-mass gap." (But there are also qualitative dimensions to "vertical integration" that are distinct from those involving boundary definition.) I suggest that the problem of boundary definition relates to the conjunctive aspect of integration. One way to describe fundamental social change is to identify the broad-scale changes in the boundaries of the political system, whether territorial or sociological.

Political systems may change in their characteristic relations with their environments from being regulative and extractive (where the political system plays a dominant role in manipulating and controlling the other social systems in the society), to being essentially responsive to the demands and needs of other social subsystems. The political system may be important in the general distribution and allocation of people, goods, and services in the society or it may be relatively uninvolved in such social processes. I am attempting here to analyze these aspects of the Cameroon governments in terms of the functional interests of the two states and communities within them, and in terms of the nature and operation of government authority in defining and allocating valuables in the Cameroon society. Chapters 5, 9, and 13 bear directly on these questions, and Chapter 12 touches on them. In Chapter 6 I discuss the forces that affected the boundaries of the system, considered in terms of who was included in it.

Change Involving Relations within the System

Political systems may change in terms of the kinds of institutions they create or permit to make, apply, or interpret rules, or they may shift from an emphasis on one or another of these three activities. They may vary in terms of the extent to which they permit or require political communication, the articulation and aggregation of interests, and what kinds of structures perform the functions. Each pattern may imply a different

29

kind of integration problem. Generally, the integrative needs of the system may be met consciously, or somewhat gratuitously as a result of the strengths of the cultural system or other social subsystems. In my analysis of the Cameroon case I approach these factors by first describing the character and operational style of the political and governmental organizations of the two Trust Territories in fact and in terms of deeply rooted preferences (Chapters 7 and 8), and how the territories came to be modified in the process of creating the Federation (Chapter 9) and developing its political life (Chapters 10, 11, 12).

CHANGE IN THE STYLE OF INTEGRATION

The style in which integrative needs are satisfied in a political system may vary from an emphasis on coercion and the direct regulation of conflict and tension to an emphasis on the creation of a coherent political culture, the force of charismatic personality or the manipulation of political and other (especially economic) interests. These themes run throughout the discussion of the Cameroon case. The nature of the changes that occurred in the integrative mechanism of the Cameroon political systems is the subject of the six chapters of Part III, most centrally, Chapters 12 to 14.

CHANGE IN THE BASIC IDENTITY (FIELD) OF THE CAMEROON SYSTEM

As we have already seen, the theoretical basis for the identity of a system is the core of invariants in it. Basic change of the system must involve some change in that normally invariant core, but slowly enough and patterned enough to permit some continuity. Both continuity and change involve integration. Change in the field of the Cameroon political system can be analyzed in terms of the same lines of behavior which I use to determine its degree and style of integration—the extent of conjunctivity and complementarity in the relations of the system. These factors must be aggregated in some way to permit an overall characterization. David Apter has developed the analytical tools that permit this.[9]

Political systems are basically congeries of structures of authority and consent. They may be classified in terms of the mix of their reliance on coercion and information, according to Apter. This is another way of saying that political activity always involves some mixture of the issues of power and legitimacy, or the larger systems of stratification and ideology

[9] Apter, *The Politics of Modernization* (Chicago: University of Chicago Press, 1965).

they imply. These two factors—power and legitimacy, or type of stratification and ideological system—are the skeletal structures which shape the two lines of behavior—conjunctivity and complementarity—I use to organize my analysis of the integration process.

The stratification patterns of a political system arise from the distribution and nature of power within it. The system determines the location, and to some extent the kind of linkages or connections between the actors in the system.

The ideological patterns arise from the values, beliefs, and cognitions of people in the system; they reflect and shape the interests of the people and determine the qualitative characteristics of the connections, or at least the perceptions people have of such connections; thus they determine the basis of legitimation in the system.

Apter has devised an analytical and classification scheme based on these two root factors of the variables. He therefore provides us with a convenient classificatory scheme for identifying the Cameroon political system and determining the direction and meaning of changes which may have occurred in it. Apter labels the two variables degree of hierarchy, and extent of consummatory values. He describes them in the following terms: "The first is the measure of stringency of control and is structurally visible in the degree of centralization of authority. The second criterion is the degree to which ultimate ends are employed in action. . . . ." [10]

Apter organizes systems of authority, or power-distribution, into three types—hierarchical, pyramidal, and segmental. The last is a type of authority system that is not important here; it is not found at the level of state organization, but is represented by some very small systems at the tribal level and by some very large ones such as the international system. Pyramidal systems are more complex types of segmental ones; such structures consist of patterns of subordinacy and superordinacy that are lim-

[10] *Ibid.*, p. 22. He calls ultimate ends in this and other works (*Political Transition in the Gold Coast*) by the term "consummatory values." He explains the distinction as one between "sacred" and "secular" ends as discussed by Durkheim. The two types of values provide the basis for differing systems, consummatory ones being ones that "cannot segregate wide areas of social relationship from the religious sphere" and secular ones "that do not evaluate social conduct in terms of its wider meanings but only in terms of its more narrow and particular ones" (p. 84). He explains further, " 'Instrumental' systems are those characterized by a large sector of intermediate ends separate from and independent of ultimate ends; 'consummatory' systems are those characterized by a close relationship between intermediate and ultimate ends" (p. 85, n. 5). The terms derive from Parsons.

31

ited to certain activities. Hierarchical systems, on the other hand, are more bureaucratic or military in character.[11]

Value systems may vary in a number of ways, of course. We have already considered the general need for the creation of a core of shared values, especially about the rules by which the political game is to be played. Systems may differ markedly in the extent to which they promote shared values on a broad basis. Apter singles out the continuum of consummatory-instrumental values by which to classify and characterize value systems. Though the literature discussing the value and belief components of the political system contain a rich variety of approaches, most often emphasizing dichotomies between "democratic" and "totalitarian" values, or "modern" versus "traditional" ones, Apter's scheme is not all that arbitrary. Many of the previous approaches to this topic can be subsumed to a large degree in his. It has the advantage of enabling differentiation among a broader range of social systems on the basis of more fundamental and distinctive value orientations.[12] I consider some aspects of

[11] Apter describes a hierarchical system as one in which authority inheres in some figure or role centrally located ("at the top") in the system and is then delegated outward (or "downward") to subordinates. This would be the structure of the typical unitary, centralized state. Segmentary systems are rather peculiar to small traditional societies but have features analogous to patterns of authority in certain modern states. In the traditional setting they are essentially balance-of-power systems which lack clear and broadly based territorial identity, relying instead on shifting alliances between lineage groups (direct genealogical relationship) of roughly equal size and "complementary opposition" (depending on similar kinds of obligations between relatives of the opponents in a particular dispute—this is a system of conflict resolution essentially). The pyramidal system is a combination of the two, involving a vertical distribution of authority, but in stages, following the logic of the segmentary system, where kinship or other social groups of like character are linked in alliance around the tasks of conflict resolution, but the whole segment may be linked in a rather stable way to other similar segments to form a new segment at a higher level. Similar powers and power-links are involved at each level of the system.

[12] The most explicit discussion of the concept of value orientation is to be found in Kluckhohn and Strodtbeck's *Variations in Value Orientations* (Evanston, Ill.: Harper, 1969). See also Talcott Parsons' *The Social System* (Glencoe: Free Press, 1951), pp. 58–67, 101–12, and *passim*. Parsons, *Structure of Social Action* (New York: McGraw-Hill, 1937), pp. 43–51; and, with Edward A. Shils, *Toward a General Theory of Action* (Cambridge: Harvard University Press, 1951), pp. 58ff., gives us the basis for a more elaborate and complex scheme of typing value and belief systems and charting change in them, but the scheme is no more sensitive to fundamental differences and change than is Apter's simplified one. Parsons' scheme tends to exaggerate differences and degrees of change. It analyzes value orientations in terms of three aspects (cognitive, affective, and evaluative) and four pattern variables (functional specificity-diffuseness, universalistic-particularistic, affectivity-

the value system beyond the mix of consummatory-instrumental orientations, such as the cognitive aspects relating to identity patterns (Chapters 2 and 4) and the affective aspects of commitments to nationalism and ideology (Chapters 6 and 7). But this scheme provides a simple and easily applied guide to the more fundamental characteristics of a system. In Chapters 7 and 8 I consider the values of the important political contingents in Cameroon in terms of these factors.

One of the most familiar modern manifestations of a value system constructed on consummatory values (and most often also valuing a hierarchical authority system) is ideology. Ideology is a peculiar cultural configuration; every true ideology embodies a political culture of a special type. It is an internally coherent and articulated cluster of values and beliefs which provide their adherents with fundamental teleological explanations for human history and the human predicament, and prescribe the political action most consistent with these explanations.[13] Ideology can be a powerful integrative mechanism, for as a society becomes infused with ideology it acquires a singular political culture. On the other hand, if the ideology appeals to only a sector of the society it can generate sharp conflict and cleavage, and perhaps competing or counterideologies. Of course, in Africa there is often a gap between the elite and the masses, each of which may have different and conflicting ideologies.

In Chapter 4 I examine the nature and role of the elements of ideology contained in the colonial impact on the two states of Cameroon, and in Chapter 7 I consider those that operated during the rise of Cameroonian nationalism, on into the postindependence and post-Federation period. My consideration of the value system of Cameroonians also encompasses values about the distribution of power and the nature of legitimate authority, which I discuss in Chapter 8. Both dimensions of political culture, the normative and the structural, are important aspects of the process which legitimizes the political system, which engenders support among the most important participants or potential participants for the

affective neutrality, and ascriptive-achievement orientations). These aspects are related to, but are not exactly comparable to, the mix of consummatory-instrumental values I consider. Parsons emphasizes a motivational factor. My discusssion, based on Almond and Powell, *Comparative Politics* (Boston: Little, Brown, 1966), p. 50, is limited to the cognitive and evaluative dimensions.

[13] *Ibid.*, Chap. 10; here Almond and Powell provide one of the best discussions of the nature and role of ideology in the process of modernizing social change. See also David E. Apter, *Ideology and Discontent* (Glencoe: Free Press, 1964); and Robert E. Lane, *Political Ideology* (Glencoe: Free Press, 1962).

system, and which shapes their attitudes about the proper nature and functioning of the system, what goals it should pursue, when and where, and by what means.

The position a system may occupy along the two lines of behavior of Apter's scheme, those concerning the power distribution and the value systems, determine its fundamental character or field. Apter elaborates two normative or "ideal" types in terms of the possible combinations of extremities and two historically significant but theoretically uninteresting alternative models.[14]

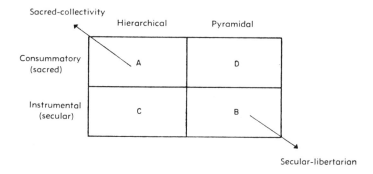

According to Apter, each type represents political systems typed according to the nature of their authority systems, which are normative systems "organized around certain structural features and incorporating particular styles of political life and civic action." Each type of system defines the conditions and the opportunities for choice differently. "The extreme model, type B, may . . . be called the secular-libertarian: *it is a perfect information model.* Its opposite, type A, is the sacred-collectivity, *a perfect coercion model.* Between these two extremes the other types have proved to be accommodated or mixed systems of choice."[15] In greater detail: (a) The sacred-collectivity type stresses the realization of potentiality, and the political community, as the key to social life, the source of morality, and the principal agency of socialization and education. It is the chief mechanism by which potential is translated into reality. Society is corporate in character; social ends are collective; unity and discipline are key virtues. This type of society "does not presume a free-flowing pattern of exchange of information between rulers and ruled" except inasmuch as coercion itself is considered the equivalent of infor-

[14] Apter, *Politics of Modernization,* pp. 24ff.
[15] *Ibid.,* p. 25.

mation. (b) The secular-libertarian type depends on the existence and pursuit of enlightened self-interest. The structural emphasis is on assuring such opportunities, and thus limited government is something of an ideal. Marketplace mechanisms provide harmony, and the public good is viewed as the sum total of private wants, rightly reasoned.

As normative types in the extreme, these two models are not perfectly matched anywhere in reality. Their interest derives not from their applicability to Cameroon or any other African political system even as a goal, but rather from some of their subtypes, representing a more heavily mixed assortment of the factors, which Apter describes with clarity and which do help us characterize Cameroon systems and the direction of change in them as a result of and by way of the inauguration of the federal union.

The subtypes which are relevant to the Cameroon case are:

1. *Mobilization:* In addition to the general features of the generic type A of which this is a specie, the mobilization system is marked by the extent to which instrumental values are elevated to the level of consummatory values through political religion. All social life is subject to politicization, and the leaders concentrate on maximizing integration by enhancing solidarity as a way of generating power, which is legitimized insofar as it betters the community morally and materially. A collective orientation becomes, in itself, a consummatory value which demands postponement of the gratification of personal consumption needs. The party of solidarity is most often the organizational means used to embody and serve the community. Political leadership acquires a charismatic base— or seeks one—and usually drifts to ideology as a way of affirming and projecting the purity, selflessness, and wisdom of the leader. Leaders often seek to consolidate this image by maintaining an atmosphere of crisis and threat of attack.

2. *Neomercantilist:* This type may appear to be a less stringent form of the mobilization system, but really is a subtype of the "C" or "Kemalist" category.[16] The crucial aspect of the type is its hierarchical structure of authority and the fact that the dominant political values remain characteristically instrumental, though the style of their pursuit may resemble the apostolic fervor associated with mobilization systems. Consummatory values subserve the instrumental ones operative in the sys-

[16] The name of this group is not important. Apter gives no descriptive name, but uses "Neo-Bismarkian" and "Kemalist" because of the historic familiarity with those systems and the more frequent recurrence of them as descriptive models in the current literature on developmental systems.

tem. Decision-making is centralized and the traditional society may be significantly restratified, but traditional norms increasingly are invoked to legitimize the new patterns and innovations. Restratification becomes less important than the process of institutionalizing the innovations or retraditionalizing political life. The system is less capricious than the mobilization system and seeks to integrate the political and technical elites as well as other competing and antagonistic strata. Those roles recognized as "careers" (which cover a lifespan, have well-defined canons of reward and explicit criteria of success and which require preparation) are the principal modernizing ones. If there is political religion, it is ritualized, and though leadership may be personal, it is not charismatic. Apter believes such systems usually arise after the failure of charisma and mobilization. The Cameroon case brings into question the necessity of that sequential development. Given the hierarchical structure of power which Cameroon and many new African states inherited from the French colonial administration, and the essentially artificial, formalistic, and shortlived sense of moral fruition and national purpose which the achievement of independence stimulated, the new states of Africa, in many cases, began their lives as neomercantilist systems. They may later drift toward the mobilizationist or perhaps even the reconciliation types.

3. *Reconciliation:* This system is a specific type of secular-libertarian system. Power is organized in a pyramidal structure and used to pursue goals that accommodate public demands. The system requires high levels of information flow within and between interest groups, voluntary associations, political parties, and government. The governmental apparatus is largely devoted to reconciling other social groups and subsystems. Economic development in such a system is sought primarily through technological change, and requires considerable initiative by local entrepreneurs and self-disciplined political participation and civic devotion among the populace. Planning is difficult because central directive institutions are weak and political structures (e.g. political parties) representative; yet planning is required to overcome the uncertainty effects arising from high levels of information available to social groups.[17] Such systems tend to disintegrate, their stratification to ossify, their technical

---

[17] Apter notes in his *Politics of Modernization*, pp. 388–89, that "the greater the degree of information in a system and the lower the degree of coercion, the greater the problem of evaluation . . . [where] the deterministic principle operates . . . [there is] less uncertainty because there is less information." Thus while perfect information systems might imply certainty, less than perfect ones entail high levels of uncertainty about interpretation and if and how groups in the society will act on their information.

elites to become estranged from the traditional ones. A high material payoff to the principal competing groups (a situation which requires considerable wealth) or some direct substitute for religious values or symbols are needed to carry the system beyond its utilitarian base.

None of these basic types or subtypes is necessarily stable. One may tend to become another. Basic change in the political system is involved when a system changes location in this scheme. The scheme provides a basis for giving meaning to the nature and direction of such change. Such change does not imply, and hardly ever involves, the complete renovation of the former society and the new construction of the later one. The shift from one type to another may be stimulated by changes in the environment, weaknesses or changes within, but the direction and pace of the shift is influenced by the original patterns. Apter argues, on the basis of theoretical argument rather than empirical evidence, that each type is more efficient and suited to particular stages in the modernization process, and thus may be stable for a given type of development strategy or need: (1) Neomercantilist societies are the optimal form of political system for consolidation in countries in the early stages of modernization. (2) Mobilization systems are optimal systems for countries that are reaching the end of a period of modernization and are about to industrialize. (3) Reconciliation systems are optimal systems for well-established and highly complex industrial states. . . . He hypothesizes the following pattern of tendencies toward change: [18]

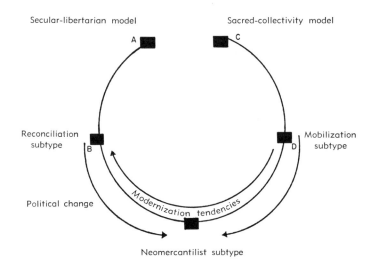

[18] *Ibid.*, p. 420.

37

I accept Apter's hypotheses as merely suggestive. My own analysis of Cameroon will characterize the authority system in terms of the mix of hierarchical and pyramidal structures of power allocation. Patterns of power allocation will also figure in the analysis as a dimension of the value system itself, inasmuch as political contingents in the two states expressed their values in terms of certain desirable patterns of power distribution between and within the states and federal government. The mix of consummatory and instrumental values in other respects also form part of my characterization of the value systems operating in the two states at the time of their union and in the overarching federal system during the course of the first five years of its life. I characterize as well the relationship between the political systems in Cameroon and the society in terms of their role in distributing economic and other valuables, and consider the original affinities and disparities between the states in these terms. Taking all these patterns and their development into account, I believe I am able to distinguish the forces that brought the two reunified political systems together, define their characters and that of the federal system which emerged out of them, and determine whether and how they changed.

PART II

The Foundations of Unity

ON THE first of October 1961 the Trust Territory of Southern Cameroons, formerly under the administration of the United Kingdom, and the independent Republic of Cameroun, formerly also a Trust Territory but under the administration of France, were joined in a federal union. The very creation of such a Federation is remarkable when the diversity it was made to encompass is considered. Its creation was a product of what one observer has termed "the Kamerun Idea," a deeply rooted belief that the 32 years of German rule, despite its harshness, had welded these diverse and sometimes warring peoples into a single cohesive unit with a distinctive, though fragile, cultural life of its own.[1] Beyond this, the existence of certain traditional, ethnic, social, and economic affinities between the peoples of this country, and the seemingly "obvious" injustices of their deliberate but arbitrary division in 1916 between British and French administrations, were taken as adequate justification for the demand of "reunification" of these territories which had formerly been a part of the old German colony of Kamerun. The so-called Kamerun Idea was based on the assumption that there had existed in the past a single "Kamerun Nation," and that despite its subsequent fragmentation into two separate state administrations, that nation persisted as an entity in the form of a cluster of generally accepted coherent values which exhibited vitality, or could easily be made to do so. Thus by all prevailing notions of justice, the new nation should have again become in fact a restored "Kamerun Nation."

How valid was the Kamerun Idea? Much of the significance of the Cameroon experience with political union and integration hinges on the

---

[1] Edwin O. Ardener, "The Kamerun Idea," *West Africa,* June 7 and 14, 1958.

answer to this question. Did a cluster of shared and coherent political values around pan-Cameroon symbols actually exist prior to the creation of the Federation, as claimed, or were the affinities between the peoples of the two Trust Territories close enough, and their social and political interaction extensive enough to give rapid rise to such a cluster once common political institutions were imposed? If either case were true, then the political union of the two Trust Territories would reflect an on-going process of political integration which already was in an advanced stage, and thus make less difficult the problems of integrating the society following federation. Under such circumstances the Cameroon case would be a much less instructive example of political union and integration for the rest of Africa, which struggles to build nations out of frag-mented societies, than if political union came about during the initial phases of integration. To answer this question we must consider the af-finities and disparities—their nature, source, and magnitude—which did exist among and between the peoples and states of Cameroon. Atti-tudinal, structural, and processual dimensions of continuity and cleavage are all important in my consideration of background factors. In turn, there are some notable differences between cognitive, affective, and evaluative aspects of attitude and value orientations.[2] No rigorous sepa-ration will be made of the various aspects of the problem, however, be-cause serious confusion would result from the duplication necessarily in-volved in such an approach. It is worth noting here, however, that ethnic (or more narrowly, tribal) factors and occasionally regional ones estab-lish the basis for cleavage and disparity. This is particularly the case for the cognitive and affective aspects of value orientations, expressed in terms of the patterns of political and social identity. Kinship based groups such as clan and tribe constitute the discrete building blocks of Cameroon society; this is reinforced by the same language. One linguist has highlighted the affective importance of the vernacular languages by pointing out that they contain "the voices of one's mother, father, brothers and sisters, and one's dearest friends." [3] Occasionally a sense of ethnic identity arises in a context broader in scope and foundation than that provided by the vernacular language. In conflict with other peoples, migrants or affronted peoples with some cultural or historic connection

---

[2] For a fuller discussion of the characteristics of these aspects and their analytic importance, refer to the discussion, Chap. 1.

[3] R. G. Armstrong, "Vernacular Languages and Culture in Modern Africa," in John Spencer, ed., *Language in Africa* (Cambridge: Cambridge University Press, 1963), p. 69.

may create and assert new ethnic definitions, a process called ethnicity.[4] This has happened in Cameroon with the Tikari peoples of the grass-fields area in the northern part of West Cameroon and with the Bamileke in the highland grassfields and Bamboutous Mountains area of East Cameroon. We shall also see that the new languages and the cultural traditions and structures that accompany them reinforce the impact of regionalism on the identity disparities between East and West Cameroon.

A second important dimension in the study of the background factors of Cameroon reunification, in addition to patterns of identity, combines the evaluative aspect of value and attitude orientation with structural features of Cameroon society. As mentioned before, there are significant disparities among the peoples and regions, not only of Cameroon but of nearly every new African state, in terms of levels of economic and social development and the rate of social mobilization and modernization. Socioeconomic disparities often coincide, thus reinforcing the patterns of identity. Consequently, such characteristics often figure significantly in the patterns of evaluation of the various ethnic and regional groups. Therefore I shall note such preoccupations in my discussion of identity patterns when they constitute an important aspect of the political outlook of particular ethnic groups or regions. Considerations of socioeconomic disparities also count for a great deal in the political orientations of the two communities of East and West Cameroon.

In Chapter 3 I consider the continuities and disparities of identity patterns that are rooted in the indigenous African cultures, along with the principal socioeconomic factors that affect the evaluative patterns of these peoples. These same socioeconomic factors, as they relate to the affinities and disparities that were introduced by the colonial powers, are considered in Chapter 4, and the major economic aspects are discussed in Chapter 5. The experience of the two communities in political interaction are treated in Chapter 6.

[4] For a fuller discussion of this process and a similar one of "supertribalism," see Paul Mercier, "Remarques sur la signification du 'Tribalisme' actuel en Afrique Noire," *Cahiers Internationaux de Sociologie* (July–December 1961), pp. 61–80.

41

$\overset{\circ}{\underset{\text{木}}{\wedge}}$ 3 $\overset{\circ}{\underset{\text{木}}{\wedge}}$

Patterns of Identity in the Indigenous Cultures

THE Kamerun Idea exaggerated the coherence of political values and identity concepts, along with the extensiveness of cultural continuities among the peoples of the two Cameroons Trust Territories. While notable affinities and continuities of this sort existed, they were insufficient to constitute a basis for national awareness or to make social and political interaction natural and the purveyor of complementary relationships. Not only were there significant disparities between the identity patterns and value orientations of the peoples of the merging states, but of various regional and/or ethnic groups within them. The new Federation would not be exempt from the problems of countering and overcoming the parochialisms that each of the two states already faced. The intensification of social and political intercourse which the imposition of common political institutions, through federalism, would impose, would not necessarily always attenuate the political importance of the cleavages between the states or within them. Indeed, the prospect of union was perceived by some groups as threatening to exacerbate the local cleavages by altering the balance of power which had been achieved between the groups.

Ardener has identified the potential consequences of the exaggerated presumption of ethnic affinity between the two Territories, a presumption inspired by so many supporters of the reunification campaign: "If all irredentist theories were allowed full rein, the Southern Cameroons would be destined to be torn asunder by its neighbors, or conversely, it would assimilate vast tracts of these neighbors' own territory." [1]

There are certain ethnic continuities between the two states of the Cameroon Federation; some tribal groups span the frontier between them. For example, the Mungo, Balong, Bakossi, and Mbo groups straddle the boundary in the Mungo Valley. The Bangwa peoples farther to the north in the Mamfe division of West Cameroon would be called Bamileke had this frontier been drawn a bit farther to the west. [2]

Several other groups, while not divided by the frontier, nevertheless have close tribal ties to peoples in the other state. The tribes of the Bamenda grassfields area are a good example; most of the peoples in this area are derived from Tikar stock located in French-speaking Cameroon.

[1] Ardener, "Kamerun Idea," *West Africa,* June 14, 1958.
[2] *Ibid.*

42

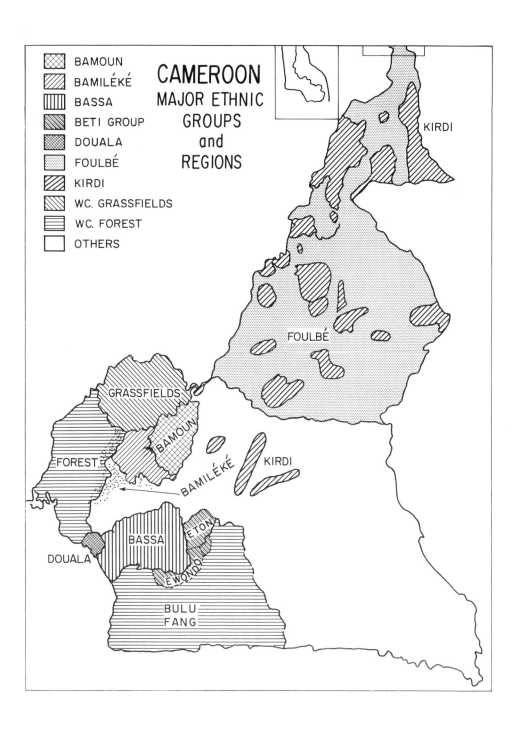

BAMOUN
BAMILÉKÉ
BASSA
BETI GROUP
DOUALA
FOULBÉ
KIRDI
WC. GRASSFIELDS
WC. FOREST
OTHERS

CAMEROON
MAJOR ETHNIC
GROUPS
and
REGIONS

KIRDI

FOULBÉ

GRASSFIELDS

BAMOUN

FOREST

BAMILÉKÉ

KIRDI

DOUALA

BASSA

ETON

EWONDO

BULU
FANG

Some of these kingdoms claim particularly close ties, such as the Bamoun and the Nsaw.[3] The Sultan of the Bamoun claims to be a "brother" of the Fon of Nsaw, and also that the Nsaw are derived from the Bankim, one of the three branches of the Bamoun.[4] The latter allegation appears heavily influenced by the ethnocentricity of the Bamoun. Anthropologists consider the ties between the two groups more distant since they place the Bankim within the Tikar group, from which both the Bamoun and the Nsaw are derived.[5] In any case, the cultures of the two groups have diverged as the Bamoun have embraced Islam, exemplified by the transformation of the traditional designation for chief, "Fon," to the Moslem title, "Sultan." Moreover, the two chiefdoms have been hostile in the past. The Nsaw once routed the armies of the Fon of Bamoun, Nsangguf (the grandfather of the current sultan), and beheaded him in battle.

Bali is the only large traditional state structure in the Bamenda highlands that is not derived from the Tikar.[6] However, as an offshoot of the Chamba of East Cameroon (and Nigeria), the Bali people also have ethnic ties to the French sector. A conquest state, the Bali structure incorporates some elements of the Tikar and Bamoun peoples picked up during their march westward, and they speak a language derived from the conquered peoples of the area.

Along the coast are located other groups with close affinities with groups across the border in East Cameroon. The most important are the Bakolle, Bamboko, and Bakweri—all offshoots of the Douala.[7]

The ethnic affinities between the two states of the Federation have come into play in political life. For example, the Sultan of the Bamoun, who is viewed as something of a paternal figurehead by the Bamenda-grassfields notables, took a keen interest in the reunification question. In April 1959, on the occasion of a general tour of Southern Cameroons, recently elected Prime Minister John Ngu Foncha was given a mammoth

---

[3] See the map in this chapter for the major ethnic groups.

[4] This assertion was made by the *adjoint* (deputy) to the Sultan of Foumban (Sultan of the Bamoun) in an interview at Foumban, November 14, 1963.

[5] M. Littlewood, "Bamun of French Cameroons," in Forde, *Ethnographic Survey of Africa* (London: International African Institute, 1954), Part IX, p. 55; M. McCulloch, "The Tikar of the British and French Cameroons," in Forde, *Ethnographic,* Part IX, p. 14.

[6] For a study of the Tikari see E. Chilvers and P. Kaberry, "From Tribute to Tax in a Tikar Chiefdom [Nsaw]," *Africa,* Vol. 30. E. Chilvers interview, Bali, April 13, 1963.

[7] Ardener, "Coastal Bantu of the Cameroons," in Forde, *Ethnographic,* Part XI; and Ardener, in *West Africa,* June 14, 1958.

reception in his Bamenda home town of Bafreng. The Bamoun Sultan was a major participant in the reception, bringing with him a retinue of about 200 men, including the mayors of Nkongsamba and Douala and the Deputy Prime Minister.[8] Each of the three eastern officials mentioned came from tribes with affinities across the border in West Cameroon.

At the time of the federal constitutional talks it was thought particularly appropriate by both delegations that the conference be held in Foumban, the capital of the Bamoun Sultanate. During the talks Prime Minister Foncha paid special tribute to the Sultan for the role he had played in the reunification movement.

The camaraderie that developed among the grassfields leaders failed, however, to obscure ancient rivalries entirely. One wonders if the Bamoun Sultan's memory of the inglorious defeat of his grandfather at the hands of the Nsaw is not of more importance than their more distant common origins. Perhaps this is the reason the Sultan's long lost "brother" opposed reunification. Neither has the Sultan of Bamoun forgotten past skirmishes with the Bali chiefdom, during which elements of captured Bamoun have been taken over. Evidence of this feeling is shown in the remarks the Sultan made to the Fon of Bali during a visit in early 1963. The Sultan thanked the Fon of Bali "for looking after my people." [9]

If ethnic ties played a part in developing along the eastern border of West Cameroon a favorable audience for the spokesmen of reunification, on the western side of the territory it had the opposite effect. The upper Cross River basin contains populations related to those found in the Ogoja and Calabar provinces of Nigeria. Among other groups, the frontier splits the Ejagham, Boki, Korup, and Efik-speaking peoples.[10] Feeling ran high against unification among many of these western border peoples.

Ardener's assertion that there is no "tidy geographical boundary" for Southern Cameroons is certainly true.[11] Along the western border of the Federation, the frontier with Nigeria, the Akpa-Yafe and Awa Rivers form a natural boundary where few trails link the two countries. But further north the Cross River basin cuts deep into the Mamfe division and

---

[8] Isaac N. Malafa, draft of article for *West Africa*.

[9] E. Chilvers interview.

[10] Ardener, "Coastal Bantu."

[11] Ardener, "The Kamprun Idea."

provides the only good road link to Nigeria. This area contains distinctive populations with stronger ties to the west than the east.[12] In the Nkambe division to the north the grass-covered hills and craggy peaks of the Bamboutos Mountains drop off into the forested basins tributary to the Benoué. This border is pierced in many places by pathways and trails. In terms of the basic geographical and indigenous cultural features, not only is there no single community that embraces the whole of the territory of the old Kamerun, but neither does such a community exist within either of the two federated states.

ETHNIC DISCONTINUITY IN WEST CAMEROON

The geographical frontier within West Cameroon between the southern rain forest and the northern grassfields is an important cultural boundary as well. The line marking the escarpment of the great Central African plateau, abruptly dividing flora and fauna, does the same to peoples, grouping the 60 or so tribal groups into broader culture areas. In the southern forest, north and west of Mount Cameroon, for example, Sudanese or Bantoid languages are spoken. Among these peoples, with strong resemblances with the easternmost peoples of the eastern region of Nigeria, "political integration does not transcend the level of the local community." [13] A headman, perhaps assisted by a council of elders, or in smaller villages an age-grade organization or small chiefs, represents political authority. But north and east of the forest line a new culture area starts, which covers most of the Bamboutos highland grassfields. The people of the grassfields speak Bantu or Bantoid languages, and are marked by a highly evolved and complicated political system utilizing conciliar institutions and by a strong central political leader.[14] Constituting councils, priesthood positions of various grades, an important role for secret societies in the polity, and court headships are all part of the pattern of the grassfield kingships from the tiny village-chieftaincies to the large

[12] The (B)Anyong, settled along the Cross River basin, are grouped in the "Bantoid Cluster" of Murdock's "Southern Nigeria Group." See Murdock, *Africa, Its Peoples and Their Culture History* (New York: McGraw-Hill, 1959), p. 243. Others in this group are the Ejagham (south of the Cross River in the area around Mamfe Station), and the Boki (but Ardener puts them with the Takamanda). See "Map of West Cameroon Tribal Boundaries," No. M280, Land & Survey Department, Buea, November 1959, from data provided by Edwin O. Ardener.

[13] Murdock, *Africa,* p. 248. The coastal peoples already discussed as relatives of French Cameroonians, e.g. Bakweri, Bata, Bomkoko, and Bakalle, speak Bantu languages.

[14] Chilvers interview. The information on the political patterns of the grassfield chieftaincies is taken from this interview, unless otherwise indicated.

and powerful city-states. These institutions are different from those found among the Bamileke and their related West Cameroon chieftaincies among the Bangwa and Ngemba. Nor is there any institutional pattern which resembles that of the grassfield chieftaincies until one gets into western Nigeria on the coast of Benin.

The line separating forest from grassfield also separates the country politically, even in "traditional" politics. On several occasions the line has marked the division between the advancing armies of the conquering chiefdoms and the indigenous clans. For example, the Bali and the Widekum clans which straddle this line have a history of conflict stretching over a half-century, which came to a head in 1951 with the Bali Widekum "war" in which seven people were killed.[15]

In reality, the unity of the "forest" occasionally exhibited in the politics of West Cameroon, especially when this area is in conflict with "the grassfields," is really a precarious, even fallacious, unity. The forest peoples, by the very nature of their traditional structures, are a fragmented collection of small clans. It is the height of folly to speak of the "forest peoples" as if they constituted a cultural community, except perhaps in terms of the anthropologist's general categories. The unity of the Widekum clans tends to crumble when there is no anti-Bali issue. Even in the grassfields the political evolution of the country, the decentralization of local government, and the evolution of a democratic structure at the center have destroyed much of the former unity of the area. This unity, never very extensive, had been imposed by conquest. Not all of the grassfields had been subject to direct Bali rule, but the Bali were a dominant influence because the Germans, perhaps inadvertently, consolidated their position by considering them their principal ally in the area. Almost all of the neighboring peoples have come to be referred to by Bali or German "mishearings" of Bali names. Evidence of the faltering unity of the grassfields, at least in terms of the traditional structures, is the fact that some of these peoples are now reverting to their ancient pre-Bali names. The *Batibur* now call themselves the *Éhué,* and the "Fon" is called the *Éhuésum.*[16]

What can become important when broader political issues are involved is that even the old conquest states such as Bali, Bafut, and Nsaw are often composite communities revealing all sorts of internal lines of cleavage between the clans making up the polity. There are usually some living

---

[15] Chilver interview. See also petitions to the Trusteeship Council and the Fourth Committee of the General Assembly.

[16] Chilver interview. (The orthography is mine.)

survivors of formerly independent political structures which were incorporated; perhaps they were made retainers in the king's court or fused with the royal lineage. The people remain competitive with the core clans of the original groups; the resulting cleavages can become important in political competition. Such cleavages may have influenced the plebiscite vote in Nsaw, for example.[17]

Ethnic Discontinuities in East Cameroon

It should not be surprising that East Cameroon exhibits a pattern of ethnic relationships and communities that is more fragmented than the border area between the two states. Among the four million inhabitants of East Cameroon, French ethnologists have distinguished as many as 136 languages.[18] There are many broad tribal or ethnocultural groups which contain several dialects. Though not every dialect represents a separate tribal group, it is obvious that such groups are extremely numerous, and in the main, quite small. Most of the Cameroon population remains caught up in these micropolities, deriving their values from the group's laws and customs and regulating their behavior by its standards.

We need not concern ourselves here with an analysis of the complete pattern of intertribal relationships throughout East Cameroon. It is important to note, however, that relationships between tribes located far beyond the frontier area between the two states bore on the question of Cameroon reunification, and these relationships continue to affect the progress and possible success of political integration in the Federation. Among the socioethnic groups there are six broad categories of tribal groups that are important to the problems under consideration in this book: (1) Bamileke, (2) Bamoun, (3) Douala, (4) the central peoples, (5) Foulbe, and (6) Kirdi. Associated with each group are factors that affected the development of the unification movement or that can affect the political development of the Federation—factors deriving from the groups' internal social and political structure and/or their mutual relationships.

[17] For a general analysis of Nsaw and its internal cleavages see P. Kaberry, "The Traditional Politics in Nsaw," *Africa,* International African Society, Vol. 29 (April 1959), 366; and Kaberry and Chilver, "Tribute to Tax," pp. 1–19. It is rumored that the Nsaw split their votes in the reunification plebiscite along clan lines, reflecting a long-standing dispute between the Ndzendzef clan and that of the king (Fon). This has been denied by J. N. Lafon, from Nsaw, then secretary of state for the local government. Private letter from Mr. Thaddy Kinga, a Cameroonian student, to the author, January 1966.

[18] D. Gardinier, *Cameroon: United Nations Challenge to French Policy* (London: Institute of Race Relations, 1963), p. 27.

1. *Bamileke*

"Bamileke" is a term applied to the nearly three quarters of a million people living on the plateau areas southeast of the Bamboutos Mountains and west of the Noun River.[19]

The Bamileke are important to an analysis of the Cameroon Federation because: (a) many Cameroonians have considered the reunification issue as essentially a Bamileke issue, (b) many Cameroonians also considered certain features of Bamileke society disagreeable, and consequently were less favorable to the idea of reunification, (c) relations between Bamileke and other groups are among the most hostile in the country, (d) much of the violence and terrorism associated with the *Union des Populations du Cameroun* (UPC) rebellion has occurred in Bamileke country.

The belief that reunification was an issue that concerned the Bamileke more than other Cameroon peoples comes from the fact that they are one of the peoples divided by the frontier between the two states of the Federation and the fact that much of the top leadership and many of the members of the UPC, the political party most strongly advocating reunification, were Bamileke. This belief is a false one, however; it exaggerates the importance of Bamileke interests in the motivation of the reunification movement. In reality, neither the separation of the Bamileke by the frontier nor the role of certain Bamileke in the UPC was overwhelmingly significant.

The frontier between British and French Cameroon *did* divide the Bamileke. However, the number of Bamileke located on the western side of the border is nowhere near as great as most East Cameroonians assumed.[20] I have already mentioned that the Bangwa peoples of West Cameroon belong to the Bamileke group. Judging from political institutions and language, their derivation from Bamileke chiefdoms to the east is clear.[21] However, this group numbers only about 20,000. It is also asserted that Bamileke chiefdoms spill over the border into the Ngemba-occupied areas of the southeastern section of Bamenda division.[22] One

[19] Tardits, *Les Bamileke de l'ouest Cameroun* (Paris: Berger-Levrault, 1960); and Forde, *Ethnographic,* Part IX. In 1961 they constituted about 25% of the population of East Cameroon.

[20] The number of Bamileke in West Cameroon has often been estimated at 300,000, i.e. corresponding roughly with the numbers of the entire Tikar-derived peoples of West Cameroon.

[21] Chilver interview.

[22] Ardener, in *West Africa,* June 14, 1958.

suspects that there are also Bamileke elements mixed in among the other areas of the Tikar and Chamba settlement in the Bamenda grassfields area, since the impingement of the invader peoples on traditional areas of Bamileke settlement is known to have driven some Bamileke west. But they cannot be numerous, and, in any case, are probably assimilated to a considerable extent into the political structures of the dominant chiefdoms.

In the later analysis of the economic affinities between the two states, the impact of the frontier on the economic life of the Bamileke will be discussed. There I call into question the significance of the frontier as a disruptive element in Bamileke economic life.

As for certain Bamileke in the UPC, it is true that much of the party's membership was originally Bamileke. The Bamileke were more heavily represented in the UPC partly because their numbers are disproportionately high among the educated, salaried, civil servant, and professional classes to which the modernizing, anticolonial program of the UPC especially appealed. The Bamileke are among Cameroon's most energetic and resourceful peoples, and are generally more successful than others in securing salaried employment. In Douala the Bamileke are reported to occupy 70 percent of the professional positions and 30 percent of the civil service positions. They constitute over 60 percent of the traders, 80 percent of the artisans, 40 percent of the laborers, and only 12 percent of the domestic workers.[23] Most of the Bamileke living in the southern areas of East Cameroon make their living through commerce. In Yaounde in 1957 they outnumbered the indigenous ethnic groups among the *commerçants* of the city.[24] On the other hand, they also figure heavily among the unemployed in the large southern cities. For example, the number of Bamileke unemployed in Douala alone was estimated in 1960 at 18,-000.[25] Since the Bamileke were so numerous among those elements most likely to respond to a political program calling for accelerated modernization and Africanization of the Territory's economic and political structure, it is natural they should constitute one of the largest tribal elements of the UPC.

Young Bamileke were driven toward the UPC for another important reason. Many felt constrained by the autocratic powers and often heavy-

[23] J. Lamberton, "Les Bamiléké," Study No. 3761 (Paris: Centre des hautes etudes d'afrique moderne).

[24] V. T. Le Vine, *The Cameroons: From Mandate to Independence* (Berkeley: University of California Press, 1964), p. 64.

[25] Lamberton, "Les Bamiléké."

handed rule of the heads of the 90 or so chiefdoms into which the Bamileke population is divided.

Some of the sentiment against the Bamileke chiefs was caused by disputes over land claims. The traditional Bamileke system of land tenure provides for succession of land titles to a single heir, usually the oldest son. Younger brothers, may be left without sufficient land to support their families, and thus may have to seek the means of support elsewhere. This is a factor bolstering the number of Bamileke in the cities (and thus in the UPC). But even those who receive large land plots may have them fragmented by autocratic chiefs acting in response to severe demographic pressures on the land.[26] Sometimes, however, the chiefs were unwilling to subdivide their extensive land holdings. Le Vine notes: "It often appeared as if everyone's holdings except the chief's were getting smaller and less productive." [27] Consequently the chiefs have come to bear the brunt of the disaffection of those forced into the towns and those who may have left for other reasons, only to have their lands reallocated subsequently. Both the detribalized elements and those with land difficulties were potentially hostile to the traditional authority system in Bamileke; in Le Vine's words, "both groups were ready to turn to political action as the internal situation worsened. . . . The UPC . . . provided that answer and grew apace, into unmanageable proportions." [28]

The antitraditional orientation of many Bamileke members of the UPC is the very factor that limits the significance of the Bamileke association with the UPC as a motivating factor in the reunification movement. UPC espousal of the reunification slogan was partially intended to win it the support of the Bamileke leadership and masses, who were by and large nonpoliticized. Though the appeal brought initial support from such elements, the antichief and traditional attitudes of much of the UPC membership and program eventually estranged them and helped make the issue of reunification virtually irrelevant to the UPC.

Nevertheless, many other Cameroonians identified the benefits of re-

[26] The density of settlement in these areas is the highest in the whole country, reaching as high as 141 persons per square kilometer, and averaging 103 per square kilometer. The highest density occurs in the Menoua department—141 per square kilometer in 1962. For one to appreciate the problem in the Bamileke departments these figures must be compared with the average density for the rest of the southern forest area (the general area of heaviest settlement in the country), which is only 17 per square kilometer, or seven for the entire country. A. Carret, J. Gorse, Y. Gillet, and F. Pattier, "Les Regroupements en Pays Bamiléké," I, Federal Republic of Cameroon (Yaounde, January 1963).

[27] Le Vine, *Cameroons*, p. 129.

[28] *Ibid.*, pp. 130–31.

unification with Bamileke interests; to the extent that they were hostile to the Bamileke, they were also hostile to the idea of reunification. Hostility to the Bamileke was caused by their impinging on other groups, and by the fact that their home areas were troubled by violence and terrorism. The Bamileke impinged on other tribal groups socially and economically because they migrated in large numbers throughout the southern areas of East Cameroon and usually preempted sought-after positions of salaried employment. I have already described the overrepresentation of the Bamileke among the professional, civil service, and salaried positions in the large southern cities. The main point is that none of the southern towns of any size has been spared the influx of the resourceful Bamileke. Massive migrations of them have occurred since the early 1930s. A hundred thousand emigrated from the traditional Bamileke areas between 1931 and 1958. By 1956 the Bamileke outnumbered the Douala in the latter's home area, and were 14.25 percent of the population of Yaounde.[29]

There is much evidence of hostility to the immigrant Bamileke communities. Intimidation and violence have been frequent since World War II. A notable incident occurred in the deep southern Bulu and Fang populous city of Sangmelima in 1956, when a major riot broke out between the Bulu and Bamileke.[30] Bamileke market stalls were scattered and pillaged and many Bamileke were beaten, seven of the eight persons injured were Bamileke.

An even more notable incident occurred four years later in Douala. Following a fight between Douala and Bamileke, almost a quarter of the city, which was heavily Bamileke, was burned to the ground.[31] At least 19 were killed and over 5,000 were left homeless.

The fact that much of the UPC campaign of terrorism was concentrated on the Bamileke departments encouraged the hostility of other groups. Those who believed that the Bamileke social structure was particularly suited to engendering violence were not entirely wrong. Also, the demographic problem contributed to violence and warfare between Bamileke chiefdoms. Tardits reports that "boundary disputes in the Bamileke country [often] become exceptionally violent, and it is frequent that conflict between bordering chiefdoms end up in armed battle, with an invasion of the nearby land and burning of huts." [32]

---

[29] Le Vine, *Cameroons,* Table 6.
[30] *Nku Nku, Le Tam Tam,* No. 7, April 1956.
[31] *La Presse du Cameroun,* April 25, 1960.
[32] Tardits, *Les Bamileke,* p. 17.

Also predisposing the Bamileke areas to violence is the fact that French administrative policy produced mutations in the traditional system which resulted in the estrangement of some important community leaders from the chiefs. Traditionally the Bamileke chief was a strong political figure, but by no means an absolute ruler. His rule was buffered by the powers of the council of notables, the *kamveu,* which was consulted on all important affairs of the chiefdom.[33] But the powers of the *kamveu* have gradually been greatly reduced. Many believe this happened as the result of the French desire to have some one person responsible for order and the execution of administrative directives in each chieftaincy. The traditional system was changed; the chief was now turned into an autocrat.[34] The notables of the *kamveu* naturally resented the loss of power, and many are believed to have profited from the general disturbances that accompanied the subsequent UPC rebellion.

Many people in Southern Cameroons feared that reunification would help spread terrorism into the English-speaking areas along the border. Most of the violence occurred among the Bamileke and Douala, and not between them and other groups, which increased the fear that the Bamileke and Douala-related peoples living in the west would be subject to terrorism for the first time.

Even in East Cameroon it was believed that the general pattern of violent tribalism hampered the reunification movement. One letter to a French Cameroon newspaper stated: "What good is it to demand unification of the two Cameroons if we must consider, at first sight, our Bamileke or Bassa brothers as strangers in our own department? In what rank will be placed a Cameroonian from British Cameroons if we are enemies between ourselves, if to say Bassa or Bamileke in Ntem [Department] becomes a hanging matter, a crime which merits death?" [35]

Hostility to the Bamileke also dampened enthusiasm among other groups for reunification; they feared it would result in the aggrandizement of Bamileke political and economic strength by adding to the vast numbers of Bamileke in French Cameroon what was thought to be the vast numbers of them in the British Cameroons. This fear was predicated on an unjustified assumption of cohesiveness and sense of community among the Bamileke. In reality, there is no such sense of community.

[33] *Ibid.,* p. 20.

[34] E. Kwayeb, *Le Droit coutumier Bamiléké au contact des droits européens* (Youande: Government Printer, 1959), pp. 142–43.

[35] Abel Eyinga, "Les Elections Camerounaise du 10 Avril 1960," unpub. thesis, Faculté de Droit et Science Economique (Université de Paris, 1960).

Even the name "Bamileke" is not part of the traditions of the people to whom it is applied; it was invented for them by Europeans.[36] Perhaps the strongest evidence of a lack of cohesiveness in Bamileke society is that it is fragmented politically into over 90 separate, autonomous chiefdoms. The peoples grouped under these chiefdoms speak approximately 13 groups of languages.[37]

Fear of the Bamileke people was unjustified mainly because the West Cameroon peoples, considered as Bamileke in the eastern sector, were really more closely related to the Tikar groups, as noted in the discussion of the peoples of the Bamenda grassfields. Thus the more understandable fear would have been of Bamoun aggrandizement.

2. *Bamoun*

Racially the Bamoun are a mixed people, descendants of an invading Tikar people who came into the plateau area west of the Mbam River about 250 years ago and of the Bamileke peoples indigenous to that area.[38] The Tikar peoples adopted the languages of the Bamileke and the two groups have intermixed, though they are still physically distin-guishable. The close historical and cultural affinities between the Bamoun and Bamileke were possibly the basis of fear that West Cameroon Tikar-derived groups would act in political harmony with the Bamileke. One test of this proposition is the *likelihood* of East Cameroon Tikar-derived groups doing so. But if the Bamoun are taken as representative of the other East Cameroon Tikar groups, the likelihood is not great.

In recent years there has been little intercourse between the two groups. Although the French administration deliberately encouraged Bamileke emigration into the more sparsely settled Bamoun areas, very few have settled there. In 1949 there were about a thousand such immi-

[36] M. Littlewood, "The Bamileke of French Cameroons," in Forde, *Ethno-graphic,* Part IX, p. 87. This may be another example of German use of Bali names for other tribes. The Bali name for the people of Dschang is *Lékeu.* The Germans may have added the normal Bantu prefix "Ba" and the name may have evolved from Balekeu to Bamileke ("people of the valleys"). Bamileke may be an appropri-ate name for about 4,000 persons living opposite Dschang in West Cameroon—it is not part of any of the languages of any of the other peoples of the Bamileke group. See also R. Delarozier, "Institutions Politiques et Sociales des Populations Bam-ileke," *Etudes Camerounaises,* Nos. 25–26, 27–28 (March–June, September–December 1949).

[37] Littlewood, "Bamileke," p. 88.

[38] Littlewood, "Les Bamum," pp. 53–54.

grants settled in the department, and a decade later the number had increased to only 120,000.[39] Compared to other areas to the south which have been subjected to heavy Bamileke settlement, Bamoun has experienced a relatively small influx; part of the reason may be hostility between the Bamoun and Bamileke.

The Bamoun and Bamileke have almost no sense of community, not even of a security community (if the absence of war or the expectation of war is the cardinal test of the existence of such a community).[40] The Bamoun department is the only one in Cameroon to have fortified and constantly guarded its borders. Its entire southwestern border of the department along the Noun River, which separates it from Bamileke department, has been constantly guarded by Bamoun warriors.[41] It was initially armed and fortified after Bamileke terrorists attacked a village in the Foumbot *Arrondissement* in January 1960, killing one Bamoun and injuring three others.[42] On the day following this attack, 1,000 Bamoun warriors "spontaneously" gathered, crossed the Noun, and razed the village and *chefférie* of Bamendjin, from which the Bamileke terrorists were thought to have come. That was the last reported incident of terrorism in the Bamoun department.

Politically the Bamoun and the Bamileke have been in separate camps throughout the modern political life of the Territory. The principal figures in national politics from each area have been associated with quite different, and often opposed, political parties. The Sultan of the Bamoun, El Hadj Seidou Njimoluh, and Njoya Arouna, recently the minister of justice in the federal government, are the major Bamoun politicians. Both have been associated with the northern-based party, the *Union Camerounaise,* since its inception. In fact, Arouna was one of the most important non-northern allies of Ahmadou Ahidjo, the founder of the UC. Probably Ahidjo was first influenced to support reunification because his Bamoun allies favored it.

The principal Bamileke political figures, on the other hand, have been associated with the southern-based UPC (with decided anti-North leanings) or have tended to form their own Bamileke political organizations.

[39] Lamberton, "Les Bamiléké."

[40] For a discussion of a security community see K. Deutsch, "Political Community at the International Level," *Foreign Policy Analysis Series No. 2* (Princeton University, September 1953).

[41] *Adjoint* (deputy) to the Sultan of Foumban (Sultan of the Bamoun), interview with the Sultan, November 14, 1963.

[42] *La Presse du Cameroun,* January 25, 1960.

For many years one of the main Bamileke political figures in "national" politics was Mathias Djoumessi, the first president of the UPC.

3. *Douala*

The Douala peoples had an important part in the development of the reunification movement and continued to be influential in the new Federation. Their importance derives from their geographical location and history.

Numerically the Douala proper are unimportant. Numbering only about 25,000 in 1965, they were not even the largest single group in their home location, the area close to the estuary of the Wouri River.[43] Several other coastal, Bantu-speaking peoples are closely related to the Douala —the Mongo, Pongo, Wouri, Bodiman, Bakolle, and Malimba groups.[44] More distantly related are the Bakweri, Bamboko, Bota, and Suba groups, which, along with the Bakolle, are found in West Cameroon.

All of these groups, located on the coast, have the longest experience of any of the peoples of Cameroon with European merchant, missionary, and military influences. They were the first to learn to respect the fiery weapons of the strange "toeless" (shoe-wearing) white men, the first to be converted, or coerced, into his religion, and the first to attend his schools. This was preeminently so for the Douala who came to occupy the banks of the estuary of the Rio dos Camaroes.[45] The Portuguese Fernão do Po visited the area 20 years before Columbus discovered America.[46] It was also in the area now occupied by the Douala that the first official British representative, John Beecroft, a Negro and "consul and agent of Her Majesty for the Bays of Benin and Biafra," established his headquarters at Bimbia.[47] A missionary station was also set up at Bimbia, to which the great British Baptist missionary, Alfred Saker, the first white man

---

[43] Federal Republic of Cameroon, Ministè de l'Economie Nationale, Service de la Statistique, *Récensement Douala—1955–56.*

[44] E. O. Ardener, "Coastal Bantu of the Cameroons," in Forde, *Ethnographic,* Part XI, p. 11.

[45] The name means "River of Prawns" in Portuguese; eventually it came to be called the Cameroons River, and now the Wouri River, after the Oli people. It is from the Portuguese name for the river that the country takes her name.

[46] They established a post for the nearby islands of Sao Thomé, one of which came to be called Fernando Po; they visited the Cameroon coast, particularly the Wouri estuary, and Kribi to buy slaves.

[47] R. Cornevin, "Aperçu Historique" (République Fédérale du Cameroun), in Gilbert Houlet, ed., *Les Guides Bleus—Afrique Centrale* (Paris: Hachette, 1962).

allowed to set up a permanent settlement in the area, came in 1845, making contact with the Douala.[48]

It was the kings of Douala, especially King Bell, that representatives of the Hamburg firms of Woermann and Jantzen & Thormalen negotiated; and it was with Imperial Commissioner Nachtigal that the "protectorate" treaties giving Germany control of the "Kamerun" were concluded.[49] The Douala, who had become internally divided (their only continued expression of unity was a council, called *Ngondo,* of the several kings), had always monopolized the commerce (in aggry stone and slaves) of the whole region with the various European powers. Their command of the coast meant all trade had to pass through their hands, and they could prevent European penetration into the interior. Their desire for a protectorate allegedly stemmed from a desire to maintain the monopoly.[50] The Douala kings insisted in the protectorate treaties that the Germans could not penetrate the interior, and could deal only with them in commercial matters.[51] Thomas Hodgkin asserts that "the history of the German occupation in its early stages is largely the history of the struggle to substitute German for Douala control over trade with the interior." [52]

[48] Joseph Bouchard, "Histoire," in E. Goernier and G. Froment-Guieysse, eds., *Cameroun, Togo,* Encyclopédie de l'afrique française (Paris: l'Union Française, 1951).

[49] For a full discussion of the role of the Douala in the establishment of German rule see H. Rudin, *Germans in the Cameroons, 1884–1914* (New Haven: Yale University Press, 1958). Also see Ardener, "Coastal Bantu," in Forde, *Ethnographic,* Part xi, pp. 19, 20; Cornevin, "Aperçu Historique"; and Adalbert Owona, "La Traite de Protectorat German-Douala," in *Revue Camerounaise,* No. 8 (March–April 1959). Owona reports that Bell, in a letter to Gladstone requesting a British protectorate, stated: "We are tired of governing this country ourselves. Each dispute leads to a war, and often to a great loss of life."

[50] Ardener, "Coastal Bantu," p. 20, states: "The Douala chiefs obtained their wealth and influence through the trade in the Cameroon estuary, and the continual fission within the Douala chiefdoms appears to have been the result, on the one hand, of the desire of more and more lineage heads to be recognized as 'Kings,' that is as persons to be dealt with directly by the English traders, and on the other, of the encouragement of 'pretenders' by these traders themselves. The insecurity and indebtedness of the Bells and Akwas in 1884 made them ready to accept European protection, which the German Doctor Nachtigal negotiated just ahead of the British."

[51] On July 12, 1884 the Douala kings asserted to either Handel or Schiff, "our wish is that white men should not go up and trade with the bushmen . . . they must stay here in [sic] this river and they give us trust that we will trade with our bushmen." This was signed as "The Chiefs of the Cameroons"; cf. Rudin, *Germans in the Kamerun,* p. 423.

[52] Hodgkin, "The French Cameroon 2: The German Period," *West Africa* (November 27, 1954), p. 1,109.

When the Germans began to penetrate the hinterland with expeditions to the east and north after 1887, the Douala protested strongly. Many petitions were made to the German administration, some directly to the Reichstag.[53] In 1911, with the grievances augmented by the addition of tax obligations and the expropriation of land for expansion of the commercial district, the Douala chiefs sent an emissary to Berlin.[54] They were the first Cameroon people to openly resist colonial rule and to attempt to manipulate the institutions of a colonial power in order to secure local interests.

The original commercial monopoly enjoyed by King Bell not only led to some of the friction within the Douala people but encouraged the opposition of neighboring peoples. Eventually the myth of Douala hegemony over all the Cameroon came to be resented by other groups throughout the south of Cameroon. When the Douala took up the call for reunification of Cameroon (much of the membership of the UPC was Douala, and the "Ngondo," the traditional assembly of the Douala, supported reunification) some leaders in other areas interpreted it as just another reassertion of old Douala claims. A newspaper partisan to political movements among the "Beti group" (or "Pahouin group") of peoples located in the forest and plateau areas around the capital of Yaounde had this to say about Douala support for reunification and independence: ". . . since 1885 when the Douala believed [themselves] to have spoken in the name of the Cameroon, according to the 'article du Ngondo' . . . Cameroon has never ceased to live in misery. . . . Here is the demagogery: for New Bell (a quarter of Douala city), no Beti, no Bamileke, no Cameroonian 'strangers,' but to combat Deputy Mbida because he is not Douala (Mbida, the first Prime Minister opposed independence and unification) one must preach unity. . . . We would . . . like to know why until now (though the Douala are preaching unification), the Beti, Boulou, Bassa, Bamileke are treated as strangers in Douala in front of Frenchmen who seem at home there. . . ."[55] A later issue of the same paper quoted J. M. Mbida, East Cameroon's first prime minister, as saying: "It is incontestable that in Cameroon the French have never wanted to favor the political evolution of the populations of the center. They have always manifested a marked and evident preference for the Douala, to the detriment of the other peoples of the Cameroon. . . ."[56] Mbida

[53] B. Lembezat, *Les Populations paiennes du Nord-cameroun et de l'adamaova* (Paris: Presses Universitaires France, 1961), p. 20.

[54] Bouchard, "Histoire," p. 55.

[55] *Nku Nku, le Tam Tam,* No. 10 (nouvelle Série) (July 1956), editorial.

[56] *Ibid.,* No. 11 (July 1956).

continued, saying that the French government wanted to give the central populations an inferiority complex, culturally, intellectually and socially, in comparison with the Douala. Their aim, in his view, was to aid the Douala "realize their place, their aspirations for hegemony and command."

4. *The Central Peoples: Ewondo, Bulu, Bassa*

For the central and southern groups, the Bulu, Ewondo, Eton, and others of the so-called Beti or Pahouin branch of the large Fang culture and particularly for the Bulu, reunification was not a particularly important issue. Such positions as they may have taken on the issue were heavily influenced by their relationships to other groups more direcly involved. Thus the Beti leaders, grouped in the *Parti des Démocrates,* in the main opposed reunification (though not actively) because they considered it to be a part of the UPC's program which they opposed and of special importance to the Douala and Bamileke peoples with whom they were in conflict. In some cases religious considerations may also have had an influence. The Ewondo and Eton are heavily Catholic; they have opposed the Ahidjo regime longer than any other group. The Bulu are largely Presbyterian; they gave early but fleeting support to nationalist and reunification programs.

What should be noted here is a pattern of ethnic conflict that may have predisposed certain groups to take a particular approach to the question of reunification. The more educated and economically advanced southern populations generally gave earlier and more vehement support to nationalist movements than the populations to the north. In view of the fact that reunification was considered basically as a means of advancing the nationalist program, one would expect that all of the southern progressive politicians would support the idea. Where such politicians were only lukewarm in their support, or even hostile, one looks for special reasons. It was likely significant that diverging positions of the southern leaders often coincided with patterns of former tribal conflict and hostilities. The statements of former Prime Minister Mbida quoted above make explicit reference to tribal animosities between the central Beti peoples and the Douala.

The Beti, as well as the Bulu (whose principal leader, former East Cameroon Prime Minister Charles Assalé, also did little to advance the reunification program), have a history of conflict with the Bassa with whom the UPC was identified until the death of its general secretary, Reuben Um Nyobe. Though there is much controversy about their origins, the Bassa appear to have arrived at their present location (between the Dibamba, Sanaga and Nyong River valleys, and north along the Wouri and Banen Rivers) before the Bakoko, Fang, and other Pahouin-related tribes did.[57]

It is not certain whether the impingement by the various Beti and Pahouin peoples on the Bassa initiated conflict between the groups, but there is modern evidence of conflict between them. The Bulu, related to the Pahouin group, allegedly call the Bassa "Mvélé," a term of disapproval in Bulu.[58] During the interwar period some of the missionary schools found it impossible to carry on their work if Bassa, Bulu, or Ewondo were housed together.[59]

The tribal hostilities between the Bassa and other southern peoples was aggravated in the mid-1920s by the burdens placed on them in connection with the extension of the old German-built railroad from Makak on to Yaounde, with a branch to Mbalmayo. Thousands of workers from all over the southern part of the Territory were pressed into labor on the railroad, and the Bassa farms were made to produce supplies to feed them. Gardinier asserts, "the requisitions imposed on the forest peoples to feed the workers produced frequent hardships and migrations. The Administration punished workers who deserted and farmers who did not produce the foodstuffs demanded of them." [60] The Bassa have been accused of refusing to grow food for the workers, in part to cause them to die, quit work, or otherwise cause the project to fail. Not only did they resent the impingement on their own food supplies and the heavy-handed tactics used to extract supplies from them but they also feared that epidemics would spread among their own villages from the workers' camps. The embitterment that resulted has never been forgotten by any of the tribal groups. Such factors could not have failed to influence the evolution of political movements and leaders in these areas.

[57] I. Dugast, *Inventoire Ethnique du Sud-Cameroun* (Youande: IFAN, 1949), p. 36. Dugast points out that the Bassa and Bakoko share a common myth about their origins. They, along with the Beti group, cite a particular cavern in present-day Bati (on the right bank of the Sanaga) as the place where their ancestors came forth (p. 37).

[58] George Ankers, missionary at the Presbyterian School at Elat (Ebolowa), who has been a missionary worker among the Bassa, Bulu, and other southern forest peoples for 43 years. See also P. Alexandre, *Manuel Elémentaire de la Langue Balu,* CHEAM (Paris: 56).

[59] Ankers, interview, Ebolowa, 1963. This was true at the missionary school at Bibia, near Lolodorf, in 1925.

[60] Gardinier, *Cameroon,* p. 17.

5. *Foulbé*

If the southern populations of East Cameroon appear to be incorrigible tribalists incapable of overcoming ethnic divisions in order to unite around a political program or leader, "the north" has the opposite image. Those holding this view of the north do not assert that the lines of division and conflict between ethnic groups are not sharp in the north; indeed, they view them as the most acute in the Territory. The popular assumption is that the north is dominated by a minority group, the Foulbé (Fulani) who prevent effective expression of political opposition among the pagan tribes who constitute the majority of the northern population.[61] The unity of attitudes regarding the north among southern political leaders was not only based on the supposition that the north was rigidly structured in a feudalistic hierarchy lorded over by the Foulbé, but also that the political leaders of the north, assumed to be the lamibé,[62] would always act together when confronted with southerners.

The bluntest statement of the charge against the north is found in the literature and pronouncements of the exiled leadership of the UPC. Typical is the following: "The Union Camerounaise, led by the puppet Ahidjo, is the party of the reactionary social classes, the party of the feudalists and of the bureaucratic bourgeois who remain loyal to medieval conceptions." [63] The point of view expressed by the UPC exaggerates a position shared by many if not most of the politically conscious elements in the south prior to independence. The northern populations were considered more backward than those in the south, not only because much of the autocratic structure of the Fulani empire still existed, but because these populations had experienced less intense exposure to modern educational communication and social facilities. About one-third of the population of East Cameroon lives in "the north," yet in 1955 out of about 252,000 children in schools, only 8,100 went to schools in that region; only 85 schools out of more than 250 were located there, and only six percent of the school-age children in the north were in school, compared with 85 percent in the south.[64] In 1955 there were four large hospi-

[61] The total population of the six administrative regions of the north (Adamawa, Benové, Diamaré, Logone-et-chari, Margui-Wandala, Mayo-Danai) was estimated in 1961 at about 1.3 million, of which the Foulbe accounted for approximately 400 thousand. Le Vine, *Cameroons,* pp. 12–14. These figures are probably low, since they have not changed from the estimates of 1957.

[62] *Lamibé* is the plural form of *lamido,* which means "chief" in Foulbé. A *lamidat* is the kingdom or chieftaincy over which the *lamido* rules.

[63] UPC, Comité Directeur, *L'Opression Française au Kamerun* (1962?), p. 15.

[64] UN Document T/1240, Chap. 5, Report of the 1955 Visiting Mission.

tals, all in the south. Most of the dispensaries, maternity clinics, and almost all of the industry are still located in the southern regions, though much has been done in the north since independence. Of all the credit advanced under the first two five-year plans prior to independence, only 18 percent went to the north.[65] The retardation of the area was incontestable. One of the high commissioners of the Territory is reported to have stated: "until now the North has lived as a parasite which disposed of only unproductive resources." [66] Sensing this, many northern leaders have expressed hostility toward the south, and consider it to have been overprivileged and their own region neglected.

This attitude was sometimes even shared by French administrators working in the north. The *Chef de Région* of the old "Northern Region" (in the far north), in his last annual report before the area was decentralized into four separate divisions, called the territory a "disinherited region" in "moral isolation." [67] Welcoming the decentralization, he stated: "One wanted this reputation to disappear which made of the North to all intents and purposes a feudal and medieval, archaic and autocratic territory, where everyone knows that it suffices to make a sign to the great Sultans in order to raise millions in taxes and thousands of workers; should one have buried pell-mell the 'vestibule of the desert,' the Foulbé Fantasia, the Toupouri dancers, the shell houses and the spires of the Kapsiki, and all this bazaar trumpery which gives so much charm to this country—on the condition, surely, that one passes forty-eight hours there in the month of December." [68]

With the increasing development of the north in the last five years before independence, the hostility of the north toward the south seemed to grow apace, rather than lessen. Part of the reason was that, as in Northern Nigeria, this development depended on southern civil servants, professionals, and teachers. The 1955 United Nations Visiting Mission was

[65] Jules Ninine, "Vers un Equilibre entre le Nord et le Sud du Cameroun," l'Economie, Supp. No. 584 (April 25, 1957). Before Cameroun independence the north had a significant cattle and livestock industry of 1½ million head. There was a model farm in Nagoundéré, in addition to meatpacking, refrigerator, and shipping companies and a cottonseed pressing plant in the north.

[66] A. Mandon, Speech, Assemblée Territoriale du Cameroun, Budget Session, March 1957.

[67] Rapport Annuel Administrative, Région du Nord, 1950 (Paul Delmond was the *chef de région* at the time); translation mine. See also P.F. Gonidec, "Questions internationales intéressant la France: de la dépendence a l'autonomie—l'etat sous tutelle du Cameroun," *Annuaire Francais de Droit International*, III (Paris: Centre National de la Recherche Scientique, 1957), note 53, p. 622.

[68] *Ibid.*

told by northern notables that they did not want the people of the south in their territory any longer, that educational opportunities needed to be greatly expanded, "in order that no official from the South should serve in the North." [69] Even the current president, Ahmadon Ahidjo, after his election to the Territorial Assembly, stated, "the population of the North remains pessimistic [about] the South." [70]

Ahidjo may have understated the issue, for many persons feared that the hostility between the peoples of the two regions would lead to partition of the Territory, though such hostility nowhere led to any significant incidents of violence or intimidation between the two.[71] One dubious report of a threat of schism between the north and the south asserts that during the inaugural session of the 1956 Territorial Assembly one deputy, Dr. Plantier, initiated an unsuccessful campaign in the press against the election of Soppo Priso as assembly president and, referring to the "problem of the North," called for the creation of an assembly just for the north.[72] Others have also referred to an attempt in the north to create an autonomous northern state in a Cameroon federation; a parliamentary commission (the *"France d'Outre-Mer"* Commission) of the French National Assembly, visiting the Territory in the spring of 1956, is reported to have discovered "a jealousy manifested among the Foulbé and the animists of the North of Cameroon regarding the regions of the South which they deem to have benefited too much from all the aid of the French Administration, which develops the South to the detriment of the North." For this reason, allegedly, the northerners are reported to have demanded a federal formula.[73]

One of the most influential of the young political leaders from the north, the first secretary general of the UC, and one of President Ahidjo's most useful and trusted lieutenants, asserts that it was really the French who attempted to divide the country. "The French did not believe that those in the North were not with the UPC-ists." [74] In the aftermath of the

[69] UN Document T/1240, p. 15, para. 120.

[70] *Nku Nku, le Tam Tam,* No. 9 (June 1957), p. 15.

[71] The report of the 1955 Visiting Mission, (T/1240, para. 115), states: "These people [Southern teachers, civil servants, etc.] appear to have been received without any difficulty, but they lived together in separate quarters, seldom associating in private life with the local inhabitants." The isolation of the Southerners serving in the north is the constant theme in the annual reports of the administrative regions of the north, from 1946 to 1955.

[72] *Nku Nku, le Tam Tam,* No. 8 (May 1956).

[73] *Ibid.,* No. 9 (June 1956).

[74] Moussa Yaya, Political Secretary, *Union Camerounaise,* Second Vice President of the Federal National Assembly in 1963, interview, June 1963.

Suez crisis, and considering the common bond of Islam, the administration allegedly viewed the young political leadership of the north as a threat, subject to influences from Egypt.[75]

The most serious threat of schism was posed by the 1957 *statut* of the Cameroon, which divided northern Cameroon into a separate province endowed with its own institutions, including an assembly.[76] The threat of Deputy Plantier matured two years later in the *Statut*. Although the new *Statut* was promulgated by decree it had been debated in the Territorial Assembly and modified there, but the provision for a northern province remained. Perhaps the inclusion of a provision for provincial councils was due to the influence of the French administration. The idea was not without precedent in Cameroon, however; as early as 1945 the cultural-youth organization, *Jeunesse Camerounaise Française* (JEUCAFRA), demanded certain reforms, among which were provincial councils.[77] The provincial councils were never established, however, probably because events moved too rapidly after the inauguration of the first "autonomous" Cameroonian government. It may also have been due to a fear among progressive leadership, even in the north, that such a system would jeopardize national unity.

It is important to note that despite appearances, the Foulbé empire in northern Cameroon was not truly unified and cohesive. Historically there are fissures running through Foulbé society that have left distinguishable marks on the political life of the area. The kingdoms established in Cameroon as part of the empire of Osuman Dan Fodio were generally dominated by one or the other of two large Foulbé families, the Vollarbe (or Bororo—pastoral Foulbé) and the Yillaga.[78] These families jealously

[75] Discussion in several annual reports of the *chefs de régions* in the northern regions of Cameroon reveal an administration interest in the potential influence of Cairo and the North African nationalist movements on the political development of the territory. A report asserted in 1951, "The cultural currents and the political cues coming from Cairo remain alive during their pause at Tchad. Fort-Lamy constitutes a sufficiently active center to absorb ideas coming from the North and North-East, but the peoples of Logone and Chari [Cameroon], exclusively rural, if they do remain attached to the letter of Islam, are refractory to every cultural notion coming from the Nile."

[76] P. F. Gonidec, *Histoire,* p. 623.

[77] Adalbert Owona, "Le Nationalisme Camerounaise," No. 5, Series II, *Etude de diverse type de nationalisme* (Paris: Association Française de Science Politique, May 1962), p. 19. At that time there were only two provinces, north and south. I discuss later the question of provincial councils in my consideration of local government structures in the Federation.

[78] Kurt Strumpell, "Histoire des Foulbé," in Abbe Thomas Ketchoua, *Contribution a l'histoire du Cameroun* (Yaounde: Imprimerie Nationale, 1962), p. 55.

sought to establish their own dominance in the areas where they had settled. Even the often nepotistic kingdoms directly established by Adama fought bitterly between themselves to increase their holdings or declare their independence from his suzerainty.[79] In short, though the various powerful *lamibé* of the north may have a common interest in countering southern privilege or in resisting encroachment upon their traditional powers by the modern institutions and leaders, there are many historically rooted hostilities in their relations which sometimes strain their relations and inhibit collaboration.

6. *Kirdi*

The cleavage in the northern society most threatening to the political stability of the state and most difficult to overcome is that which distinguished the immigrant Foulbé and the mostly pagan (called "Kirdi" by the Foulbé) communities which originally occupied the northern plains. In 1957, of the nearly 1.3 million persons living in northern French Cameroon, 500 thousand were Moslem, and of these perhaps only two-thirds were Foulbé.[80] Thus the Kirdi are by far the majority in the north, but they do not constitute a monolithic bloc of potential voters. The Kirdi community, much more than the Foulbé *lamidats,* are small isolated, tribal, or clan groups, with little in common other than their similar experience of displacement and domination by the Foulbé.

Most of the Kirdi have had relatively little contact with the Foulbé in the last century and a half, since they were driven out of their former habitat into the mountains or away from the principal Foulbé settlements

Modibo Adama, the military commander of the expeditions sent out by Dan Fodio's son, Mohammed Bello, was of the Bororo (Vollarbe) family. But before his efforts eventually led to the establishment of Foulbé-dominated kingdoms, there had been at least two waves of Foulbé migration into the north Cameroon area. One group came from Jaffoun near Kano by way of Baoutchi; the second, the Kest-chouen, came from Bornu.

[79] The *lamido* of Rei-Bouba is the chief representative of the Yillaga family, and remained juridically independent, even under the French, until 1950. Ngaoundéré and Banyo are the chief representatives of the Vollarbe. Historically none of these various kingdoms would pay tribute to the other. J. O. Froelich, Centre des Hauts Etudes d'Afrique Modernes, Paris, interview, Paris, December 17, 1963. See also Strumpell, "Histoire des Foulbé," p. 55; and E. Genin, "Le Lamidat de Banyo," administrative report dated March 1929, Archives, District Office, Garoua, Cameroon.

[80] M. Arnould, "Transformation des Structures Traditionelles du Nord Cameroun," Study No. 2877, Centre des Houtes Etudes d'Afrique Moderne (Paris, November 23, 1957); See also: *Rapports Administrative Annuels: Région du Nord,* 1950, *Région du Diamare,* 1951, *Région de Margai Wandala,* 1951, *Région de l'Adamoua,* 1951, *Région de Benoué,* 1951.

on the plains. Among those having experienced close contact, there are two groups, the vassal pagan tribes of the plains, called "Machudo," who pay heavy tribute to the Lamibé but who continue to live in their own villages and preserve much of their tribal consciousness and former customs and structures; and the descendants of *"Matchoubé"* slaves, or those who were captured in war, who lived with the Foulbé families. Despite laws against slavery, many of the *Matchoubé* remain in servitude. Detribalized, living in close association with the Foulbé in the towns and cities, yet only partially incorporated into the Islamic community (since full accession would bring freedom with it), the *Matchoubé* have exhibited neither the structural organization nor the psychological inclination to challenge Foulbé preeminence and thus have not constituted as much of a political threat to Foulbé domination as have the plains peoples and those who fled to the mountains. After the French-inspired reformation of local government institutions in the north, which was central to French policy in the area between 1953 and 1955, the Foulbé notables began to include *Matchoubé* in the new expanded "Councils of Fada." One French administrator serving in the north during this period stated that in all 10 of the new councils he had installed, the new dignitaries added to the old councils were chosen from among the *Matchoubé*.[81]

Those most suspicious of the Foulbé, and who thus pose the greatest problem of political reconciliation are the peoples who fled to the mountains to escape Foulbé domination during the *jihad* of Osuman Dan Fodio in 1804–1811. In reality, not all of those found in the mountains today —e.g. the Matakams, Mofu, Kapsiki, Margui especially, and perhaps the Fali farther south—were chased off the plains by the Foulbé. The mountains have been too transformed (terraced, for example) and the societies too well adapted to the conditions (totally unlike the plains) for some of the most respected students of these societies to accept the proposition that they have occupied their present location for only a few generations.[82] Some of the pagan tribes of the plains and foothills must also have been invaders, driving some of their predecessors farther into the hills. At any rate, whether deserving of the honor or not, the Foulbé have inherited much of the hostility and suspicion of the displaced peoples. Only very recently benefiting from the *pax gallica* and later from the appeals of the new political leadership among the Foulbé, have some of the *montagnards* descended and resettled on the plains to employ their considerable farming skills on land much more fertile and pliable than the

[81] Arnould, "Transformation."
[82] Lembezat, *Les Populations,* pp. 12–16.

rocky crevices from which they have eked out their existence for over 150 years.

So far the Foulbé leadership of the UC has successfully avoided a political split between the Kirdi and Foulbé communities in the north, but one suspects this has been due in part to the low level of political mobilization among the Kirdi peoples. As these groups become more exposed to modern communications and economic activity, it is expected that the dangers of open political conflict between the two communities will be heightened. The young, progressive UC leadership appreciate these dangers and are moving to head them off by working to make both Islam and the UC serve as a framework within which these communities can be regrouped.

IT IS obvious from this discussion of the relationship between the disparate ethnic communities within the frontiers of the old German "Kamerun" that the ethnically based affinities between the two states in the new Cameroon Federation were meager prior to their reaffiliation in the new federation. While these affinities and continuities may have given a certain stimulus to the reunification movement, they were not so extensive as to account for the success of that movement or to provide a significant basis for the cluster of coherent values and sense of common community necessary for the construction of a nation among all the peoples inhabiting the new federation. Moreover, neither of the two states taken individually could meet this test. The political and social life of each state was fragmented into a complex myriad of ethnic groups which in the past have been, and which in the future may continue to be, hostile to each other. If reunification lessened the disruptive impact of tribal grievances by reuniting ethnic groups in the area of the frontier, it threatened to increase them elsewhere by altering the delicate political equilibrium among the various ethnic groups of each state. Thus the viability of the Federation depends in part on the resolution or suppression of grievances and hostilities, not only between the broad cultural groups of the two states, but between the tribal groups and cultural regions generally.

✿ 4 ✿

Colonialism as a Culture Carrier

THE GREAT truth Western students of the developing areas are prone to
see in the relatively brief European experience with direct colonial rule is
that it spread the revolution of the rational, science-based society to almost all the rest of the world. This view prevails despite the perversities
of the experience, which some students have found only in the brutality,
exploitation, and abuse of power that unfettered control usually breeds
and which others find only in the ageless "old abuses" of a "savage" tradition whose resurgence seems to them guaranteed by a "premature" independence of the colonies. These students seem to think traditional Africa
was made up of petty, parochial worlds, embodying a life style Hobbes
might have described, whose people were isolated and fearful, constantly
preying on each other's problems, persons, and possessions.

Colonialism is supposed to have penetrated these worlds and laid them
open to new forces of change and progress which splintered them, and
from the pieces built an order more productive, powerful, and participant. Ironically the same view was shared by disparate groups of people:
those for whom the moral revulsion derived from the cruel upheavals of
change itself and the oppressions of an unfinished incipient order (e.g.
Karl Marx), and those for whom it was the result of unrepentant attitudes
of people enmeshed in a stable, un-Christian, traditional order (David
Livingstone). Both groups saw the necessary hardships of the transition
as progressive.[1]

Wittingly or not, both groups were agents of colonialism. They, their
followers, and accomplices were the modern Romans, carrying the imperial torch in the name of Civilization. They were different from present
and future analysts of the process, not only in their remarkable understanding of their own age, but in their unwillingness to consider the cultural diffusion as simply the "Westernization" of Africa and Asia. They
were different because they sensed that the differences between the cultural, religious, and ideological strains of the "European tradition" (rep-

---

[1] Marx discussed the progressive revolutionizing impact of British colonialism in
a series of articles in the *New York Daily Tribune* in 1853. Livingstone popularized
the notion of the civilizing mission of Britain in a number of anti-slave trade and
anti-slavery speeches in Britain. See William Monk, ed., *Dr. Livingstone's Cambridge Lectures* (Cambridge, England: Deighton, Bell & Co., 1860).

resented by the differences in national cultures) were of considerable significance. After all, agents of the European powers stumbled over each other—often quite literally, and sometimes violently—in a "scramble" to stake out their exclusive claims in Africa. It seemed to matter to them whether Africa became British, French, or German, Protestant, Catholic, or Mohammedan. It is therefore worth enquiring into the differences to determine how much they really did matter.

THE first fully colonial power to rule the Cameroonians was, of course, Germany. The German colonial period can, nevertheless, be dismissed, because, though it created a myth of some value to Cameroonians, it did not create a durable legacy. Apparently little appreciated by the nationalist movements which were rooted in the myth of a German-created "Kamerun Nation" is the fact that the German colonial administration had only a decade of relatively peaceful administration of the territory—too little time to elicit a sense of "national" identity.[2] The Cameroon nationalists also tend to exaggerate the German contribution to the economic development of the territory. Despite greater material gains during the longer mandate-trusteeship period (truer of the French-administered sector than that of the British), Cameroon nationalists speak better of their German masters than of those who succeeded the Germans.

However, the Germans did begin to establish the foundations of a modern state in Kamerun, of which much evidence remains. The major portion of the railway system still in use was constructed by the Germans. The railroad, as well as the land road system, were designed to integrate at least the southern portions of the Kamerun. Also, the Germans began plans to extend the railroad into Adamawa and on to Tchad. Discussed by the French administration, this proposal was not put into operation until the French Cameroon achieved independence. The Bamenda grass-fields still have their most direct link to the sea via the Douala-Bafoussam road which skirts the internal frontier on the East Cameroon side. However, relative to its contribution to other colonial possessions, the German administration did not bring significant road or railroad development to the Cameroon. Among German colonies in Africa, Cameroon stood last in number of miles of railroad track. The first permanent land

[2] Rudin, *Germans,* p. 96, asserts that the territory was fairly well explored and pacified by 1905, but that there remained "much work in local exploration and in local military measures to establish complete control."

69

roads were not built until 1905.[3] Though road construction was one of the obligations of the plantations, most roads and pathways were constructed by native forced labor.

Though many German investors expected great rewards from their efforts in Cameroon (the colony was sometimes called the "pearl of the German Colonies"), the territory was not the most significant recipient of German capital investment, nor was it often the most important of its trading partners. By 1912–1913 the colony had received only 19 percent of Germany's colonial capital investment and was third among the four colonies in the importance of its trade with Germany. German grants-in-aid and loans to the territory amounted to only 71,144,000 marks by 1911, less than that received by Tanganyika or Southwest Africa.[4]

The most impressive and important residue of German activity in the Territory is the collection of agricultural plantations that still dominate the economy of West Cameroon. Much of the agricultural development of West Cameroon was accomplished during the German period. By 1913 German planters had bought over 100,000 acres of land for plantation development, though only about one-third was then under cultivation. In 1913, 58 plantations employed 17,827 workers. At the time of independence, about 45 years later, the Cameroons Development Corporation (CDC) which administered almost all the formerly German plantations, employed fewer workers (17,236) than were employed on the German plantations in 1913, and the acreage under cultivation had only doubled.[5]

Present-day Cameroonians seem to be most impressed by the fact that what little the Germans accomplished was intended to last. Examples are the impressive array of hilltop and mountainside forts and castles that

---

[3] *Ibid.;* see pp. 280–85 for a discussion of "the Economic value of the Cameroons." Figures for German contributions are from Rudin unless otherwise indicated.

[4] The Germans established the basic framework for a communications network, linking Douala to Europe by telegraphic cable in 1893. These lines were extended (including telephone) to Buea and Victoria in 1898 and into the interior by 1900. Other German installations still in operation in the territory are the complex of experimental livestock and agricultural farms in Buea and the Botanical Gardens in Victoria.

[5] The CDC administers only 49 of the 58 plantations. Elders & Fyffes Ltd. has leased the estates in Likomba, and in 1955 employed 3,435 African workers. For more on the history of the CDC and the impact of the plantations on the social patterns of the Africans indigenous to the area in which plantations were established, see Ardener et al., *Plantation and Village in the Cameroons* (London: Oxford University Press, 1960).

remain as the principal symbols of prestige. The prime minister of West Cameroon, like the British commissioner for the Southern Cameroons and the German governor before him, lives in the stately German-built "Schloss" halfway up the slopes of Mount Cameroon. Several of the district officers in West Cameroon have their offices and/or homes in old German forts. Even in East Cameroon, a former prime minister has his hometown residence on the commanding site of the old fort, whose tower still stands sentry over the city of Ebolowa. These provide material evidence of a colonial superculture common to the two states; in the post-World War II period they confirmed the idea among those who needed to assert it that the two territories were one.

There are also certain human testimonies to the previous unity of the imposed colonial culture. In Buea and Ebolowa one can still get something of a crowd of old men together, ex-clerks, translators or military assistants, to converse in German about *"die ereignisse in unserem Zeitalter."*

The impressive, sturdy old German forts and castles, and a dwindling number of German-speaking ex-*Beistände* is about all of the German cultural heritage that has survived the British and French efforts to remove the image of the heritage. These few shared symbols of status, and the diminishing number of nostalgic *Deutschfreundliche* are hardly a foundation for a real nation.

THE British colonial tradition arose from British nationalism, both of which are subject to considerable distortion through stereotyping, auto-deception, and hypocrisy. The core of the English political philosophy at home and abroad is proclaimed to consist of a commitment to liberty wedded to a fundamentally Christian and liberal moral undercurrent.[6] English nationalism, which, like many other nationalisms, was the mother of imperial expansion, has been described as "closer than any other nationalism to the religious matrix from which it arose. . . . it always put a great emphasis upon the individual and upon the human community beyond all national divisions." [7] These values presumably were established by the Glorious Revolution and consolidated by the works of John Locke, who toppled the moral edifice built by Hobbes and the Stuarts and laid the foundation for modern England and Western liberalism. Locke's *First Treatise of Government* begins with the most explicit

[6] Hans Kohn, "The Genesis and Character of English Nationalism," *Journal of the History of Ideas,* Vol. 1, No. 1 (1940), pp. 69ff.
[7] *Ibid.*

71

statement possible of the new spirit: "Slavery is so vile and miserable an Estate of Man, and so directly opposite to the generous Temper and Courage of our Nation, that 'tis hardly to be conceived that an *English-man,* much less a *Gentleman,* should plead for't." Yet this was said at a time when England had displaced Lowland and Iberian powers as the principal agent of the most extensive and perverse organization of slavery in recorded history, and over the course of the next century England's role in it grew.[8] How seriously can one take the pronouncements of English philosophy when measured against the behavior of Englishmen? Ignoring the perversities of slavery in the New World perpetrated by people most of whom were no longer Englishmen, and despite libertarian values used to legitimize colonial and imperial missions, and sometimes used even in support of "the trade," it is safe to conclude, as one high British official of the Gold Coast did in 1853, that from their first settlement on the coast of West Africa until the abolition of the slave trade in 1807, the British "did not confer one lasting benefit upon the people." [9] Indeed, no more forceful challenge to the unalloyed libertarian proclamations of England need be found than her inability to reconcile them with the demands of her transplanted subjects in the American colonies for self-government and the full enjoyment of "the rights of Englishmen." [10]

[8] By the time Locke wrote his *Treatises,* England, through the Royal African Company, controlled almost all the slave coast of West Africa, on which it maintained a tight monopoly. Shortly thereafter the company monopoly was terminated in favor of a general 10 percent tax on the slave cargoes of English merchants, still insufficient to save the company, although the trade itself became ever more prosperous. Treasury subsidies for the English forts along the West African coast replaced company subsidies after its demise in the mid-1700s.

[9] D. P. Mannix and M. Cowley, *Black Cargoes: A History of the Atlantic Slave Trade, 1518–1865* (New York: Viking Press), p. 33.

[10] The eminent student of nationalism, Hans Kohn, suggests "The Genesis," p. 69) that Americans, like Continentals, were and are prone to consider as cant English professions of high moral purpose, and to accuse them of serving God and Mammon. However, it seems reasonable to consider the American Revolution an affirmation rather than a denial of English values, a revolution which, in the words of Louis Hartz (*The Liberal Tradition in America*), lacked an *ancien régime,* American society "begins with Locke, and thus transforms him, stays with Locke. . . ." Inasmuch as American society carried to its fullness the hideousness contained in the slave system, we can conclude that American society was also an affirmation of the contradictions and perversities of English culture. Hartz errs only in his unwillingness to see these perversities as the moral counterpart of the *ancien régime,* a fundamental denial of the liberal order and sure to destroy it if given half the chance. Hartz tells us that, "The task of the cultural analyst is not to discover simplicity, or even to discover unity, for simplicity and unity do not exist, but to drive a wedge of rationality through the pathetic indecisions of social thought. In the American case that wedge is not hard to find. It is not hidden in an obscure place. We find it in what

Individual Frenchmen may deserve less than Englishmen or Americans the accusations of hypocrisy their victims hurl at them, but the French tradition is none the more coherent for it. Perhaps no Frenchman claims more than one France, and for each its fundamental character is precise and easily perceived, but it is a different France for several groups of them, perhaps for each of them. Which France came to Africa —the France embodied in the ideas of Voltaire, Montesquieu, and their friends, or the idea of France that blazed in the minds of Robespierre and Tom Paine? Rousseau's ideas mix with each, and those of Compte, Bonald, and de Maistre have remained generally irrelevant, at least to the France that had much to do with Africa.[11]

In its prerevolutionary origins, French colonial expansion followed much the same logic and pursued many of the same objectives as the British—an outlet for the energy and curiosity of the various groups of their nationals, the exaggerated promises of fabulous wealth in the form of precious stones and metals one need only scoop up, or grab from their weak and easily beguiled owners across the seas, or in the forms of the commerce these societies knew how to organize so well. But after the great events that truncated French history the colonial enterprise took on a distinctly moral flavor. Unlike the British colonies, most of those under French control did not consist of large numbers of French settlers, for Frenchmen, in the words of Deschamps, are pushed into foreign travel primarily by "a taste for the new . . . not by material need. France offers them resources enough; it is a beautiful country . . . which one leaves only for a time, in order to sow one's wild oats." [12] With such attitudes in

the West as a whole has always recognized to be the distinctive element in American civilization: *its social freedom, its social equality*" (emphasis mine). These are jarring words for anyone who looks at the American experience from a vantage point other than Europe, for they perpetuate the egocentricities and shortsightedness Hartz deplores in standard American self-interpretations, but which all Western Europeans and their immediate descendants seem to share. The one value American society has so far failed to affirm as universally valid is that of social equality.

[11] France's visions for Africans have fluctuated greatly between, on one hand, the crystalline egalitarianism of the Jacobins who freed the slaves of Santo Domingo and made them, along with the residents of the Senegalese colonies (technically the communes of Dakar, Goree, St. Rufisque, and St. Louis), French citizens; and on the other, the paternalistic mercantilism, however liberal, of the Girondins championed by Napoleon, which made them subjects again in Africa, and, by threatening to make them slaves once again in Santo Domingo, stimulated the Haitian revolution (pursued *in defense* of the French Revolution of 1789). See C. L. R. James, *The Black Jacobins* (New York: Random House, 2nd ed., 1963).

[12] H. Deschamps, *Les Methodes et Doctrines Coloniales de la France* (Paris: Collection Armand Colin, 1953), p. 11.

the background, French colonialism came to terms as early as the Revolution with the situation Britain would confront and face up to only much later—of suzerainty over peoples and lands with cultures starkly different from its own. In terms of doctrine the French response, nurtured by the objectives, styles, and impulses of the Great Revolution, has been described as: "On the whole . . . as early as the time of the Restoration (French) colonisation . . . takes on a very determined character: it ceases to be an exploitation pure and simple to become a guardianship and an education, it endeavors to conciliate the interests of the metropole with those of the indigenous populations, it seeks to be an instrument of human progress." [13]

This was a spirit that derived from and at the same time nurtured the French emotional commitment to the revolutionary slogans of *liberté, egalité, fraternité*. However, that commitment was not strong and clear enough to sustain its promises to the subjugated peoples in the charge of France; thus the Revolution freed the slaves and then tried to restore their chains; it proclaimed citizens of its subjects only to subjugate them over and over again.[14] The spirit survived the convolutions of practice and doctrinal disputes and inspired spokesmen for the "colonial mission" to state, near the turn of the 19th century, that its objective was "to create new societies [in the colonial areas] morally and politically similar to our own as much as possible, ultimately united with it by a very close friendship, which should be for our fatherland an augmentation of economic power, and in the long run an [integral] part of it." [15]

This spirit took the doctrinal form of "assimilationism," the commitment to bring the subjugated subjects into the full dignity and freedom of man through their acquisition of French culture, on a basis of fraternal equality, and their subjugated lands into a fuller measure of wealth through their union with France.

The natural administrative concomitant to these doctrines would be for France to transplant its hierarchical and centralist bureaucratic traditions into the colonies, ruling the local areas directly through its own administrative staff. The evident French predilection to rule in this fashion has inspired the term "direct rule," in such widespread use as a contradis-

[13] George Hardy, *Histoire sociale de la colonisation française* (Paris: Larose, 1953), p. 252.

[14] Citizenship was conferred, or new procedures were instituted to make real a previous conferral, only to be reversed in a few years thereafter, in 1794, 1848, 1870, 1916, and 1946.

[15] Marcel Dubois, *Systemes coloniaux et peuples colonisateurs* (Paris: G. Masson, 1895), p. 33.

tinction to the principle "indirect rule" ascribed to British colonial policy.[16]

In reality, neither British nor French policy was ever coherently direct or indirect, at least not over extended periods. Some have suggested that the British empire was founded in a fit of absentmindedness and perhaps administered in the same way. French policy, according to some students of it, was motivated by "a thousand and one goals . . . and often the absence of [any] goal." [17] In any case, it is clear that doctrines and practices seldom accorded, and certainly did not always, if ever, exhibit a causal relationship. The driving forces of French colonialism were "Personal impulses, methods improvised to fit the change of circumstances, announced intentions which founder before the unforeseen, practices which give rise to doctrines and doctrines destined to justify [ongoing] practices. And in all of this, periodically, [there appear] radiant ideologies. [There is] utter chaos, which, after long intervals, organizes itself into relatively durable structures." [18] Those who staked out the colonial territorial claims were usually military men, or men necessarily preoccupied with the practical requirements of pacification and rule; they were not much concerned with doctrine. Direct or indirect rule depended on local exigencies, the availability of strong yet amenable indigenous political institutions, the availability of sufficient personnel and resources to permit rule in any way other than through indigenous authorities. Britain was disposed to have the colonies pay their own way, following Draconian and Gladstonian principles which held that the colonies, like the Crown in previous days, should be "self sufficing." [19] This reflected the limited moral commitment to the transformation of indigenous society recognized by the English colonialists. The great driving impulses behind British expansion and rule historically are said to have centered on commerce in terms of (a) the expansion of British trade, (b) provision of adequate security for worldwide commerce, and (c) expansion of the power and prestige of Great Britain.[20] Yet French policy also occasionally em-

---

[16] See esp. Frederick D. Lugard, *The Dual Mandate in Tropical Africa* (Hamden, Conn.: Shoestring Press, 1922), Part II, Chap. 10. An excellent discussion of the application of the doctrine of indirect rule is in Martin Kilson, *Political Change in a West African State* (Cambridge: Harvard University Press, 1966), Chaps. 2–4. William Malcolm Hailey, *An African Survey, Revised* (London: Oxford University Press, 1956), discusses both traditions of colonial administration.

[17] Deschamps, *Les Methodes et Doctrines*, preface.

[18] *Ibid.*

[19] Perham, *Colonial Reckoning* (New York: Knopf, 1962), Chap. 5, *passim.*

[20] *Ibid.* Emigration was another theme, not altogether separate from these three.

phasized financial self-sufficiency on the part of the colonies.[21] About 1890 the French began to look to the British model, which they regarded as singularly dedicated to the pursuit of commerce and economic growth for the colonial power. They began to look as well to British methods of native administration, like rule through local chiefs, and especially to the work of the anthropologists whose findings supported these methods. Many accused France of having failed because of an erroneous belief in the moral unity of mankind.[22] Assimilationism was labeled a colossal mistake, resulting from the ideas of "latinisme classique" and from the Revolution which imbued people with the false dogma of "l'unite humaine" and an erroneous belief in France's "mission providentielle." Oddly enough, it was also in the late 19th century that British colonial commitments began to change and give broad reflection to a moral stream of concern which the antislavery forces had introduced into colonial policy at the beginning of the century.[23] As in France, part of the British "philanthropic" support for colonialism reflected the rising force of Social Darwinism and the idea of superior races. But the idea of the rights of the "natives" and the duty of deference toward them by rulers was established as a standard in British public life with the 1837 Select Parliamentary Committee on Aborigines; "the standard has never been wholly lost. It . . . was maintained by individuals of all parties or of none, and especially by the churches. . . ." [24] The idea of the colonial enterprise as the "white man's burden," or, in the words of T. J. Alldridge, a travelling district commissioner in Africa, "the thin edge of the wedge of civilisation" [25] was not deemed to be a principle in conflict with

[21] Deschamps, *Les Methodes et Doctrines.* A financial law passed in 1900, for example, suppressed all subventions to the colonies, making them rely on locally generated resources. This came in deference to the forces of the rural-based right wing in France, but by that time the radical left had also condemned assimilationist theory and begun to support the views of those who viewed colonization in economic terms. Only the Socialists, led by Juares, held to something like an assimilationist's position. Colonialism had the duty, he said, "to proceed, by degrees, toward the unification . . . of the human race."

[22] Deschamps, *Methodes et Doctrines,* p. 145, attributed to L. de Saussure, a follower of Gustave le Bon who spoke of "psychological races" and "heredity of mental makeup," factors which generate different national temperaments and make certain races and peoples fundamentally unassimilable. De Saussure claimed that attempts at assimilation by conversion or education lead only to the lowering of standards of morality and the disorganization of indigenous society. He regarded Black Africans as irredeemably inferior.

[23] Perham, *Colonial Reckoning,* pp. 132ff.

[24] *Ibid.*

[25] Alldridge, *The Sherbo and Its Hinterland* (London: Macmillan, 1901) quoted in Kilson, *Political Change,* p. 15.

the pursuit of material interest and development. Quite the contrary, for Alldridge stated that although "I am a great admirer of missionary efforts . . . I believe primarily in showing to the people the need of individual work and of working to a paying end. With greater comforts about them, procured by their own labour, we may certainly hope that higher ends will be attained, and that the obstacles which encompass missionary enterprise and retard civilisation will be materially modified and more successful results obtained." [26]

Throughout the first half of the 20th century Britain and France found themselves pursuing a mixture of identification and differentiation, assimilation and association policies, in pragmatic response to local conditions. The moral and "philanthropic" strain of British policy led to the transference to the colored dependencies, initially and especially India, of the principle of self-government, which formerly had been applied only to the dominions settled by "Kith and Kin." [27] Yet the implications of the change, that the dependent areas of the empire would press for full equality of political rights—in other words, for independence—was missed or only dimly foreseen: ". . . if we cannot successfully attempt to convert them [the territories of the Dependent Empire] into Dominions and yet do not want them to become Foreign Nations, what is to be done?" [28] In any case, the British commitment to a deliberate and steady guidance toward self-government, which was implied in a declaration by Lord Devonshire in 1923 promising the paramountcy of "native interests," did not involve any haste. Britain still somewhat leisurely followed a "protective policy," one focused on building social and economic infrastructure.[29] As late as 1939 a high-ranking British colonial official stated: "Well, at any rate, in Africa we can be sure that we have unlimited time in which to work." [30] On the French side, the policies of association went down, in part, under the weight of debts to Africans most Frenchmen recognized as a result of the African war effort in behalf of the French. But the institutions of the French Union, which was created to settle that debt, turned out to be a mixture of the principles of assimilationism and association, unity and federalism, revolution and restoration—in short, it reflected the pattern of dualism in French history since 1789.

---

[26] *Ibid.*

[27] This change occurred in 1917 in response to the birth of Indian nationalism.

[28] Lord Milner, as quoted in Kenneth Robinson, *The Dilemmas of Trusteeship* (London: Oxford University Press, 1965), p. 13.

[29] *Ibid.*

[30] Perham, *Colonial Reckoning,* p. 141.

DIFFERENCES are distinguishable in the value systems Britain and France implanted in Africa, despite the contradictions and incoherencies in them. This is especially evident with respect to the kinds of ultimate or long-range goals that were embedded in these systems. The systems differed not only in the extent to which consummatory rather than instrumental values predominated, but also in the kinds of objects or activities made the subject of such values. The British colonial mission was far less dominated by consummatory, "sacred-like" objectives than was the French; those that did figure in the British mission were more strictly religious, in an orthodox sense of the word, than was the case in the French colonial situation.

The dominant purpose of the French colonial mission was to spread French culture and associate the colonies to a French domain; that of Great Britain was to spread British rule and commerce and subject the colonies to British law. French administrators tended to measure their accomplishments and the progress of their subjects by the standard of acculturation; in the process they made French culture itself something of an object of worship. The British measured theirs by the stimulus colonialism gave to their commerce. They inspired envy for the privileges of Englishmen, but did not engender a large-scale commitment to English culture per se.

The promulgation and propagation of French culture as a consummatory value is revealed in the approach of French colonialism to the nature and role of language, in contrast to the British approach. Language symbolizes much, not by virtue of its serving as a cognitive carrier of the culture, but to the extent that it is revered as a "sacred" object, something that embodies the fundamental worth and achievement of a people, as it is by many Frenchmen at home and overseas, white or black.

The most striking evidence that the known reverence of Frenchmen for their language was central to the value system of the colonial regime is that the educational system they constructed for the Africans from the beginning emphasized the French language. How different this is from the British, who approached language in a mundane instrumental way, and often permitted, even encouraged, initial formal instruction in the vernacular.[31] A hundred varieties of an English-based pidgin around the world attest to the willingness of Englishmen to focus their attention on their own ultimate purposes—trade and the conditions most favorable to it—utilizing whatever scraps of language were available and neces-

[31] See *The Use of Vernacular Languages in Education,* Monographs on Fundamental Education, VIII (Paris: UNESCO, 1953).

sary to establish and maintain trading contacts. In contrast, the limited occurrence of Creole or dialect varieties of French, which have developed almost exclusively in those areas where France lost or never acquired a dominant influence, would suggest that for the French spreading their ways counted for as much as spreading their wares. Even Christian missionaries, who preceded the colonizers of Africa by a century, ultimately came to approach their tasks differently in the areas of colonial contact between the two powers. Church services, translations of the Bible and other church literature, even the educational enterprise under the dominion of British missionaries, continued to use local languages or pidgin, whereas local languages came to depend almost exclusively on the French language for broader contact wherever France was strong.[32]

In Cameroon the early work of the missionaries, Catholic and Protestant, who prodigiously developed scripts for one vernacular after another and translated the Bible and other works into them,[33] did not suddenly disappear without a trace. Those literate in French could continue to use these skills, and a few people acquired literacy only in their mother tongue. Moreover, some of the missionary establishments in Cameroon were not French. The American Presbyterian missions that operated in the south-central and southeast sections did not share official enthusiasm for French language and culture, or at least not to the same degree.[34]

During the colonial era enthusiasm for French was especially, but not

[32] V. Thompson and R. Adloff, in *French West Africa* (London: Allen & Unwin, 1958), remark (p. 513): "Persuaded by tradition that they had a 'civilizing mission' to fulfill, the French colonizers of the late nineteenth and early twentieth centuries were certain that West Africa was, from the cultural standpoint, a *tabula rasa*, upon which the political and social institutions of the Metropole should be traced. 'Assimilation' was the term frankly applied to this process, whose most conspicuous manifestation was the setting up of an educational system that employed French as its sole linguistic vehicle." This pattern was not limited to Africa, but applied to Asia as well, despite more codified and coherent records of civilisation. See Deschamps, *Les Methodes et les Doctrines.* . . . pp. 144–45ff.

[33] Engelbert Mveng, *Histoire du Cameroun* (Paris: *Présence Africaine*, 1963). See also C. P. Groves, *The Planting of Christianity in Africa* (London: Hewat, 1958).

[34] Newspapers in the vernacular still appear, mostly from missionary centers. Many missionary schools, especially the non-French ones and the Protestant affiliates, introduce second languages or offer vernacular training later. However, education in French Cameroon, whether missionary or state, is tightly regulated and has been since the July 25, 1921 decree which provided the general legal framework for the educational system. In the words of Le Vine, in H. Kitchen, ed., *The Educated African* (New York: Frederick Praeger, 1962), p. 521: "It [the decree] stipulated that the schools should bring the indigenous population into a closer association with the colonists by teaching the French language to the Africans and by familiarizing them with the methods and policies of the Administering Authority."

solely, among officials; it continues to enjoy a certain currency among many African intellectuals content to consider themselves part of "Francophone Africa." These same intellectuals reject and disdain what they call "Saxophone" Africa. The realities of cultural development with respect to the spread of the French language lay somewhere in the large void between the ideal formulated in the doctrines of French colonialism and the limited rates of scholarization achieved by it. A few Africans learned the language very well indeed, in the process becoming *enfants terribles* to the apostles of the French civilizing mission; those whose command of it elicited only affronted winces in Paris are numerous enough to demonstrate the historic connection. At the time of independence, however, seldom did more than 10 percent of the African population know French, and of these perhaps only two percent could speak it fluently.[35] Such figures mislead, as much by denying the importance and prestige of French as by exaggerating it. It does matter that a commitment to French was part of the French definition of the progress their civilizing mission was to bestow on Africans. The attitudes of many of the colonizers has been stated by P. F. Lacroix: "Loyal to the old centralist and unitarian propensity which has always been one of the characteristics of our governmental policy, consciously or unconsciously imbued with a complex of linguistic superiority all the more ardent because realities do not always correspond to their desires, French functionaries are to be found who think that the essence of our activity in Africa must be to "sell [or give] French," without considering either the real desires of the Africans or of the conditions imposed by the facts." [36]

The values of the emergent African modern elite often reflect such attitudes, although they can hardly be considered sterling reproductions of them. The prevalent view among West African intellectuals, especially those with great ability in the French language and culture, is that one's attitude toward the indigenous languages is closely linked with the problem of "the acceptance of one's culture." The brilliant historian, Dr. Joseph Ki-Zerbo, by his educational achievement a perfect example of the ideal of the assimilationist idea, states: "to accept the death of African languages is to commit cultural suicide." [37] Such sentiments are shared by Africans from the areas of British influence. A Nigerian put it: "Our feelings, our thought, our whole personality are expressed and shaped by the languages that we use so that to lose one's native lan-

[35] P. F. Lacroix, "Le français et l'Afrique," in *Le Monde,* September 1965.
[36] *Ibid.*
[37] Joseph Ki-Zerbo, "Education and African Culture," in *Présence Africaine,* Vol. 10, No. 38 (1962), 67.

guage is to lose one's native personality." [38] This feeling notwithstanding, a sense of the intimacy between language and particular cultural traditions is almost inherent in the African reality of superdiversity. Moreover, there is also the equally real and extensive multilingualism of most Africans, which ought to make it evident to them that one can partake of several cultures at once without necessarily losing one's "identity."

Many factors inhibit the adoption of the vernacular languages as national languages in Africa; most inhibiting factors are of a practical nature: the limited demographic and geographic scope of most of the thousand or more vernaculars, coupled with some potential for conflict between the ethnic groups they differentiate; the limited development of *lingua franca,* especially in western and central Africa; the lack of a technical or artistic literature in the vernaculars; the momentum behind the existing and growing school and administrative systems; the need to retain easy access to the scientific, technical, and cultural products of the "developed" world. The question penetrates strictly utilitarian levels of considerations, however. African intellectuals, especially—only *they* have the freedom to choose their language—confront a moral dilemma rooted in the dualism of their purpose. They desire to modernize African society and make it relevant to the mainstream of the "universal" culture of mankind; for this the state apparatus and the incipient "nation" are the sacred symbols, ones imparted to Africa by the colonial situation. The intellectuals also desire to affirm and develop the dignity of their indigenous African tradition, which is symbolized by language. The new nation-state cannot be made authentic symbolic referents of African civilization except as it embodies the values and insights only African languages can express, and it cannot be considered authentically modern except as it embodies the values and insights of the latest science and technology the European languages monopolize.

The dilemmas of language have inspired widespread debate, but so far very little action.[39] The debaters carry it on primarily in French, sometimes with frantic insistence on the affirmation and promotion of indigenous languages as "national" languages.[40] This stand ironically contrasts,

---

[38] See W. Johnson, "African-speaking Africa," in *African Forum* (New York: AMSAC, 1965), Vol. I, No. 2.

[39] In ex-colonial tropical Africa, except for Tanzania and Mauretania, the language of the former colonial power has been retained as an official language. Several countries—Burundi, Kenya, Ruanda, and Tanzania—have made indigenous languages official or co-official.

[40] See Johnson, "African-speaking Africa"; and Cheikh Anta Diop, *Nations, Negres et Culture.* Also Diop, *Présence Africaine,* Vols. 24–25, on the Rome Congress of African Artists and Writers.

not only with the linguistic medium through which it is expressed, but with the position sometimes taken prior to independence by French-speaking African leaders in opposition to the efforts of Metropolitan Deputies in the French National Assembly to introduce vernacular language instruction in the African schools. The leaders considered the move a trick designed to deny the African child an education the equal of that given to children in France.[41] Others have argued that the interest of non-Africans in promoting the use of indigenous languages reflects a desire to "maintain Africa at the folkloric and picturesque stage." [42] Oddly enough, both Leopold Senghor (one of the most competent masters of French anywhere) and affiliates of *Présence Africaine* (who, while ranking among the most highly educated French Africans, militantly promote the idea of developing an authentically African culture) dissented in the vernacular debates in the Assembly. But even these circles also argue that the European language continues to serve the purpose of national salvation and construction in the face of the international forces at work within and without African communities.[43] Whether the debaters insist on the use of the "world language" or the "national" one—and no doubt both sides are deeply conditioned by the core of African values their European educations have failed to stifle—their attitude is more fitting to the French than to the British tradition, precisely because of its recognition of language as a sacred object.

I would expect a more telling French impact on the cultural values of Cameroonians than on the values of most other African subjects of French colonialism, due to the more extensive spread of formal education in Cameroon. Table 1 indicates this greater educational advance.

Whether the impact of the French will be more durable in Cameroon than elsewhere in French-speaking Africa is questionable, however, given the extraordinarily severe drop-out rate which Table 1 indicates occurs over the course of the primary and secondary levels of education.[44] Of course, the size of Cameroon's primary school population is important; in 1958 it was larger than any other French African territory

[41] Pierre Alexandre, in John Spencer, ed., *Language in Africa* (Cambridge: Cambridge University Press, 1963), p. 54. This book contains reports and papers from the Leverhulme Conference on Language Problems of Tropical Africa, University College, Ibadan, Nigeria, December 1961–January 1962.

[42] *Ibid.*

[43] Alioune Diop, "Political and Cultural Solidarity in Africa," in *Présence Africaine*, Vol. 13, No. 41 (1962), 69.

[44] Le Vine notes (*Cameroons*, p. 76) that only one-fifth of those starting finish primary school.

except Madagascar, and it is reasonable to assume that it is easier to sustain a given level of achievement in a society that contains a relatively large number of schooled people than where there are only a few, whatever proportion of the school-age population they may represent. Even so, it is known that the deterioration of literacy and the other skills imparted in primary school is rapid in Cameroon.[45] On the other hand, Cameroonians were among the most numerous African student groups in French universities; only Ivorians and Malians were more numerous in 1962; [46] and the attachment to and competence in French language and culture is greatest among this group.

TABLE 1

Percent of School Age Children in School in Selected
French-African Countries, 1958

	Cameroon	Gabon	Dahomey	Ivory Coast	Senegal	Togo
Primary	69.2	78.2	34.1	35.6	31.5	52.7
Secondary	1.5	3.4	1.2	1.3	2.5	1.5
Technical	0.6	0.2	0.4	0.2	0.4	0.25
Higher[b]	a					

[a] Cameroon had 1,050 students abroad in institutions of higher education in 1958; the local university was not opened until 1962, when it had 588 students.

[b] In local universities.

Sources: Calculated from data provided in Rapport sur la situation sociale dans les pays d'outre-mer associés a la CEE. Communaute Econ. Europ. Commission.

The differences between the British and French approaches to their colonial mission, as exemplified by the role of the colonial language, was much the same in Cameroon as in most other areas of Africa under the control of these two powers. This is less the case for the differences in these legacies with respect to the role of organized religion, particularly the Christian missionary organizations. The special circumstances of British and French entry into the area, through the military displacement

[45] The high drop-out rate is compounded by the low level of qualifications of many teachers, especially in private schools and some mission schools. Over 70 percent of teachers, even in public schools, are uncertified; the figure rises to over 80 percent in the private schools. (*Ibid.*, p. 82.) Moreover, a media-penetration study conducted by André Celarie for the Office de coopération radiophonique in Paris (Les Moyens d'Information au Cameroun, Vols. I, II, 1965), indicates (Vol. I, pp. 90–91) that outside the largest cities, including the developed southeastern part of the country, the capacity of the local population to speak French, as estimated by 150 medical attendants, was limited to about 50 percent in the towns, down to a handful in the townships. In many quarters of Douala it was estimated to be about 50 percent only, and perhaps 75 percent for Yaounde.

[46] See the official publication, *Coopération France-Afrique, Madagascar* (Paris: Ministère de la Coopération), 1964.

of German rule, gave each power a shorter period of rule and confronted them with established patterns of missionary activity, which they had either to accommodate or dismantle and replace. As a result, the secular orientation of French colonial rule elsewhere in Africa was attenuated in Cameroon, and the extent of Christian missionary penetration and activity did not differ significantly between the two areas of the country. The history of the expansion and activity of the Christian missions in Cameroon has been discussed by others.[47] What I wish to signal here is the impact of these efforts on the values of Cameroonians. This impact was considerable in both territories, and, unlike many other French-controlled areas in Africa, involved the significant activity of Roman Catholic orders. For all faiths in each territory the most significant vehicle for carrying its beliefs to the people was education. The Christian missions dominated the educational effort in the country, until the post-independence period. At the end of the German period, for example, there were nearly 50,000 pupils in some 631 mission schools, compared with only 833 pupils in 4 government schools. There has always been a large private sector to the educational system in Cameroon. In 1919 fully 60 percent of the students attended such schools. This figure has fluctuated from 90 percent in 1938 to 65 in 1962—evidence of unusual French willingness to rely on missionary organizations in Cameroon, but not typical of their approach elsewhere.

At the time of reunification, the voluntary agencies, most of which were missionary-related, provided education for nearly two-thirds of the pupils enrolled in Cameroon schools. In West Cameroon they provided education for nearly 90 percent of the students. Only three of 650 schools were not run by missionary organizations. Not only have the mission organizations controlled a much larger portion of the schools in West Cameroon than in East Cameroon, but more of the program in these schools as well. Though there has been more extensive regulation of the curricula by the government of West Cameroon and by the Federal authorities in recent years, in West Cameroon the missions still have considerable latitude. Moreover, the Westerners are deeply committed to continuing religious instruction in the schools, whether they are run by voluntary organizations or by the government.[48] The East Cameroon, and federal, government (at least with respect to schools in East Camer-

---

[47] See Le Vine, *Cameroons*, pp. 69–73ff.; and Mveng, *Histoire du Cameroun*, pp. 451–71.

[48] The Secretary of State for Education, L. M. Ndamukong, pledged to keep religious instruction in all West Cameroon primary schools, in a speech which otherwise promised far reaching reforms. *Cameroon Times*, 26 July, 1963.

oon) continues the practice, started by the Germans in 1910 and taken over by the French, of having the government establish rather strict guidelines for the school curricula, which missionary schools were obliged to follow if they received government subsidies.[49]

Despite the marked difference between the two states on the extent of church and missionary control of the schools, there is not the same kind of disparity in the intensity of the impact of Christian organizations. There is some significant difference in the scope of the impact, due to the large Moslem areas of East Cameroon, where there has been little Christian proselytizing until recently—a situation encouraged by both German and French policy. There are few areas of West Cameroon that have not been affected by missionary work, but Christianity has had a less profound impact than in East Cameroon, for two reasons: (a) the educational system, the principal purveyor of the faith, was less extensive in the Western state, as I have indicated; (b) more effort was put into post-primary level education by the religious organizations in East Cameroon. As early as 1923 the first junior seminary was started, and in 1927 the higher seminary was opened in Yaounde. By 1961 there were seven seminaries, junior and senior. Fine secondary schools (colleges) had been opened by then in several cities by the Catholics—Collège Libermann and Vogt in Douala, Saint-Paul in Bafang, Mazenod at Ngaoundere, Sacre-Coeur at Makak, and four others, as well as five normal schools for boys and two for girls and several technical schools. By 1961 Protestant groups had also developed some outstanding secondary and higher schools, especially the American Presbyterian mission, whose school at Foulassi is one of the best in the country and perhaps in all of West Africa. They collaborate with French missionaries in running a good higher school at Libamba.

Not only has the more intense effort at Christian education occurred in East Cameroon, but it seems to have distinguished the Catholic from the Protestant churches. Education offered by the Catholic seminaries, the only secondary schools in the country until 1940, has acquired a notable reputation. Owona Adalbert, in a masterful study of Cameroon Nationalism, stated: "the seminarians and ex-seminarians were the only Cameroonians to receive an education worthy of the name." [50] While Protestant members of the elite might disagree, even they respected the liberal training of the seminarians.

It is somewhat puzzling that the Catholic missionary orders, which

[49] Le Vine, *Cameroons*, p. 72.
[50] Adalbert Owona, "Le Nationalism Camerounaise," *Association Française de Science Politique* (May 25, 1962), pp. 15–16 (mimeo.).

were the last among the more energetic and better equipped missionary organizations to enter Cameroon, emerged with the largest, most organized and committed Christian communities in both states.[51] This reflects not only the more insistent and disciplined approach taken by the Catholic church in such matters, but, at least in East Cameroon, probably favoritism also on the part of colonial administration.[52] Catholic missionaries were direct and forceful in their attempt to displace African customs with the new faith. Owona notes: "The last on the scene, the Catholic missionaries were the ones to attack the traditional customs the strongest . . . [they] opposed polygamy in particular [and thus helped to destroy the prestige of the village chiefs] . . . against 'paganism,' against slavery, against child marriage, against ritual murders and cannibalism; in general, they waged all-out war against everything which called to mind the ancient ways. Sorcerers and festishists were chased after, humiliated and ridiculed; traditional dances were prohibited." [53]

If the proselytism of the Catholics was abusive, it was nonetheless effective. The graduates of their schools acquired a dominant position among the ranks of teachers in the Territory; the geographical regions of Catholic influence were virtually exclusively so; and, given their entrenchment in the political capital of Yaounde and the commercial capital of Douala, at least during the preindependence period, the Catholic hierarchy determined many of the rules governing all missionary activities of any faith. By the time of reunification, nearly half the population of Yaounde was Catholic, as was over a third of Douala. Nearly one-fifth of the citizens of East Cameroon were Catholic, and even in West Cameroon there were more children attending Catholic schools than those of any other faith.

West Cameroon is fundamentally Protestant, despite the large Catholic contingent (which is much younger), a fact which is evident enough when West is compared with East Cameroon, though the Protestants are divided into two or three large sects. The Protestant churches throughout Cameroon have had a more unsettled life there than have the Catholics. This is particularly true of the Baptists, whose first and greatest missionary to the area, Alfred Saker, arrived in 1845 and stayed for 32 years. When the Germans established their rule in the colony, all the missions

[51] The first Catholic missionaries came in 1883, but were not permitted to establish a station until 1890.

[52] C. P. Groves, in Vol. IV of his *The Planting of Christianity in Africa*, states that Roman Catholic missions were in the ascendancy throughout the interwar period, and the larger part of mission education was in their hands (p. 120).

[53] Owona, "Nationalism Camerounaise."

were forced to transfer their holdings to German organizations. Thus the Basel Mission acquired significant holdings in Kamerun, but due to its efforts to enforce stringent and narrow practices, several of the Baptist congregations under African leadership in Douala broke away and established "national," or African, churches.[54] This provoked yet another schism among Baptists, as the German Baptist Missionary Society then came into the Territory to try to restore the mission field. It remained as a separate organization until all missionary stations were once again transfered to new owners. The German administration had nearly destroyed its missionary organizations anyway, by pressing the missionaries into military service.[55] The French sequestered the German mission holdings, and turned most of them over to the *Société des Missions Evangélique* of Paris. In 1924 the Basellers were permitted to resume their operations in British Cameroons, with indemnity for lost possessions.[56] Only the American Presbyterian missions were exempted from the periodic disruptions that war and change of colonial rulers had occasioned in Cameroon. The Americans came into the Territory before the Germans, and were treated as neutrals during the First World War. German colonial administration had leaned heavily on the missionary organizations, not only for educational development but for administration; they had divided up the country into administrative districts along tribal lines, which the missionary organizations were to honor.[57] The Presbyterians got the lands of the Bulu, Bassa, and the scattered Baya and Kaka groups to the east. The Baptists remained in Douala and the coastal areas around Mount Cameroon. They have generally respected the territorial divisions. Thus religious cleavages tend to coincide with ethnic, geographical, and to some extent economic cleavages.

As one might expect, given such coincidence of lines of fragmentation, the religious differences have affected the political life of the country. Religion became an important aspect, or at least defined a pattern during the rebellion. Most of the Bassa leaders of the UPC were raised in the self-reliant tradition of the American Presbyterians and trained in its excellent liberal schools. The UPC leaders' claims to political power struck a sympathetic cord among the Presbyterian missionaries, who as early as 1925 had committed the church to a policy of supporting African evolu-

[54] Mveng, *Histoire du Cameroun,* pp. 457–58.
[55] Rev. Kruger, Secretary, Société des Missions Evangéliques, interview, Paris, December 1963.
[56] Groves, *Planting of Christianity,* Vol. IV, p. 86. £10,000 was paid by the British government for all Basel losses in British Africa.
[57] Kruger interview.

tion toward self-government. Most of the Bamileke and many of the Douala members of the UPC were Catholic or came from areas heavily influenced by the Catholic church. Generally the Catholic hierarchy opposed the UPC because of its militant program and the communist orientation imputed to it. It was all the more important, therefore, that church leaders—namely the five Cameroonian bishops—all signed a letter at the time of the April 1955 disturbances supporting the general claim Cameroon nationalists were making, to "progressively take in hand the direction of their country and to guide it towards a free, honest and prosperous life." The Catholic clergy constituted a political force in the country; for example, even influential Catholic politicians saw fit to criticise Bishop Etoga for participating in politics. The results, some noted, were that "the Nyong-et-Sanaga [department] is provided with parliamentary representation of your own choice." They further accused him of nepotism, of practicing tribalism and furthering division. During the rebellion itself, eight Catholic priests and many lesser officials were the targets of assassins. Many Catholic installations were attacked or burned. In the capital the opposition *Démocrates* based their party on the Catholic institutional structure, which fact seems to account for its ability to survive efforts to crush it for so long.

In conclusion, I note that while many special features of Cameroon history had attentuated the differences that existed elsewhere in Africa between British, French, and German colonial legacies, and though many of the supposed disparities between legacies did not in fact exist, there were some noticeable ones which might affect the nature and prospects of the new Federation. The most important discontinuity in the political superculture which colonialism had developed concerned the attitudes of Cameroonians toward language. This difference symbolizes a number of other ones of greater subtlety. The spread and character of modern education, the pattern of diffusion of religious faiths, and the intensity of their penetration are also factors that tend to fragment Cameroonian society.

$$\overset{\circ}{\underset{*}{\pi}} 5 \overset{\circ}{\underset{*}{\pi}}$$

Patterns of Functional Interests

POLITICAL stakes are not only the valuables available for distribution, but
also the means (power) by which individuals or groups affect the authoritative (collectivity-sanctioned) allocations of them. In this chapter I am
considering such stakes as "interests." Functional interests are those interests that are relevant to the operation of the whole system, as distinguished from those that affect only the individuals who enjoy or seek
control of them.

Among the major interests motivating social activity, at least politically
relevant activity, are material valuables, the structure of their distribution, and the power relationships capable of altering that structure or
generating increments of valuables. The functional interests in the Cameroon case that were relevant to the achievement and success of political
union were of three types: (a) *economic interests,* that is, the nature,
quantity, and distribution of valuables among the general populace; (b)
financial interests, the valuables (mostly monetary) available to the governments of the two states; and (c) *power interests,* the winning of home
rule and the distribution among local individuals and groups of authoritative positions gained thereby. To avoid repetition and confusion I will
consider the last set of interests in later chapters, where I discuss the activities and value orientations of political groups. In this chapter I shall
consider the first two sets of interests in terms of affinities and disparities
between the two states with respect to them.

THE domestic economies of East and West Cameroon prior to reunification were relevant to the motives of those espousing the cause of reunification and to the potential for rapid success in achieving political integration in the new federation. Many claims advanced in support of reunification concerned the advantages that allegedly would accrue to traditional
trade between the border peoples, especially those of common ethnic
stock. Though there was a substantial clandestine trade across the
border, even when it was enforced the existence of a customs frontier is
supposed to have restricted a potentially extensive interchange of people,
goods, and services.[1] The Bamileke in particular are known to have car-

[1] UN Document T/798, p. 18. It is widely admitted, even by district officers who
served in Southern Cameroons, that there was significant smuggling of goods (espe-

ried on trade over the border when custom restrictions were lenient. Reportedly they depended heavily on the plantains, yams, and palm products produced on the western side of the border, and sold (or exchanged) meat and skins of the animals they raised on the eastern slopes of the Bambutos Mountains.[2]

The kola nut was an important item in the trade across the boundary. The largest kola markets in all the grassfields were located in the Bamileke highlands; these markets attracted small traders from British Cameroons who carried the nuts as far as Northern Nigeria.[3] Bamileke traders who dealt in kola, as well as in all forms of small commerce, were particularly strong advocates of reunification, because their major competition came from Hausa and Nigerian traders. Tardits reports that keen interest in the traditional cultivation of kola nut trees in Bamileke was not motivated simply by the importance of the revenues from kola nut production in areas deprived of a palm industry, but because it offered the opportunity for the Bamileke to capture an important commercial market by eliminating non-Bamileke competition, which in East Cameroon came mostly from Hausa and Bamoun.[4] Bamileke traders in West Cameroon found it difficult to take advantage of the trade, however, because of difficulties of passage across the border. The 1949 United Nations Visiting Mission noted the special case of the traders in the Southern Cameroons who were "placed at a disadvantage through being unable to move freely among peoples of their own racial stock."

cially coffee) across the frontier during the period of Trusteeship Administration. Some smuggling of import items continued long after federation, due to price differentials between the two states. See Chap. 13.

[2] Gardinier, *Cameroon,* p. 59. However, one of the leading ethnographic surveys of the Bamileke mention grazing and animal-raising as an insignificant part of the Bamileke economy. Littlewood, "Bamileke," in Forde, *Ethnographic,* Part IX, p. 97, asserts: "The Bamileke are agriculturists, and the small numbers of livestock which they possess play a very minor part in their economy." Tardits, *Les Bamileke,* p. 75, suggests that while cattle-raising is of little importance, the raising of small animals is widespread among the Bamileke, and sustains a commerce which some administrators have considered the principal resource of the high country. He quotes an administration report from Dschang for the 2nd half of 1925, which states: "The natives who go to Victoria, Beua and Calabar in order to sell livestock and poultry there become more and more numerous. . . . They find, in effect, at Victoria and especially at Calabar, . . . numerous buyers for poultry and small livestock, buyers who, profiting from the crisis in exchange rates, can easily pay for their purchases in shillings at a price . . . superior to the prices of the same products at Nkongsamba and even at Douala (pp. 80–81; my translation). Whether this trade continued to be important in the postwar period is uncertain.

[3] Chilvers interview, Bali, April 13, 1963.

[4] Tardits, *Les Bamileke,* p. 74.

Petitions to the visiting missions and those sent directly to the United Nations almost invariably mentioned the trade difficulties and especially the difficulty of social intercourse among those of common ethnic backgrounds or those who were linked through intermarriage.[5] Yet there has been considerable controversy about the impact of frontier regulations; not only the two administrations, but many students of Cameroon political and social development, have said the border was not a serious impediment to such intercourse.[6] Gardinier asserts that the frontier caused little dissatisfaction until World War II, when each side restricted the passage of people, goods, and currency: ". . . France instituted forced labour to help the war effort and tried to prevent Africans from fleeing to British Cameroons where obligations were lighter. After the war, both territories faced labour shortages and currency crises, so that many restrictions remained in force." [7]

What in fact *were* the boundary restrictions? They were not uniform throughout the length of the border between British and French Cameroons. In some cases the bordering administrations worked out a modus vivendi between themselves. One example is that between Bamileke-Bamoun and Bamenda, which provided that:

1. Tax certificates and identity papers of all sorts are equally valid in both zones.
2. Customs:
   a. Foodstuffs carried to supply frontier populations are exempt from all Customs duties.
   b. Foreign currency is admitted without formalities or exchange up to a total of £5 per person.
   c. Free export of cattle to British Territory is allowed under a local exception to the Customs regulations.[8]

In northern French Cameroon customs authorities generally ignored frontier movements and merely supervised lorry traffic. No identity

[5] UN Documents T/798, pp. 18, 55, T/1109, p. 9, T/1239, p. 15, T/1110, p. 17.

[6] Dr. Chilvers (interview, Bali, 1963) asserted that "during the British period there was really extraordinarily little difficulty about the frontier. The Administration winked its eye . . . because there was no outlet for palm oil . . . on the northbound road; nobody was ever stopped from taking his goods to Nkongsamba." The French administration has said that the frontier had no bearing on the lives of these peoples, except insofar as it represented the difference between the two systems of administration (UN Document T/798, p. 20).

[7] *Ibid.,* pp. 58–59.

[8] UN Document T/798, p. 56 reports the situation as of 1949.

document or administrative pass was required to cross the frontier into Nigeria.[9] However, a *laissez-passer* (an identity card good for six months) was required for persons crossing into the French sector.

Although the British and French claimed no serious difficulties along the frontier, they informed the 1952 Visiting Mission of measures taken to liberalize the system.[10] The measures apparently remained in force, with increasing laxity, until independence, or until the widespread violence in the border regions of East Cameroon. Neither the 1955 nor the 1958 Visiting Missions reported major complaints specifically about frontier problems.

The flow of workers across the frontier seems to have been more important than the familial or commercial intercourse between the two areas. Frontier restrictions probably provided little impediment to the flow of "French"-Cameroonians into the British-administered Territory to work on the plantations of the Cameroon Development Corporation (CDC). This community of Easterners played a significant role in the political controversies of the Territory, as we shall see later. However, they never approximated the numbers or the political impact of the Nigerians who came into the Southern Cameroon plantation areas (there were no restrictions on the flow of persons between the Southern Cameroons and Nigeria). In 1955 only 1,711 of the CDC's workers were from French Cameroon, while 7,767 were from Nigeria.[11] The terrorist campaign in the Bamileke *Départements* and throughout the littoral area of East Cameroon between 1956 and 1962, perhaps reinforced by a policy of Cameroonization (presumed to mean Southern-Cameroonians) by the Endeley-led Southern Cameroons government, reduced normal French Cameroonian immigration to almost nothing.[12] Perhaps these factors are the cause of the nearly 50 percent decline from 1955 to 1958 in the num-

[9] According to French reports to the first Visiting Mission, but the British administration claimed that currency exchange restrictions were technically in force, although unofficial exchange was widespread and freely accessible.

[10] UN Document T/1109, p. 10. The number of customs posts had been reduced from 24 to 11 on the UK side and from 11 to 7 on the French side. Local agricultural and handicraft products, small livestock on lead, up to three head of large animals (cows and horses), and manufactured articles regarded as customary gifts, of a value of not more than 15,000 francs could be imported or exported freely. Frontier dwellers could import or export up to £15 per person (or export in addition to the £15 some 20,000 francs).

[11] Ardener *et al., Plantation and Village,* Appendix B. About 325 French-Cameroonians were employed by other large employers in the Southern Cameroons in 1955 (3,737 Ibo and 2,584 Ibibio-Efik).

[12] Except, of course, the influx of refugees and exiles, who, because of the nature of their entry, were not counted.

ber of French Cameroonians employed by the CDC.[13] The drop-off in numerical strength of the Easterners may also have been influenced by the fact that the Endeley government, as a consequence of its shift in 1957 from support of to opposition to the idea of reunification, also switched its position on the enfranchisement of French Cameroonians and passed in the House of Assembly a motion disfranchising them immediately.[14] There was also a decline between January 1955 and 1958, though not nearly so great, in the number of Nigerians employed by the CDC. Even so, Nigerians constituted over 30 percent of the CDC labor force in 1958. If the nearly 7,000 Nigerian workers employed by the major plantation firms had remained after reunification, they would have constituted nearly one-sixth of the salaried work force of the Territory.[15]

One significant disparity between the two states of the Cameroon Federation prior to their union is the extent to which the government services were staffed by the indigenous inhabitants of the Territory. Despite the policy of Cameroonization of the civil servants staffing the government departments, Nigerians constituted 12 percent of the staff when the Foncha government came to power.[16] They filled nearly a quarter of the positions in the federal services operating in Southern Cameroons, nearly one-fourth of the positions with the ports, one-third of those with post and telegraph offices, one-half of those with the customs services, and three-fourths of those in the technical services. Over 400 positions were vacant. Only 19 positions out of 950 in the federal services were filled by expatriates, and about 100 in the regular department were so filled.

A smaller percentage of the staff positions in the French administration of Cameroon were filled by nonindigenous personnel than was the case in the Cameroons under United Kingdom administration. That this was so is ironic, since one would have expected the reverse to be true, given the difference in the colonial policies of the two administering powers. French colonial policy during its "assimilation" and "association" phases did not envision complete independence (a strict separation

[13] Ardener *et al., Plantation and Village.* Cf. Table 1 with Table 2 of Appendix B. See pp. 196–97 for a discussion of the French-Cameroon contingent; the authors point out that their numbers had been declining steadily since the beginning of World War II. Cf. also Tables 1 and 2 of Appendix H of this work.

[14] Southern Cameroons, House of Assembly Records, February 12, 1958.

[15] The salaried work force was estimated at 38,000 in 1961; see also the official report of the Chambre de Commerce et d'Industrie du Cameroun, December 1961, p. 61.

[16] Phillipson, *Report.* The figures cited show a gap between the total number of positions and the number of Cameroonians (both French and British), of about 104 persons plus Nigerian personnel. I assume this gap was filled by British expatriates.

from France) for her overseas territories and associated states until 1958. The French continued to demand and receive close association between France and her former colonies and dependencies. Thus one would expect more French nationals in the government service of the territory than in British areas, where the aim of colonial policy was supposedly to prepare the inhabitants to run their own show eventually.

There is still a widespread impression that in the French-speaking states Frenchmen occupy most of the important positions and run the government from behind the scenes. Yet in the Cameroun Republic, after independence, only about 640 French technical assistants were placed at the disposition of the Cameroon government.[17] Considering the difference in size of the two territories and of their governments, this compares favorably with the 120 or so British expatriates in the Southern Cameroons (even if one adds to these figures the approximately 400 Nigerians).

These figures suggest that not only were the British Cameroons less advanced than the French sector in preparation of indigenous personnel to take over the government, but also that Nigeria and not the United Kingdom was the real colonial power in the Territory. We shall see that the nationalist movement in Southern Cameroons directed its attack against the subjugation of the Territory by the political institutions of Nigeria and that the alien personnel it sought to expel from its institutions were Nigerian rather than British. There was much truth in the jest often made by French-speaking Cameroonians about the Southern Cameroons: *"C'est une colonie d'une région d'une colonie."*

If relatively more Cameroonians were able to enter the administrative services in the eastern state than in the western, opportunities for them to enter the business and commercial world were about equally limited in each. Although Africans in the British Cameroons perhaps had more freedom and were encouraged to become small traders and small-scale entrepreneurs, the Africans were usually not Cameroonians. It has been estimated that before reunification Nigerians, particularly Ibos from the Eastern Region, controlled 85 percent of the small commerce of the Southern Cameroons and most of the African-run transportation services.[18] In the east even small commerce was usually subject to European

---

[17] *Europe France-Outre-Mer,* xxxviii, No. 379, p. 28. One hundred and forty-nine technical assistants were assigned to the general administration, 43 to the Justice Department, 167 to Public Health, 140 to Agriculture. Even in the area of education the number of Frenchmen serving in the Cameroon under government agreement was not high—248.

[18] Phillipson, *Report.*

domination right up to the creation of the Federation. Commerce in cattle and other livestock, tourist artisanry, and trinket and similar small trade outside the big cities was in the hands of Hausa and Bamileke traders. But in the towns of any size most imported items were sold in European or Levantine-owned and operated shops. Most of the 16,000 or so non-Africans living in East Cameroon depended on commerce for their livelihood. On the 1,336 French living in Yaounde in 1962, for example, at least 481, almost half of those employed, were involved in commerce, industry, or activities involving essentially business-management skills. Of the 574 in the public or semipublic sectors, 122 were employed in the general administration; most of the rest (205) served with the army, the gendarmes, or research services. Out of the 332 non-Africans from countries other than France nearly two-thirds were in commerce, industry, or artisanry. In 1962, among the nearly 23,000 Cameroonians in paid employment in Yaounde, only a little over eight percent—about 1,850 persons—were employed in modern commerce, banking, or insurance. About 13 percent were in commerce associated with artisanry.[19] Few of the Africans in commerce or business are managers or own their shops. Europeans dominated industry, commerce, and banking in East Cameroon. Prior to federation, construction, contracting, and ownership of rental property was the only field that offered Africans in either state opportunities to become entrepreneurs.[20]

COMPETITION rather than complementarity denotes the relationship between the export economies of East and West Cameroon. Both states produce much the same products for export. Table 2 compares the export

[19] All figures for the Yaounde non-African population are taken from "La Population de Yaounde, 1962," Ministere de l'Economie Nationale, Service de la Statistiques, September 1963.

[20] In East Cameroon by far the most successful African businessman was Paul Soppo Priso, a Douala who is considered by most Africans and many Europeans to be a millionaire (in dollar equivalent). He owns a construction company and has landed a number of important building contracts in Douala and Yaounde. He was once a strong force in Cameroonian politics, but with the rise of the Ahidjo-led movement for a single political party and the jailing of various opposition leaders, Soppo Priso chose to retire from politics entirely. His wealth gives him a position of independence enjoyed by perhaps no other Cameroonian.

In West Cameroon there is no comparable figure to Soppo Priso. The most important businessman among the Cameroonians also works in the construction field. D. A. Nangah's company is not nearly so big as Soppo Priso's, and was organized only in 1963, but was for some time the biggest outfit owned and managed by Africans in West Cameroon (save perhaps for the transportation companies owned by nonresident Nigerians).

figures in the chief crops of the two territories on the eve of reunification.[21]

Although both states tended to produce the same agricultural crops for export, until reunification there was almost no competition between them for customers, because each sold the great majority of its exports to different, protected markets. In 1958, 75 percent of British Cameroons exports (both northern and southern sections) went to the United King-

TABLE 2

1961 Exports Compared

	West Cameroon	East Cameroon
AGRICULTURAL	*Short Tons*	*Metric Tons*
Bananas	84,975	51,280
Cocoa	8,225	58,302
Coffee (Arabica)	4,260*	7,281
Coffee (Robusta)	—	28,203
Palm Kernel	4,803	14,564
Palm Oil	9,458	—
Peanuts (shelled)	—	9,924
Pepper	47	—
Tea	79	—
Timber	177,044	148,260
Rubber	4,552	4,940
Hides & skins	1,092**	1,290**
Cotton	—	10,307
INDUST.		
Aluminum	—	46,144
Cocoa Butter	—	3,027
Cut Lumber	—	7,753
Tobacco & Cigarettes	—	1,021

* Most of the West Cameroon coffee is arabica (1960 Arabica 3,500, Robusta 1,500). There is much smuggling of coffee to the East (estimated at 1,500 tons). Documentation Française, No. 2,946.

** 1962 figures.

dom.[22] Despite important tariff advantages associated with membership in the Commonwealth (leaders in the two states agreed that the Cameroon Federation would not become a member of either the Commonwealth or the French Union), some European countries figure signifi-

[21] West Cameroon figures are from Hon. A. N. Jua, "Budget Speech," West Cameroon, House of Assembly Records, June 17, 1963. East Cameroon figures are from *Rapport Annuel, 1962*, Chambre de Commerce et d'Industrie et des Mines du Cameroun.

[22] Documentation Française, Document No. 2756, p. 8.

cantly in the exports of some of the formerly Southern Cameroon's products.[23] About 80 percent of her cocoa exports went to Europe, mostly the Netherlands, despite a Commonwealth preference of £²/₄ per hundredweight. A substantial percentage of the Territory's palm products went to Europe despite a 10 percent imperial preference. The Southern Cameroons enjoyed imperial preferences of £⁷/₁₀ per ton on bananas, but the European Economic Community has also offered a 20 percent tariff preference on bananas from the Associated States. (The preference is estimated to have been more than that offered by the Commonwealth.) Coffee enjoyed an imperial preference of £⁹/₄ per hundredweight, which might have been offset by the 16 percent tariff reduction the EEC offered.

Thus, though the two export economies consisted of many of the same items, the loss of imperial preference for Southern Cameroon goods in many cases need not have produced severe hardship if after reunification the European market had been able to absorb the combined Cameroon exports. As we shall see in Chapter 13 this did not happen, and West Cameroon suffered severe economic disruption as a result of the loss of the Commonwealth market.

The Cameroon Development Corporation dominates the economy of West Cameroon. When it played its greatest role in the economy, it accounted for 65 percent of the export tonnage and 55 percent of export earnings (excluding trees and lumber).[24] By reunification CDC production had dropped to about 41 percent of export tonnage (excluding wood exports) and about 28 percent of the total export earnings, yet the CDC continues as the major employer. Its labor force of 17,236 in 1961 was about half the paid labor of the Territory.[25] In 1964 it was still the largest employer in the Federation besides the federal government, although its work force had dropped to about 13,000.[26] In addition to the part played by the CDC as a chief exporter until the federal government took it over in 1962–1963, it provided important educational and health services and community centers for employees and nonemployees, and administered the ports, and continues to offer housing for its workers, and operate water supply, roads, and railroad systems. As the 1952 United Nations Visiting Mission noted: "It was sometimes difficult to draw a line in

[23] *Ibid.,* No. 2946.
[24] *Ibid.,* No. 2946.
[25] CDC Report, 1961; cf. Jua, "Budget Speech."
[26] *Entreprise,* Supplement No. 602, March 1967, p. 12, note 1.

the Trust Territory between government services and the corporation's duties and functions." [27]

The CDC was created in 1946 to take over and administer most of the former German plantations which had been confiscated for the second time at the beginning of World War II (they were confiscated after World War I, but were eventually resold to the original owners). The plantations were purchased by the governor on behalf of the government of Nigeria and leased to the CDC for 60 years at a nominal rent.[28] A statutory corporation, the CDC was initially required to pay taxes to the Nigerian government, as if it were a private corporation, but after payment of the taxes and certain other charges, the net profit was to be paid to the governor for the benefit of the inhabitants of the Trust Territory. After 1954 Southern Cameroon was given regional status, payments were made directly to the Southern Cameroons government, and its annual report and account were submitted to its House of Assembly.

Sweeping changes in the organization of the corporation were scheduled to be made in 1960. Beginning January 1 of that year the British Colonial Development Corporation was appointed the managing agent of the CDC, and the leases on the plantations were extended to 99 years (the option to re-lease was also extended to 99 years). The managing company granted a loan of one million pounds and agreed to grant up to two million more in equity and loan stock after the CDC was reconstituted. The reconstitution of the CDC was to make it a joint stock company with equal representation between the federal government of Nigeria, the government of Southern Cameroons and the CDC, but the reconstitution did not take effect and the £2 million loan fell through.[29] Though the new managing agent took over in 1961, the scheduled reconstitution depended on a complete evaluation of the assets of the CDC; before that could be completed, reunification took place. Despite the separation, however, for four years Nigeria continued to be technically eligible for a representative on the board of representatives, though according to officials of the CDC their appointee never participated.[30]

The Nigerian government's interest in the corporation continued, represented by its one million pound loan (repayable in 18 annuities at four percent interest beginning in 1970). The West Cameroon government

[27] UN Documents, T/1109, p. 18.

[28] Ardener *et al., Plantation and Village,* p. xxix.

[29] Mr. Moss, assistant to the chairman of the board, CDC, interview, Bota, April 3, 1963; and Mr. Rogers, secretary and assistant to the general manager, CDC, interview, Bota, August 1965.

[30] Moss interview.

has an unsecured loan of the same type amounting to 519 million CFA francs. Though all of the initial £1 million loan of the CDC had been drawn by April of 1963, the additional credits promised were not paid because of the retardation in the reconstitution of the CDC, and ultimately the offer was withdrawn. The need for immediate financial assistance led the CDC to procure a loan of £400,000 from the Cameroon (federal) Development Bank in 1963. Longer-run plans for the CDC are enmeshed in uncertainty; as one CDC official explained: "The intention, as expressed in the annual report of 1962 is that the evaluation should be completed and that consequent upon the evaluation then the corporation should be reconstituted. [But] the intention of the parties concerned is hard to judge. The original [plan for reconstitution] was stated previous to the plebiscite, previous to independence, and previous to the reintegration [reunification], previous to the Common Market, previous to the ending of colonial preference." [31]

Discussions in London were held around mid-1963 between representatives of the Cameroon federal government, the West Cameroon government, and the CDC. The outcome of the discussions, and subsequent ones, seems not to have altered the basic status of the CDC as a semipublic corporation under the West Cameroon government.[32] It was decided in 1965 not to have the CDC become a joint stock (mixed public and private) company.

Given the nature of its activities, especially the use of new acreage (out of the 200,000 acres of land taken over from the Custodian of Enemy Property, about 60,000 are planted), and the redirection of its productive efforts (since 1956 the CDC has steadily reduced the acreage in bananas and diverted it to rubber and tea), the CDC cannot avoid seriously affecting development-planning undertaken at the federal level. Moreover, when one considers that federal authority potentially extends over laws regulating the status of persons (natural and moral) and property (personal and real), it is not difficult to imagine many pressures operating to reconstitute the CDC as a federal and not a state body. This may ultimately result in the net profits accruing not to the government of West Cameroon but to the federal government.

Another factor complicating the future of the CDC is the fact that it has administered programs and services that come under the authority of

[31] Moss interview.

[32] Rogers interview. The federal government processes all dealings with foreign governments and companies, but the CDC operates under the jurisdiction of the office of the West Cameroon prime minister.

the federal government, e.g. medical services. In reality the CDC has been anxious to turn over most of these "ancillary services" to someone else, and probably didn't care whether it was to the state or the federal government. Medical services cost the CDC the onerous sum of 83 million francs in 1962. However, one of the forces acting against turning over the medical services to the government has been the CDC Workers' Union which has expressed fears that the government could not run them as efficiently as has the CDC.[33]

More central to the interests of the CDC is the problem of long-range development planning. The word "development," as used in the title of the CDC, is sometimes misconstrued as referring to its role as a source of finance for government projects (perhaps development projects). Since it contributes financially to the government of West Cameroon, which has a capital development program, there are pressures for the CDC to embark on similar projects directly, to build additional schools, dispensaries, and especially open up new roads and communications facilities. The CDC views its development role as one of bringing into cultivation the lands leased to it, increasing its production, so as to be able to provide a higher net profit for the government, the real development agency. In fact, the CDC does engage directly in what one would term "development projects," its expansion often does mean new roads, etc., and even more directly, it has considered a plan of stimulating, in association with the government, small-holder and outcropping ventures, the production of which would be partially local, partially corporative. The CDC's activities along these lines must now be integrated into the overall development plan for the state.

A SUPPOSED lack of solid financial foundations for the government of the Southern Cameroons is one of the factors that produced a reunification movement in the Territory. From the time the Southern Cameroons was administratively and financially disengaged from the Eastern Region of Nigeria, the caveat of the Nigerian financial secretary, Sir Louis Chick— that the Southern Cameroons would be unable to run its government without external financial aid for a number of years—was used as an argument for continued association with Nigeria or for continued association with Great Britain under an extended Trusteeship, and finally, as an argument for reunification. The partisans of reunification first made feeble attempts to counter this initial warning and a reassertion of it

---

[33] Rogers interview.

made three years later, but they ultimately bowed to the conclusion that the Territory needed a stronger partner on which to lean.

Before 1954, when the Trust Territory of Cameroons under United Kingdom administration was administered as an integral part of Nigeria, no separate budget was prepared for the Territory and public accounts were not kept separate for it. The UN Visiting Mission of 1949 reports: "government revenues accruing there are included without distinction in the budgets of Nigeria as a whole and expenditures are allotted to it not on the basis of its overall need but on the basis of the various Nigerian regions with which it is administratively integrated." [34] This arrangement made it impossible to accurately determine the capacity of the Territory to finance its own way. Because of its size and stage of development, it was generally assumed that the central Nigerian government and the Eastern Region government had put more into the Territory than they took out. In an attempt to counter accusations of financially neglecting the Territory, the Nigerian federal minister of finance asserted before the House of Representatives that between 1922 and World War II (during which statistics were not properly kept) the Nigerian government spent more than it received in revenues.[35] During the period 1943–1949 the Nigerian government claims to have subsidized the Trust Territory (both North and South) by over a million pounds (i.e. expended that much more than the revenues derived in the Territory). When the old German estates operated by the CDC began large-scale production, the Territory the first time had a surplus of revenues over expenditures. A special fund was created to be used for the benefit of the Territory; into it was deposited about £1,163,000 over the next six years. However, when the Southern Cameroons was made a separate administrative unit in 1954, a fiscal commission studying the financial implications of the reform reported that the Territory would not be viable without external financial assistance, despite the surpluses later claimed to have accrued to the Territory in the six years prior to the separation. The expectation of the fiscal commission proved correct. The Southern Cameroons budget for the first full year showed a deficit of about £285,000.[36] To guard against such deficits, Fiscal Commissioner Chick had worked out a special formula for stabilizing the finances of the new government. A federal constitutional grant was instituted which would pay to the Southern

[34] UN Document T/798, paragraph 61.

[35] F. Okotie-Eboh, Speech to Nigerian House of Representatives, February 17, 1959.

[36] Budget estimates: Southern Cameroons, 1955–56.

Cameroons government, "every penny the Federal Government gets from the Territory and does not spend on Federal services for the Territory." [37] This system of revenue allocation was deemed more advantageous to the Trust Territory than that applied to the Eastern Regions. In addition to the constitutional grant, a special advance of £300,000 was made to supply the government with working capital.

The "Chick formula" was a failure, however, because it was based on the assumption that the CDC would be a major source of revenue for the Territory. In fact, the revenues of the CDC have seldom fulfilled the original expectation of its capacity to finance the Territory's government and development program. Though its net profits declined sharply after the 1949 period, they took a turn for the worse in 1954, falling to less than a third of the level of the previous year. Table 3 indicates net profits in the years prior to reunification. [38]

TABLE 3

Cameroon Development Corporation Net Profits, 1947–1961
n.d. = no data

	Pounds Sterling		Pounds Sterling
1947	nil	1954	19,204
1948	54,352	1955	nil
1949	n.d.	1956	15,117
1950	n.d.	1957	38,028
1951	55,559	1958	16,078
1952	n.d.	1959	nil
1953	60,285	1960	25,788
		1961	47,620

The wide fluctuations in CDC revenues and its heavy tax obligations to the Nigerian government undermined the "Chick formula" and resulted in a new arrangement designed to guarantee the Southern Cameroons government a fixed minimum of revenue. The Nigerian federal government accepted the obligation in 1955 to guarantee that the revenues the Territory would receive from the Federation would not be less than £580,-000 over a three-year period. [39] Should the normal constitutional grant,

[37] UN Document T/1239, p. 25, paragraph 214. The 1954 system for allocation to Southern Cameroons is embodied in Section 163 of the Nigeria (Constitutional) Order in Council 1954.

[38] These funds were paid directly to the government of Southern Cameroons after 1954. Compiled from figures in the United Nations Visiting Mission Reports, UN Documents T/798, T/1109, T/1239, and T/1440, *Cameroons Champion*, December 8, 1961; and CDC Report and Accounts, 1960, 1961.

[39] UN Document T/1239, p. 25, paragraphs 215–16.

combined with distributed profit of the CDC, fall short of the £580,000 figure, the federal government would make up the difference. For the two fiscal years 1956–1957 and 1957–1958, federal grants were £450,000. The system of revenue allocation was still deemed unsatisfactory, how- ever. The size of the federal subsidies ran much higher than expected. Moreover, it was estimated that greater revenues would have accrued to Southern Cameroons from the system applied in the other regions of the Federation. A new fiscal commission (the "Raisman Commission"), which studied the actual and estimated financial situation in the Territory during the years 1956–1959, brought the change about.[40] The 1958– 1959 budget therefore benefited from the new scheme, which allocated to the Southern Cameroons its estimated proportionate share of the total Nigerian revenues from imports of motor spirits (gasoline); its estimated share of half of the import duty on tobacco; one percent of all other im- port duties; its apportioned share of half of the excise and export duties; and all personal income tax, mining royalties, and certain miscellaneous revenues derived from within the Territory.[41] In addition to the new sys- tem of revenue-allocation, advances totaling over £700,000, plus accrued interest, made under the old system, were written off by the Nigerian fed- eral government. Even so, the first budget estimates applying these changes showed a £200,000 deficit.[42] Only through unexpectedly high revenues was the budget finally balanced.[43] The British government also granted the Territory £450,000 in early 1958.[44]

The Nigerian federal government made significant contributions to the capital expenditures of the Territory. Annual averages of federal con- tributions to this category of expenditures were £300,000 between 1955 and 1958.[45] Road development in the Territory was allegedly also a large beneficiary of Nigerian support—the 1959 "Economic Programme" of the Nigerian Federation foresaw an additional allocation of £1,200,000 for completion of the Victoria-Bamenda road.[46] A great part of the re- sources for such development actually came from the CDC (i.e. British sources). In 1956 the Colonial Office reportedly allocated for the first time funds (£1.3 million) for road, communications, technical education,

[40] British Government Document, Cmnd 481, September 1958.
[41] UN Document T/1440, pp. 9–10.
[42] E. M. L. Endeley, Speech to Resumed Constitutional Conference, London, 1958.
[43] UN Document T/1440, p. 10.
[44] Endeley speech.
[45] Phillipson, *Report*.
[46] Okotie Eboh speech.

103

agricultural, and other development projects.[47] Independent estimates have conflicted with Nigerian claims of the extent of the latter's capital investment in the Territory. It has been suggested that for the 37 years prior to 1959 the investment was no more than £2,700,000.[48]

Recurring deficits, periodic revision of the scheme of revenue allocations, and repeated disappointments over the level of revenue from CDC profits and from customs and other taxes contributed to the constant worry among Southern Cameroons officials about the financial stability of the Territory. If Dr. E.M.L. Endeley, the first Cameroonian "Leader of Government Business," advocated autonomy out of a conviction that the Territory was being exploited by Nigeria, the responsibility for balancing his budget quickly convinced him of its financial weakness. Though the Territory's financial position was by no means its only, or even principal concern (cf. Chap. 6) in the 1957 and the 1959 elections, when the question of the Territory's relationship with Nigeria was at issue, "associationist" forces stressed the financial factor as an argument for continued association with Nigeria.[49] The 1958 United Nations Visiting Mission noted their argument: ". . . we need hardly emphasize the fact that the Southern Cameroons is one of the under-developed areas on the west coast of Africa and needs extensive external financial aid if the Territory is to keep pace with her neighbours in all fields of human endeavour. The Mission will recall that we have repeatedly laid strong emphasis on this unenviable situation. . . ."[50]

The Kamerun National Democratic Party (KNDP), as did the Kamerun United National Congress (KUNC) before it, stressed its belief that the Territory was able to make its own way financially and that deficits had been incurred because the Territory did not receive the full benefit of the resources it had. "If the Southern Cameroons had its own customs this would provide money for the poorer districts of the Territory."[51] The KNDP felt that as a separate state the Territory could increase its revenues by retaining all its customs collections and by reducing competition from other regions for customs revenues on Cameroon imports by having more imports enter the Territory through its own seaports. (Pre-

[47] Kameroon National Congress, Manifesto, March 1957 elections.

[48] *Ibid.*

[49] Kamerun National Congress, Manifesto, March 1957 elections. The congress calls attention to the 1954 Fiscal Commission's conclusion that the Southern Cameroons would be unable to run its government without outside help. A considerable portion of this document is devoted to the Territory's financial position.

[50] UN Document T/1440, Annex II, p. 54.

[51] KNDP, *Newsletter,* July 1957.

viously, over three-fourths of their imports first entered Nigeria through one of the other regions.) But as if to nullify all these arguments, the party also pressed the British government for a guaranteed annual grant of £2 million for the recurrent budget and a long term grant of £5 million for the capital budget.

If John Foncha and the other partisans of reunification were not convinced of the financial incapacity of the Territory, they nevertheless did not consider that it could stand alone. They did expect, however, that external assistance for the Territory would be greater than that provided by Nigeria if it came directly from the United Kingdom, or even from the Cameroon Republic. Much of the complaint of the reunificationists was that the development of the Territory was restricted to the level of the financial help provided by the Nigerian government, when responsibility for its administration was rather that of the government of the United Kingdom. Thus much of the effort of the spokesmen of this idea was directed toward producing the realization, as Victor Mukete put it to the Nigerian House of Representatives, that its status as a Trust Territory meant, "responsibility for the well-being of the Southern Cameroons also extends far beyond the confines of this Honourable House to Governments or States, most of which are far more developed than the Federal Government of Nigeria." [52]

What incensed the reunificationists most, however, was the belief that the Territory had not received its just due even from the government of Nigeria. Foncha, shortly after his accession in 1959 to the prime ministership, ordered a study of the financial, economic, and administrative consequences of the Territory's separation from Nigeria; the study confirmed this belief.[53] Sir Sydney Phillipson, who headed the study team, concluded that it was impossible to say whether Southern Cameroons was a net creditor or debtor to the Federation of Nigeria, or to establish the real extent to which the Territory's government had been subsidized by the Federation, but he thought that at least since 1954, during the application of the "Chick formula," its contribution to the Federation's revenues had been underassessed and thus perhaps it was a net creditor to Nigeria.

If the report had vindicated, however mildly, the KNDP charges of in-

[52] Nigeria, House of Representatives, Official Report of Debate, March 4, 1957, p. 150.

[53] Phillipson, *Report*. The fact that the possibility of reunification with French Cameroon was not part of the frame of reference for the study is one of the strongest indications that Foncha considered such union to be remote. His interest in ordering the study was to bolster his demand for an extended period of trusteeship.

105

equitable allocations of Nigerian revenues, it discredited certain KNDP contentions concerning the financial viability of the Territory. The federally contributed revenues which the Territory would lose amounted to £571 thousand annually. Though it might expect to gain about £960 thousand in revenues which usually accrued to the federal government, the cost of replacing the federal supported services (£488 thousand), together with loss of revenues, would leave a deficit budget. In Sir Sydney's opinion, only by dropping the scheduled £175,000 payment into the reserve fund and sharply reducing the normal £250,010 contribution to the Development Fund could the Territory balance its budget in the first year of separation. If the administering authority contributed the sum scheduled for the expenditure on development and welfare on the recurrent side of the budget, the recurrent expenditures might even be modestly expanded.

These remedies would only meet the immediate problems of separation, however. Eventually the cost of services supplied directly or indirectly by the federal government, would have to be taken over by the Territory. Certain of them, such as postal and telegraph, customs and excise, and inland revenue services, might continue to be supplied by Nigeria on a "paid agency" basis. The Territory would presumably have to compensate the Nigerian government for fixed and mobile assets left in it. Then too, there was the question of paying off Southern Cameroon's share of the obligation for the Nigerian public debt.[54] Separation would also require considerable new capital expenditures which did not then figure into the budget estimates, such as expenditures for new office buildings and quarters for the increased staff needed to run an autonomous administrative unit.

The author of the report deemed that if: (1) prices remained stable, (2) the rates of taxation then in force continued to be applied (or increased), (3) revenues for most of the capital expenditure came from external sources, (4) the government possessed revenue-collecting machinery adequate to tap the local resources, and (5) civil conditions in the Territory were favorable to foreign and internal investment, the Territory would *potentially* be viable. As an independent state, at its present state of development, the report stated, the Southern Cameroons was not viable.

The KNDP leadership, in control of the government only since early

[54] The Phillipson *Report* recommended that instead of paying this off at a rate determined on a per capita basis, the Territory should pay only for a portion of capital expenditures actually made in the Territory, which had been raised through public subscription.

106

1959, apparently felt that the conclusions of the report would advance neither the cause of "secession" from Nigeria or their continued control of the government, and the report was not made public. The ostensible reason for its suppression was that it had been made under the assumption of continued trusteeship, and before the decision was made to conduct a plebiscite on the question of reunification. However, one might have expected that the report would be used in the plebiscite campaign for reunification, since it indicated that the Territory might not have received its just due from Nigeria and that it would continue to need external assistance. Foncha may have felt that admitting the extent of the Territory's dependence would undermine the expectations he had built up in his followers of a considerably autonomous state in a Cameroon Federation, or that it might scare off the leadership of the Cameroon Republic.

Despite the extensive efforts of the KNDP at self-reassurance, it took little research to reveal the financial difficulties the Territory had experienced throughout the postwar period. The leadership of the Cameroon Republic could not have been blind to the financial threat to the success of their own programs posed by the prospect of reunification of the two Cameroons.

GREATER diversity in its economy, a higher per capita income, a relatively larger budget notwithstanding, the Cameroon Republic had its own financial problems. France had certainly invested more, publicly and privately, in the Cameroon Trust Territory under its administration than Britain and Nigeria combined had invested in the British Cameroons. The nationalist movement in French Cameroon did not punctuate its propaganda with so many charges of neglect. During the first decade of the Trusteeship France contributed 71.5 billion CFA francs ($286 million) to the budgets of the Territory, over 95 percent of the total government expenditures.[55] The French government contributed heavily to the Cameroon capital budget as well; during the period 1946–1958 the *Fonds d'Investissements pour le Développement Economique et Social des Territoires d'Outremer* (FIDES, later renamed *Fonds d'Aide et de Coopération,* FAC) poured nearly 77 billion French francs ($154 million) into the Territory. Semigovernment organizations such as the *Bureau de la Recherche des Pétroles* (which invested five billion French francs during this period), and the European Economic Community also made significant contributions to Cameroon's capital. During the Trusteeship

[55] UN Document, T/1441, p. 10, paragraph 41.

107

period, from all French public sources, about 200 billion French francs were spent in the Territory, and an additional 2 billion came from private French investment.[56] Thus nearly $450 million, more than 10 percent of the Gross National Product for this period, or about $12 per Cameroonian per year, was invested in the Territory from French sources. Table 4 summarizes these investments, except for private investments.[57]

TABLE 4

French Aid to Cameroon, 1946–1958
(in French Francs)

Year	Metrop. Budget *	Fr. Treasury	FIDES	CCFOM **	BRP †	Total
1946						
1950	2,570	—	25,841	3,222	—	31,633
1951	1,248	—	7,721	2,060	180	11,209
1952	2,246	—	3,873	3,454	217	9,419
1953	1,925	—	7,772	3,393	253	13,343
1954	2,188	780	4,731	14,359	398	22,447
1955	2,504	1,259	8,509	3,355	1,526	17,154
1956	3,432	2,506	6,817	2,009	1,080	15,843
1957	8,632	1,393	7,084	3,924	775	21,809
1958	8,792	2,000	4,997	318	454	16,560
Total	33,545	7,938	76,956	36,094	4,874	159,426
Grants	33,545		56,428		4,874	94,847
Loans		7,938	20,547	36,094		64,579

* Excludes military expenditures.

** *Caisse Centrale de la France d'Outre-Mer,* later renamed *Caisse Centrale de la Coopération Economique.*

† *Bureau de la Recherche des Pétroles.*

If the high rate of French investment and contribution indicates an accelerated rate of development for the territory, it also indicates the extent to which it was dependent on external financial resources to maintain the rate. With "autonomous" powers under the 1957 *Statut* and the first Cameroonian-prepared budget, the level of French assistance was reduced, and the "austerity budget" was balanced only by sharply cutting back development expenditures.[58]

As French Cameroon approached independence its financial situation became more difficult, because increasingly services formerly financed

[56] Kjell Andersen, *Report on the Fiscal and Economic Implications of Union.* Gardinier, *Cameroon,* p. 29, puts the figure at 95.4 billion CFA.

[57] Andersen, *Report.* It was estimated that the 1959 government grant would equal that of 1958.

[58] UN Document T/1441, paragraph 42.

by the French government as part of the authority of the high commissioner fell on the Cameroon budget. In response to this situation Cameroon authorities attempted to reduce government expenditure to eliminate programs that were not urgent; an atmosphere of realism about the financial consequences of self-government permeated the government. The prime minister declared: "a country which wishes to be free and aspires to independence must follow a sound financial policy so that the local budget may progressively take over from the lenders. . . . We are staggering under the weight of our recurrent expenditure, particularly expenditure on personnel, while our investment budget is notoriously inadequate. We shall constantly strive to curtail, and indeed eliminate, unprofitable or superfluous expenditure, while at the same time doing everything possible to increase revenue in accordance with a fiscal policy whose primary objective will be a more equitable distribution of taxation." [59] The last budget before independence benefited from a French grant of nearly 1,500 million CFA francs ($6 million). The grant fully covered the cost of the services now transfered to the Cameroon government.

The preindependence rate of capital accumulation and expansion in the recurrent budget could only be approximated after independence through large-scale assistance from France or elsewhere. Such assistance was now a problem of negotiations between independent governments or between the Cameroon government and various international financial institutions. France was generous with her former ward; the 1958 UN Visiting Mission was informed by the French high commissioner for the Territory that, "while the legal obligations binding France and the Cameroons would cease to exist as of January 1, 1960, that did not mean that the obligations of friendship would likewise disappear." French assistance to Cameroon increased after independence; her contribution to the 1960 budget was about 600 million CFA francs in the first three months,[60] twice the amount granted in the year prior to independence. In addition to the normal budgetary assistance, a special grant was given (*Aide exceptionnelle du budget*) which amounted to 1.3 billion CFA francs (for the whole year), and the expenses of certain personnel were met by France. In all, France's contribution to the Cameroon in 1960 was about 3.2 billion CFA francs ($13 million).[61] In the second year of inde-

[59] *Ibid.*, paragraph 43.

[60] Republic of Cameroon, *Budget,* exercise 1960–61, p. 20.

[61] *Europe France-Outre-Mer,* No. 379; Gilbert Comte, "La Coopération avec la France." The figure includes a grant of 300 million CFA for maintenance of order (i.e. military).

pendence, the French budgetary aid alone was 1.9 billion CFA francs (roughly $7.6 million).[62] By 1965, when French budgetary aid ceased, France had provided Cameroon with nearly $80 million in aid.[63]

It seems ironic that Southern Cameroons partisans of reunification should have insisted so strongly that the new federation would belong neither to the British Commonwealth nor the French Community, given the dependent position of each state concerned.[64] This demand was probably intended to counteract the pro-Nigerian CPNC, but UPC-inspired, arguments that the French still ruled "independent" Cameroon, that they dominated the economy and maintained military bases in the country which would allow them to take over the country at any minute. Though it had been part of the French Union as an Associated State, technically the Cameroon Trust Territory had never been part of the French Community. This is a point leaders on both sides of the reunification issue misunderstood. The Cameroon Republic did sign bilateral agreements with France which provided for military and economic assistance, and by the *Accord de Coopération Économique Monétaire et Financière,* signed in November of 1960, Cameroon entered the Franc Zone. By this treaty Cameroon agreed, among other things, to keep her foreign exchange in the *Banque de la France,* to grant French products preferential tariffs, and to consult French officials in drawing up her annual import program. In return for these obligations, Title II of the agreement provided that France would grant financial assistance, carry out studies, furnish equipment, send experts and technicians, and help in the training of Cameroonian civil servants.

IN SUMMARY it is evident that only with external aid could the Cameroon Republic hope to meet not only its own needs but the expanded needs of the Federation and particularly those of its new partner, the former Southern Cameroons. However, there is little evidence that the leadership of either state really understood the financial implications of reunification. Indeed, it was not until the eve of the plebiscite that the Republic's government commissioned its own study of the fiscal and economic

[62] Republic of Cameroon, *Budget,* exercise 1961–62.

[63] UN Document. *Industrial Development in Africa* (New York: Doc. No. ID/CONF.1/RBP/1, 1967), p. 254.

[64] Foncha repeatedly promised his followers that the "United Kamerun" would not belong to the French Union. Ahidjo was made to agree that "in no case . . . [would the Federation] be part either of the French Community or the British Commonwealth." Cf. Joint Declaration, October 17, 1961, in *The Two Alternatives,* Administering Authority Southern Cameroons, 1961.

implications of the union.[65] Certainly none of the main partisans of re-unification on either side of the Mungo appreciated the extent to which not only resulting problems of financing the budgets of the three governments but also the consequent decline and disruption of economic activities generally, would plague the leadership of, and peril the enthusiasm for, the new Federation.

The situation with respect to the general economies was similar; though there were some opportunities for economic advancement through reunification of the two Cameroons, these were primarily limited to small commerce and the subsistence economy, especially among the border peoples. For the broader economy, particularly the export economy, reunification threatened serious disruptions of the patterns of production and commerce in West Cameroon. In any case, a merger of the economies of the two states certainly promised to give rise to myriad problems, the solutions of which, or even the recognition of which, are barely evident in the preplebiscite pronouncements of the partisans of re-unification.

[65] Kjell Andersen, who made the study, did not visit the Southern Cameroons for research until February 5, 1961, six days before the plebiscite.

⚚ 6 ⚚

Patterns of Political Interaction

WE HAVE considered the conjunctive aspect of the relationship between the two Cameroon Territories prior to union insofar as patterns of identity, culture, and economic life were concerned. I have characterized some of the complementary and conflicting features of these relationships. It is important to do the same for the relationships between Cameroon political leaders and organizations, for such relationships usually provide the catalysts for political union. In this case, was there the high level of interaction and undistorted and responsive political communication which the Deutsch school considers so important a motive to political union and integration? Which forces facilitated such interaction? Which hindered it?

The following points about the general situation should be noted: (1) the continuities that existed in the patterns of political leadership and organization between the Territories were nearly as meager as were those in the other fields; (2) though their political interests were not as disparate or conflicting as their economic and financial interests, leaders in the two states lacked extensive contact with their counterparts; (3) to be sure, there was joint activity on several occasions during the 13-year course of the reunification movement, but for the most part the leaders pursued their parallel if not always common objectives separately; (4) a sense of mutual acquaintance developed among the leaders, but no sense of intimacy.

The salient factors inhibiting close collaboration were the very ones which also most strongly engendered a need and desire for it. The way in which the Administering Authorities ruled the two Territories determined this.

The two states of Cameroon, during their life as mandates and as Trust Territories, were administered under an "administrative union"—British Cameroons as part of the Nigerian protectorate, and French Cameroons initially as part of French Equatorial Africa and later as part of the larger French Union. In the British case, the union was especially intimate; no separate representative institutions were created in the Trust Territory until 1954. Even after the creation of representative councils in the regions of Nigeria, no special seats were reserved in either central or regional assemblies for Cameroonians; and until 1951 no Cameroon representative was elected to the central legislature even as part of the Eastern or Northern Regional delegations. Before the 1951 "Macpherson Constitution" of Nigeria, the two provinces of Southern Cameroons had 2 of the 18 unofficial (popular) seats in the House of Assembly of the Eastern Region. Northern British Cameroons was represented in the Northern House by one member of the House of Chiefs. No separate budgets were prepared for the Trust Territory; its public accounts were indistinguishable from those of the two Regions with which it was administered.[1] Cameroons was supposed to develop politically within the framework of Nigeria.

French Cameroon was subject to a similar administrative arrangement, although it enjoyed greater autonomy. The trusteeship agreement provided that the territory could be administered "as an integral part of French Territory."[2] The French Union grouped Cameroon along with Togo as two Associated Territories of the French Union; the other French colonies in Africa were Member Territories of the Union or Overseas Departments of the French Republic.

The French Union was established by the October 1946 constitution of the Fourth French Republic. Though some Africans participated in its framing, the French did not incorporate much of the Africans' aspirations or program for Franco-African collaboration. African views had figured much more importantly in the Constituent Assembly which drafted the first constitutional proposals, but French voters defeated the proposals in the May 1946 referendum. In a study of these developments Thompson and Adloff have noted: "There is no doubt that it [the October constitution] marked a step backward so far as colonial emancipation was concerned. The concepts of federalism and decentralization advocated at [the conference of] Brazzaville, lost out through a reassertion of the established French policy of centralization and assimilation"[3]

It appeared to many Cameroonians that the constitutional structure of the French Union incorporated Cameroon directly into the French Republic on a basis no different from that of the "overseas territories," despite the special international relationship Cameroon was supposed to enjoy. Though the Union had an assembly of its own, within which Cameroon participated, the fundamental legislative and administrative

[1] UN Document T/798, paragraph 64.

[2] Trusteeship agreement for Cameroons under French Administration, T.C. 62nd meeting, 1st session, 13 December 1946, Art. 4, Sec. A.1.

[3] Thompson and Adloff, *French West Africa*, p. 34.

powers were vested in organs of the French Republic—the *Assemblée nationale* and the *Conseil de la République*—within which Cameroon also participated.[4] Cameroon's administration was responsible directly to the Ministry for Overseas France.

In short, the system of the French Union seemed particularly designed to sustain the colonial relationship between a dominant France and her dependent territories. The relationship contradicted the terms of the Trusteeship Agreement and the system of international accountability for colonial rule which the trusteeship system and the United Nations Organization embodied, in the eyes of informed Africans. Africans of this persuasion looked to the UN Charter and the Trusteeship Agreements, both of which affirmed the objective of progress toward "self-government or independence" for the peoples of the territories involved.[5] The libertarian implications of these words grew stronger in comparison with the provisions of the Covenant of the League of Nations and the terms of the old mandate system, which affirmed only that "the well-being and development of [dependent] peoples form a sacred trust of civilization." [6]

The realization of the African nationalists that the UN documents could be interpreted as firm support for their aspirations came slowly, nurtured by the affirmations of vociferously anticolonialist soviet bloc delegations, because nothing in the Cameroonians' experience with the French during and following World War II promised anything other than continued French domination, despite the wartime African assistance. De Gaulle himself, while promising significant reform, held fast to the traditional French tutelage. French policy, as defined at the often mentioned 1944 Brazzaville conference of French colonial officials, held: ". . . the goals of the civilizing work accomplished by France in the colonies puts aside all idea of autonomy, any possibility of evolution outside the French bloc of the empire. The eventual constitution, even in the distant future, of self-government in the colonies is to be averted." [7] Dr. Louis Aujoulat, a noted apostle of the ideal of Franco-African federalism who would one day sit in the French Assembly representing Cameroonians on the African roll, stated in 1945 as he prepared to represent the Territory in the first 1946 Constituent Assembly: "No portion of the

[4] See the Constitution, Republic of France, 1946, Article 60.

[5] See Article 76 of the Charter of the United Nations; and Trusteeship Agreement, Cameroons under French Administrations, UN, 1946.

[6] Gardinier, "Movement to Reunify the Cameroons," African Studies Association, 1960.

[7] Quoted in Eyinga, "Les Elections Camerounaise du 10 Avril 1960."

114

French empire intends to lead its international life apart, to have its own army . . . its own independent legislative power. Paris remains the heart of France. . . ." [8]

French officials insisted in United Nations circles that when the time ultimately came the peoples in the Trust Territories would be free to choose their own future. French sincerity was to be doubted, and was certainly doubted by African leadership. The French claimed, for example, that the Africans had voiced no objection to the Territory's inclusion in the French Union: "The system of the French Union could therefore be regarded as having the wholehearted support of the inhabitants of the Trust Territories." [9] It had nothing of the sort; there had been no opportunity for Africans in the Territory to form or express a public opinion on the matter.

Delegates to the United Nations eagerly debated the whole question of the compatibility of the promises of the trusteeship system, with the provisions for "administrative unions" contained in the Trusteeship Agreements, and the specific institutional structures of the French Union.[10] Anticolonialist delegations argued that the colonial peoples would face a fait accompli at the end of the trusteeship period. Such a close-knit, interlocking network of economic infrastructure, bureaucracy, and marketing patterns would arise that the inhabitants would be left with no alternative but to accept the continuation of these ties. As one delegate stated in a UN debate, "it is extremely difficult to unscramble eggs."

Anticolonialists expressed even greater concern about the meaning of the term "self-government," which the French administration promoted as the objective of its tutelage, as opposed to independence. Neither the UN Charter nor the Trusteeship Agreements provided a clear definition of the term. Nothing in these statutes prohibited the achievement of "self-government" through either free association with or full integration into another territory so long as such changes reflected the freely expressed wishes of the indigenous peoples. The United States provided the first example of a termination of nonself-government through association when

[8] *Ibid.*

[9] T. Hodgkin and R. Schacter, "French-speaking Africa in Transition," *International Conciliation,* Carnegie Endowment for International Peace (May 1960).

[10] The provision for administrative unions had a precedent in the mandate system. Several mandates were administered in this way, and six trust territories were subject to clauses which permitted their administration as an integral part of some other territory, possibly even the metropolitan country. Eight agreements (including the six already mentioned) allowed the Administering Authority "to constitute this Territory into a customs, fiscal or administrative union or federation with adjacent territories . . . and to establish common services between [them]. . . ."

115

in 1953 she demanded and received from the General Assembly approval of her relationship with the Free, Associated State of Puerto Rico.[11] A year later Denmark received approval to terminate her reporting about Greenland on the grounds that Greenland had been incorporated into Denmark. There was considerable controversy about such interpretations; the committees of the General Assembly made repeated attempts to establish some guidelines for determining when states were no longer obliged to report to the General Assembly on the affairs of nonself-governing territories under their administration. In 1955 the Assembly adopted a list of principles to guide the states, and it reaffirmed the principles in a definitive statement on the subject in 1960.[12] By that time the problem had lost much of its importance, because most of the areas concerned were already independent or scheduled to become so.

In the early days of the Trusteeship System, however, few imagined that the drive for independence would proceed so rapidly. What troubled African nationalists and non-African anticolonialists alike was the apparent intention of France to twist the promises of the system to suit her own purposes, which in no way encompassed independence for these peoples and the apparent British intention to have Cameroonians become Nigerians. In the two states of Cameroon, therefore, those who aspired to freedom realized the need to organize themselves to articulate their own aspirations before the United Nations and to expose the intentions of the administering authorities. Cameroonians had to find a way to buffer the two Territories from the forces that had worked to integrate them further into the colonial empires of Britain and France. It is not hard to appreciate why (I will explore the variety of motives in the next chapter); in both states the leaders called for unification of the Cameroons.[13]

THE EMERGENCE OF THE REUNIFICATION MOVEMENT

In order to formulate their claims and press them effectively, Cameroonians in both Territories had to organize pressure groups and political

[11] "Issues before the Seventh General Assembly," *International Conciliation* (October 1952), p. 444.

[12] See UN Documents A/465, A/AC100/2, plus Addenda 1 and 2, A/AC 100/1 Addenda 1. These principles affirmed the three ways in which dependent states could achieve self-government: "(a) Emergence as a sovereign independent state; (b) Free association with an independent state; or (c) Integration with an independent state."

[13] The term "reunification" was not used until later—in the early 1950s, when the symbolism of old Kamerun became more explicit. Indeed, it is probable that many early advocates of "unification" meant only union of the north and south of British Cameroons.

parties, which naturally were oriented to the de facto political arenas in which they had to operate. There was no single political arena within which all Cameroonian leaders could participate effectively. Neither the Mandates Commission of the League of Nations nor the Trusteeship Council provided anything; they were dominated by the Administering Authorities. The African organizations with political potential were often parochial in orientation. There were the many voluntary associations that sprang up in the new towns and cities in the interwar period, but they catered almost exclusively to the interests of urban dwellers, and usually only in terms of common ethnic or geographical origins.

There did develop a number of more explicitly political organizations during and immediately after World War II, but they modeled themselves on Nigerian groups or metropolitan French organizations. Such groups in the two Territories functioned in virtual isolation. In Lagos, for example, young well-educated Cameroonian civil servants organized the Cameroons Youth League (CYL) in 1939; it was modeled on the Nigerian Youth Movement (NYM) which had been organized in Lagos about a year before, when it had achieved an impressive political victory in the 1938 elections for the Legislative Council. Members of the CYL were probably also members of the NYM, and certainly later did follow Naamdi Azikiwe's leadership in forming the NYM offshoot party, the National Council of Nigeria and the Cameroons (NCNC).[14] The CYL leadership worked closely with and in some instances were the leadership of the Cameroons Federal Union (CFU), which also functioned principally among the small Westernized elite group working in Lagos and Enugu. Both organizations articulated the broad interests of the Trust Territory as such; but this initially took the form of claims for greater autonomy, at least for Southern Cameroons. Sporadically they demanded the unification of Northern and Southern British Cameroons, but never explicitly advanced a claim for a pan-Kamerun organization.

With one notable exception, the story was much the same on the other side of the Mungo River. The first organization to provide Africans in the French-ruled Territory with a vehicle through which to express themselves on social and public affairs was the *Jeunesse Camerounaise* (JC), which was established in 1933 as a cultural and social improvement society. Because French policy did not permit Africans to form political asso-

---

[14] Claude E. Welch, Jr., *Dream of Unity* (Ithaca: Cornell University Press, 1966), p. 160; and Coleman, *Nigeria,* pp. 293–94. The most prominent members of the CYL were Paul Kale, who had helped to found the organization, and Dr. E. M. L. Endeley; both were prominent in the NCNC.

ciations, the JC pursued its political interests clandestinely. Its leadership included many who became prominent political figures in the postwar nationalist period.[15] As early as 1936 the members of the JC considered the advisability of demanding a reunion of the Territories through the creation of a British-French condominium. They thought that the more progressive British policies regarding African political and civil rights might attenuate the French system, and eliminate the harsh *indigénat* penal procedures and forced labor practices. This leadership finally rejected the scheme out of consideration that two masters would probably be worse than one. In fact, after Hitler began to reclaim Germany's former colonies, and under pressure from the French, the organization was transformed into the *Jeunesse Camerounaise-Française* (JEU-CAFRA) with French membership.[16] Following the war, the JEUCAFRA leadership, including liberal French figures such as Dr. Aujoulat, and more radical elements in the nascent trade union movement, created a series of successor organizations—the *Union Camerounaise Française* (UNICAFRA, 1946); the *Rassemblement Camerounaise* (RACAM, 1947), which the radicals created after their failure to fully control UNICAFRA; and finally the *Union des Populations du Cameroun* (UPC, 1948), the first truly nationalistic political party in either Territory. Neither the UPC nor any predecessor had included representation of British Cameroons elements, however; with the exception of ephemeral family, friendship, and improvement-association ties among the Bamileke, these groups had no connections across the western border.

Naturally political leaders in both Territories, fearful of being submerged in the institutions and organizations of Nigeria or the French Union, and desirous of power and recognition of their distinctive rights as part of the international Trusteeship System, should recognize the need to coordinate their efforts and create common organizations that could operate on a pan-Kamerun basis. But there was no effective opportunity

[15] E.g. Paul Soppo Priso (president), Jean Faustin Betayene, Charles R. Okala, Andre Fouda, Paul Monte, and Reuben Um Nyobe. Information from Betayene (ex-foreign minister) interview, Yaounde, October 1963.

[16] Paul Soppo Priso, who engineered the transformation on the African side, claimed (interview, Douala, August 1963) that the French were never permitted to be full members. They were not given membership cards, for example. He interpreted the move as a response to a generational conflict between displaced officials of the old German service, who seemed to favor a return to German rule, and the new Gallicized African elite. JEUCAFRA actually demanded an end to the mandate and recognition of Cameroon as a full French colony. It was thought that in this case the Africans would enjoy the rights of full French citizenship as in other French-African colonies. See Gardinier, *Cameroon,* p. 36.

to do so. These leaders were largely unfamiliar with each other and had no easy channels of communication. The idea that there were distinctive rights to claim in the name of Cameroon (or Kamerun) did occur to them during and immediately after the war, especially after the inauguration of the Trusteeship System. But it was the Trusteeship Council's decision in 1949 to send a Visiting Mission directly to the Territories that provided the first basis for effective collective effort by both groups.

Despite their lack of mutual familiarity or contact, as the time for the visit of the first UN Visiting Mission approached, the demands of African political forces in the Territories began to converge. In British Southern Cameroons Dr. E.M.L. Endeley, a Bakweri medical doctor who had been expelled from practice in Lagos for alleged malpractice, subsequently returned to Buea and Victoria to launch a number of social development and quasi-political organizations. He succeeded in uniting nearly 20 tribal unions, along with organizations advancing special claims, such as the Bakweri Land Committee (which demanded a return to Bakweri of all the lands taken by the Germans for plantations) and later the French Cameroons Welfare Union (FCWU) and the Cameroons Federal Union into what was called the Cameroons National Federation (CNF). This organization made the first written demand for Cameroon reunification.[17] The CNF included at least one organization that represented French Cameroonians, though only those resident within the British-controlled Territory. This group, the Baminyang Improvement Union, along with others representing border peoples divided by the frontier, presented their own resolutions to the inaugural meeting of the CNF, which focused specifically on the problems caused by the frontier between the Territories and which called for immediate endorsement of the idea of reunification, with specific modalities for achieving it to be worked out later.

The UPC also petitioned the Visiting Mission about reunification. From its central executive and from over 20 branch organizations petitions and communications flooded into the Mission's hearings. They strongly emphasized the evils of the "administrative union" provisions of

[17] All of the resolutions of the inaugural meeting of the CNF, held on the 14th and 15th of May 1949, were later presented to the UN as petitions. See T/Pet. 4/16-T pet. 5/7. One resolution was introduced, ironically, by N. N. Mbile (who much later pledged his people to fight to the last in resisting reunification) who claimed that the existing system tended to cut Southern Cameroons "finally from the rest of her brothers under the French, Adamawa and Bornu." The resolution continued to state that "After three decades of British Administration, the economic development of the people . . . has not made the slightest advance from where the Germans left it."

119

the Trusteeship Agreement, the hardships involved in the enforcement of the frontier between the Territories, and the desire of the party and the Cameroon people for independence. It may be that the communications emanating from the UPC central leadership to the branch organizations, instructing them to demand reunification and independence, constituted the party's first explicit endorsement of the reunification idea.[18]

Despite the similarity of demands, which acquired added effectiveness through the fact that the Mission visited both Territories and made contact with the African spokesmen, the groups had not coordinated their plans. More than the visit of a UN mission would be needed to stimulate the creation of a Pan-Kamerun organization; this would require that an organization have very direct and deeply rooted stakes in reunification itself.

EFFORTS AT PAN-KAMERUN ORGANIZATION

One of the factors which did stimulate and facilitate cooperation and coordination between political leaders in the two Territories was the presence in Southern Cameroons of a large migrant and immigrant community of French-speaking Cameroonians who exerted strong pressures on the leaders.[19] The politicians of Southern Cameroons were constantly aware of the significance of this block of potential voters in the Territory. Leaders of the community who played a leading role in organizing the reunification movement have asserted that interest in the vote was what induced political figures like E.M.L. Endeley to support reunification. One indication of the political importance of the French Cameroon elements is the fact that politicians who favored reunification tended also to favor enfranchisement, but those opposed to reunification also opposed enfranchisement. Before 1956, for example, when Dr. Endeley was committed to reunification, he pressed for the elimination or relaxation of naturalization requirements for French Cameroonians residing in the Territory, in order to have their votes. In 1957, when he opposed full reunification, he pressured the Parliament to disfranchise them. The pro-reunification forces, led by the KNDP, pressed for their enfranchisement at that time, but later, during the plebiscite campaign in 1961, the pro-Nigerian forces led by Endeley and the proreunification forces of the

[18] The communication is reproduced in the Mission's report, UN Document T/798.

[19] Ardener *et al., Plantation and Village in Cameroons,* pp. 409–10, estimated their number at 13,500. At the 15th session of the Trusteeship Council (569th meeting, para. 19 of Official Record) mention was made of 17,000 French Cameroonians being denied the vote in Southern Cameroons.

KNDP switched positions again. The KNDP thought there were more Nigerian migrants (antireunification) in the Territory than French Cameroonians, and their cause (reunification) would be advanced by having both groups removed from the voting rolls.[20]

One of the most important political spokesmen for the community of French Cameroonians living in the British-controlled area was R. Jabea K. Dibongue, one of the country's most interesting personalities. Dibongue was a member of the Akwa clan of the Douala peoples; he was one of the brightest members of the emerging young educated elite during the period of German administration. In 1911 he won the coveted Governor Puttkamer Prize as the top student in the colony. By the time the Germans were expelled from the country Dibongue had risen to the highest ranking African in the Kamerun government, as clerk to the German district commissioner at Douala. Soon after entering the German colonial administration he had been stationed in the capital, Buea, as a clerk and made many contacts with leaders of the Bakweri, Balondo, and other coastal peoples of what would later become Southern British Cameroons. After the German defeat Dibongue resided in his home city of Douala, but began to learn English from a Nigerian friend, and sometime later moved to the British-controlled zone and entered the British colonial service, in which he achieved another spectacular career, rising to the top ranks available to Africans. There is little doubt that he would have become a district officer had he not resigned in 1947 to return to Douala. To my knowledge Dibongue is the only African to have achieved a significant career in two different colonial administrations.[21]

Dibongue may have played a key role in initiating the reunification movement in British Cameroons. It is known that he returned to Douala in 1947, having resigned abruptly from his civil service post to live in his native city for nearly two years. He was there when Cameroon's first radical nationalist UPC was organized, and he returned to British Cameroons shortly thereafter, zealous in his advocacy of Cameroon reunification, one of the goals of the UPC.

Soon after Dibongue's return to Buea he either established or began to work with the FCWU, one of many new voluntary associations organized on a regional or ethnic basis which sprang up especially among urban Cameroonians, as they did among such Africans in most of the colonies, to advance the social and economic position of particular ethnic groups.

[20] *West Africa*, May 14, 1965, May 8, 1958; and *Report*, Mamfe Conference on the Plebiscite Questions and Register, November 1959.
[21] For a biographical sketch of Dibongue see *West Africa*, August 6, 1960.

121

The French Cameroonians were interested in winning the vote for themselves in British Cameroons and protecting their interests generally, but they also concerned themselves about political and social conditions back home on the French side of the border. This group quickly came to support the demands for Cameroon reunification.[22]

It is probable that Dibongue influenced the FCWU's activities in support of reunification, though apparently from behind the scenes. The FCWU was one of several groups that petitioned the First UN Visiting Mission in late 1949 to unify the British and French Territories "in a very short time." [23] The petition was written in a style suggestive of Dibongue, though it did not bear his name; it invoked St. Thomas Aquinas, Aesop, and the Treaty of Versailles in pressing its claims. Curiously, however, the petition was directed almost exclusively to the conditions which obtained in the French-ruled Territory; it claimed that the French had done virtually nothing to improve the Territory, that France practiced the color bar there, that the people lacked public liberties and representative institutions. It called for a time limit to Trusteeship and for initiatives to keep the Cameroon peoples, for whom language, customs, and laws had been "almost identical," from becoming progressively estranged from each other.[24]

Dibongue gave a sharply different direction to the reunification movement when he took over the leadership of the FCWU as its "Honorary General President" in 1950 or early 1951. He tried to give the movement a broader framework than that which had been offered by either the FCWU or the CNF. He appears also to have been motivated by a disagreement with Dr. Endeley over voting rights for French Cameroonians in the Territory.[25] In August 1951 he combined forces with Nerius N. Mbile, who had been secretary of the CNF and a close associate of Dr. Endeley's in several endeavors, but who had become embroiled in a per-

[22] It has been asserted that the FCWU was the group that initiated the idea of Cameroon reunification (1948). (See Gardinier, *Cameroon,* p. 59.) This is doubtful. Dibongue himself has stated to me (interview, Buea, April 1963) that the FCWU was organized because the Cameroon Federation Union, organized in Lagos in 1941 or so, was not following through on demands for reunification. It is not clear when the CFU might have advanced such demands (Gardinier suggests they did so in 1948, *Cameroon,* pp. 60–61). The CFU and the CYL, which worked closely with it, had expressed their concern about the rights of the Trust Territories and the dangers of the administrative union with Nigeria, but probably limited their claims within Nigeria until 1948, if not later.

[23] T/pet. 4/19, T/pet. 5/8, in UN Trusteeship's Council Official Records, VI, Annex Vol. II.

[24] This is more in keeping with Dibongue's perspective than the rest of the petition.

[25] Welch, *Dream of Unity,* p. 177.

sonal feud with him, to host a general conference to consider the question of reunification. The top leadership of the UPC was invited to the conference and the meeting was held in Kumba, the Southern Cameroons town most accessible to French Cameroonians. Despite these efforts, only two members of the UPC executive were able to come, although they were two very prominent members and, significantly, the leaders of the Bamileke faction of the party—Ernest Ouandié and Abel Kingue.

The most important result of the conference was the establishment of the Kamerun United National Congress, a new political party led by President Dibongue and General Secretary Mbile. The conference reiterated and sharpened the details of the by then customary arguments for Cameroon reunification. But it failed to spell out a specific program for the achievement of reunification or the constitutional mechanisms that might affect the union or be used to govern it.[26] The resolutions of the conference reflected a worse failure—not appreciating the need to coherently structure the Kamerun Nation. The closest it came to suggesting common political institutions was the assertion that the British government (and the resolutions were addressed only to the British administration) should welcome the chance to rule a unified Cameroon jointly with France, since it had so often complained of the difficulty it faced in administering the Territory alone. But the institutional structures the conference demanded suggest that most of the participants still thought simply in terms of winning autonomous political institutions for Southern Cameroons. For example, they demanded a house of assembly with full legislative powers *in each Territory*. But practical steps *were* demanded which might have prepared the people for a later merger.[27]

It may be that the conference participants were reacting to the earlier failure of Dr. Endeley to obtain full regional status for Southern Cameroons on a scale won by the Eastern, Northern, and Western Regions of Nigeria during the 1949 review of the Nigeria constitution. Endeley and other Cameroons leaders pressed for a regional house of assembly of their own at preliminary hearings held in the Territory in May and later at the Eastern Regional meeting in July and the final constitutional conference held in Ibadan in January 1950.[28] In the latter two meetings the

[26] See UN Document T/Pet. 4/29, T/Pet. 5/105, 30 October 1951 and Sup. of 26 November 1951.

[27] The conference demanded that English and French be made compulsory in the schools, both primary and secondary, in both Territories, and that the customs union which had existed between the two from 1916 to 1921 be reinstated.

[28] See Welch, *Dream of Unity*, pp. 171–72, for a fuller discussion of these meetings.

123

British administration and other delegates rejected the Cameroons' plea on the grounds that the Territory was too poor to support a separate government, and the difficulty of what to do about Northern British Cameroons. Instead, it was decided by these Conferences to grant the Territory 13 seats in the Eastern House of Assembly.

The KUNC soon became firmer in its position on reunification, perhaps because of more substantial UPC participation or perhaps as the result of more affirmative leadership from Dibongue. In December 1951 a second general meeting was held in Kumba, to which not only the UPC came in substantial numbers (26 representatives), but to which other French Cameroon political groups also sent representatives.[29] Here at last was an opportunity—what was in fact the last opportunity—for Cameroonians to create a grand pan-Kamerun platform of militant if not also moderate nationalists. The conference came out strongly in favor of reunification, as part of a program of accelerated political development leading to independence within five years.[30] Unlike the conference held four months earlier, this one elaborated a skeletal program for implementation of reunification by demanding a single legislative assembly for the whole of the Kamerun.

Perhaps more important than the decision of the conference to envision reunification as a program of imminent political union is the fact that serious consideration was given to the question of creating a common political organization of proreunification parties and spokesmen. The UPC leadership threw both fire and water on the deliberations. Um Nyobe made an impassioned speech denouncing the colonialists' game of divide-and-rule, and signalling the advances unity was bringing to independence movements in Morocco and Algeria. Um Nyobe pleaded for unity among the nationalists in Cameroon; "we can't do anything without unity." [31] Having said that, however, he immediately brushed aside the idea of any immediate fusion of the nationalists' parties: "However, for the moment, it seems to me that unity in a single movement would offend certain susceptibilities. That is why I should constrain myself to propose that which is more realizable, because, in such matters it is better to do less . . . than to take decisions which won't get past the doors of this hall." Um Nyobe then proposed that a coordinating committee be estab-

[29] The Kumze, Ngondo, and ESOCAM were also represented. ESOCAM declared itself opposed to reunification and left before the congress ended.
[30] Unification Immédiate, UPC, Imprimerie speciale des Étudiants Camerounais (Paris, 1953).
[31] Unification Immédiate, pp. 17–18.

lished outside all the existing organizations which would set a common direction for them, but not affect their structural independence or freedom within their own areas. No member organization would take a line of action or policy that contradicted the program on which this committee, to be called the Kamerun United National Committee, would be based, namely: (1) immediate unification of the Territories of Cameroon; (2) setting a time limit on the Trusteeship Agreements; (3) elimination of the provision for "integral part" (administrative union); and (4) opposition to any inclusion of British Cameroons in Nigeria.

Nationalist leaders of neither British nor French Cameroons put much effort into effecting their joint call for a pan-Kamerun organization to advance the cause of reunification. Preoccupation with the March 1952 elections for the Territorial Assembly in the French territory may have prevented Um Nyobe and his cohorts from doing so, or they may simply have been unwilling to sacrifice their organization to any new movement over which their own control might be weakened. In any case, the decision taken by the Trusteeship Council in March to send another Visiting Mission to the Trust Territories, with explicit instructions to investigate the unification question in Togo and to consider the various problems raised in petitions from the Territories, which included the claim for Cameroon reunification, rekindled Um Nyobe's and Southern Cameroonian reunificationists' resolve to coordinate their efforts more effectively. Dibongue, as president of the KUNC, and representatives of the FCWU, met with Um Nyobe and Abel Kingue at Tiko, Southern Cameroons, in August 1952 to discuss the imminent visit of the UN delegation. They renewed their earlier call for close cooperation between the two national movements (UPC and KUNC), and expressed their desire to create an executive committee for Cameroon unity as soon as possible. This decision went beyond the call of the December KUNC meeting, inasmuch as it envisioned a superordinate organization with powers to act on behalf of the national movement. Um Nyobe seems not to have been willing to give up very much, however, for he extracted from the Southern Cameroonians support for the idea of convoking a general congress for Cameroon unity, but this time in the French Cameroons. In fact, such a congress was already planned, in the form of the Second National Congress of the UPC itself, which took place less than a month after the Tiko meeting in the Bassa town of Eseka.[32] The UPC congress made some important decisions about the reunification program; it focused principally

---

[32] The Second Congress had been postponed the year before because of factionalism. See *La Voix du Cameroun* (Cairo), No. 9, August–September 1952.

on the reunification question, but it was not a meeting organized outside the framework of the UPC, and it failed to advance the movement toward a truly pan-Kamerun organizational base. Though there were 80 observers at the congress apparently none was an important leader from Southern Cameroons. At least two members of the newly elected executive bureau claimed to live in British Cameroon, but they were not leaders of organizations there.[33]

The Second UPC Congress managed to spell out its program for achieving reunification in greater detail than any group before.[34] A legislative assembly was to be elected by universal adult suffrage for all of the reunited Territory, which would be authorized to establish any governmental bodies necessary to implement the various administrative, judicial, economic, educational, and social reforms involved in merging the two societies into one. The united Territory was to be governed by a mixed government council composed of Europeans and Africans in the proportion of one to four. Independence was to be granted by January 1, 1957.

The UPC leadership paid virtually no attention at the congress to the problem of creating a larger organization that would include British Cameroons elements. Rather they affirmed the suitability of the UPC itself as the principal instrumentality for advancing the cause of reunification. It should be noted, however, that the UPC was concerned primarily about its relation with other political organizations in French Cameroons. The UPC claimed an advantage over other such groups on the basis of its belief that the Cameroonian masses considered the UPC to be the only organization capable of defending the higher interests of the country, and on the basis that it alone had any meaningful contacts with British Cameroonians.[35] That some connections existed between the UPC leadership and the leaders in Southern British Cameroons is unquestionable, but time proved them much less important than Um Nyobe had presumed. The absence of even these elements at the UPC congress is left unexplained by either the temper of the times or the commentaries and speeches made by the UPC or KUNC leadership. It is plausible that French Cameroon officials may have made it difficult for the Southern Cameroonians to get to the Congress site—the UPC was often harassed and travel across the border was controlled by the French.

---

[33] *Ibid.* Éka Martin and Éka Market, both farmers or perhaps brothers, were among those named as Executive Bureau members.

[34] Unification Immédiate, p. 40.

[35] *Ibid.*, p. 29.

The most likely reason for the failure of the Cameroonians to create a pan-Kamerun organization to press for reunification was that the Southern Cameroons leadership involved in the movement were weakly committed to the objective. The KUNC had been formed at the instigation of Dibongue because he felt that the other political organizations, especially the Endeley-led CNF, were faltering or insincere in their support of reunification, something to which Dibongue was highly committed. But Dibongue had to form a coalition with Nerius Mbile in order to win broad support for the new organization and Mbile turned out to be even less in favor of reunification than Endeley.[36] More importantly, Dibongue has claimed that he became disenchanted with the UPC leadership as he learned of their Marxist convictions and their connections with communist organizations abroad.[37]

For whatever reason, the rhetorically potent attempts to achieve a unified movement failed, as a result of UPC desire for hegemony, or lack of real commitment to the objective of reunification among British Cameroonians. In the two years following the UPC's second congress and the visit of the Second UN Visiting Mission, which occurred at the same time, the UPC monopolized advocacy of the issue and gained considerable prestige at home and abroad by doing so. During the congress and immediately thereafter, the UPC submitted several petitions to the UN Visiting Mission, but was not effective in winning sympathy for its objective.[38] The KUNC also submitted petitions to the Mission, more forceful and detailed than those submitted by the UPC, but they too received little sympathy from the visitors.[39] The Mission's blasé response belied the real

[36] The following year Mbile was expelled from the KUNC because he had supported a minority faction among the Cameroons block of 13 representatives to the East Nigerian House who wanted to maintain an affiliation with the National Council of Nigeria and the Cameroons. The majority, led by Endeley, were pushing for autonomous structures and declared their "benevolent neutrality" in Nigerian politics. Shortly thereafter Dibongue teamed up with Endeley to launch the new Kamerun National Congress (KNC), with Dibongue as president general and Endeley as head of the parliamentary wing.

[37] Interview, Buea, April 1963.

[38] The Mission received 71 communications from organs of the UPC. UN Document T/1110, para. 91. The Mission repudiated the UPC claim that reunification was a popular objective, however: ". . . the question of the unification of the two Cameroons is not at present an acute problem . . . the masses of the population were not interested in the question" (Para. 104).

[39] UN Document T/1109. Also see T/Pet. 4/79, T/Pet. 5/105 and Addenda 1, and T/Pet. 4/83. The Mission concluded in its report on British Cameroon: ". . . the demand for unification is localized in some parts of the Southern Section of the Trust Territory and even there the question is neither a popular demand among the people nor a lively issue."

importance of the reunification issue, if only as a stratagem for gaining other more immediate objectives. Though it was true that the parties supporting these demands were still peripheral, they represented the future and, at least in the case of the UPC, would become major political forces in a few years.

Um Nyobe took the boldest step in presenting the case for reunification, and nationalists' claims generally, when he pressed the Fourth Committee of the General Assembly in December 1952 to grant a personal hearing on the question. He made the most vehement and eloquent plea for reunification that had been made up to that time, and did so in representing not only the UPC but also the reunificationists in British Cameroons led by the KUNC which cabled authorization to the UN for Um Nyobe to speak on their behalf.[40] The speech and ensuing debate, largely sympathetic as a result of the interventions of the anticolonialist bloc, was printed in a pamphlet, "What the Cameroon People Want." Thousands of copies of this document were then circulated throughout Cameroon; the UPC's fame and support grew apace. Um Nyobe made other visits to the UN to work for the cause. In subsequent years many other Cameroon politicians were sent by the administration to counter the UPC or who were desirous merely to share in the prestige of attending UN sessions. The UPC continued to dominate the political propaganda concerning reunification and independence until the disturbances of April–May in 1955, after which it was banned.[41]

UPC Exile

The ban on the activities of the UPC in French Cameroons occasioned the closest and most broadly based contact between the militant nationalists of the two Territories which had been achieved at any time prior to reunification itself. However, the contact failed to generate any effective coalition between the two groups; it also inspired animosity for the French-speaking militants which Foncha and others in his camp were never able to overcome. What each camp expected to be an easy and natural collaboration developed into direct competition as each group sought to make of its own structure the organizational embodiment of Kamerun nationalism. The competition was based on and reflective of the transformation of the nationalist movement itself from the first phase, in which the objective of winning home rule had been paramount, to the second, when Africans began to realize the objective would be achieved

[40] Um Nyobe's speech is contained in UN Document A/C.4/226, Add. 1.
[41] See Chap. 14.

128

before long and they came to concern themselves more with the question of who would rule at home. Winning a power base was the chief objective of every major political party; for the UPC, banned in the French Territory, this required direct entry into the electoral politics of the British controlled sector.

Soon after the French outlawed the UPC organizations several of its leaders, almost all of them from the Bamileke or Douala factions of the party, made their way across the border.[42] Dr. Roland Felix Moumié, the president of the party and its most violence-prone leader, Ernest Ouandié and Abel Kingue, the two stalwarts of the Bamileke contingent, and a number of other members of the executive bureau reassembled in the largest town in Southern Cameroons, Kumba, near the border. Many hundreds of their compatriots also fled across the border.[43] Though many accounts of this development vary, it seems that Um Nyobe, Mayi Matip, and the principal Bassa leaders of the party never left the French-ruled Territory. They remained in hiding in and around Eséka and soon thereafter began to organize the rebellion.

The exiled UPC leaders who reached British Cameroons knew little about its political leadership. Evidence of this is the fact that Dr. Moumié went first to Dr. Endeley, the head of the KNC, which had by then acquired the support of the proreunification forces which Dibongue led in the now defunct KUNC, but had lost the wing of the KUNC led by Mbile. Endeley is alleged to have been quite unsympathetic to the UPC group and their forceful advocacy of reunification. Moumié then went to Bamenda where he conferred with John Foncha, who had by then split from the KNC and created the KNDP as a party unalterably devoted to breaking away from Nigeria and ultimately reuniting with the rest of old Kamerun. Foncha's program and aims accorded with the ostensible objectives of the UPC; so Foncha personally provided Moumié and his friends with a house and provisions. Soon thereafter the two leaders established another reunification committee, reminiscent of the 1951–1952 efforts between the UPC and the KUNC. Moumié was made president and Foncha secretary.[44] This committee was no more successful than its

[42] Adalbert Owona, in his unpublished paper, "Le Mouvement d'inspiration marxiste: UPC," suggests that the only Bassa among the escaping UPC leaders was Jean Paul Sendé.

[43] The 1956 Visiting Mission noted the presence of "an unknown number, perhaps many hundreds" of persons from French Cameroons, "many of them ostensibly as political refugees," and considered them to constitute a new element in the political life of the Territory. UN Document T / 1440, Para. 83.

[44] Abel Kingue, interview, Accra, December 1963.

129

predecessor had been. It set about studying the predicament of the two Territories and the means of achieving independence and reunification. The committee soon came apart over the issues which should come first, and whether violent tactics, if only verbal violence, would be useful in the achievement of these ends.[45]

The KNDP leadership apparently felt that the Territory was not ready for independence, something the UPC demanded with insistence, taking their stated demands for continued Trusteeship as evidence.[46] Foncha is alleged also to have preferred that reunification come simultaneously with or even before independence; in either case, he wanted both in the distant future. The UPC leadership, aided by some local converts like Ndeh Ntumazah, insisted on obtaining both immediately.

The views of the two leaders were even further apart on how to advance their cause. The UPC had already stimulated riots in the French sector and had organized a clandestine guerilla army there. Shortly after the reunification committee was established in Southern Cameroons, the UPC leadership also established the *Comité d'Organisation nationale* which would embody the armed campaign.[47] Foncha and most other English-speaking Cameroonians would have been appalled at such tactics, but they knew little of them.

Collaboration between the Foncha and Moumié camps broke down completely in the prelude to the March 1957 elections to the House of Assembly. The UPC desperately needed a forum from which to speak and a base from which to continue to petition the United Nations. Moumié succeeded in enticing Ndeh Ntumazah, a KNDP branch secretary from Foncha's own locale, to join the UPC in touring the country and helping build up an organization in its own name. The party put up several candidates in the elections, all campaigning vociferously for immediate reunification to be quickly followed by independence. Several candidates opposed those running under the banner of the KNDP, including Foncha himself, who never forgave Moumié and the UPC for this embarrassing challenge. However, the UPC failed to establish a base of any significance outside the areas heavily settled by French Cameroonians; all UPC candidates were easily defeated.

After the defeat Moumié proclaimed himself and his party the cham-

[45] Renée Ngapeth (former member of the executive bureau of UPC and one of the exiled contingent at the time), interview, Yaounde, September 1963.

[46] The Administering Authority, in its 1958 Report to the United Nations, para. 204, indicated the KNDP's desire to continue trusteeship while arrangements for reunification were worked out.

[47] See Chap. 14.

130

pion of reunification with waning sincerity. Rather than take a back seat to the KNDP, which had made impressive gains in the elections, Moumié began to talk of a Cameroon government in exile and attempted to present an oral petition to the UN Fourth Committee, taking up where Um Nyobe had left off three years earlier; but Moumié found himself unable to get a passport. Ntumazah made the trip instead. The UPC now had little to gain—except perhaps legal dissolution in Southern Cameroons—from immediate reunification. It dropped the demand from its propaganda and concentrated instead on making broad-based attacks on the French and their "stooges" in the French sector. The shift did not save the exiled leaders from reprisal, however. Probably at the instigation of Foncha, and certainly with the acquiescence of Endeley, the British administration also banned the UPC from the Territory on the grounds that there existed "a grave possibility that in order to achieve its political objectives the Party may have to resort to violence in the Southern Cameroons." [48]

THE FINAL PHASE

By late 1956 almost every one of the political factions of Southern Cameroons had come to consider the exiled UPC leadership an unwanted, troublesome influence in the Territory. No doubt even Foncha felt a greater anxiety about the prospects of unity with the Easterners. The one exception was a small band of young activitists who, with more than adequate financing and good organizational instinct, established the One Kamerun Movement (OK) to take over from the banned UPC. Almost everyone considered the OK to be the old UPC under a new guise. But there was one important difference; this party was more indigenous to the Territory. It continued to maintain close contact with the exiled wing of the UPC, however. For the rest of the reunificationists, and occasionally even for people like Dr. Endeley, who by now had publicly stated his preference for permanent association with Nigeria with regional status, different kinds of contacts had to be established with Cameroonians across the border.

There had been some contact between some of the leading personalities of Buea and Victoria on the one side and Douala on the other, which had not been restricted to the militant leaders of the UPC or KNDP. These contacts began as deliberate efforts to promote the exchange of information, at least on a social level; but they had not been sustained

[48] UN Document T/1440, para. 83.

and did not involve a great many people. Late in 1956 Cameroonians established two friendship societies, the Committee of Ladies and Gentlemen to Promote Friendship Between French and British Cameroons, in Victoria, and *Des Amis du Cameroun britannique* at Douala. The Western hosts, including Endeley, Dibongue, other KNC leaders, and some of the younger or more distinguished civil servants, received two delegations of Eastern Region visitors for dinners, dances, cocktail parties, and sightseeing. A delegation from the Western Region returned the visit over the Christmas holidays.[49] It is not clear whether such visits continued over the course of the next few years, but Dr. Endeley, for one, claimed in his electoral manifesto for the March 1957 elections that he had "established useful contacts with influential people in the French sector." [50]

As he prepared for the third general elections in Southern Cameroons, to be held in January 1959, Foncha succeeded in developing some important contacts in the French sector outside the UPC by traveling through the Bamileke Mungo and Douala *départements* across the border in May 1958. Foncha traveled with the simple people, by taxi and *camion* (small truck), bus and railway. He spent hours talking and drinking palm wine with people in various walks of life, in his characteristic way. He was stopped by *gendarmes* who demanded an identity card and unsuccessfully tried to extort 2,000 francs from each member of his party. Foncha felt that wherever he went there was a spirit of optimism following the fall of the Mbida government, that "reunification et indépendence immédiate" had lost its insistent appeal. He came to the conclusion that "the quickest approach to reunification was through independence"; it "is a matter within the competence of Cameroonians acting as a free people, and not one to be referred to the Administering Authority or even the United Nations." [51]

Foncha spoke of meeting with a recently organized reunification committee of undefined character and of meeting the members of the opposition, which dubbed themselves simply the "Group des huits," including the eloquent and well-off Paul Soppo Priso, a persistent spokesman for UPC nationalists' objectives who had never joined that party. It was Soppo Priso who donated the money with which Foncha bought presses

[49] According to invitation cards in the possession of Isaac N. Malafa (CDC, Bota), one of those involved as host during one of these visits.
[50] KNC Manifesto for Elections, 1957. Endeley also claimed therein that he was still an advocate of eventual reunification, and had invited all the parties to a conference to discuss the question, but that only the UPC leadership had accepted.
[51] *KNDP Newsletter,* July 1958.

for the first printed newspaper in the Southern Cameroons, *The Cameroons Times,* the organ of the KNDP. Foncha also met the more progressive Douala notables who later patronized the reunification effort; he may have met Douala Yondo for the first time, though Yondo had been a key figure in the earlier friendship society efforts.[52] Douala Yondo, who spoke English and French, eventually proved to be one of the most committed and energetic supporters of reunification.[53] He organized fundraising campaign after campaign during the preplebiscite period, and served as Foncha's principal contact with immigrant or itinerant British Cameroonians, as well as Eastern sympathisers.

Foncha also set up tours through important or responsive districts in his own state for sympathetic people from French Cameroon. In April of 1959, for example, he held a mammoth reception at Bamenda for the Sultan of Foumban, who came with the deputy prime minister, the mayors of Nkongsamba and Douala, and a retinue of about 200. This was followed by a three-day visit from Foncha to Prime Minister Ahidjo in Yaounde, during which he was presented with the *Commandeur de l'Ordre de la Valeur Camerounaise.* Subsequently Foncha unsuccessfully attempted to persuade Ahidjo to help campaign for reunification in Southern Cameroons.[54] Meantime, Foncha would again visit the East on the occasion of its independence celebrations, January 1, 1960. During the plebiscite campaign, Foncha and his aides, with the help of local Préfêts, officials of the Bamileke Welfare Union, or leaders like Douala Yondo, were able to raise several thousand dollars (CFA francs equivalent) through solicitations in the eastern border districts.[55]

In summary, these patterns of political interaction between the leaders of the two states during the prereunification period may be characterized by noting their lack of continuity and scope. There did not develop a thick network of contact, communication, and movement between the two. There were some powerful forces pushing for close and harmonious collaboration: the political pressures and appeals of several thousand immigrant workers and refugees from the French sector who resided in the border cities and plantation camps of Southern Cameroons, the parallel

[52] There is no evidence that Foncha was involved in the friendship society meetings.

[53] Given his later activities on behalf of the reunification campaign, it is likely that Douala Yondo was connected with the Reunification Committee mentioned by Foncha.

[54] J. N. Foncha, letter to Douala Yondo, February 13, 1961.

[55] Letters between J. N. Foncha and Douala Yondo, October 1960, January and February 1961.

interests nationalistic leaders in both Territories had to present a united front to the United Nations and the local administrations, the actual commitment groups on both sides had to the idea of reunification. But there were also powerful forces preventing close collaboration: the forced participation in neighboring political systems, the resultant preoccupation with the politics of winning home rule, the strong desire on the part of each political faction to secure itself in power, the marked disparities in organizational needs, capabilities, and orientations. When close contact did occur, it sometimes engendered more animosity than existed between groups not in close contact. If united Cameroon was to come into being as a mature union, during the advanced stages of integration, it would have to do so on the basis of high levels of complementarity in the areas where English and French-speaking Cameroonians did affect one another through common objectives, or widely shared values, whether regarding ultimate ends or the means to their achievement. We shall see that it could do neither.

7

The Value System of Ultimate Ends

THE ideology of modernization has taken deep roots in Cameroonian politics. Both the ideas of Cameroon independence and reunification are derived from and in turn nurtured by this ideology and the related one of nationalism. Since every important political force in the country finally embraced the two objectives of independence and reunification, it can be said that ideology permeated the Cameroonian political arena and provided the basis for a common political culture among modernized elements. However, the attitudes, values, and programs of the major political forces are in stark contrast to those of the traditional elites of the parochial societies in Cameroon. By comparison the orientations of the emerging elite reflected the ideology of modernization. But for most of the groups the specific content of the modernization program and the details of the new society they envisioned remained ill-defined. Only a few groups evolved an explicit and fundamental set of objectives for the social, economic, and political renovation of their society, along with a radical program for realizing those objectives. What seems to be important about the relationships between these political groups is that some of them determined the issues around which the debate about political and social change turned and the terms in which they were expressed. Thus while it may be appropriate for limited purposes to consider as ideological the orientation toward change of most political groups, the full implications of the term apply only to those few groups and programs with radical aims and implications, even in the short run.

The penetration and consolidation of European power in Cameroon, the subsequent substitution of new European powers for the German regime, the initial African adjustment and the later advance of "Westernization" leading to the final outburst of militant, even violent, nationalism is a story well treated elsewhere.[1] It should be noted here, however, that

[1] The best study of the German period in Cameroon—indeed, one of the very best case studies of colonial rule—is Rudin's *Germans in the Cameroons*. The rise of African nationalism in French Cameroon is ably analyzed by Le Vine in his *Cameroons;* his chapter on the Cameroon Federation in G. M. Carter, *Five African States; Cameroons* (Ithaca: Cornell University Press, 1963), and his discussion of political parties, in Coleman and Rosberg, *Political Parties.* Gardinier, *Cameroon,* presents an excellent historical analysis of these themes in French Cameroon. Welch, *Dream of Unity,* discusses the reunification movement. My own Ph.D. dissertation, "Cameroon Reunification: Political Union of Several Africas" (Harvard University, 1964), is devoted to this subject.

135

the general themes and characteristics of the modernizing ideology, as discussed above, were shared by those who pressed for immediate independence and who were willing to delay it for some years, by those sympathetic to the UPC and those opposed to it, by those for reunification and those for continued association with Nigeria. Let us therefore concentrate on determining the distinctive aspects of the militant nationalists.

The militant nationalistic parties and leaders stood apart from the rest of the Cameroon political scene prior to independence on the basis of their perceptions and attitudes regarding two matters: (1) the compatibility of the interests and intentions of the Administering Authorities with those of the Africans; and (2) the need for and prospect of significant internal social restratification.

The Compatibility of Interests

More than any other political faction in the two Territories, the militant exiled wing of the *Union des Populations du Cameroon* (UPC) and its supporters believed the objectives and interests of the Africans and colonial authorities to be irreconcilable.

The UPC was established in 1948 on the heels of the refusal of the French administration to grant legal status to a precursor organization, the *Rassemblement Camerounaise* (RACAM), because it had directly attacked the assimilationist policies of the administration. UPC leaders were therefore careful to avoid any allegations that their objectives conflicted with those of the administration in any fundamental way. The charter of the organization did not speak of breaking away from the French Union; rather it stated: "The UPC is not a movement standing in opposition to the French nation, the interests of the French Union or even the existing Constitution." They stated their objectives simply as being to assist the masses organize themselves for social and economic improvement "within the framework of the French Union." These conciliatory phrases may have sufficed to secure legal approval, but they neither eliminated nor veiled for long the direct conflict that was intended between the UPC's real goals and those of the French administration.

For its local sections the UPC leaders soon elaborated a program that revealed this conflict. The basic program centered on the dual but intimately related objectives of gaining complete independence and reunification of the "Kamerun." The word independence did not appear explicitly in the early written propaganda of the party, but it was clearly implied.[2] Given the provisions of the Trusteeship System, it can reasonably be assumed that the UPC's goal of independence conflicted with French policy, not in the fundamental question of independence, but what timing and mode of achieving it the French would permit. But as we have seen, the French did twist the Trusteeship Agreement to their own ends. Thus Cameroonians who thought of the Territory as part of a system singularly designed to perpetuate indefinitely its subordination to France, perceived correctly. To aspire to full independence was in fact to invite irremediable conflict with French policy.

It is not generally appreciated how central to the nationalist objective of independence for Cameroon the question of Cameroon reunification was. Reunification, it was thought, would inaugurate a condominium of British and French power in the Territory, and through the workings of colonial jealousies in a check-and-balance fashion, prevent the permanent incorporation of any part of the combined country into the British Commonwealth or the French Union. This plan was not new to the formal nationalist or to "reunification movement," however; it predated them by several years. The UPC leadership rejected the positions taken by earlier organizations (some of whose leaders were also among the UPC leadership), and also considered the prospect of a condominium in a new light. The secretary-general of the UPC, Reuben Um Nyobe, based the rationale for the strategy on the supposed fear of each colonial power of the subjugation of their own colonial possessions to the power of the other.[3] The fact that both colonial powers expressed opposition to the idea of reunification seemed to them to confirm this view.

Um Nyobe and the rest of the UPC leadership advocated reunification for other reasons, as well, some of them mundane: it would eliminate the injustices and inconveniences caused by the border restrictions on trade and travel between the two sectors; it would attenuate the imposition on

[2] The program was outlined in letters to local chapters in preparation for the visit of the First United Nations Visiting Mission in 1949. The objectives were: (1) the unification of the two Cameroons (British and French); (2) the establishment of a time limit for Trusteeship; (3) termination of the Trusteeship Agreement provisions permitting administration of the Territory as "an integral part of French Territory"; (4) the participation of the indigenous population in special supervisory machinery to be established under the auspices of the United Nations; and (5) the establishment of local and territorial deliberative assemblies.

[3] An article entitled "Comment faire pour gagner la bataille du referendum pour l'unification du Cameroun," in *La Voix du Kamerun*, No. 16 (August–September 1954), signed by MPODOL, Um Nyobe's symbolic name, taken from a Bassa secret society.

137

Cameroon society of two alien and disparate cultures. However, part of their reasoning was based on a firm dedication, almost religious in character and expression, to the notion of the existence of a Kamerun nation with moral rights equal to those of the colonial powers. They argued that Kamerun in a strict legal sense had already achieved its independence at the termination of the original German treaties with the Douala kings, presumed to have contained a provision limiting its life to 30 years, that is, until 1914.[4] On this basis it was argued that when British and French troops defeated the Germans in the Territory 1914–1916, the legal authority for German rule had already lapsed. British and French rule consequently were deemed to be based on de facto control only, or on military conquest. Moreover, Nyobe and others considered that the Mandate Agreement did not regulate the relations between France and Great Britain, on the one hand, and Cameroon on the other, but rather those between France and the League of Nations (United Nations). The colonial powers had become internationally accountable in the exercise of de facto control; morally sovereignty was deemed to remain with the local people. In any case, it seemed clear to the UPC that there existed only one Cameroon, subject to two administrations but with one moral identity. As Um Nyobe put it, "Everyone will recognize, speaking in Christian terms, that God created only one single Cameroon." If there existed this one Cameroon nation, and if the termination of trusteeship over it was to accord with the wishes of its people, then this divided "Cameroon people" had to be brought back together in order to express their wishes. By all logic (at least in terms of French tradition) such wishes should be expressed in a constituent assembly, but there could be no such assembly until reunification was achieved. Thus reunification was initially as central an objective to the UPC program as was independence itself, for achieving the one was considered to be a necessary prelude to achieving the other, and both reflected the burning aspirations of nationalists to assert and develop the Cameroon nation.

The impulse toward self-assertion was widespread among French-

---

[4] The myth of a 30-year limitation on the German treaty is widespread in Cameroon, but is rejected by several scholars. Adalbert Owona, in a letter to the *Revue Camerounaise* of the Cercle Culturelle des Etudiants Kamerunaises (Paris), No. 8 (March–April 1959), cited the work of J. R. Bruach (*Etudes Camerounaises*, Nos. 477–48) and a translation of the treaty contained therein. The treaty mentioned no such condition, but did contain a clause (No. 5) not included in many other versions, which stated: "During the initial period of the establishment of an administration, our local customs and our usages must be respected." Such phrasing does not suggest the authors expected a limited duration of German rule.

speaking Cameroonians, thus the UPC's slogan "reunification and independence" enjoyed great currency, especially among the more sophisticated southern peoples. After Reuben Um Nyobe presented the UPC's claims before the General Assembly of the UN in 1952 and exploited UN prestige by widely publicizing his appearance and the ensuing and generally sympathetic discussion, every important Cameroon politician tried to obtain a personal hearing in New York, and nearly every party appropriated the UPC slogan. One important political party that did not develop a genuine commitment to the goals of the UPC was the Catholic-oriented *Bloc démocratique Camerounais,* which had been organized by the French medical doctor Louis Aujoulat in 1951 when he won a seat in the Territorial Assembly from the African electoral college. Aujoulat was deeply committed to the assimilationist ideal of a genuine Euro-African partnership under French tutelage. He succeeded in attracting to his party two of Cameroon's most interesting and important leaders—André Marie Mbida from the aloof, Catholic, Eton-Beti ethnic group in the environs of Yaounde; and Ahmadou Ahidjo, the half-Fulani and Moslem inspiration behind the emergence of a number of politically oriented progressive unions and cultural associations in the major northern cities. Neither of these areas had a real interest in the Kamerun idea. Moreover, Catholic church leaders had instilled a deep suspicion of the "pro-communist" UPC among Catholics.

The more general idea of African nationalism was acquiring enthusiastic support throughout both the north and the Catholic areas of the south and central highlands. Evidence of this was the successful bid by Mbida in the 1956 elections to displace his former mentor, Aujoulat, from the Assembly, and the leadership of his party's (now renamed *Parti des Démocrates*) representatives in it. Mbida became the first prime minister of the Cameroon "state," which was brought into being by the reforms contained in the June 1956 *loi cadre* of the French Assembly. Ahidjo had formed his own northern-based party, as we shall see in a later chapter; despite the fact that this party controlled 11 more seats than did the *Démocrates,* Ahidjo chose to take the position of vice premier in a coalition government. Mbida had always kept his distance from the other political movements, having refrained from joining either Soppo Priso's *Union National* or Assale's *Action Nationale.* As prime minister he continued to pursue an independent course by attempting to forcibly suppress the UPC-influenced rebellion, rejecting the goal of reunification, and introducing legislation to retard the attainment of independence for at least 10 years. This program was very unpopular;

coupled with Mbida's personal clashes with nearly every other important politician, including several government ministers from his own party, it led to the early demise of his government.

With a program of reconciliation with the dissident forces, and embracing the claims of reunification and independence made popular by the UPC, Ahidjo took up the reins of government. As he moved to consolidate his position by espousing the aspirations of the southern groups outside his own party, the militant exiled wing of the UPC itself moved away from its commitment, not only to reunification which had ceased to have any strategic importance to it, but also to an early independence for the country, because it remained outside the circles of power and did not wish to see the UC or any other party consolidate its hold on the government through the achievement of this popular aspiration.

Reunification was more central to the ideology of the UPC than to the nationalists in the British-controlled sector.[5] This was due largely to the fact that the conflict between the objectives of the English-speaking Cameroonians and those of the Administering Authority, Great Britain, was less fundamental than that between the Francophone nationalists and authorities. The militant leaders of the UPC burned with a passion to rid themselves of every vestige of French power and tutelage, whereas most Anglophones did not reject all ties, per se, with Britain, the Commonwealth, or Nigeria, at least not initially. The reunification movement on both sides of the Mungo River was an expression of nationalism, but the character of the nationalism differed. In the western territory the movement remained preoccupied with instrumental values and objectives, rather than being consumed by a fervor for activity or blinded by a passion for power, right up until the eve of the UN plebiscite of 1961. In both territories the initial concern was for winning a greater measure of home rule, the devolution of authority to locally based and manned representative and executive institutions. In both territories these movements fed on general and diffuse desires of the people to be rid of alien rulers and to share the privileges the latter had so conspicuously and arrogantly enjoyed. In both cases the earliest leadership for the cause came from highly educated individuals who represented southern or coastal,

[5] For a fuller discussion of the development of nationalist ideas and organizations in British Cameroons see Johnson, "Cameroon Reunification"; Welch, *Dream of Unity;* and M. P. Mukoko Mokeba, "Cameroon Reunification: A Case Study in Political Integration," unpub. Master's thesis (University of Pittsburgh, 1966). One of the most zealous Cameroun nationalists in Southern Cameroons was Samson A. George. His pamphlet, "Kamerun (Unification)" (London, 1956), is one of the best examples of the ideology of this movement among the English-speaking group.

140

rather heavily Christianized, somewhat "Westernized," and relatively wealthy populations.

ON THE French side the colonial power was the main target of nationalistic abuse, but it was an irony of the British Cameroons that an African system and its leaders should share the spotlight with Europeans as the "colonial enemy" in nationalist demonology. Winning a greater measure of home rule meant prying the Territory loose from the contiguous Eastern and Northern Regional institutions of Nigeria and demanding greater responsibility over local affairs. The strong emotions that drove the English-speaking Cameroonian nationalists resulted from a sense of affront and discrimination about the retardation of the Territory compared to other areas of Nigeria.

During the initial phase of the birth and growth of Cameroon consciousness, the demand for reunification served as a tactical weapon which strengthened the moral claims of distinctiveness and quickened the pace of politicization in the Territory.[6] The demand also highlighted administration abuses of the Trusteeship Agreement. The British response was equally pragmatic: a refusal, if not an inability, to repudiate such claims outright and a willingness to strengthen the political voice of Cameroonians (at least in the southern provinces). Reunification per se was a useful but not necessary claim to make in order to achieve the most urgent objectives of local leaders. This is not to imply, however, that for some leaders reunification in its fullest sense was not a real objective. In reality, throughout the reunification campaign the objective was real for one group or another, but it was never the only objective for any group, save perhaps for the One Kamerun Movement. The effort to achieve reunification was nearly always a part of an effort to achieve other always more immediate and compelling objectives. Not a single person, political organization, or ethnic group partisan to the idea of Cameroon reunification made it the sole theme of political expression or activity. But reunification did feed into the broader concerns of the nationalists' movements; to the extent that Cameroon nationalism became a dominant symbol in itself, reunification was elevated to like stature.

Since "nationalism" refers to a process whereby "the nation" asserts its will to power, one can consider the basis of every militant political group in Cameroon, however broad or narrow its geographical and ethnic focus, to be insubstantial. We have seen that the brief period of German

[6] Cameroon Youth League Newsletter, Vol. 1 (1945).

rule did not precipitate a national awareness, that the cultural and practical affinities between the two Cameroons were minimal, and that the mandate-trusteeship period did not introduce substantial economic interchange between them or the basis for it in the future. Thus there was no "Kamerun nation." Nationalists were therefore left with no choice but to advance essentially normative claims. They tended to create the people's aspirations rather than to reflect them. But in the process they sometimes became the prisoner of their own creations. The leading elements of any popular movement tend to mold its "character" to conform to their own conceptions of the interests and aspirations of the community they invoke. Yet to the extent that the community actually exists as a coherent cluster of values and commitments, the latitude given the leaders to determine the community's aspirations is limited. Claims which spring from the base of genuine grievances tend to elicit a unity of purpose among the individuals of the community and to consolidate the organizational structures through which the claims are articulated. But if the objective basis for consensus is narrow or diverse, differences in the conceptions of the community's needs and desires, which are bound to exist among potential leading elements, inspire claims and activities that transgress the limits of consensus and promote the fragmentation of the movement. This process has been quite evident in the Negro freedom movement in the United States since 1966, and in the broader liberal– "Great Society"–civil rights movement since perhaps 1965 under the onslaught of not only the black power forces but those of the new left and the anti-Vietnam war movements. The process was also evident in the development of Cameroon nationalism.

In their initial phases on both sides of the Mungo, the themes of nationalism and reunification were based on broad and diffuse objectives. They made legitimate a wide range of specific demands, most of them relating in some way to the assertion of the African or Territorial community's claim to power. Ironically, however, these themes invoked and adjured loyalties to a community larger than either of those for which home rule was actually sought. When a measure of such rule was achieved the themes had become highly successful slogans which served to differentiate competitive political groups and individuals in their efforts to amass popular support for their control of the newly created political structures. This second phase was one dominated by the question, "Who will rule at home?" It led to the emergence into power in each territory of a new group of people, hinterland and northern-based, less well educated, less privileged and "Westernized" than the first groups to emerge into politics. In both states the theme of reunification became more specific, thus an unimportant, even threatening, rejected claim for those who had first launched it. Even in this phase reunification was not in and of itself the compelling objective for any group. It remained an accessory to other objectives; it had initially served to differentiate each Trust Territory from larger administrative and political structures; now it differentiated competitive political elements within each Territory. One significant difference in the impact of reunification in the two Territories, however, was that in the western state it abetted the subterritorial nationalism or parochialism of the grassfields populations who had a more authentic interest in reunification, whereas in the east it was made to serve the interest of a group that started as a regionalized political force but sought an everwidening sphere of influence through espousal of this theme which was so popular in the south. Even in the east the two phases of the nationalist movement hinge on the period, reached about 1957–1958, when the reunification slogan ceased to unify the entirety of political opinion, and came to fragment it. On the eve of achieving reunification the chief beneficiaries of the slogan's appeal in each Territory (Foncha in the west and Ahidjo in the east) seemed to be most uneasy with its success; it is doubtful that reunification would have come about had not the United Nations intervened.

In British Cameroons the latter-day reunificationists had a firmer and more honest commitment to the idea of reunification than the initial group led by Endeley, Mbile, and Kale. To be sure, the new leaders had been prominent in the older groups. Men like J. N. Foncha, A. Jua, and Solomon Muna were among the first important political figures; but with the exception of Muna they had remained underlings and had not built up a movement of their own. The history of their political organizations and activities is presented elsewhere.[7] The point here is that despite their greater sincerity in espousing reunification, the commitment of these men to achieving it was more ideological than the earlier leaders' commitment only with respect to the narrower questions of winning power for heretofore submerged "grassfielders" and separation from Nigeria. Cameroon reunification required a prior disentanglement from the institutions of Nigeria, more certainly than it required a similar disengagement from the French Union for French Cameroon. Thus it is difficult to judge the strength of commitment to reunification independent

---

[7] See Johnson, "Cameroon Reunification"; Welch, *Dream of Unity;* Mukoko Mokeba, "Cameroon Reunification"; and Le Vine, Chap. 4, in Carter, *Five African States.*

of the strong and growing desire for a full measure of self-government (since Northern British Cameroons lagged so much behind the Southern Cameroons in its nationalist awakening, what the southern leadership really expressed was a Southern Cameroons nationalism).

In the 1959 elections, which brought John Foncha and his KNDP to power, the preeminent theme of KNDP propaganda was "secession" from Nigeria. As early as September 1957 the KNDP had focused the KNDP–KNC–KPP debate on this issue, when it entered a motion in the House of Assembly calling for secession and the attainment of full self-government for the Territory by 1959. During the 1959 campaign the KNDP issued a "Secession Charter" which asserted: "There exists no pronounced social relation between the people of Southern Cameroons and Nigeria. We differ in culture, tradition and in all our general outlook . . . therefore making it a different and distinct people from those of Nigeria. We therefore want to maintain our identity as a Cameroons Nation." [8] But the charter mentioned reunification of all parts of old Kamerun only as the "ultimate objective," and stated, "we know we can only achieve this ultimate goal by first seceding from the Federation of Nigeria before her independence." [9]

Foncha interpreted his election as constituting a mandate to disengage from Nigeria, and quickly moved to implement the mandate. The United Nations Visiting Mission, which left the Territory shortly before the elections, failed to see the narrow victory (two seats) as a mandate; thus the debate over the issue shifted to a consideration of the proper modes for terminating the Trusteeship Agreement. [10] The Visiting Mission recommended a plebiscite unless general agreement could be reached among all the major political parties regarding the constitutional future of the Territory. Agreement was not forthcoming, either at the resumed session of the Thirteenth General Assembly which met in February 1959 on an

[8] KNDP, "Secession Charter Spelled Out," Ofomata's Press (Oba, Nigeria, 1959).

[9] Welch notes that there was never any serious suggestion made to associate a reunified Cameroon with Nigeria (*Dream of Unity,* p. 150). Actually there was at least one occasion on which such a suggestion was made, though it is hard to judge its sincerity because it was mentioned in the context of a wider union of independent West African states. See *Debates,* House of Representatives, Nigeria, 26 March 1957.

[10] Foncha's hold on the Assembly was tenuous indeed, for one of his supporters soon "crossed the carpet" to the opposition, equalizing government and opposition strength. The switch was allegedly made because the deputy in question thought Foncha favored only secession from Nigeria and not reunification with French Cameroon. It is not clear whether this rationalization was spontaneous on the part of the M.P. or induced by opposition offers.

exclusively Cameroon agenda, or at a subsequent meeting of all the parties in Bamenda. In both instances Foncha insisted that if a plebiscite were to be held the choice involved was only to be that between secession from and integration into the Federation of Nigeria. This was a fleeting position of the opposition coalition, which proffered to the Visiting Mission the idea that the proposal for a plebiscite should be dropped entirely or restricted to the clear-cut choice. But the KNC-KPP changed its mind; at both the resumed General Assembly and a subsequent all-party conference held at the forest town of Mamfe, it insisted that reunification be the alternative to "continued association" with Nigeria. The UN was able to decide only that a plebiscite would be held before April 1960. Foncha continued to attempt to limit the issue to the Territory's relationship with Nigeria, and even suggested the Trusteeship be extended: "Why should separation and continuation of [the] Trusteeship Agreement be the next alternative? Because it is the immediate thing that matters. Without it our identity as a nation, small or great, would never be a reality. . . . Why continue under the Trusteeship Agreement? Because the ultimate objective of the United Nations Charter has not been achieved. . . . The British Cameroons still needs development, politically, economically, culturally." [11] Allegedly what Foncha feared was not reunification itself, but losing the plebiscite, and perhaps also losing control of the government.[12]

As the implications of the familiar slogan "reunification" became more precise, confusion over where people really stood grew apace, until all sides began to reject the alternative of integration with either Cameroon or Nigeria and to seriously consider full independence. Paul Kale, who had lit the spark of patriotism for Cameroon in John Foncha years before, argued for terminating the Trusteeship Agreement even if it left Southern Cameroons on its own: "By the terms of the Trusteeship Agreement the right to the enjoyment of self-government or independence had been guaranteed the Cameroons even if Nigeria had not set the ball rolling. . . . I have even wondered why a plebiscite should be called at all. . . . [I] hope that after the said plebiscite the Cameroons ll be granted self-government without ties or apron strings either way. On the face of this one would therefore assume that the Cameroons has a right to the enjoyment of self-government independent of Nigeria." [13] This position was supported in more colorful language, as is illustrated by the remarks

---

[11] Southern Cameroons, *Report,* Mamfe Conference on the Plebiscite Questions and Register, August 10 and 11, 1959, Buea, 1959.

[12] Foncha stated in an interview with Claude E. Welch, Jr., September 1963. "It was better to keep trusteeship than to rush in and lose the plebiscite."

[13] *Report,* Mamfe Conference, p. 10.

at the Mamfe Conference by the Fon of Bafut: "To me the French Cameroons is 'Fire' and Nigeria 'Water.' Sir, I support secession without unification." [14]

Even Dr. Endeley would later, if only briefly, take up Kale's position, but his burning desire was to embarrass the government by revealing a lack of dedication to its long-avowed program—despite the fact that Endeley disclaimed any interest simply in bringing ruin to a particular party. Consequently he tried to force Foncha to tie his position firmly to that of reunification, a position Endeley thought lacked the popularity of the evident anti-Nigerian sentiment in the country: "Does [Foncha] want secession by itself or does he want secession with immediate unification? . . . We are trying to advise that we must be together with one of our neighbors. Is it [to be] the French Cameroons or . . . Nigeria? . . . The Premier very ably said in his answers in the United Nations that secession can only end in unification. The KNDP have a policy which is secession and unification. . . ." [15]

Foncha vociferously resisted the tactic. To a "Pan-Kamerun Student Conference" held in the summer of 1959 just prior to the Fourteenth General Assembly, Foncha said: "Reunification should not be made a condition of secession [from Nigeria]. Reunification is a simple matter for round-table discussion by the two governments. Everybody who makes reunification a condition of secession is an enemy working in favour of integration in the Nigerian Federation." [16]

The two principal groups were unable to resolve their differences at the Mamfe conference; they returned to the Fourteenth General Assembly having made no progress on the questions to be put in the plebiscite or the nature of the voting registry. They therefore invited pressure from other African and anticolonialist delegations. After many heated discussions Foncha and Endeley decided to call for a deferral of the plebiscite.[17] For a brief moment, at Endeley's suggestion, Foncha agreed to rally around Kale's suggestion and request complete independence for Southern Cameroons.[18]

What both Endeley and Foncha feared most was neither reunification nor integration into Nigeria but rather losing their political following and thus power or the opportunity to gain it by having their indecision and

[14] *Ibid.*

[15] *Ibid.*

[16] Quoted in Welch, *Dream of Unity,* p. 206, from Pan-Kamerun Student Conference, Yaounde, August 1959 (Prague: International Union of Students, n.d.), p. 18.

[17] UN Document A/C 4/414.

[18] *Kamerun Times,* December 16, 1960.

146

abandonment of their own programs too openly exposed. Endeley quickly bowed before the pressures of African delegates to the UN who were fearful of the Balkanization of Africa through a separate independence for tiny Southern Cameroons. He returned to his earlier position and also pressed for an immediate plebiscite. Foncha was persuaded to accept the two alternatives (integration with Nigeria or Cameroon) if Endeley agreed to compromise and accept a delay in the conduct of the plebiscite.[19] The compromise was embedded in General Assembly Resolution 1352 (14th G.L.), which required that the plebiscite be held not later than March 1961. Only persons born in the Territory (this applied to the southern part only) or of one parent who was born there, were to vote; separation from Nigeria was to take place not later than October 1, 1960.

Foncha's supporters at home were extremely dissatisfied with the timing of and the alternatives involved in the plebiscite. Augustin Jua, acting premier in Foncha's absence, wired him at the UN to indicate that the party leaders considered the compromise unacceptable. It is alleged that the party leadership was considering replacing Foncha as premier.[20] Rather than the joyful dreams of full independence which the Endeley-Foncha communiqué at the General Assembly inspired, or even a significant delay in a public vote on the matter, which they deemed to be crucial to the success of such a vote because French Cameroon still suffered the ravages of a violent rebellion and the efforts to suppress it, the KNDP leaders faced the bleak prospect of an early referendum on two distasteful alternatives. Now they were required to develop support for a proposition they doubted themselves, with little time to organize such a campaign, no deep thought having been given to the precise nature of the reunited country they wished to create, and confronted with daily reports of violence and brutality just across the border. The success of such a campaign is strong evidence of the existence of deep-seated commitments to the idea of Cameroons nationalism, if only within the context of Southern Cameroons. The plebiscite campaign and results turned around a number of issues: xenophobia toward Nigerians and particularly Ibos, subnationalism among grassfields people who had come to consider Foncha and his KNDP as their own special spokesmen and consequently his government as their own private instrument, and a surprising and consuming if vague commitment to the idea of being Cameroonian.

It has been asserted by an eminent student of Southern Cameroons of

[19] UN Document A/Cr/414.
[20] See Le Vine, *Cameroons*, p. 210.

long standing that the politicians had five fundamental realities to deal with in the plebiscite campaign: [21]

1. A deep-seated antipathy toward certain Nigerian peoples, especially the Ibo peoples, by much of the Southern Cameroons population.
2. A general attachment to "British ways."
3. A feeling of community with certain French Cameroon peoples.
4. A general antipathy toward "French ways."
5. A fear of terrorists (and the military) from the Cameroon Republic.

Each protagonist had to juggle perceptions of these realities in order to produce favorable attitudes. Endeley based his campaign on emphasizing the second, fourth, and fifth themes. He hoped that the second would neutralize the first and that the fourth and fifth would do the same to the third. The following examples of the rhetoric used to deal with these questions by the pro-Nigeria (CPNC—Endeley and Mbile) group follow:

Theme No. 1. Separation from Nigeria will close these natural and only outlets [the ties of the Balondo peoples to those in the Calabar area of Nigeria] to our people and strangle us economically. To us, association with Nigeria is not just a political desirability, it is basic to our very existence.[22]

Theme No. 2. It will be senseless to drop the British way of life for a French way of life. Never has England bowed before France and we of the Southern Cameroons shall never bow to France.[23]

Theme No. 3. The Southern Cameroons, like the Congo on the outside, may look like one people. It is NOT, I repeat NOT a people. It is a European arrangement which has not had time to gain concrete form, and which can only succeed to keep together after in-

---

[21] E. O. Ardener, "Crisis of Confidence in the Cameroons," *West Africa,* August 12, 1961.

[22] N. N. Mbile, Statement to the 1,142nd meeting of the General Assembly's Fourth Committee, following the plebiscite and in reiteration of demands made before it that the Territory be partitioned according to the ethnic groups voting one way or the other in the plebiscite.

[23] "Mr. Foncha's False Jerusalem," *Cameroons Champion,* February 8, 1961.

dependence through agreement between the tribes to work together.[24]

Theme No. 4. I have heard the KNDP say we must teach the Cameroun Republic the modern art of proper government. Madness! [25]

Theme No. 5. With Nigeria . . . you can be assured of the security of the rule of law, the protection of your lives and houses and farms. . . . And now ask yourselves what is the alternative. You would throw your lot in with a country . . . which unfortunately has been torn in recent years by civil wars.[26]

or:

Twenty-five thousand Cameroonians have fled that Territory, but none has fled British Cameroon for French Cameroons. People are killed daily on the streets of Douala and Yaounde.[27]

Foncha and the KNDP forces used the first four themes to neutralize the fifth. By arguing that the second (love of British ways) was compatible with the fourth (a community between peoples of both areas) the first (hatred of Nigerians) and the fourth (antipathy to French ways) could be used to enhance the desirability of this combination (a community in which British ways would be preserved). Some of the more interesting, and not atypical, statements on these themes are:

Theme No. 1. Plenty t'ing Nigeria do, we no savvy! [28]

Theme No. 2. We've been with Nigeria for forty years under British Administration. We have no roads, no Government-secondary schools, no NOTHING. It is about time we tried the other side of the border.[29]

Theme No. 3. [There is a] Cameroonian, who, whether speaking French, English or German or any of the hundreds of languages of its peoples, is undeniably and unmistakably Cameroonian. His sense of hospitality,

[24] Mbile, Statement.

[25] *Cameroons Champion*, February 8, 1961.

[26] Balewa, Sir A. T., Prime Minister of Nigeria, "Broadcast on the Southern Cameroons Plebiscite," January 22, 1961.

[27] *Cameroons Champion*, February 8, 1961.

[28] UN Document T/1440, para. 88.

[29] *Kamerun Times*, February 11, 1963, quoting from its plebiscite issue of two years earlier.

his directness of manner and irrepressible sense of humour, and other qualities, not necessarily always noble, combine to make him what he is.[30]

Theme No. 4. But we are faced with a peculiar problem, Sir, a real problem which I think it is very difficult for even our most sympathetic friends to appreciate. We feel we must salvage the Cameroons; the French Cameroons from the French Union. This is the sacred duty to which Cameroons Nationalists are dedicated.[31]

Theme No. 5. (The proreunificationists did not discuss the question of terrorism in the French-speaking Republic.)

To this list of five realities should be added two more: the fact that Foncha represented the government in power, and the name "Cameroon." The proreunificationists placed heavy emphasis on the name they advanced as proof that the country should join with the Republic and reject Nigeria: "Cameroonians are not Nigerians." The argument was difficult for the opposition to break down; it permitted an indirect appeal to anti-Nigerian sentiment without identifying it as such. Those opposed to reunification could thus be labeled "traitors to the Kamerun Nation" (the term "Kamerun" was used throughout the campaign to emphasize that it was the restoration of the former German state that they sought). Appeals to this kind of patriotism, which asserted the existence of a Kamerun nation, or of an opportunity through the plebiscite to create one, constituted about 12 percent of the arguments expressed on behalf of reunification in the pro-KNDP newspaper during the plebiscite campaign.[32] However, by far the most frequently used theme was equating support for reunification with loyalty to the government (or to the state,

[30] "Kamerun Society and the Nigerian Constitution," Kamerun Society, mimeo. pamphlet, 1958.

[31] Victor Mukete, Cameroonian minister in the Nigerian Federal Government, in a speech to the House of Representatives, Lagos, March 26, 1957. Note that this speech was made before the plebiscite, but it reflects the attitudes of many West Cameroonians at the time of the plebiscite, who considered that the French influence was still the dominant one in the east. In order to counter assertions that they would exchange one colonial master for another, they tended to assert that Southern Cameroonians could "educate the East Cameroonians to more peaceful ways of doing things" and show them, by example, that Africans could be masters in their own homes.

[32] Based on my content analysis of the *Cameroons Times,* December 9, 1960 through February 18, 1961, with the exception of Nos. 5, 6, 8 of 1961.

which many saw as the same thing).[33] Endeley himself later claimed that the plebiscite vote was invalid and inappropriate as a test of the true wishes of the people, because "the plebiscite was generally understood only as an issue between those tribes controlling the Government and those tribes whose leaders are in the Opposition and who wish therefore to unseat the Government." [34] On this he had a point, one not different than that cited by Foncha to discredit the results of the plebiscite in Northern British Cameroons which were the opposite of those in the south.[35]

The members of the opposition party were not alone in revealing serious doubts about it, if not certain rejection of, the immediate union of the two Cameroons. Foncha himself attempted to hedge on his commitment to union as late as three months before the plebiscite. At a special conference in London called by the British Colonial Office to discuss with Foncha, Endeley, and other Southern Cameroons leaders the security problems of the Territory following the plebiscite, Foncha requested the British government to grant the Territory full independence immediately following the plebiscite on the basis of a constitution to be written especially for the circumstances. It is also reported that Foncha requested a grant of several million pounds to permit an independent administration until suitable arrangements for union could be worked out.

In effect, what Foncha sought was British agreement to an interpretation of the plebiscite that would permit a delay in the implementation of reunification. It would seem that at that time there was ground for agreement between Endeley and Foncha. Indeed, Endeley did propose to Fon-

---

[33] *Ibid.*

[34] Endeley, speech to 1,142nd meeting of the Fourth Committee of the UN General Assembly, 1961.

[35] See Appendix II for the official results of the plebiscite votes in the North and South, February 11 and 12, 1961. The Southern Cameroons parties repeatedly attempted to stimulate organization around the theme of reunification, or at least of "unification" between North and South but they never received much support from the Northern leaders. Historically a part of the Islamic emirates of the Fulani empire (Northern Nigeria) the traditional Moslem leadership of the area favored even closer association with the Northern Region. Not until the UN plebiscite of 1959 was there a significant expression of opposition to the idea of amalgamation with the Northern Region. Voters in that first plebiscite unexpectedly rejected immediate incorporation, however, and decided instead to delay a determination of the Territory's future status. Many observers attribute this result to desires, especially among pagan groups, for local government reforms, and to the fact that suffrage was not extended to females. The Northern Kamerun Democratic Party, inspired by the secessionist, proreunificationist KNDP in the south, began to campaign for merger with Southern Cameroons during the 1959 plebiscite and then continued to work for a break with Nigeria but was unable to get such a campaign going.

cha that they issue a joint demand to the UN for independence. However, each leader continued to try to work the other into an embarrassing position which would compromise his chances of success in the plebiscite. Endeley charged that the plebiscite questions required reconsideration because the second alternative (Cameroon reunification) could not be implemented at all, because he thought the Cameroon Republic was unable or unwilling to take over the full responsibility for governing the territory.[36] British officials rejected the propositions of both sides and stated that "the people of the Southern Cameroons should be told plainly that if they voted to join the Cameroun Republic this would definitely happen in a short time." In this the British sided with Endeley, perhaps consciously; they concluded: "The United Nations, in adopting the two alternatives . . . clearly ruled out a period of continuing Trusteeship or separate independence for the Southern Cameroons."

Indeed it had! It is apparent that the long campaign for home rule, for control of the authoritative institutions created thereby, and for the plebiscite, had awakened a spirit of nationalism in the Territory but had also fragmented what were initially united and popular organizations which gave body to that spirit, and had reduced this spirit to its tribalistic, almost nativistic foundations. In forcing a choice of political union to the east or to the west, the United Nations had forced on Southern Cameroons the achievement of goals its wayward leaders had come to repudiate.

Thus, in a sense, there was also a major conflict between the objectives of English-speaking Cameroonians and the various other authorities which shared responsibility for colonial rule, Nigeria, Britain and the UN. However, the conflict was not ever fundamental. Though there was some resistance, British and Nigerian authorities quickly bowed to Cameroonian pressures for regional autonomy. In insisting on a showdown on the question of reunification versus integration, the British and the UN forced on Cameroonians only what they themselves had first and continually demanded.

The Ideology of Modernization and the Restratification of Traditional Society

The basic tenets of the ideology of modernization seem to imply a thoroughgoing restratification and reorganization of traditional society. Ideology differentiates Cameroon political groups less neatly in this re-

[36] *Cameroons Champion,* November 21, 1960; see also *The Two Alternatives* (Buea: Government Printer, 1961).

spect than do the questions of reunification or independence, however. Several factors contribute to this result: (a) the similarity of rhetoric for most groups; (b) the failure of the ideological nationalists to gain power and thus the limitation on opportunities to demonstrate convictions in action; and (c) social realities that forced leaders desirous of a following to respond to particularistic claims, such as those of clan and tribal groups.

The logical core of the nationalist campaign was the proposition that the Cameroon peoples ought to, if they did not already, constitute a single mass imbued with a spirit of solidarity. To the extent that other political parties adopted UPC slogans and the objectives they symbolized, all political groups tended to speak the same language of modernism. It was a language that stressed "democratic ideals," the "equality of all Cameroonian citizens," the "will of the people," and other such phrases which would, if carried to a logical conclusion, dissolve most of the status and power hierarchy of traditional society, as well as the colonial yoke. However, the UPC leadership assaulted the promoters and signaled the peril of tribalism more eloquently than most; though their targets were often traditional authority, their propaganda concentrated on themes intended to unite the masses of all tribes against the colonial power:

> They [the colonizers] set one tribe against another in making the one believe that they are more intelligent and the other believe they are richer and will dominate the country. They both naïvely believe this and throw themselves into vain civil wars which finally lead to everybody's ruin, and the only ones to profit are the colonisers. They set the chiefs against the intellectuals in making the ones believe they are the holders of tradition and that power belongs to them, and the others believe that they are "just like the whites" and that the privileges of modern civilisation belong to them. But the colonisers believe in neither the power of the chiefs nor the intelligence of the so-called evolué. They seek simply to draw out of these people's hatred more profit and the prolongation of everybody's misery.[37]

The UPC fished both sides of the tribal stream, however, and found it rewarding. Its leadership revealed their awareness of the ethnic base to Cameroon politics from the start; in naming the organization, for example, they rejected "Union of the Cameroon People" on the grounds that this people did not yet exist,[38] and achieving ethnic balance was a quite

[37] Reuben Um Nyobé, speech to Kamerun United National Congress, Kumba, December 15, 1951, in *Unification Immediaté*, p. 16 (my translation).

[38] Owona, "Le Mouvement."

explicit motive in the selection of the members of the first executive bureau.[39] Ethically based organizations which affiliated early with the UPC included the Ngondo of the Douala and the *Kumze* of the Bamileke, whose founder, Mathias Djoumessi, was an important chief and the first president of the UPC. Part of the stimulus to turn to traditionally oriented or inspired organizations for support no doubt came from the character of most of the opposition to the UPC and its program, which came from scores of mini-parties, most of which were established along tribal lines at the instigation and with the financial support of the administration.[40] Even the original UPC supporters quickly fell away into opposition ranks, either frightened by administration charges against it of communist affiliation or antichief, antitradition sentiment, or simply attracted to the glittering prospects of electoral success on the basis of unalloyed tribal support. Pragmatism dictated accommodation to these factors. Though the UPC was less pragmatic than other groups, it was enough so to win backhanded compliments even from the administration: "It (the UPC) has always been at pains to avoid making a head-on attack on the local social structure, its alleged aim being, on the contrary, to protect and strengthen it, and its attempts to gain the backing of the most important traditional chiefs.[41]

UPC leaders had few opportunities to implement any anti-traditionalist principles they may have had, because none of them—except young Mayi Matip of the Bassa, the former head of the youth wing and successor to Um Nyobé's leadership of the Bassa after his death in 1958—ever successfully contested an election. The principal UPC spokesmen (Um Nyobé, Abel Kingue, Ernest Ouandié, and Dr. Roland Moumié) tried in various elections—in 1949 for the Representative Assembly, in 1951

[39] Um Nyobe, speech, p. 22.

[40] Victor Le Vine has treated the nature and activities of the most important Cameroon parties in a number of studies—in Coleman and Rosberg, *Political Parties;* his Chap. 4 in Carter, *Five African States;* and in his book, *Cameroon.* There were, at one time or another, nearly a hundred organizations participating in politics, almost all of them associated with particular tribes or clans. Every party had an ethnic base, especially those receiving administration support, such as the Union Bamileke (set up to oppose the *Kumze*-UPC until its disaffiliation in 1959), the Evolution Sociale Camerounaise (among the Bassa and some Douala), the Renaissance Camerounaise (among the Ewondo), Paysans Independants (ex UPC Bamileke), Action Paysanne (Bulu-Fang). Even the larger political parties which later acquired a broader base started as ethnic referents—the Bloc Des Democrates among the Ewondo-Beti Catholics, and the Union Camerounaise among the Fulani dominated Northern peoples and the Bamoun (Moslem groups).

[41] Administration communication to the First UN Visiting Mission to West African Trust Territories, UN Document T/798, p. 52 (1949).

for the National Assembly, in 1952 for the Territorial Assembly—as they and other trade unionists had in local elections in 1946 and 1947, but without officially recognized success. The party claimed victory for Um Nyobé and Kingue in 1952; in the former case it may have been justified in doing so,[42] but power did not accompany the victories. Thus the UPC leadership was never able to make use of the sanctions and rewards of the state apparatus as an instrument in support of a modernizing revolution, as the militant revolutionary leaders of other black African states were able to do. Their general orientations can be judged only by their actions within the party and in the areas that fell under their control. From this perspective it appears that the UPC was split into at least two camps with different orientations, or at least different accomplishments.

EVIDENCE of the differences in the attitudes of UPC leaders regarding the traditional society is to be found in their conduct of the rebellion the party directed in Cameroon from 1956 through 1962 and after. I shall return to the general motives and methods of the rebellion, but wish to single out here the relevance of the traditional structure and customs.

During the whole period of the rebellion the UPC operated essentially as two organizations with little coordination or cooperation. The split between the two reflected a difference of opinion about the prospects for nationalist objectives, whether they could be accommodated by the procedures and institutions established by the Administering Authority, or whether they required a violent showdown with the administration. The division had an ethnic base, with Um Nyobé and his Bassa following generally more optimistic about the potential for gaining their objectives through open participation in politics than the Bamileke wing of the party, led by Moumié, Ouandié and Kingue. Whether or not the two wings differed in their general policy orientation during the early phases of the rebellion, the character of the guerrilla campaign differed appreciably with respect to its willingness or ability to utilize indigenous structures. The campaign in the Bassa and Bamileke areas was shaped by the tribal cultures and structures, but the consequences differed because the traditional cultures were different.

Um Nyobé was able to give the "*maquis*" (guerrilla campaign) in the

[42] A political officer in the French colonial administration at the time of the 1952 elections has stated to me that it was the administration that refused to permit Um Nyobé access to an elected position of authority. The mechanisms used to do so are not entirely clear, but included tactics such as a careful enlargement of the electorate among more traditionally oriented strata. The French were notorious for rigging elections in some of their colonies (e.g. Algeria).

155

Bassa regions a coherence and effectiveness that was unmatched else-where in the country. This was accomplished by meshing the rebel orga-nizations with traditional institutions, and by using traditional authority and influence. It was necessary to have absolute control of large tracts of land in order to quarter, train, and feed guerrilla bands, but almost all the land was controlled by the corporate lineage groups of the society. The cooperation of lineage notables would be necessary to obtain access to, ownership or usufruct rights in this land. Um Nyobé relied on the connections and influence of members of various Bassa secret societies to accomplish these objectives.[43] He was not a member of the most powerful, the *Um Nkoda Nton* (*Jông*) society, but was able to buy membership into a lesser one, one of the *Mbo* societies. This latter society was no longer a secret one; it held public meetings in which eloquent speaking was an asset. In this Um Nyobé was a master. Many members of the soci-ety were also influential figures in lesser societies, and Um Nyobé was able to use these connections to get personnel and supplies.

To acquire influence in the top society, Um found his associate, Theo-dore Mayi Matip, invaluable. Only the notables of a small number of so-called Grand Bassa clans belonged to the *Um Nkoda Nton;* preeminent among them was the clan of *Ndog-Njoué,* which was headed by the Matip family. Mayi Matip happened to possess the family fetishes and other symbols of chiefly authority from his grandfather, Matip Ma Mbondol, the last authentic clan chief, who had been succeeded by someone the French installed in a manner contrary to Bassa custom. Consequently the symbols of authority had been retained in Matip's family, and he now used them adroitly to reassert the traditional influence of his family in the *Ndog-Njoué* society, claiming successorship to the titles of Mbondol. In this manner he was able to marshal the full influence of Bassa tradition behind the rebellion and the *Comité Nationale d'Organisation* (CNO) which Um Nyobé had established to direct it.

There existed no pan-Bamileke set of societies that could serve the purpose of imposing discipline on these people. Even so, the conditions and nature of the traditional Bamileke society profoundly affected the course of the rebellion by making it more chaotic and less controlled for explicit political or military objectives. In the homeland areas and the

---

[43] This discussion of Bassa clan and secret society is taken from "La Pacification de la Sanaga Maritime," Col. J. Lamberton, Centre des Hautes Etudes d'Afrique Moderne, Etude 3760. The view of Bassa society therein presented is confirmed in G. H. Schwab's monumental but still unpublished study of the Bassa, "Etudes sur les coutumes Bassa," 1936.

settlements of emigrants, the society provided a readymade reservoir of conflicts and grievances into which the UPC could dip at will. Thus it was not hard for it to gain recruits or to encourage violence. As I have already mentioned,[44] violence has been an endemic feature of Bamileke society for years, encouraged by the political and social structure and by the plight of the 100 thousand or so Bamileke who have emigrated. But these are the very features that make control of the violence difficult.

The moderate nationalists, many of whom had helped to found the UPC or sympathized with its objectives, and most of whom were by virtue of education or professional occupations members of the emergent elite, were highly successful at utilizing traditional institutions or symbols to marshal electoral support. Their view of politics and vision of modernizing change in the country was not mediated by the prism of ideology. To the man, they constituted a group distinguished by their pragmatism, and in some cases, opportunism.

The politician who most successfully exploited tribal loyalties was Charles Assalé, who joined the Efulumeyong (tribal union) of his Bulu people in 1948 at its second annual meeting, and in four years transformed it into his personal political machine. The organization was founded by a deeply religious and prosperous clan notable who claimed to have been inspired by God in order that the Bulu "expose the will of God through their meeting, show respect due to authority and realize the unity of the Nation." [45] In this case they seem to have used the word "nation" to refer to the Bulu tribe, whose traditional life had disintegrated under the pressures of Christian missionary work and the impact of cash cropping. Later, under Assalé's prodding the idea of nation was expanded to encompass all the related peoples of the "Pahouin" (Fang) group and then finally, under the new name of *Union Tribale d'Ntem et Kribi,* it identified the ethnic referent by a purely administrative-geographical designation. This is an excellent example of super-tribalism or ethnicity at work, where new ethnic loyalties that have little if any historic reality are made politically relevant. In the elections of 1952 this mechanism produced an "almost plebiscitary majority" vote for Assalé.[46] He continued to successfully tap this support for his subsequent party *Mouvement d'Action Nationale Camerounaise* (MANC) and for the UC, with which he merged it in 1961.

[44] My discussion of Bamileke society in Chap. 3.

[45] David Medjo Mvondo, founder of the Efulumeyong, interview Ebolowa, May 1963.

[46] Le Vine, *Cameroons,* p. 151.

157

The success of Ahmadou Ahidjo in manipulating traditional structures is almost equally spectacular. His success was a source of much of his trouble with southerners, however, for they tended to regard him as a prisoner of the reactionary feudalistic *lamibé* of the north. Southerners tended to perceive the north as monolithic, an area dominated by the Foulbé, Islam, and the relics of the empire of Usuman dan Fodio. As the largest voting bloc, the northern representatives in the legislative assemblies of the Territory, just as in the case of their ethnic and historic relatives in Northern Nigeria, were regarded as threatening to the progress and integrity of the country because they were strong enough to dominate the rest despite the fact that they represented peoples who were geographically quite delimited and who accounted for a mere plurality of the population.

The degree of political unity actually achieved in the north is striking. The unity was first demonstrated to the rest of the country in the aftermath of the 1956 elections, when Ahidjo succeeded in gathering all of the deputies from the northern regions into a single parliamentary grouping. Another display of northern solidarity, which seemed more threatening to the southern-based political groups, came with the 1960 referendum to ratify the constitution of the first republic. The vote split roughly along geographical lines—the north approved the constitution overwhelmingly, and a large majority of voters in the south, encouraged by moderate and militant nationalists, opposed its ratification.[47] The contrast between the degree of political unity achieved in the north and in the south is most evident in the electoral campaign for the April 1960 elections to the first National Assembly. For the 44 seats in the northern (including Bamoun) constituencies, there were only 44 candidates, but for the 56 seats open in southern districts there were over 400 candidates.[48]

The UPC charged that such unanimity resulted from government discrimination in disallowing alternative lists of candidates to that of the government party, the UC.[49]

Northern solidarity was thought in the south to mean much more than interference and discrimination in favor of UC candidates on the part of the government and the state apparatus. It was also presumed to arise

---

[47] The constitution passed by a narrow margin—786,957 to 529,007. In the north the results were 562,000 to 13,000 opposed. The constitution failed to carry a majority of votes in 10 of the 21 districts, all 10 in the southern area.

[48] Eyinga, "Les Elections du 10 Avril, 1960."

[49] UPC, *Le Kamerun sous un Régime de Dictature fasciste* (1962?). The *annexe* quotes an article by Herve Montant in *Echos d'Afrique Noire*, April 9, 1960.

from the very social structure of the north, and thus to produce a group of deputies in the National Assembly who were all of a single stripe politically. It was this fact more than anything else that seemed to threaten unity in the country. The schism between the north and the southern areas appeared to be fundamental. In reality, as the political secretary of the UC has pointed out, "the division between the North and the South is a false one; there are many divisions within these two [regions] as important as that between them." [50] For one thing, though the northern deputies all felt a certain common interest in speeding up the development of their part of the country in order to achieve a position of equality with the south, they were not in agreement on how this was to be done. There is a distinction to be made between the progressive forces of the north, represented by Ahidjo and Moussa Yaya, for example, and the more conservative elements, represented by many of the *lamibé* who have occupied positions in the Assembly.

It is less surprising, however, that the northern deputies, once elected, would group themselves into a common organization, than that the progressive leadership of the organization should have been elected in the first place. In the south there was a widespread belief that the northern deputies were hand-picked by the Foulbé *lamibé*. In an area where the traditional system remains strong and where the chief traditionally was almost an autocrat, it is a natural assumption that no one could achieve an elective office without their support. The validity of this point of view in the 1956 elections is evident in the testimony of even the progressive northern deputies in question. One of them explained: "it was necessary in order that your candidacy be approved, that the Administrative Authorities know that you were not a person [pushing] for independence. . . . That was the program of the UPC. All that they [the Administration] were concerned about at the time was to combat this idea. It was necessary to convince these authorities that you were not for independence. If they thought that you were for this idea your candidacy would not be allowed [now]. . . . The *lamibé* were very close to the Administration. . . . [therefore] your candidacy had to be supported first by the Chef de Circonscription and then by the *lamido*." [51] It was necessary to deceive the officials, he explained, in order to convince them you were with them, when in fact you may not have been. One had to be "souple," flexible, and complaint until the elections; afterward it didn't matter.

[50] Moussa Yaya, interview, June 1963.
[51] Malam Yero, formerly president of parliamentary group UC and its youth secretary, interview, Yaounde, May 1963.

It seems doubtful, however, that this process could be repeated all over the north in 1956, as the deputy quoted above asserted. In splendid isolation, one from the other, the candidates in nearly every *circonscription* who had been "souple" before the elections, supposedly became solid progressives after them. That some of the northern progressives, the most important leaders of the UC, have pursued a progressive policy once in office is undeniable. But included among the northern deputies in 1956 were more than 10 Foulbé *lamibé,* and several others were the sons of *lamibé.*[52] One suspects that some if not most must have felt their interests to lie with the preservation of the ancient privileges of the *lamibé,* of the impressive political hierarchy which they headed, and of Foulbé domination generally.

If a number of the members of the UC bloc in the Assembly cultivated the prerogatives of traditional authority, it is clear that Ahidjo and his closest associates from the north—Moussa Yaya, Malam Yero, and Mohaman Lamine—did not. They were eager modernists who sometimes took bold action to constrain if not eliminate the power of the *lamibé.* Several recalcitrant *lamibé* have been deposed.[53] Some sources of financial support such as the "Zakat," or "Oussoura," taxes in the Fulani areas, or other forms of traditional tribute, were suppressed by the party, as well as the powers of sanction the chiefs had through the maintenance of private police forces and private prisons.[54] Sometimes the chiefs and *lamibé* were given leadership posts in the party, either as its candidates to the Assembly or other remunerative positions, or at the local level. But as Malam Yero explained: ". . . if the traditional chief is a good one and beloved by his people (we allow him to be president of the *comité de base*). . . . But if not, and we can tell by the looks on their faces and the general agitation that the chief is unpopular, . . . we see to it that another man of the village is elected to lead the party there." [55] Ahidjo him-

[52] *Revue Camerounaise,* No. 8 (March 1959). The following *lamibé* were members of the Assembly: The *lamido* of Maroua, Banyo, Guidder, Tcheboa, Bogo, Zamay, Mayo Oula, Wangai, Mokolle, and the Sultan Logone-Birni.

[53] In 1963 the *lamido* of Ngoundere was removed, allegedly strictly for reasons of administrative malfeasance, but the removal was politically convenient. The *lamido* of Maroua, who made life difficult for the UC, was deposed in 1959. As difficult *lamibé* died off, the party moved in to replace them with ones more pliable, loyal to the UC or with weak personalities who could not bring much power to bear against party purposes.

[54] These institutions were denounced by Ahidjo at the Third Congress of the UC, Maroua, September 1960.

[55] Quoted by Richard Matheron, Political Officer, U.S. Embassy, Yaounde, interview, 1963.

self always directly approached the subject of the position and proper role of the *lamibé* and chiefs. To the younger elements in the party, those who regarded the chiefs as a break in development and a threat to the coming new world, he stated: "I earnestly ask you to calm your impatience, knowing that the future belongs to a younger generation which faces problems head on and which elaborates the programs for tomorrow in peace and with discipline, taking into account the experience of the elders." To everyone involved, young and old alike, he demanded: "Our party must proceed to make some choices . . . men must adapt themselves rapidly to new ideas. . . . It is not to be permitted that, under pretexts of the conservation of misinterpreted traditional structures, the North of Cameroon should remain outside the currents of the general growth which the whole of the country experiences." And lest the chiefs misunderstand: "In their own interest, as in the interests of their peoples the traditional chiefs must remain the artisans of evolution in our country, they must even place themselves in the avant garde of this evolution. What I am asking of them is that they act in such a way that this evolution comes about with them, for in the contrary case, they will be vanquished by it." [56]

Though these words reveal a determination to foster modernizing change in the country, especially in the north, Ahidjo was not rigid in his approach to the traditional structures. Indeed, he continued to need their support. Nor was he by nature insensitive to the plight of all parties to this controversy. He constantly tried to assure the chiefs of an honorable place, were they to regard the inexorable process of social change as opportunities created rather than birthrights denied. "Traditional structures . . . cannot be effaced with a stroke of the pen," Ahidjo said. He believed that hasty action could destroy structures that have proved useful and efficient over a long period of time, but he thought it necessary to find valid and efficacious ways of replacing them.

Another of Ahidjo's concerns was the pagan community in the north which harbored explosive anti-traditionalism of the Foulbé variety, but which, as a majority of the population, had the leverage to pry loose Ahidjo's grip on the north and perhaps on the government. Ahidjo and his modernizing associates were therefore concerned that social mobilization and change proceed at a temperate pace and in a controlled manner. Both Islam and the party could be key instruments in bringing this about, so the regime pursued a policy of courting the *kirdi* (pagans) bring-

---

[56] A. Ahidjo, speech to Second Congress, UC, Ngaoundere, July 1959. The same themes were echoed at each subsequent congress of the party.

ing some of them into the national government, democratizing the structures of local government especially, giving the mountain-dwelling Kirdi assistance in settling on the plains and setting up farms, and recruiting them into the ranks of the party, as well as encouraging their conversion to Islam.[57] The latter approach worked to lessen the impact of change on traditional Moslem institutions.

Nationalists among the English-speaking Cameroonians also successfully exploited traditional institutions and sentiments. We will have occasion to see that the rise to power of the KNDP did much reflect and involve a fragmentation of the political arena along regional or ethnic lines. The KNDP came increasingly to speak for the grassfields, and the KNC-KPP (CPNC) opposition to speak for the forest areas. John Foncha, the uncomplicated, devout Catholic schoolteacher who perhaps felt more secure in speaking pidgin English or indigenous languages than standard English and who would walk all day to reach a remote village of voters, was much more successful at marshaling traditionalism to his cause than was the highly educated and articulate medical doctor, Endeley. Endeley made many mistakes in dealing with the symbols and spokesmen of tradition in the Territory: he would offend the *fons* by shaking their hands, sitting at their side on stools reserved for their fellow *fons,* or by addressing them by the wrong title or at the wrong times. Foncha eschewed such offenses. Endeley found it difficult to turn a good phrase in pidgin and consequently was ridiculed for haughtiness and for "spikin da big Inglish."

As Southern Cameroons' most highly educated citizen at the time, Endeley did project himself during the postwar period as the symbol of African competence, and attempted to organize Africans in the Territory to make their rights and aspirations respected by colonial authorities. He was widely respected throughout the territory for this, not only in the areas settled by his own people but in all sections of the country. He tried to inspire the young members of the emergent new Westernized elite, but obtained the support of traditional elements as well, so that in 1953 when he organized the first electoral competition on party lines, his Kamerun National Congress carried 12 of the 13 constituencies.

On the other hand, Endeley's tribal loyalties were strong; they some-

[57] See Chap. 3 for identification of Kirdi. The party, through its control of the state apparatus, required party membership of those demanding normal government services, such as the issuance of birth certificates or marriage licenses. There was also a concerted effort to staff the bureaucracy in the north with Moslems, whether initially of pagan stock or not. Chiefs and *lamibé* were brought into local councils or the central assemblies, but tended not to be given administrative functions.

times combined with his own personal pride to generate hostility among other groups. On one occasion he is reported to have bragged to a Mamfe audience that its peoples would never produce someone of the standing of the leaders produced by the Bakweri (refering, no doubt, to himself).

Endeley's general attitude toward chieftaincy and traditionalism was complicated. It concerned primarily the support or opposition of the chiefs. He was certainly not unaware of the prestige of chiefs, for he was himself the son of the most important Bakweri chief. But he was also a modernist, a highly educated person who lived in an era when power was obviously shifting to nontraditional institutions. Even so, during the first period of his leadership as Leader of Government Business (1954 to 1957), when he was charged with the responsibility for local government, he did not oppose the demands of the chiefs that they have a House of Chiefs.[58] Endeley supported the idea of the chiefs meeting in their own conference prior to the 1956 "Bamenda Summit Conference" of leaders held to work out a position for the coming London conference on the constitutional future of Nigeria and Cameroons. The chiefs supported Endeley's position on that occasion. Endeley even made the Fon of Bali a member of his delegation to the London conference, but this turned out to have been a mistake because the two became antagonists thereafter. In the campaign of 1957 Endeley continued to campaign on a prochief platform: "The Kamerun National Congress believes in maintaining the long-established institution of Chiefs, and will continue to work hand in hand with them in carrying out the modern democratic responsibility of lawmaking. . . . We shall, therefore, press for the establishment of a House of Chiefs." [59]

After the defection from his party of the important Fon of Bali, Endeley sought to recapture the support of chiefs (the Fon had systematically set about organizing all of them against Endeley) by begging the administration to establish the House of Chiefs ahead of schedule and before the elections so that he could take credit for the innovation.[60] This ultimately made matters worse, because Foncha, suspecting the motives for this move, claimed Endeley intended to interfere in the Chiefs' affairs by putting his own stooges into the House, or would use the promise of a

---

[58] Endeley and his cabinet abstained on this issue and the request was vetoed by the commissioner. See *West Africa*, April 9, 1955.

[59] KNDP Election Manifesto, 1957.

[60] It is not clear why the Fon of Bali deserted Endeley's ranks, but one widely believed story has it that Endeley treated the Fon like an errand boy in London. The abruptness of the Fon's shift in loyalties from the KNC to Foncha's KNDP would suggest that personal relations between the Fon and Endeley were the key.

163

position in it to pressure the chiefs. The Fon of Bali, aided by Foncha, assembled most of the country's chiefs at Kumba, where they formally rejected the idea of inaugurating the House of Chiefs before the elections.

As the Fon of Bali stepped up his campaign to organize the chiefs against Endeley's KNC, Endeley shifted his position on the role of chiefs and traditionalism in politics. He stated in May 1958, shortly after being installed as prime minister, that, "we shall also expect that in their own interest chiefs and traditional rulers must keep clear of party politics. . . . Any chief who persists, despite this timely advice, to participate in party politics does so at his own risk." [61]

Foncha and Agustin Jua moved quickly to consolidate the opposition of the grassfields chiefs to Endeley. They proclaimed that the KNC had no regard for "natural rulers," that Endeley was full of hatred for the Bali peoples particularly and grassfielders generally. They had villagers dig trenches or build obstacles in the roads to prevent Endeley's touring the Native Authority areas of the grassfields. Jua even succeeded in turning a revived ancient secret society of Bikom women, the Anloo society, into a special instrument of attack on the KNC.[62] Initially aroused by administration rules requiring contour plowing, the women of Bikom eventually set upon the compounds of KNC supporters, pressured their men into joining the KNDP under threat of denial of food and other services, and finally conducted a grand march on the district office, clad only in leaves, according to ancient custom, while beating sticks, rustling branches, and denouncing not only the new regulations but the KNC government. Though traditionally the Anloo had been loosely structured, under the goading of the grassfields politicians the society acquired a formal executive and set up local branches. Its support of the KNDP became fanatical in some localities; opponents were sometimes beaten and intimidated, cars were stoned and houses torn apart. The movement produced a large turnout for the KNDP in the 1959 elections which brought that party to power; it then atrophied, no doubt discouraged by the KNDP politicians.

Dr. Endeley and his supporters were also capable of using ancient tribal institutions and playing on tribal loyalties. Perhaps it was simply because Endeley sensed defeat, but fully two months before the 1961

[61] *KNDP Newsletter*, July 1958.

[62] For a discussion of the nature and consequences of this movement see the works of Robert E. Ritzenthaler, *Cameroons Village* (Milwaukee Public Museum, 1962), and "Anlu: A Women's Uprising in the British Cameroons," *African Studies* (Johannesburg), Vol. 19, No. 3 (1960), pp. 151–56.

plebiscite he led the CPNC executive to request that the United Nations partition the territory according to the vote of the different ethnic regions.[63] He and his colleague, Nerius N. Mbile, then whipped up frenzied support for the idea among the Bakweri and Balondo peoples. In order to do this they revived an ancient and now moribund association, the *Molongo,* or the supreme council of Bakweri clan chiefs.[64] A week after the plebiscite, 6,000 Bakweris met on the slopes of Mount Cameroon to suffer the fulminations of Dr. Endeley and P. Motomby-Woleta, another CPNC stalwart from that tribe. The ad hoc assembly passed a number of resolutions setting forth the following demands: (1) the Bakweri are to be administered according to their unanimous vote during the plebiscite; (2) the United Nations should receive a delegation from Molongo to state their case; and (3) the Molongo should be extended into the kindred tribes of "New Bantu extraction" in Kumba, viz. Balondos, Bakossi, etc.

The climate of opinion in which the *Molongo* flared to prominence was a distinctive xenophobia, as a discussion of the phenomenon in the pro-CPNC (and Bakweri owned) press indicates: "The revival of the Molongo today is a welcomed step . . . these foreign influences, unknown to our forefathers, have brought in hatred, disunity, and disloyalty among the Bakweri, which is responsible for the present handicapped state of this formerly united tribe. . . . [The job of the *Molongo* today] is to revive and regain the past glory and place of Bakweri people. It will demand also that all lands in the Victoria Division be recognized as belonging to the Bakweris." [65] The society sent a delegation to the postplebiscite discussions at the United Nations, but its leader dropped the land claims and demanded merely that the plebiscite results be set aside and the Territory given a "kind of separate status under the supervision of a special

[63] *Kamerun Times,* December 22, 1960.

[64] See the *Cameroons Champion,* March 8, 1961. This article described the *Molongo* as the supreme council and stated that it used to be the highest tribunal of appeal to those sentenced by Bakweri village councils. It acted "to prevent the spread of evil practices" and was the principal instrument for decision making with respect to war. The council, in name and function, is reminiscent of the *Ngondo* organization among the Douala, a people related to the Bakweri. Ardener, "Coastal Bantu of the Cameroons," in Forde, *Ethnographic,* Part XI, makes no mention of this institution in his description of the Bakweri, however.

[65] *Cameroons Champion,* March 8, 1961. The demand for a return of Bakweri lands repeats longstanding claims which Endeley himself helped to give prominence in the UN through the Bakweri Land Committee, which he helped organize after World War II. The committee petitioned the UN insistently after the war. For fuller treatment of these claims and of the Land Committee, see Ardener *et al., Plantation and Village,* esp. Chap. 16.

U.N. commission." [66] Dr. Endeley echoed these themes in elaborating on his demand for full independence, not under the Trusteeship System but under a UN commission with Britain as administrator for another three to five years. In this, he was returning to formulas he had discussed with Foncha, but which he had finally rejected during the previous (Fourteenth) General Assembly session. The most threatening and ardently tribalistic presentation to the committee was made by Mbile, who claimed that his people were "irrevocably [decided] NEVER to accept union with the Cameroun Republic." "If on this we shall have to be killed to the last man," he pledged, "it should rather be better that history records how a race of men died to the man fighting for their freedom." Of course, neither Mbile nor the Balondos physically resisted implementing reunification, but his wild threats did reflect the extent to which the initially unifying idea of reunification had come to reduce politics to its ethnic, almost nativistic foundations in West Cameroon.

IN SUMMARY I would like to note that while all major political factions in both states shared a commitment to the precepts of the modernization ideology, more so for those in East Cameroon, only the militant nationalist grouped into the various factions of the UPC raised the precepts to positions of consummatory values. The UPC militants, and the French-speaking nationalists generally, pursued goals more sharply in conflict with colonial policy than did even the strongest supporters of the Kamerun Idea in the English-speaking areas. The right to be master in their own house was the goal that dominated the motives of the nationalists, and in both areas the theme of reunification was thought to be an instrument to its achievement. Reunification, or the Kamerun Idea that inspired the claim, thus became a tenet in the ideology of self-assertion. It was a more autonomous tenet for the KNDP leadership in British Cameroons; but even for this group it remained a secondary one. As soon as the campaign for home rule achieved some success, it gave way to the more demanding one of determining who would rule at home, which party or faction would command the authoritative institutions established thereby. In both states those who launched the modern nationalist movement and the reunification campaign associated with it were overtaken by events and either denied or displaced from power. One important difference between the two areas was that whereas the militant reunificationists ultimately won power in the English-speaking west, they

[66] Presentation of E. K. Martin to the 1,142nd meeting of the Fourth Committee, UN Official Records, 15th General Assembly.

were totally denied it in the east. This fact, combined with their initially greater distrust for traditional institutions, led the militants in French Cameroon to work for a more profound and perhaps truly revolutionary renovation of indigenous society. In Southern Cameroons the more modernistic leaders from the forest areas were never driven to resort to territorism and rebellion, perhaps because they had enjoyed real power and continued to occupy important positions in the political system, or perhaps because they were less genuinely estranged from the traditional systems. In any case, the westerners of all factions were more nearly like the moderate nationalist in the east, who came late and somewhat ingenuously to embrace the idea of reunification, than they were like the militant UPC leadership, whose frustration could be mollified only in fruitless debates in foreign capitals or in rather aimless violence and sabotage within the country.

⚵ 8 ⚵

The Value System of Means:
The Distribution of Power

MY APPROACH to the aspect of value consensus that concerns the distribution of power among Cameroon political figures is akin to that taken by Apter.[1] Rather than treating the structural characteristics of the society as given, however, or appropriate in any preordained way to particular mixes of instrumental and consummatory objectives, I am proposing here that deep rooted preferences respecting the distribution of power are an important dimension of the value system itself. The fact that the elite groups of the two Cameroons faced the task of building the structures of a new and overarching state makes the dimension especially important in this consideration of the obstacles to integration that would have to be overcome, and helps identify the features of the new system helpful to the integration process. I am concerned, then, with identifying the patterns of conflict, complementarity, and continuity in the values relating to the distribution of power. Was there agreement about the distribution of authority? What distribution of authority did each side or politically important group prefer? Did they all accept a hierarchical distribution, or did some seek something like a pyramidal or segmental distribution?

A hiatus of considerable proportions and significance existed between the values of the major political leaders of the two merging states. There were also important disparities between the values of groups within the two state elites, insofar as the distribution of authority is concerned. These disparities were clearly revealed in the constitutional discussions that preceded federation, and are vaguely evident in the meager discussions of structural form found in the literature of the reunification campaign. The most important characteristic of the difference between the values of the two leadership groups was that one of them—the French-speaking east—desired a tightly centralized federal structure, and the other a loosely structured federation with a real fragmentation of power in something like a pyramidal distribution of power between local, state, and federal levels of authority. Another important aspect of the difference was that the eastern officials had a fairly precise and detailed conception of their structural program for the federation, whereas there was not only disagreement but confusion in the ranks of the westerners.

[1] Apter, *Politics of Modernization,* Chap. 3.

Perhaps the disparities in the constitutional conceptions of the various political groups could have been lessened, or more fully understood and thus perhaps more functional in terms of facilitating knowledgeable choices among structural alternatives, if they had been clarified earlier. Much of the confusion and some of the conflict evident in the constitutional discussions might have resulted from the paucity of concern with such problems explicitly in the early stages of the discussion about reunification. Initial discussions between leaders from the two Territories on the desirability of political union and the means of achieving it perforce concentrated on the organization and popularization of a political campaign. Though the constitutional viewpoints expressed foreshadowed the difference between the French-speaking eastern bias toward a centralized system and that of most westerners for a federal arrangement, the position of each side was incoherent and unstable.[2] The fact is that little attention was given before the plebiscite to such questions, and little time remained after it to consider them.[3]

[2] As we saw above, political groups campaigning for reunification in each territory failed to achieve a united platform or organization. The first KUNC meeting in August 1951 did not elaborate a detailed program, but did seem to opt for a federal system given its demand for a separate House of Assembly in each sector. The UPC advocated at its own second congress in the summer of 1952, and at the second KUNC in December 1951, a unitary structure with a single legislative assembly for the whole country. The latter program was akin to one advocated by Dr. Endeley to the 1949 Visiting U.N. Mission, when he called for a joint constituent assembly of leaders from the two Territories in order to elaborate a constitutional system for the reunited Cameroon. Even the KNC, the western successor to the KUNC, advocated a unitary system, through a select committee appointed in 1955 to study the reunification question. It recommended explicitly that the ultimate form be unitary, but initially a quasifederal one. See the Kamerun Society pamphlet, "The Nigerian Constitutional Conference—The Unification Question." President Ahidjo, as a latter-day reunificationist, was even less precise than his western counterparts in specifying his conception of suitable constitutional arrangements. Neither in his maiden speech as prime minister nor his first progress report (see Prime Minister Ahidjo, *Discourse d'Investiture*, 18 February 1958 and his *Communication a l'Assemblée Legislative*, 18 October 1958) did he mention modalities for union, though he placed himself firmly in the camp of reunificationists on these occasions.

[3] The terms of the union of the Cameroon states might have remained undefined prior to the plebiscite unless the pressures of the campaign itself, and of the Administering Authority of Southern Cameroons had not pressed Prime Minister Foncha to make his intentions clear to the voters. The development of the reunification idea itself had the effect, if not the objective, of elaborating and refining the constitutional structures of the Nigerian federation, and thus of Southern Cameroon's position within it. Thus it was easy to predict the status of the territory within Nigeria —it would be a full region with the rights and duties of the other regions. Endeley and the CPNC procured from the Nigerian leadership statements detailing these features, but in no way changing them from what applied to the other regions. See

169

It may be that KNDP opinion on constitutional arrangements was divided, for its own propaganda was a source of confusion about these aspects of reunification.[4] It is certain that they perceived and feared the divergent views of leaders in other parties. Consequently they called an "All-Party Conference" for Southern Cameroons leaders in Bamenda, near Foncha's hometown, in late June, just before the official constitutional conference with eastern leaders. Foncha's aim was to elaborate a well thought out set of proposals to present to the eastern delegation, proposals which might replace those of the Republic, which some participants insist had already been secretly submitted to him.[5] For some unexplained reason, however, Foncha chose not to reveal the nature of the eastern proposals.[6] Perhaps he feared revelation of the disparities between the type of system proposed by Ahidjo and those promised in the KNDP plebiscite propaganda, which might be politically costly at a time when he needed to speak from a position of strength, or even worse, which might provoke the opposition parties to revive their demands for partition or some other action compromising to the impending union or to his rule.[7] In any case, the proposals his government submitted to the all-

the official plebiscite pamphlet published for the UN Plebiscite Commission by the Administering Authority, *The Two Alternatives.* In an effort to counter the CPNC propaganda with their own describing the constitutional position the Territory would enjoy in a Cameroon state, Foncha and advisers met with President Ahidjo and members of his government on four occasions during the latter months of 1960. They came to a vague general agreement that the union should be federal and loose, with a minimum number of items subject to federal authority, including (1) public freedoms, (2) nationality, (3) national defense, (4) foreign affairs, (5) immigration and emigration, (6) higher education, (7) postal and telecommunications services, and (8) the federal budget. See *Two Alternatives.*

[4] Differing versions of the Foncha-Ahidjo agreements were published by the KNDP and by other sources. The version published by the Administering Authority (cf. *Two Alternatives*) did not match one published by the opposition party press (see *Cameroons Champion,* November 12, 1960), nor that published in the pro-KNDP press (see *Kamerun Times,* January 20, 1960) nor any KNDP pamphlets. The party versions came closest to each other, and were most unlike the "official" plebiscite version, especially concerning provisions for guarantees of civil rights and liberties, "second stage" powers for the federal government, merger of the legal systems, and the resolution of disputes between the states.

[5] This was claimed separately and independently by Ndeh Ntumazah in an interview with me in Accra, December 1963, and by Moussa Yaya, political secretary of the UC, interview, Yaounde, June 1963.

[6] Foncha insists that the proposals had not been submitted to him prior to the Bamenda conference, only that he had a copy of the Republic's constitution (on which the federal proposals were modeled). Interview, Yaounde, August 1965.

[7] Despite earlier demands for partition of the Territory the opposition leadership had reconciled itself with the government by the time of the Bamenda conference. Endeley refrained from attending the conference lest his presence impede progress

170

party conference failed to prepare the delegates for the shock that awaited them at the constitutional conference held a month later in the lovely highlands town of Foumban.

THE proposals submitted to the Bamenda conference by the government party reflected the spirit of its earlier pronouncements and the general values of westerners concerning the allocation of power and prerogative. They envisioned a parliamentary democracy at state and federal levels, with the federal government endowed with a bicameral legislature of limited powers.[8] The executive was to be weak, headed by a president of largely ceremonial functions and limited in his actions by the requirement to act with the agreement of his ministers who in turn would be chosen from and responsible to parliament. Protection for state interests derived from (1) quota allotments of ministerial portfolios to residents of each state; (2) provision for a presidential veto over federal legislation having a discriminatory or harmful effect on the citizens of one of the states; and (3) a federal tribunal which would arbitrate all disputes between the states or between one of them and the federal government. A supreme court could eventually "coordinate" the two legal systems (not necessarily "unify" them, as stated in the Administering Authority's version of the Foncha-Ahidjo agreements). All matters not specifically allocated to the federal government were to come under state jurisdiction.

There were also some points of divergence between these proposals and earlier KNDP pronouncements, occasioned in part by the greater de-

toward a common program; Deputy Leader Mbile pledged the cooperation of the CPNC, but exclaimed, "nobody has ever been asked to give cooperation in the dark." There was considerable criticism of Foncha for conducting his discussions with the Republic's government in secret. Such procedures aroused suspicion and inspired continued apprehension about the impending union. The CPNC argued at Bamenda, for example, that the people of Southern Cameroons should not be "incapacitated forever by the results of the plebiscite." Though they were equally disturbed by the secrecy of the Foncha-Ahidjo discussions, the leaders of the OK tried to consolidate support for the plebiscite results. They cited the widespread rumors that Foncha and Ahidjo were in serious disagreement and argued that they must concentrate on resolving *that* disagreement. Declaring Southern Cameroons independent was out of the question. "We cannot declare sovereignty because we cannot assert it and defend it," stated Ntumazah. "When the Kamerunian people opted for . . . reunification . . . it was complete and entire . . . there was never a condition attached thereto." See *Record of the All Party Conference on the Constitutional Future of the Southern Cameroons.*

[8] KNDP, "Constitutional Proposals of the Government Party," in *Record of the Bamenda Conference.* All quotes and references to discussions of the conference are taken from this source.

tail demanded at this time. For the first time there appeared a list of powers which would initially continue to concern the states, but which would at a "second stage" accrue to the federal authorities, powers that concerned economic and foreign relations matters, for the most part.[9] Inclusion of such items in a list of federal powers in surprising only by virtue of the allocation of many of them to the list of state (regional) powers in the Nigerian Federation (on the constitution, of which all the Southern Cameroons' proposals were modeled). The most conspicuous example concerned external loans and financial aid for a state.[10] Significant changes from earlier proposals were also made respecting the list of powers initially to be assumed by the federal government; these were considerably broadened.[11]

The KNDP proposals reveal great concern for autonomous powers for the states in the federation. Fourteen of the clauses in the constitution were to be "entrenched" (as in the Nigerian constitution), in order to make their amendment exceedingly difficult, and impossible without the concurrence of two-thirds of the members of each state parliament, or a majority of votes cast in a referendum in each state. No powers were to be exercised "concurrently" by federal and state governments, a feature Foncha thought would weaken the federation, but which actually strengthened it, due to the preponderance of powers allocated to the federal level. In many other respects the states were to remain nearly autonomous.[12]

THE serious differences in the points of view of political factions in Southern Cameroons regarding the constitutional order for the federa-

---

[9] Included in the "second stage" list were (a) trade agreements (a provision later withdrawn by Foncha, implying he intended this to remain a state responsibility); (b) development planning and the direction of economic policy; (c) statistics; (d) weights and measures; (e) technical assistance; (f) external finance; (g) federal transport facilities; and (h) taxation for federal expenditures and customs regime.

[10] Nigeria Federal Act No. 20, 1963 (Constitution of the Federal Republic of Nigeria 1963—not significantly changed from the earlier Act) Schedule I, section 69, item 5, for example, permits the regions to borrow externally for a period of less than 12 months on the security of any funds or assets of that Regional government held outside Nigeria.

[11] The following were added: (a) responsibility for external security; (b) federal information services; (c) scientific research; (d) civil aviation and meteorology; (f) all services relating to items mentioned in this schedule of powers. A system of federal-state nationality was included, and federal jurisdiction restricted to defining the character and consequences of "federal nationality."

[12] The states were to have their own military forces, legal systems, public services, and revenue sources. Traditional rulers were to be recognized by both federal and state authorities.

tion all concerned the status of the states in the new federation. They expanded from and deepened the cracks and crevices in the commitment to the Kamerun Idea among the westerners. But more important, they reflected the gaps in the westerners' understanding of the nature of federalism. Many western political leaders found it difficult to conceive of the new reunified state as a single nation-state; their image of the federation shifted from that to one of a loose league between two states. Their problem is rooted in the perplexities of the federal idea, perplexities that have troubled political thinkers since the French political philosopher Bodin elaborated the idea of sovereignty, the hallmark of the modern state, but a notion which is made to fit that of federalism only with some strain.[13]

Three types of issues reveal the dilemmas these leaders faced as they attempted to structure the federal union—(1) legal procedures and structures for the transition; (2) citizenship; and (3) provision for legal secession of states.

As much a confrontation of confused forces as the crumbling of consensus, the discussion of procedures for the transition from the termination of Trusteeship for Southern Cameroons to the new reunified Cameroon revolved around the new ambiguities, not only of the KNDP proposals, but of the legal implications of the plebiscite. Despite the straightforward language of the plebiscite questions, the meaning of the results was not clear. Presumably something called "sovreignty" was to pass out of the jurisdiction of Great Britain (or the United Nations, or both) on October 1, 1961, but to where?

The government party proposed that sovereignty pass to a special temporary body of representatives from each state, chosen in numbers roughly proportional to their population ratios. This body would exercise

[13] "Sovereignty" as conceived by Jean Bodin, *Six Books of the Commonwealth* [1576], abridged and translated by M. J. Tooley (Oxford: B. Blackwell, 1955), is the power to legislate (make law) for the whole community. Federalism involves the idea of plural loci of ultimate authority. Bodin believed that the state had come to embody the "supreme power over citizens and subjects, unrestrained by law" and that there were no mixed states where such power was divided. One state never truly shared sovereign power with another; sovereignty was made to reside in some one place—parliament, king, or the people. Yet Bodin had great difficulty in applying his ideas to specific cases. When he examined the Swiss Confederation, for example, he couldn't decide whether it represented one state or a league of several. Others concerned with sovereignty, the state, and federalism were able to view the Swiss case with greater coherence. See Carl Friedrich's discussion of Johannus Althusius, in Arthur Whitter MacMahon's *Federalism, Mature and Emergent* (Garden City, N.Y.: Doubleday, 1955). For one of the best modern studies of federalism see K. C. Wheare, *Federal Government*, 3d ed. (London: Oxford University Press for the Royal Institute of International Affairs, 1935).

the powers of a parliament until elections could be held for a national assembly. But it was not clear whether the constitution that the conference was attempting to draw up would regulate the activities of the transitional body. Did the transition refer to a period between the end of extant constitutional statutes and the inauguration of new ones, or merely to that period, after the birth of the new order required to fully implement the provisions of the new constitution? One fact that complicated the discussions was the shortness of time remaining before Trusteeship would terminate—three months. It was not clear that full agreement could be reached with the eastern leadership and the legal language worked out by that time. Thus the government's preference to install an interim body appeared to offer a way around the obstacle; yet some delegates wondered what would be the use of their efforts at constitution-making if they were not to bind the interim body. What assurances could be given that the interim structures would not elaborate a new constitution along different lines? Should Cameroon leaders fail to produce a final constitutional document by October, advised the attorney general (an expatriate official soon to leave the territory), the existing laws and institutions would continue in force. This answer satisfied few delegates since it was evident that the existing institutions failed to provide for a central government between the two states. If time was too short to permit a final version of the permanent constitution, how much shorter still was that available to devote to the determination of interim arrangements? The problem was to find a way of achieving a known, agreed-upon and stable distribution of power between the existing state structures and a new central government.

It was the unspoken consensus of the conference that their work concerned both the interim and permanent constitutions, but this did not eliminate confusion over procedures for the interim period. The dilemma of federalism was at the heart of the confusion. The One Kamerun Movement delegation, for example, suggested that neither the existing Southern Cameroons legislature nor any "interim body" had a mandate to establish a "sovereign" transitional body for the new federation. Could the interim body enter into agreements with foreign powers which would bind later federal institutions, for example? The attorney general insisted that the transitional arrangements must enjoy sovereignty: "You have got to have sovereignty somewhere . . . you have got to have somebody capable of entering into foreign relations . . . and trade agreements," he stated. But some delegates thought this would make the interim body stronger than they intended the final federal government to be, because to them federalism implied divided powers distributed between the existing state structures and the new central ones. A federal arrangement with "sovereignty somewhere" seemed to threaten elimination of the existing states, an eventuality that would betray all the promises made during the reunification campaign and amount to the handing over of Southern Cameroons to the Republic, in the words of a One Kamerun delegate, "like a sop to Cerberus." [14]

The logical basis of the OK's insistence on the lack of a mandate for the creation of a "sovereign" interim body was their firm belief that the constitution for the federation must be discussed and approved by the general public in some kind of referendum. "The Kamerun people all told cannot abdicate their democratic responsibilities to others," they stated. Behind the rhetoric was not only a commitment to the idea of popular sovereignty, but the tactical objective to prohibit the strengthening of power in the hands of President Ahidjo whom the OK leadership, as the closest western affiliate of the UPC, despised. The near failure of the constitutional program of Ahidjo in April 1960 probably inspired the OK leaders to believe that the inauguration of federalism in Cameroon would decentralize power and lessen the hold of the Ahidjo regime, by giving the people a new chance to discuss and vote on the constitution. [15]

The other parties, with less clear anti-Ahidjo tactical objectives, but with some belief in the requirements of popular sovereignty, thought they could circumvent the problems spelled out by the OK by stipulating that the representative delegations to the interim body would be selected from and by the existing legislatures, which already enjoyed representative legitimacy. This was the view of the CPNC, for example. But the view failed to dispose of the problem of sovereignty, for the only way this could be done required that one consider sovereignty as having passed from the two separate bodies politic to the combined one of the whole Cameroon nation, a moral unity which would be symbolized by the new constitution and given expression through popular consultation. But time was perhaps insufficient for either to come into being.

The fine theoretical distinctions remained inarticulate in the discussions, though their consequences are evident. Most delegates simply felt uneasy about the uncertainty of the transitional period and wished to de-

---

[14] *Record of Bamenda Conference,* p. 65.

[15] The Cameroon constitution submitted to a public vote in February 1960 failed to carry a majority of the voters in 10 of the 21 electoral districts, all of which were located in the Southern areas formerly influenced by the UPC. See Le Vine, *Cameroons,* p. 224.

fine as precisely and narrowly as possible the powers of the central government, transitional as well as permanent. Most of the delegates shared the view of OK leader Ndeh Ntumazah, that the interim government should have only caretaker powers. If such were to be the case, however, there was no reason to have proportional representation between the two states on the transitional body. Since each state would have an equal stake in the local implementation of constitutional agreements reached between them prior to federation, each should be equally represented. Thus the KNDP later changed its proposals to accord with this principle. The KNDP would also insist that legislative acts of the transitional body require specific reenactment by the first regularly elected national assembly in order for them to remain in force. As we shall see below, little of the letter or the spirit of the provisions for the interim period would characterize it in fact.

THE issues of the dilemma that confronted the Bamenda conference—to create one new superstate, or link two existing ones in a collaborative alliance—was explicitly revealed in the discussions on the question of citizenship in the federation. The discussion produced, or revealed, a conflict of viewpoints, perhaps reflecting underlying values, which could not be resolved at the conference.

The government party proposed that dual citizenship be confered on the indigenous inhabitants of the federal territory, that is, both state and federal governments would have the authority to enact legislation defining citizenship requirements, benefits, and obligations. This suggestion was in keeping with the earlier Ahidjo-Foncha agreements which had stated, "Nationals of the Federation States will enjoy Cameroon nationality." Purely practical reasons lay behind the government party proposals, and the viewpoints of most delegates, concerning how to properly identify West or East Cameroonians for their respective state level elections, or for service in federal agencies where state quotas might be involved. However, the provision for dual citizenship raised questions that in their import went far beyond the practical considerations to touch on the very basis of the commitment to the Kamerun Idea.

Viewed as a whole, the issue returned the conference to the problem of stabilizing the elusive compound of the ideas of sovereignty and federalism. The attorney general, with the above wording of the Ahidjo-Foncha agreement in mind, argued for dual citizenship as if the will of the two states, as moral collectivities, rather than that of the whole "Kamerun people," was what gave birth to the federation. In this light, it seemed

176

clear that "in order to be a Cameroonian citizen it is necessary first to be a national of one of the [two] states." The implications of the argument did not escape the opposition party leader, Motomby Woleta, who stated that the argument meant that each citizen would belong to two nations instead of one. Would the Cameroon be one nation indivisible or not? The issue has a long history in the life and evolution of federalism.[16]

The Bamenda conference left the many questions raised or suggested

[16] The experience of the United States of America with federalism involved the same issue. Those who argue that the birth of (in effect, the legitimacy of) the American union is derived from an act of will on the part of the uniting states suggest that sovereignty was and remains divided between the states and the central government. The proponents of this view find it difficult, nonetheless, to accommodate the idea that the federal government is truly "sovereign" (free from limitations imposed by state action), even respecting powers explicitly designated as federal in the Constitution. Throughout the history of the American federation this viewpoint has consistently been used to justify "states rights" in interference with federal action. The implication of such a position is that the union is not real, that is, generative of a unit, but is rather a form of cooperation among the several states on specific matters of mutual concern. For an excellent account of the early debates on this issue see Alpheus T. Mason's *The States Rights Debate* (New York: Prentice-Hall, 1964), esp. pp. 27–55.

The opposite approach supposes that the union was effected by the will of the collective community, by "the whole American people." This is the notion of "popular sovereignty," one that preserves the conception of sovereignty as a singular and unitary attribute located in one place—with "the people." Both the federal and state governments derive their legitimacy, their right to "exercised sovereign powers," from this common source. This notion was made judicially secure as early as John Marshall's opinion written for the Supreme Court majority in *McCullough v. Maryland*. See Robert G. McCloskey, *The American Supreme Court* (Chicago: University of Chicago Press, 1960), pp. 66–67. The option avoids rather than settles the question of the compatibility of federalism with the classic idea of sovereignty, for although it respects the integrity of the latter as a principle, by way of dividing the right of the exercise thereof, nothing in the approach guarantees the stability of this division. As need for government action changes and society becomes more complex, the burden of action generally shifts to the central authority, which comes to exercise, as it has in the United States, the preponderant share of the rights of sovereignty. See E. A. Corwin, "The Passing of Dual Federalism," in Robert G. McCloskey, ed., *Essays in Constitutional Law* (New York: Vintage, 1957), pp. 158–210. This has been so in the U.S. even with respect to the question of the source, definition, and consequences of citizenship. Initially the U.S. constitution did not define national citizenship, and it was generally assumed that it was because of the citizenship rights conferred by or embodied in the states. It became clear in the aftermath of the Dred Scott decision (which asserted that neither the states nor the federal government had been authorized to confer citizenship on Negroes, of slave or free background), that in this, as in so many other instances, the viability of the union required that standards be set at the national level for and by the whole community. See John H. Ferguson and Dean E. McHenry, *The American Federal Government* (New York: McGraw-Hill, 1953), p. 197. The Constitution was amended to define citizenship for the states and the nation.

177

by the issue of dual nationality unanswered and the conflict of values un-resolved. The KNDP retained the original wording of its proposals, but in doing so merely postponed the problem to the later constitutional con-ference, where this indecision would place the West Cameroon delega-tion at a serious disadvantage vis-à-vis their eastern compatriots.

THE conference discussions raised the same issues in connection with the question of the possible secession of a state in the federation, whether provision should be made for legally and unilaterally doing so. Inclusion in the constitution of such a provision would reduce the basis of the col-laboration between the states to that of the lowest denominator of their interest, granting the states a veto, in effect, over federal action and ren-dering the union impotent. It would make of the federation a league rath-er than an independent state.

Some of the proponents of legal secession, especially the CPNC dele-gates, erroneously thought that other federations contain effective provi-sion for legal secession.[17] Although the exact wording of the proposal is not known, it would appear that the form in which it was put forward at Bamenda, if adopted, would have nullified its intent. The CPNC sought to add a provision for "right of secession" to the clauses that were to be placed in the constitution. These clauses would require a two-thirds ma-jority vote in every legislative body in the federation, both federal and state; the attorney general considered that this voting procedure would apply to the process of legalizing the act of secession also. Under such circumstances, of course, "secession" would be no different than volun-tary dissolution of the federation or renunciation of sovereignty over a portion thereof, if successful, and if pursued despite the lack of appropri-ate legislative backing, would no longer be a "legal" act but rather one of civil war or treason.

The real issues turn not on the technicalities of what is or is not appro-priate or legal in a federal union, but on the question, what were the in-tentions of these uniting parties? Did they or did they not mean to create a united Cameroon? The prime minister, who on many occasions had re-vealed a reluctance to take his people into full and final union with those of the Republic and who thus may have desired some constitutional pro-

---

[17] Head of the CPNC delegation, Nerius Mbile, specifically mentioned the Mali Federation constitution, but in this he was mistaken. Only the Soviet federal consti-tution provides for legal secession, but the provision is rendered a dead letter by the control of the Communist Party over the governments and societies of the states. The Soviet system is generally considered quasi-federal. See Wheare, *Federal Gov-ernment*, pp. 85–87.

178

vision such as that proposed by Mbile, nevertheless appreciated the delicacy of the situation and the likely negative reaction among "brother" East Cameroonians. Foncha sought to avoid the impression that he considered the union to be less than permanent. Mbile, on the other hand, explicitly stated his belief that Southern Cameroon's commitment to union, embodied in the plebiscite vote, was not permanent; the people there had not been "incapacitated forever and . . . tied hand and foot to that alternative." His values in this respect were directly opposed to those of the One Kamerun Movement. The KNDP, perhaps with embarrassment, sided with the OK.

There were a number of other items on which various delegates or parties disagreed initially, but which disagreements they were able to resolve to their mutual satisfaction. All parties agreed that the federal president's responsibilities should be almost exclusively ceremonial, but there was some temporary disagreement on the most appropriate means of selecting the president. All parties rallied to Foncha's suggestion that the president be elected by popular vote. All agreed that there should be a "head of state" for West Cameroon, a position considered to be the successor to the high commissioner, but in reality a redundant post. Failing to clarify the need for or the powers of such a post, all parties nevertheless agreed to have the president appoint him on the advice of the prime minister. There was a dearth of clear thinking about the appropriateness of a provision permitting the states to initiate and conclude trade and military agreements with foreign powers. Mixed in with this issue was the related one of determining what the condition of being "outside the French Union and the Commonwealth of Nations" really meant; this was a condition vigorously proffered by the KNDP. Were the military and financial aid ties between the Republic and France in violation of this condition? If not, shouldn't West Cameroon have its own similar arrangements? Discussion weaved in and out of the dilemmas already considered above but the parties did reach agreement. All parties asserted the right of the states to initiate treaties and conventions with foreign powers, though they seemed willing to accept the attorney general's opinion that any such agreements would require approval of the appropriate federal authorities to be valid.[18]

[18] The principles and practices of international law prohibit substate prerogatives in foreign affairs. Such provisions would have denied to federal Cameroon the accepted prerequisites for membership in the international community. Even where federal constitutions permit the regional governments independent powers respecting the ratification of treaties (such as Canada), these are negative powers only, the power not to ratify. The regions have no powers to conclude foreign treaties on their own, and when regions may refuse to ratify a treaty negotiated and properly ratified

The OK was more vehement than the other parties in its insistence that "Kamerun" be absolutely unaligned internationally.

All the delegates agreed that the union ought to serve the most pressing needs of West Cameroon for general economic development, but they were sometimes rather far apart and often confused about the best way to realize this common objective. The KNDP initially proposed restricting all federal expenditures to services directly under the control of federal authorities, provision which would have prohibited federal subsidies to the states. The curious nature of the proposal is evident when considering the experience of Southern Cameroons in the Nigerian Federation, where it received very little federal financial assistance and almost always less than its just due.[19] Indeed, it was this experience which Foncha and other exponents of reunification had used to such great political advantage, so much so that even the opposition party was willing to point out the KNDP's error. It is equally curious, however, that in doing so Motomby Woleta linked his proposition of federal support for state activities with one for a 50-50 split between the two states in revenue support to the federal budget. A member of his own party pointed out that such a provision would be highly discriminatory against West Cameroon, given the severe disparity in the economic resources of the two states. Woleta's initial objective seems to have been to secure a stronger basis for a 50-50 division in the membership of the federal legislature. The KNDP position paper actually submitted to the constitutional conference at Foumban contained no reference to any of these proposals.

The legal community of West Cameroon was not involved directly in the Bamenda conference, but its advice, through a newly organized bar association, was solicited on a number of unresolved questions. In fact, the bar association rendered opinions and suggestions on almost the entire range of the KNDP constitutional proposals. In doing so it revealed a significant disparity in objectives and values between the legal community and the political party leadership.[20] They made a number of sugges-

by the central government, that government is still held responsible by the International Community for the proper execution of the treaty even if it involves the recalcitrant region. See Herbert W. Briggs, *The Law of Nations* (New York: Appleton-Century-Crofts, 1952), p. 889.

[19] See Great Britain, Command 9026; Phillipson, *Report;* and Andersen, *Report on the Economic Aspects of Reunification.*

[20] It is not clear to what extent the bar association recommendations reflect the indigenous Cameroonian legal community. The association's membership was about 35 at the time, but only 12 were Cameroonians. Their report, Minutes of the Emergency Meeting, Southern Cameroons Bar Association, July 12, 1961, does not indicate which of its members actually shaped the proposals.

tions about the judicial system which can be considered technical and not necessarily in conflict with the views of the politicians, but they differed from the KNDP in suggesting that the top federal tribunal have original jurisdiction in the review of legislation discriminatory to the interests of one or more states. Also, the courts and not the president should decide if legislation violated the constitution. Also, this tribunal, or a separate supreme court, should coordinate and not simply link the two legal systems. A federal high court was called for, which would have full civil and criminal jurisdiction on appeals from the magistrates courts in each state, having the effect of incorporating into the federal court system the existing high court of the state. These proposals would have had the effect of making the federal union more real and more far-reaching than the KNDP envisioned, insofar as the judicial process was concerned, though less threatening to the British legal tradition as such.[21]

It is important to note that the disparity of views between the political and legal communities was of relatively little consequence since not one of the bar association's suggestions was taken seriously enough by the government party to be incorporated into the proposals they presented to the Foumban conference. Perhaps there was not enough time; the two meetings occurred only a week apart. In addition, the KNDP did make a few slight modifications in its proposals between the Bamenda and Foumban conferences, which had the effect of bringing their views closer to those of the bar association, though they were probably made before the bar association met.[22]

The basis for the differences in values among West Cameroonians was not simply a difference in the extent to which various leaders and groups believed in Cameroon or the Kamerun Idea, though this certainly was a factor of some importance and clearly marked off the OK leadership from the rest. Only they consistently differed, if sometimes only slightly, with the prevalent desire for a union so loosely joined and decentralized

[21] The bar association strengthened the place of the separate legal traditions from what would result from the KNDP proposals by suggesting that the high court, when hearing appeals on cases between citizens of a particular state or different states, always have a majority of judges from the state in which the case originated. The KNDP initially envisioned a stable, evenly divided membership in the top federal appellate court, but later dropped the proposal.

[22] The KNDP withdrew reference to evenly divided membership on the federal supreme court, modified its demand for the jury system in criminal trials to require this only when it could be implemented, and amended its reference to linking the two legal systems by stating instead: "There shall be no alternation of the legal system without reference to the state electorate." This can be interpreted as a more rigorous defense of the existing system than given by the bar association.

as to approximate nonunion. Only they insisted that the federation come into force immediately without any "transitional body." They opposed allocation of federal ministries or any other federal posts on a quota basis, and they would have the president remain in office so long as he enjoyed the support of the people, despite the fact that the most likely occupant of that post was a man they thoroughly despised. They opposed dual nationality and in this were joined by the opposition party, and they opposed as well any provision for legal secession, in which they were joined by the government party. Even so, the One Kamerun Movement gave its support to the bulk of the KNDP suggestions at the Bamenda conference. The CPNC did likewise, despite the fact that only they openly expressed the view that federalism was not the ideal constitutional format for the country: "The ideal constitution for a country of the size, population and resources as the one envisaged is unitary." Motomby Woleta's newspaper, usually an outlet for the CPNC point of view, specifically denounced federalism, ironically on the Fourth of July, by calling it "an expensive venture . . . to the detriment of the common man and a mockery to democracy." As a single unitary state Cameroon would be strong and capable of raising "one common army against any foe. . . . But divided [through federalism] I wonder if we shall not remain in perpetual servitude." [23]

The discontinuities in political values should be measured principally in terms of the disparity, not in their general belief in Kamerun, but in their view of how power should be distributed in it. Foncha and the KNDP—whose positions had generally fallen somewhere between those of the CPNC and the OK, the former willing to remain within Nigeria and the latter ardently supporting the reunification idea—found themselves on opposite ends of the spectrum when it came to their willingness to accept a hierarchical distribution of power. Indeed, much of the thrust of Foncha's long political career came from his demand for greater power, almost absolute power, not only for Southern Cameroons but for the grassfields area within it. His was the most parochial outlook of all those of the major political figures; in keeping with the tradition of spokesmen of local interests, he argued for strong local governments in a pyramidal structure of power. His view of the new Cameroon was illusory. The spokesman for the opposition party was quick to penetrate the protective shell of self-deception with which the KNDP had cloaked itself

[23] *Cameroons Champion,* July 4, 1961. Recall, however, those CPNC proposals discussed above, which suggest a union more decentralized than that envisaged by the KNDP.

by stating in his opening speech to the Bamenda conference that federalism had the "great advantage over the other [forms of government] of preventing the stunning impact of reunification, but to be realistic it will only act as cushion to minimize the inevitable collision [between the] opposite" cultures of the two uniting territories.

THE political values of the East and West Cameroon elites were different and often conflicting. They collided in the official constitutional conference held in mid-July 1961 in the pine-forested, artistically and historically rich capital of the Bamoun Sultanate. The collision was inevitable, although the Eastern government and the regal host and patron of the reunification movement—El Hadj Seidou Njoya Njimouluh, Sultan of the Bamoun—went to great lengths to obscure and cushion it. The KNDP's fragile and illusory world of dreams was shattered in the aftermath, though its leaders were not altogether aware of it at the time.

The atmosphere in which the conference convened was one of uninhibited gaiety and celebration. The full splendor of the ancient though relatively recently Islamized kingdom was proudly displayed to the 25 delegates from West Cameroon and 12 from East Cameroon. Colorful squadrons of Bamoun warriors, frenzied and untiring dancers performing the explosively happy yet controlled dances that are the ancestors of the "watusi" and the "frug," driving rhythms and a permeating clangor from a variety of drums and bush xylophones—these built up a festive façade ill-fitting to the grave body of work the conference was called on to do.

The leaders of both delegations opened the conference on notes of caution, realism, and a spirit of family. They stressed their commitment to a federal form of government.[24] Their purpose, according to President Ahidjo, was neither to propound abstract theories of government nor to construct an ideal state. They had only a "restricted margin in which to work if we wish that our institutions should answer to our needs," he argued; thus only a federal system would be appropriate in light of the linguistic, administrative, economic, and cultural differences between the two regions. Foncha echoed these themes in asserting that they required, and federalism offered, a system which would "keep the two cultures in the areas where they now operate and . . . blend them in the centre." He went on to express the hope that ultimately an indigenous culture

---

[24] West Cameroon, *Record of the Conference on the Constitutional Future of the Southern Cameroons, held at Foumban, 17th to 21st July, 1961*. All subsequent references to the Foumban discussions are taken from this source unless otherwise indicated.

would evolve to replace those inherited from colonialism, but that in the interim they needed to accommodate the differences, thus whatever might happen to the cultures, "we will keep the form of government [federal] now envisaged." It would appear, however, that Foncha's ample use of the royal we when refering to the commitment to federalism was premature and overoptimistic, for the commitment was not shared by his eastern compatriots.

Once the preliminary courtesies and anxious affirmations of familial respect for each other were disposed of, it became clear that most of the preliminary discussion among westerners had been in vain and that the Bamenda conference had not prepared the delegation to deal intelligently with the comprehensive and starkly different set of propositions advanced by the host government. The western delegates decided that they would have to meet by themselves to consider the eastern proposals point by point and attempt to form a position about them. In short, they had to repeat the Bamenda conference all over again. The process took much longer than any of them expected, nearly the whole of the five days during which the conference lasted. In fact, the official conference of both delegations meeting together lasted only an hour and 35 minutes.

The western delegates were hampered by two problems during these discussions which ultimately prevented them from articulating a satisfactory compromise with the eastern officials productive of a federal structure more loyal to their own values: the severity of the disparity in their conception of the federation, and their contradictions in the West Cameroon position reflecting continued failure to understand the basis of that disparity.

WE HAVE SEEN that the West Cameroon delegates anticipated a loose federation with a diminutive and weak government at the center, and robust states endowed with nearly every power they had formerly exercised. This vision and the values that inspired and nourished it could not have contrasted more with what the Ahidjo regime proposed and achieved at the Foumban conference and a few secretive discussions which followed.

That the federal government of Ahidjo's vision would be anything but weak and diminutive is revealed in a cursory examination of the list of federal prerogatives included in his set of proposals. The list contained 15 items that did not appear in the KNDP proposals, five of which were subjects over which the federal authorities would gain jurisdiction immediately following federation.[25] The remaining items were contained in a list of "second stage federal powers," which would remain under state jurisdiction until the federal authorities chose to take them over.[26] A number of powers which Westerners envisioned as "second stage" federal powers were placed in the "first stage" list in Ahidjo proposals; three of them concerned matters that would prove to be of great importance to West Cameroon and to entail serious problems in the adjustment of its people to the new conditions. The matters in question are jurisdiction over trade agreements with foreign countries, development planning and control of the economy, and foreign technical and financial assistance. In other instances the westerners anticipated much more narrow federal jurisdiction over certain matters than were provided for by Ahidjo. This was true of the question of nationality, for example, concerning which the westerners, as we have seen, desired dual federal-state nationality status. They wished to restrict federal authority to the definition of federal nationality. Similarly, as concerns security questions, they desired to limit federal jurisdiction to protection of the federal state from external threats only; consequently they sought to drop the item "maintenance of law and order" from the list of federal responsibilities in Ahidjo's proposals.

The western delegates, led by opposition spokesmen, repeated much of the Bamenda conference discussion of the powers of the president. In order to cut the strong presidency proposed by Ahidjo down to the size of the ceremonial figure they had envisioned at Bamenda, the West Cameroonians sought to limit the president's discretionary powers to a few items (not spelled out), to limit his prerogatives in questions of clemency to the advice of a council of the magistracy and to tie his exercise of all other powers to the accord of his ministers. Inadvertently they thus sought to continue the system of the Republic, a system Ahidjo intended to transform. One important difference between the federation projected in the discussions of the westerners and the Republic was that in the former the president would be elected by direct popular ballot and would be

[25] These powers, listed in Article 5 of the federal constitution, are: (a) rules governing the condition of aliens; (b) rules governing legal disputes; (c) responsibility for the maintenance of law and order; (d) protection of the internal and external security of the Federation; (e) telecommunications.

[26] These powers, listed in Article 6, cover the following jurisdictional areas: (a) the status of persons and property; (b) obligations and contracts in civil and commercial matters; (c) rules governing the judicature, including rules of procedure for and the competence of all courts; (d) penal law; (e) control of currency; (f) prison administration; (g) labor legislation; (h) public health; (i) primary, secondary and technical education; (j) administrative services.

185

eligible for reelection only once, and in the latter by the national assembly with no restrictions on reelection.

There were a number of important differences in the views of the two elites concerning powers of the states in the federation. Reconciliation was needed in two broad areas, state executive functions and state legislative functions. With respect to the executive, Foncha had originally proposed that there be a "head of state" at this level, but the activities he envisioned for the post were ones Ahidjo thought the federal head of state could carry out. Foncha therefore substituted the president in this role. This arrangement would empower the president to dissolve the state assembly under certain conditions.[27] Other powers of the federal president in state-level government included authorization to promulgate the state laws, to call for a second reading on bills he thought inappropriate, or to repeal a state bill he deemed to violate the terms of the constitution. With respect to the legislature, the westerners were quick to amend Ahidjo's proposal for a unicameral state assembly. This would have eliminated the western House of Chiefs, an institution Ahidjo agreed to retain and guarantee in the constitution.[28] Of course, the westerners desired a much wider range of legislative powers for the state parliament, but the extensive list of federal prerogatives preempted this.

The western contingent sharply disagreed with the Republic's proposals concerning the judicial system. Foncha's plebiscite propaganda had promised that the English legal system would be preserved, at least in the west, and he now wanted this guaranteed by the constitution. But it was not so guaranteed. Instead, the responsibility for the entire judicial system in the federation was allotted to federal authorities, with the sole ex-

[27] In the case of persistent discord between the legislature and the state executive branch, or in case of a successful "no confidence" or "censure" motion. The CPNC insisted at Foumban that Ahidjo's proposition that a two-thirds majority be required to pass such motions be changed to a "simple majority" and "absolute majority" respectively. Otherwise, they argued, the prime minister could retain his post with the support of only one third plus one of the members of the legislature. Ahidjo rejected this suggestion at Foumban but it had been incorporated by the time the draft was submitted to the Eastern Assembly. There an attempt was made by the government party to reinsert the two-thirds majority provision, but it was defeated.

[28] It appears that this proposal had been made out of ignorance of the western system. Another innocent but important proposal was that which provided for a House of Assembly of only 32 members in the west. Foncha had promised that the House should be expanded to 37 members, to which Ahidjo agreed. Formerly the House had only 26 elected members, but three ex officio and two members appointed to represent special interests.

186

ception that the West Cameroon Customary Courts were to be preserved and regulated by state rules, except for appeals from these courts.

The states would enjoy starkly different powers to assert their collective interests against federal authority according to each of the two sets of proposals. Foncha had long pledged that federal laws discriminatory to the interests of the citizens of either state would be vetoed by the president upon the demand of the appropriate state prime minister.[29] The spirit but certainly not the letter of the pledge was honored by the Ahidjo proposals. The interests of the states could be safeguarded in two ways: laws which violated the constitution could be repealed by the president, and the president, upon the urging of the prime minister concerned, could demand a "second reading" of a federal bill, in which case its passage would require majority support within the contingent of federal deputies from each state. While such a provision might protect the interests of the states, as such, it could not insure the interests of minorities within the states. Such minorities would not likely command a majority of the federal legislative delegation, and in fact might not be represented in it at all, and also would have no opportunity to mobilize sentiment within the state or state assembly. Indeed, the situation that did obtain in the federation during the first few years was akin to this, where Catholic and militant southern minorities in the east, represented in the state assembly by the Démocrates and UPC, had no representation in the federal assembly. Another feature of the Ahidjo proposals which weakened the collective position of the states contrary to West Cameroonian delegates desired was the lack of "entrenched" clauses. Constitutional revisions can be made by a simple "qualified" majority of the federal legislature (comprising majorities of each state delegation). Here again, minority interests are left unprotected, for as few as six deputies from the west and 21 from the east may alter the ground rules of politics and government throughout the whole country. The states are not involved, as such, in the process of constitutional revision.

Constitutional guarantees of individual liberties were another item of controversy among westerners and between them and the eastern delegation. The guarantees concerned a cause Southern Cameroonians considered, not altogether justifiably, lost at Foumban. KNDP pamphlets persistently had pledged: "Human Rights, in accordance with the U.N. Charter will be protected by the Constitution and enforced through the

[29] KNDP, "United Cameroons' Federal Constitution by KNDP," 1960.

courts." [30] Moreover, the constitution of the Cameroun Republic not only embraced the Universal Declaration of Human Rights and the U.N. Charter, but specifically spelled out about 20 principles and rights taken from these. Most western delegates at Foumban wanted to incorporate such guarantees into the constitution, not just mention them in the preamble; they also wanted the courts to repudiate laws that failed to conform to the principles. Ahidjo agreed to include the guarantees in the Constitution, but unlike the terms of the existing constitution or his proposals, and as a mere reference to the UN documents. In the federal constitution Article One states that the Republic "affirms its adherence to the fundamental freedoms" set forth in the UN Declaration and Charter. The leader of the opposition party, Dr. Endeley, later claimed that adopting this procedure had been a great mistake, that it represented a defeat for their position and a difference in their values: "We tried to argue the definite inclusion of the Declaration . . . but they [Ahidjo and possibly Foncha] argued that such things were never written into a constitution." [31] Despite Endeley's pessimism and the evident burden on the courts to establish their own prerogatives with respect to enforcing human and civil rights and liberties, there is no need to consider the Cameroon procedures unworkable.

THE records of the constitutional debates provide little evidence that the western delegates recognized the nature of the disparity between their view of the federation and that of the Ahidjo regime, namely that it involved the difference between a decentralized federation, almost a *con*-federation, and a highly centralized one, almost a *non*-federation. The first view was rooted in a strong desire for power in the hands of the Westerners, and at local levels, wedded to a very real respect for the capacities of the average man to participate in politics. The second reflected a desire for power ordered in a strict hierarchy, with the eastern leadership at the top of a relatively weak state and local governments. Though the leaders were not as far apart in their democratic ideals as Ahidjo's critics assume, the Eastern leadership had come to distrust widespread and genuine mass participation in politics, particularly among the southern peoples so involved with the UPC rebellion.

The debates of the westerners were replete with contradiction. Even

[30] Item 31 of the KNDP pamphlet, "United Cameroons' Constitution." Substantially the same wording appeared in the KNDP proposals to the Bamenda and Foumban conferences.
[31] Endeley interview, Buea, April 1963.

188

where they explicitly involved questions of centralization of power the Western delegates gave little evidence of recognizing the nature of the conflict involved. Most of the items on Ahidjo's list of federal powers that did not appear in their own were nevertheless accepted with little debate; or the debate would concentrate solely on the need to align wording of the eastern proposals with that of the Bamenda discussions, with no debate of the underlying issues.[32]

The opportunity to come to grips with the conflict of values and attitudes between the two delegations was greatest with respect to the question of presidential power. Here, too, the debate failed to make the western delegates achieve a coherent position or a clear idea of their differences with the east. The Southern Cameroons attorney general realized the mixture of uncomplementary features in the position of the Buea delegation and tried to stimulate some basic decisions which would have made it more congruent. He argued that it was "essential" that "certain fundamental political decisions" be made before it would be possible to draft any realistic constitution; they needed to decide on the type of president: "Whether he . . . [is] to be an executive head of government or merely a ceremonial one." The CPNC reiterated its desire for a ceremonial president, but then proposed that the president be elected by universal adult suffrage precisely because of the extensive powers to be accorded him in the Ahidjo version of the constitution. The other delegates rallied to this position, but ironically, on the basis of provisions in the Ahidjo proposals which they subsequently sought to eliminate.

We shall see below that this procedure only purified the system as conceived by Ahidjo rather than attenuating it; Ahidjo quickly accepted the proposition of direct election of the president.

Other revisions the westerners made in the Ahidjo proposals also had a boomerang effect, strengthening rather than weakening the federal government and the federal president. They suggested a "transitional period" of 18 months instead of the 12 they had formerly decided on or the four suggested by Ahidjo. The probable intent of this was to lengthen the period during which the states could continue to exercise the powers

---

[32] The westerners sought to leave education under state jurisdiction, but there was no discussion about why this was important. Even where the potential for federal domination was recognized, such as in the case of a large federal police power, the argument against such provisions was not carried to its logical conclusion. The attorney general warned the delegates against Ahidjo's inclusion in federal powers of the item "maintenance of law and order" and interpreted Ahidjo's intention to be federal control of *all* police forces but failed to say that such an arrangement would be altogether inappropriate to a real federation. *Record, Foumban Conference,* p. 9.

scheduled to become federal ones in the "second stage." In fact, their proposal would have had—in fact did have—the effect of prolonging the period of time during which the president could monopolize the exercise of federal powers, and nothing would have prevented the president from federalizing the second stage powers early on and exercising the powers himself without the control of other federal institutions. The westerners did not anticipate such a possibility because they did not intend the president ever to exercise power unilaterally, during the transitional period or otherwise.[33] During the transition they at first foresaw a "transitional body" equally divided in membership between the two states. Though they accepted Ahidjo's proposal that the president of the Republic automatically become the president of the federation, they decided at Foumban to demand that the two prime ministers and 14 others appointed by the state legislatures constitute the federal government's sole decision-making body during the transitional period. As with every western proposal to limit the powers of the president, Ahidjo dismissed this one outright and agreed instead to an interim arrangement providing for a federal assembly elected on a proportional basis by the two state legislatures. He also rejected an 18-month transitional period, but did settle on one of six months' duration. This resolution of the problem of interim powers failed to accommodate West Cameroon objectives, however, because it left the president with extensive almost undiluted powers, and an interim legislature with no stronger position during the transition than in normal times. And by accepting the role of the president as a functional part of the state-level executive and legislative process, they inadvertently undermined their own proposals for strong states' rights.

PRESIDENT Ahidjo's proposals to the Foumban conference reveal a disparity of political values not only between himself and his followers, on the one hand, and the Western leadership, on the other, but also among various groups of East Cameroonians. The federal union as envisaged by those proposals centralized powers not only more than desired by Foncha and others, but more than had the structures of the first Cameroon Republic, structures about which there had already developed a lively controversy. To appreciate the disparity of political values among the easterners, it is useful to compare Ahidjo's proposed federal arrangements

---

[33] They continued to think in terms of parliamentary democracy, wherein the president's action would be limited to decisions made within the Council of Ministers. As noted, this feature was dropped from Ahidjo's proposals.

with those of the Republic in an effort to identify the innovations for political life in East Cameroon which they embodied.

The most important consequence of federal union for easterners was the establishment of a "presidential system." The new system concentrated power in the hands of the top executive to a greater degree than had been the case in the Republic, through eliminating a bicephalic executive (with a prime minister and president), reducing the role of parliament, and through making the judiciary less independent and civil rights and liberties less secure.

Ahidjo's proposals transformed a parliamentary system into a presidential one by combining the position of head of state with that of head of government. To determine what powers the presidency would gain in this way, it is necessary to consider first the scope of legislative powers within the general list of federal prerogatives. The federation would retain the feature of the Republic's constitution that restricted legislative power to a specific list of prerogatives; all powers not contained in the list would accrue to the presidency. The implications of this procedure were not fully understood by the Southern Cameroons leadership, but were understood all too well by many of Ahidjo's adversaries in East Cameroon. In the new proposals the list of legislative powers of the federal assembly was the same as it had been for the assembly of the First Republic with the exception of only four items. This is surprising, because the federal assembly would operate on only one level of a two-level legislative hierarchy, yet it would be empowered to act in nearly every area in which the Assembly of the Republic, a unitary state, had been empowered to act. This fact alone should have indicated to West Cameroonians and any others who feared a strong center in the new federation that just such an arrangement was in the offing. Moreover, only two of the four items dropped from the former list of legislative powers would remain with the states; both concerned the institutions governing localities. The final two areas would accrue to the president, and they concerned significant powers—the regulations governing the judiciary and those governing the civil service. While the president was not required, and would not in fact elect, to exercise this authority alone and directly, it was to be his responsibility to establish the institutions that would organize, regulate, hire, and fire all judicial and administrative officials of the federal state. Clearly the legislature would play a much less important role in the life of the federation than it had in the Republic.[34]

[34] Another indication of the reduced importance of the federal legislature is the fact that its legislative session was shortened by over 100 days.

The diminished role of legislative power would serve to benefit executive authority in the federation. The nonlegislative federal powers passed directly to the president, rather than to a council of ministers selected from and collectively responsible to parliament.[35] Executive authority would be streamlined, shorn of the encumbrances of ministerial leverage against the President.[36] It would also enjoy a larger measure of freedom from legislative control, in the area of foreign affairs, for example, where the Assembly's powers were limited to ratification of only those treaties touching on subjects normally within the domain of legislative authority.[37] Presidential power would also grow as concerns "special powers" during declared states of emergency,[38] and most important of all, the president would acquire new rights for the enforcement and interpretation of the constitution.[39] His authority in this domain would not be exclusive and

[35] The prime minister and ministerial council (cabinet) were not directly responsible to parliament in the Republic. The president could appoint and dismiss members of his government, including the prime minister, irrespective of parliamentary investiture. However, a parliamentary vote of "no confidence" in the prime minister's government required his resignation, but it could also lead to presidential dissolution of the Assembly. See Constitution, 1940, Republic of Cameroun, Art. 36.

[36] Elimination of the Council of Ministers and the prime minister is an important innovation. These institutions enjoyed genuine legal authority under the Republic, although they were buffered by the political reality of control of the Assembly by the president's party, and cabinet dependency on and loyalty to him. The Council was constitutionally required to be consulted on all matters relating to (a) the general policies of the Republic; (b) agreements with foreign powers; (c) legislative bills; (d) ordinances and regulatory decrees; (e) nominations to higher public posts. Moreover, every presidential act affecting one of the ministries or concerning its domain required the countersignature of the minister in question.

[37] Ahidjo initially proposed to continue legislative ratification of treaties and conventions with foreign powers, but some time after the Foumban conference and the inauguration of the federation he restricted this power.

[38] Under the first Republic the legislature enjoyed significant powers with which to regulate emergency situations and the actions of the president during them. States of emergency required Council of Ministers approval and conferred on the president certain "special powers" determined by an "organic law." This type law could be passed only after a 15-day delay. Under the federation special powers would continue to be subject to the limits determined by the legislature, but the features of the "organic law" no longer would obtain. In situations of particular peril, "état d'exception" could be declared; in these the president would gain considerably. Formerly the procedure required Council approval and endowed the presidency with only those powers normally enjoyed by the executive. In the federation declaration of such an emergency was to be subject to the president's discretion, after conferral with the state prime ministers, and would endow the president with any and all powers he deemed it necessary to have. Cf. Art. 10 of Constitution 1960, and Art. 15 of Federal Constitution.

[39] Formerly, the constitution contained only vague references to the problem of constitutional interpretation. Nowhere was it mentioned that this would be a duty of

192

would bring the system perhaps closer to that envisioned by West Cameroonians of all factions. Ahidjo proposed that the president, in consultation with a Court of Arbitration, could repeal *ex officio* statutes and regulations of either federal or state governmental institutions if they were found to violate the terms of the constitution. The Federal Court of Justice, the highest court, would play a role in guarding the constitution by interpreting statutory acts should state courts give different interpretations to them, or by ruling on charges of "abuse of power" on the part of federal authorities. This would not be full judicial review, however, because the courts would not be independent. The president could determine the composition and procedures of the courts, even those involved in constitutional review.[40]

Ahidjo's proposals submitted to the Foumban conference embodied a significant departure from the provisions of the 1960 Constitution with respect to the selection of the president. His proposal was that the president be elected by an electoral college composed of the two state legislatures. The former constitution contained the odd provision for the election of the president by an electoral college comprising not only the National Assembly but also representatives of the general councils of provinces and of the municipal assemblies.[41] President Ahidjo had never liked this provision, and its inclusion in the Republic's constitution was probably due to French pressure.[42] In any case the provisions are modeled on the Fifth French Republic.[43] The reason Ahidjo did not like these procedures is that under the circumstances that obtained during the early months of the Republic, and probably continuing right on into those of the federation, they would have operated in a way prejudicial to his own

the courts, or even of the president, who was charged with simply "upholding the constitution." The most explicit reference to such matters endowed the legislature with self-regulatory responsibilities, as was the duty of the president of the legislature to determine if a law were "receivable" or not (if it contravened provisions of the constitution). Nowhere were the courts charged with more than the protection of individual liberty and private property in the Republic's constitution.

[40] Presidential decrees would establish and regulate the Federal Court of Justice, as well as the Council of the Magistracy. Formerly, though the president was the guarantor of the independence of the judicial authority, the composition and jurisdiction of the courts and the rules of administering justice were established by organic laws of the Assembly. See Art. 41 of 1960 Constitution.

[41] Art. 12, 1960 Constitution.

[42] Jean Faustin Betayeye, former Minister of Foreign Affairs, in an interview with the author in October 1963, Yaounde, asserted that these provisions were the results of direct French pressure.

[43] See Le Vive, *Cameroon*, p. 225. Cf. Dorothy Pickles, *The Fifth French Republic* (New York: Praeger, 1966), pp. 135 ff.

election as president, due to the strong voice the local councils would have in the process. The local councils tended to remain an instrument for the expression of relatively conservative ideas. In the north this might have strengthened Ahidjo's hand—at least it did not weaken it—but there were few such councils in the north. Ahidjo himself noted to the 1960 Commission that drafted the constitution that the whole of the territory was not then covered by the network of *communes* (urban areas with elected councils) which was supposed to give to the presidential election "son équilibre et son ampleur." [44] Thus if the president had been elected by the procedures actually proscribed in the constitution, the heavy representation of the southern-based *communes* would probably have nullified Ahidjo's strong margin of strength in the National Assembly. Using the excuse, then, that the system of provinces and communes had not been completely established, Ahidjo suspended the constitutional provisions and placed the election solely within the National Assembly. He now proposed to make the earlier expediency the permanent rule.

It is evident that Ahidjo's proposals contained many innovations for the structure of power in Cameroon, certainly at the highest levels of government, but also, in effect, at the state level for East Cameroon, since most governmental prerogatives would be transfered to federal institutions. It is reasonable to assume that those political forces that had opposed the constitution of 1960 might also have been opposed to the federal one and on the same grounds. Indeed, the federal reforms strengthened many of the features singled out for criticism three years earlier. The prior version might well have looked much more like the later one had not the pressures of French advisers and those of the political and security situation compelled a compromise.

The opposition to the 1960 system was intense but geographically localized. Almost all the opposition came from the south, but there were a variety of views voiced and approaches taken among opponents. The exiled UPC leadership called for massive abstention in the constitutional referendum held in April 1960. Most of the moderate nationalist opposition counseled participation in the referendum but rejection of the consti-

[44] *La Presse du Cameroun*, January 18, 1960. In 1960 all eight of the *communes de plein exercise* were located in the southern areas of the country, areas heavily influenced by parties and leaders in opposition to Ahidjo and the UC. In the north there were only two *communes de moyen exercise* (elected councils but still with appointed mayors) and none of the country's three *communes mixtes urbaines* or the 12 or so *communes rurales*. For a list and description of the attributes of the *communes* on the eve of Cameroon independence see *Marchés Tropicaux et Mediterranèens*, No. 732 of November 21, 1959, pp. 2,617–19; and *Citoyen Actifs Dans une Commune Vivante*, Federal Republic of Cameroon, Ministère de l'Intérieur, 1963.

tution. Among the former UPC elements who had quit the rebellion or broken with the party, only the Douala leaders in the quasi-traditional association, *Ngondo* (led by Betote Akwa), and the Bamileke deputies in the Assembly supported both the referendum and the constitution.

It is not easy to translate opposition to the constitution into a real conflict in political values with those who drafted it. Most of the opposition was motivated by short-range considerations such as procedures for elaborating the constitutional draft or the lack of an effective general amnesty for the rebels and UPC leadership.[45] The UPC demand for a constituent assembly composed of all significant political factions and for a roundtable of all parties to prepare such an assembly produced a strong reaction among a diversity of political leaders and groups. Many of the southern-based members of the constitutional commission resigned or refused to accept appointment in deference to the UPC's claims and demands.[46] The rhetoric of the attack was that of liberal democracy and parliamentarianism. The exiled leadership of the UPC, for example, complained of the lack of effective guarantees for public and individual liberties and denounced the centralization of power by the president.[47] The Paris-based student leadership expressed the same themes, with strong emphasis on the evident borrowings from the constitution of the Fifth French Republic. From the militant left the most vehement criticism was that the constitution was a product of Frenchmen, imported merchandise, and at that, merchandise which had not been "tropicalized." [48] It is not clear that had the critics of the 1960 constitution con-

[45] UPC sympathizers among the Cameroonian students in Paris, moderate nationalists with formerly close ties to the UPC such as Soppo Priso and *rallie* UPC deputies such as Mayi Matip and Inack Njoki, all stressed the need for a roundtable of all factions to prepare for a true constituent assembly. These views came on the heel of considerable violence in the country and reflected a desire for a return to calm. It was widely thought that the only way to achieve internal peace was to accommodate the UPC, grant a real amnesty to its agents and base the new political system upon a consensus of all strong political forces. See *La Presse du Cameroun* for the period of mid-January through March 1960, esp. 15, 16, 17, 20 January.

[46] *La Presse du Cameroun,* January 20, 21, 1960. Some of the members of the commission resigned because of a disagreement, or more properly, misunderstanding, about the place the draft constitution would give to religion.

[47] See the *Declaration* of the Bureau du Comité Directeur of the UPC, Accra, March 16, 1960.

[48] See "Débat contradictoire sur la Constitution," *Cahiers d'Education Civique,* No. 1 (Spring 1960). Abel Eyinga, a lawyer and leftist critic of the Ahidjo regime, but also a person with strong support among the Catholic-influenced Démocrates, argued before the student foyer in Paris that the constitution had been written by French technicians, "[who were] yesterday the zealous defenders of the colonial regime, but [who are] today the builders of our independence, [something] which they never desired" (p. 17 of "Débat contradictoire").

trolled the government, either the structure of power or the style and ends of its exercise would have been any different than what developed under the rule of Ahidjo and the UC.

These points notwithstanding, it is important to note that a number of the disagreements expressed in the popular debates over the 1960 constitution probably do, or did, represent true value differences. The foreign-based student community, and the pro-UPC elements within the country argued eloquently, if at times with contradiction, for a greater measure of democracy in the political structure of independent Cameroon. Abel Eyinga, an opponent to the constitution and the regime, appearing in a debate at the Student Cultural Center in Paris defined his concept of democracy as a regime "wherein power rests with the people . . . where the people control at all times those to whom they have confided the exercise of sovereignty." He then compared the conditions in Cameroon with this definition, pointing to the many powers of the president, the lack of parliamentary control over him and his government, the lack of popular election to fill this post, and concluded: "Here [in the president] we have a man, provided with complete power, who escapes any control by those who conferred it upon him, those to whose profit this power is supposed to be exercised. It is from this [fact] that the paradox of this regime springs: a President of the Republic who can do anything in the name of a people who did not elect him and who cannot demand of him the least accounting, who have no means to make him change policies or force him out if he refuses to submit himself to [the will of] the sovereign people. . . . The situation will be ripe for *coup d'états*. . . . [The official claim is that this is democracy.] No doubt it concerns a democracy such as exists nowhere else. . . ."

After the advent of federalism this critic continued to take to task the Ahidjo administration and all those who speak of "African democracy"; he charged that the new African political life lacked democratic principles and conditions. "What is the value of a democracy in which freedom of choice for the people is not effectively recognized, where what figures on the balance sheet is the will of an individual only, however representative he may be, or simply of a fraction of the people, or of a clan?" [49]

It is impossible to say—in fact it is rather implausible, given the general post-independence trend toward authoritarianism in Africa [50]—

[49] Abel Eyinga, "L'Espoire de la Democracie en Afrique," typescript of paper presented to the International Congress on French-Speaking Africa, Washington, D.C., August 1964.
[50] See Francis X. Sutton, "Authority and Authoritarianism in the New Africa," *Journal of International Affairs*, Vol. xv (1961), 7–17; and M. L. Kilson, "Author-

that the populist spirit that imbued the opposition to the Ahidjo regime and its constitutional program would have persisted had these opponents won power; but it is clear that it was real enough at the time. It is also clear that, proclamations aside, there was little evidence of the regime's willingness to put its own populism and democratic ideals to the test of an unfettered popular vote. President Ahidjo has echoed many other African leaders in stating: ". . . there is no universal standard of democracy. To be sure, in contact with the coloniser, we acquired a certain conception of democracy and republican principles. . . . For heaven's sake, let us acknowledge the need to adapt this democracy to our realities, which are not the same as those of other countries. . . . We have extolled the single and unified party in order to achieve indispensable national unity. . . . In the old [established] countries . . . it was also necessary for them to achieve national unity. In order to achieve it, what did they do? Certain ones had to resort to dictatorship. The monarchy which existed there was, in my estimation, worse than the single party. . . . It is known that, in these kingdoms and empires, the citizens, because they were against the policy of the king or emperor, paid for their opposition with their life, and were decapitated. . . . Thank God, we haven't yet come to that." [51] Such sentiments have been so widespread in postindependence Africa that one must suppose that the underlying social and economic conditions with which the politicians have had to work quickly wear smooth the cutting edge of liberal and democratic convictions. Certainly the critics of Ahidjo's constitution, exemplified particularly well by Eyinga, shared his realization of the need for "strong government," but they expressed this attitude with an impressive faith in the capacities of the people and of the instruments for consensus formation present in their society: "Strong government [*un pouvoir fort*] is absolutely essential for our society at the present moment, in part in order to curb corruption and set the country on the course of development, and in part to bring order into the house. But what do we mean by Strong Government? My conviction is that the strength of a regime or a government does not derive from the fact that it can, from the Capital, pass ordinances which one applies more or less successfully by means of proclamations of a state or siege or of alert; the propensity to use force or extraordinary measures does not denote the strength of a regime, but rather its weakness, its lack

itarian and Single Party Tendencies in African Politics," *World Politics* (January 1963), pp. 262–94.

[51] President Ahidjo, speech to party meeting, opening of UC building in Yaounde, September 1963. Also quoted in Eyinga, "L'Espoire de la Democracie en Afrique."

197

of roots in the masses. A strong regime, in my opinion, is one which, above all, rests on a large popular foundation, on [the support of] a majority, if not on unanimity. . . ." [52]

Eyinga followed this eloquent statement of democratic ideals with a plea for direct popular election of the president, a procedure Ahidjo finally accepted at Foumban for the federal presidency. The fact that the adoption of such procedures has not significantly enhanced the opportunity for unfettered and undirected participation by the masses in the making of political decisions in federal Cameroon may be the strongest evidence available that the values of the leaders, whether democratic or not, are not much help in explaining the course of events in postindependent Cameroon.

[52] Eyinga, "Débat contradictoire," pp. 30–31.

PART III

The Integrative Advance

WE CONCEIVE of political integration as an advance along two dimensions of political change—an increase in the extent to which political actions and symbols are mutually related, and an increasing singularity in the significance of these relationships. Both dimensions reflect a growing interdependence, or "systemization," of political action, first through revealing the broadening range of conjunctiveness, the degree to which political actors are caught up in a common web of activity and concern, and second by revealing the rising levels of complementarity of the activities and concerns, the extent to which they involve mutually beneficial consequences or are free of mutually disruptive or threatening ones. Movement in either direction can represent progress and development, and can expand the capacities of the system to initiate or control change within or without the system, though not always without short-run difficulties.

All the issues that have preoccupied the leadership of the three Cameroonian governments—indeed most of the new governments of Africa —submit to analysis along both dimensions. Some of the issues are more directly associated with one or the other of the two, however. In the chapters which follow I shall consider the major issues of integration in Cameroon, emphasizing first the conjunctive aspect, in terms of which I shall examine the problems of elaborating and embellishing a constitutional order, of establishing viable procedures and political traditions, of apportioning power and resources in such a way that the two states and all areas of significant political power within them are linked into a common structure of decision-making and political activity. In later chapters I shall consider the problems of increasing the complementarity of political activities in terms of animating and operating political structures so that the system should work to the satisfaction of all the principal (powerful) groups and so that the interpenetration and competition of political groups and other formal organizations should bring mutual benefits.

199

⚡ 9 ⚡

Conjunctive Allocations of Authority

THE most important aspect of the allocation of authority, the distribution of decision-making jurisdiction, was that which affected the capacities of the two states of Cameroon to define and pursue their interests as collectivities vis-à-vis the central government. There was a second dimension to the question, however, which affected more local levels of government and thus the legal right of regional and parochial groups to assert themselves or manage their own affairs. The first aspect was directly involved in the allocation of responsibility and prerogative regarding the general conduct and finances of government, and especially the maintenance of law and order and control of development resources. The second came into play in the allocation of resources and in the structure of the administrative services.

THE constitutional order that the federation inaugurated for Cameroon grew out of the interaction of political elites in each state, but the western leaders bore the heavier burden of adjustment because of it. Juridically these officials found themselves hedged about and generally unaware of the extent to which the new order impoverished their offices. The union produced a highly elitist system. Moreover, the dominant political elite was initially relatively imbalanced between representatives of the two states. The composition of integrative power in the federation is thus more utilitarian and coercive than identitive, in the words of Etzioni.[1] It represents extensive internalization of powers in the eastern elite.

The term "federation" is perhaps a misnomer for the structural organization or the style of political life in the country. Cameroonians call it federalism; but despite the fact that both central and state governments exist, the constitutional order concentrates jurisdiction in the chief executive of the central government. In this respect it is important also to note that federalism centralized the political structures for the eastern state more than had been the case previously in a unitary state.

West Cameroonian partisans of reunification did not expect or desire such an outcome. We saw earlier that the constitutional discussions preceding federation indicated that serious disparities existed between the

[1] Amitai Etzioni, *Political Unification: A Comparative Analysis of Leaders and Forces* (New York: Holt, Rinehart and Winston, 1965), pp. 37ff., 48ff.

political values of the leaders of each state.[2] It is clear that a hiatus of considerable proportions and significance existed between the values of the communities. I will return to a consideration of the meaning of that hiatus in terms of the emergence of complementary relations and the reduction or elimination of incompatible relations between the various political actors in the federation. We must first note the ways in which the actions of Cameroonians were brought into relation and mutual determination through the structures the federation created, and the de jure allocation of prerogatives and resources.

The two governments at the state level enjoy almost none of the prerogatives of government. The constitutional text—the conscious and unconscious application of that text by the federal authorities—concentrated in the federal institutions the juridical authority to regulate and carry out most political or economic activities. The list of federal powers in the constitution was long and covered a multitude of specific activity areas.[3] More important than the fact that the allocation of powers between central and local institutions founded a juridically close-knit system is the fact that many of the federal powers enabled if not required a precise delimitation of the initiatives and activities that can be carried out in the name of the separate states. Moreover, the allocation of constitutional power provided authorities at the federal level with the juridical right to substantially affect the lives of the average citizen. Groups with vested political interests, such as the ruling parties and their opposition in the states, found themselves potentially constrained by federal authority. In short, the jurisdictional structure realized in the transformation to federalism provided an adequate basis for exercising control over the political life of the states from the federal level.

IT IS not surprising or unimportant that the powers of the federal authorities embraced the internal and external security of the federal state and matters of national defense. Circumstances in each merging state attributed distinctive implications to patterns that are nearly universal in the practice of federalism.

At the time of federation the tiny state of Southern Cameroons had no police or security forces to speak of. Cameroonians serving in the Nigerian police or armed services numbered less than 150. Despite this, fear of external military threats had not been a motive for Cameroon reunifica-

[2] See Chap. 8.

[3] Federal powers are delineated in Arts. 5 and 6, of the October 1961 Constitution, Federal Republic of Cameroon.

tion. The reverse was true; an armed rebellion in the Republic of Cameroon generated widespread fear in "gentle, peaceful" Southern Cameroons of a spread of the terrorism and violence. In response to these threats, the Administering Authority stationed Grenadier Guards at Buea in 1960, but it was announced on several occasions prior to federation that these would be withdrawn on the termination of trusteeship.[4] These facts, combined with the widespread occurrence of violence in ex-Belgian Congo in the months prior to the UN plebiscite, right up to the time of Cameroon federation, caused considerable anxiety about security throughout Southern Cameroons. The embassy staff of at least one foreign country drew up plans to evacuate its nationals.

THERE was widespread recognition in Southern Cameroons of the need to acquire well-equipped and trained police and armed forces. During the consideration of constitutional proposals the government and opposition parties issued a joint appeal to the government of the United Kingdom to help provide such forces, and failing this, they determined to call up all able bodied ex-service men in the area for immediate training and active service. They also requested that all Cameroonians serving in Nigerian forces be given the option of repatriation for service in Cameroon. These forces were too small to meet Southern Cameroon's security needs, however; its leaders had to request additional forces from the Republic of Cameroon.

The availability of additional forces from the sister state was viewed in Southern Cameroons as a mixed blessing. Some West Cameroonians warned of the "dangers of armies of occupation" should the state be "flooded" with troops from the east. Many people considered the Republic's *gendarmes* to be as brutal as the terrorists. Travelers returning from the Republic told of having seen the heads of alleged terrorists impaled on stakes in front of *gendarme* camps and along the roads of troubled areas. The fear generated was enhanced by the massacre of 12 unarmed Southern Cameroons plantation workers near the eastern border about six weeks before reunification. Many have attributed the massacre not to the terrorists, whom official reports blame for the incident, but to over-zealous or drunken *gendarmes*. A promised inquiry into the affair mysteriously was never convened. The fears of Southern Cameroonians not-

[4] Such an announcement was made in the British House of Commons on February 7 and May 4, 1960 and repeated in a message to the Government during the All Party Conference on the Constitutional Future of Southern Cameroons, Bamenda, 26–28 June 1961.

withstanding, about 400 *gendarmes* were stationed in West Cameroon following reunification. As much as two years later two companies of the forces were still stationed there. Though one could hardly say the state was "flooded" with *gendarmes,* there were serious consequences of the action.

It is not my purpose here to analyze the allocation of security jurisdiction for what it may reveal of the disparities in values, beliefs, and attitudes between the two elites. The important point is that the way in which police and security responsibilities were defined and allocated affected the behavior and perspectives of a great many ordinary citizens, as well as the state government of West Cameroon. Western enthusiasm for the federation was seriously strained as a result not only of the jurisdictional provisions but the demeanor of the security forces stationed in the west.

One consequence of the jurisdictional provisions was that the allocation to federal authorities of the ultimate responsibility for security matters foreclosed the opportunity for either federated state to legally raise armed forces capable of challenging the central government. There is no evidence that officials in either state ever attempted to use armed forces toward this end, but some western leaders did indicate in their prefederation deliberations a desire to have the capacity to do so. It is unorthodox of federalism to have regional components endowed with an independent military capacity, together with the jurisdictional freedom to conclude military assistance agreements with foreign powers, yet many western leaders considered these as concomitant aspects of their vision of the impending federation as the loose association of morally equal states.[5] In fact, not only did the federal constitution centralize control of the military forces at the federal level; it also established the machinery for maintaining the internal security of the federal state, which required the collaboration of state police with federal security officials whenever and wherever they were called on to act in security matters. Though these matters supposedly relate to the security of only the federal state, there is no precise boundary between federal and state security. During declared emergencies state police automatically come under the jurisdiction of the appropriate federal administrative officials. At other times security officials may commandeer personnel and materials for security operations. At all times the security branch, the "special" branch, of the West Cameroon police operates directly under federal command, and the police continually participate in the gathering of intelligence.

[5] *Record, Conference on Constitutional Future of Southern Cameroons.*

A potentially wide range of restrictions on public and individual liberties may also result from the declaration of an official state of emergency.[6] The possession and use of arms, the mobility and liberty of persons and goods, the security of home and person from search, the rights of residence, the exercise of freedom of assembly and speech may all be rigidly controlled. These controls can be exercised by officials throughout the federal administrative hierarchy.[7] Another consequence of the provisions for security is that power in this field is more centralized than it has ever been before, even among East Cameroonians. The power to declare emergencies, for example, is concentrated, though not exclusively, in the office of the president. Only the president may declare an emergency, after consulting the prime minister of the state wherein it is to take effect. The prime ministers may initiate a request for such a declaration. It is not clear what the legal consequence would be of the refusal of either party to concur in declaring an emergency. The laws regulating these procedures are contained in a presidential ordinance established during the "transitional period" and subject to but void of any subsequent legislative amendment. The Federal National Assembly is empowered to end states of emergency, but only when their initial six-months duration has expired and presidential action has extended it. In the absence of legislative acts to terminate renewed emergencies, there is no limit to the number of six-month renewals the president may declare.

Situations of extraordinary peril, threatening the life, independence, institutions, or territorial integrity of the national-state, may occasion a presidential declaration of "special emergency." [8] This requires "consultation with" but not necessarily approval of the prime ministers, and empowers the president to take any and every measure he deems necessary to deal with the situation. Though the national legislature remains convened throughout an emergency, it is not clear what it would be empowered to do. These provisions represent a significant change from those of the first Cameroon Republic, wherein special powers accruing to the president in emergencies were confered on him through the action of a council of ministers and were regulated by "organic laws" requiring certain specified delays. The normal legislative and judicial prerogatives remained in force during such occasions.

[6] The demarcation of security responsibilities are found in Decree 61-DR-15 of October 20, 1961 and Ordinance 61-OF-5 of October 4, 1961.

[7] See Chap. 11 for an analysis of the federal administrative system and its impact on and relationship to the state administrative apparatus.

[8] Art. 15 of the Federal Constitution. Normal emergencies may be declared in the event of a serious public calamity, repeated disturbances impairing public order of the security of the state, or foreign aggression. See Ordinance 61-OF-5.

Some of the regulations established during emergencies may carry over into the next period. Controls placed on the residence of individuals, for example, may continue for up to five years. Orders requisitioning people and goods may also continue, as may administrative acts bearing on the jurisdiction of military tribunals. This latter provision is important, in that it affects the repartition of jurisdiction between civilian and military tribunals at the federal and local levels. Emergency regulations permit the extension of the jurisdiction of special military judicial bodies into the territory affected. Temporary military tribunals have been established, which are authorized to try all cases involving offenses against the internal security of the state and against any legislation regulating the bearing and use of arms by persons over 18 years old.[9] Thus the restrictions on the regular courts in these fields may outlive the emergency which gives rise to them.

The legal potential for the exercise of powerful federal muscle at the level of the federated states, especially within West Cameroon, was quickly realized. Due to the continuing disruption of peace in the highlands areas of Bamileke country bordering West Cameroon, a regular state of emergency was declared in four of West Cameroon's six administrative divisions almost immediately after federation.[10] Emergency regulations were in force for some time throughout most of the southern portion of East Cameroon; the regulations were renewed every six months in both states for several years following federation. The eastern security forces which were stationed in West Cameroon upon federation were therefore not restricted to a passive role, or isolated in scattered army or *gendarme* camps, but rather exercised considerable geographical and jurisdictional scope.

The range of the *gendarmes'* activities went beyond a narrow reading of the constitution or the security laws and regulations. This derived from the traditions of that force in colonial times. For example, the *gendarmes* were used to maintaining general law and order; despite the deliberate deletion of the phrase "maintenance of law and order" from President Ahidjo's initial constitutional proposals for federal powers,[11] the *gendarmes* continued to consider this their own domain.

[9] Ordinance 61-OF-5.

[10] Decree 61-DF-23 of November 6, 1961.

[11] The Administering Authority reported in 1956 (*Rapport Annuel pour le Cameroun*, Quatrieme Partie) stated that the *gendarmerie* "est une force instituée pour veiller a la sûreté publique, pour assurer le maintien de l'ordre et l'exécution des lois. . . . Elle constate les crimes, délits et contraventions." The *gendarmes* operated particularly in the countryside and along routes of communication. Responsibility for public security and the maintenance of order were shared with the

Overzealous *gendarmes* were often insensitive to the legal, or supposed, limits on their jurisdiction and thereby occasionally came in conflict with the West Cameroon police. On one occasion *gendarmes* reportedly forced their way into a West Cameroon jail to retrieve one of their suspects. The prisoner was forcibly removed from the jail and allegedly beaten and hospitalized. Western parliamentarians and high-ranking government officials were allegedly not immune from roadside search or seizure by *gendarme* contingents. The residents of a quarter in Buea reportedly were once driven from their homes at night to sit, hands over heads, in the street while their houses were searched.

Needless to say, the demeanor of the *gendarmes* stimulated considerable public protest. Despite *gendarme* misbehavior or public protest, however, many people recognized that the presence of these forces was made necessary by the scarcity of local police. A factor that compensates for the few Cameroonians serving in Nigerian forces was the fact that the tiny state inherited from Nigeria a fine college for training police officers. The college was put into operation almost immediately, and the first class of 51 "passed out" of the college in early May of 1962, eight months after federation. Apparently a number of the newly recruited police took the eastern *gendarmes* rather than the Nigerian police as their model and began to act in as heavyhanded a manner as the *gendarmes* had been charged with. This, coupled with an alleged tendency of the police to bear down harder on those not affiliated with the ruling party in the state, inspired charges of administration-inspired discrimination against the opposition and of a serious deterioration in the quality of police action with the increasingly rapid growth and Cameroonization of the force. The leader of the opposition once suggested in the House of Assembly that a possible solution to all the problems connected with the provision of security would be to centralize all such forces under federal control.[12] A

Cameroonian Guard, but these forces were generally restricted to rural centers and minor roads. The police were usually found only in the larger urban areas. The *Sûreté* was responsible for external and internal security and linked all the police and security forces, including the military. In the discussions for a constitution Ahidjo had included "maintenance of law and order" and "internal and external security" among federal responsibilities. The Southern Cameroons attorney general warned the Buea delegation of the dangers of federal domination in these areas, including federal incorporation of all police powers. The law-and-order provision was later dropped by the eastern government, and maintenance of internal security restricted to the federal state. The *gendarmes,* a federal force, nevertheless operated throughout West Cameroon, especially in the districts under emergency regulations; their standing orders, no doubt, failed to reflect the modifications.

[12] Endeley, interview, Buea, August 1963; and *Cameroon Times,* June 25, 1963.

change in the policy of the *gendarmes,* along with a general decline in the threat to security (real in the east and only perceived in the west), and the establishment of federal predominance gradually reduced the importance of this issue.

Federalism introduced new security forces and practices into the life of West Cameroon, affecting governmental institutions and ordinary citizens alike. Reducing the range of incompatibilities and establishing and enhancing complementary relationships between federal and local police and security forces became a major concern of officials at both levels.

THE federal system of territorial administration instituted throughout the new federation a few days after its birth increased the ability of the federal executive to supervise political life closely at the local level, especially in West Cameroon.[13] To be sure, the ability existed in the former Republic, but there were provisions of the constitution of the First Republic which, had they ever been implemented, would have considerably restricted such a capacity. The new system reversed a trend toward administrative decentralization in East Cameroon.

The administrative system initiated by presidential decree was not altogether new, despite its deviation from the promises of the first Republic's constitution; something similar had existed in Cameroon during the Trusteeship Period. The new system established six administrative regions, each to be headed by a Federal Inspector of Administration. One of the six regions corresponded with the territory of West Cameroon; the other five fell within East Cameroon, one each for the north, east, central south, the Wouri district (Douala), and Bamileke country (which had been decentralized into five departments only about a year before). During the days of the colonial administration there was also a system overarching administrative regions, of which there were only two, one for the north and one for the south.[14] The constitution of the First Republic promised three provinces (adding a separate one for Bamileke Department) corresponding in function to the regions, but they were never established. Unlike the new Inspectorates, the provinces were supposed to operate with a general council composed of elected local representatives

[13] Decree 61-DF-15 of October 20, 1966.

[14] A service of Inspection of Administrative Affairs was created in 1958 (Decree No. 58-12/CAB/PM of February 8, 1958). This was modified in 1960 (Decree 60-252 of December 31, 1960). The powers of the inspectors were similar to those described here, but the inspectors were responsible to the prime minister, not the president. They were also concerned with watching over the administration of credit and financial resources given to administrative or local government institutions.

and the members of the National Assembly from the area. The administrator, representing the central executive, placed at the head of these provinces was to execute the decisions of the councils. In the new system no provision is made for provincial councils, and the inspectors are not restricted by the decisions of any locally based representatives. Rather, the inspectors are themselves the local representatives of the federal executive, which means, in effect, the president.

The innovations instituted in the transition to federalism severely restricted the capacity of local officials for initiative and independent action. The Federal Inspectors of Administration not only supervised but coordinated the work of all federal officials and departments within the region. They could establish their own rules and regulations within the framework provided by general executive powers and jurisdiction. They were charged with the maintenance of order, application of federal laws, and coordination and control of the activity of federal services. They could initiate an investigation into the activities of federal officials in their area. They could carry out their tasks forcibly, if need be, with the help of the police (a state force) and the armed forces. They became the liaison between local federal officials and federal ministries and bureaus. All reports and correspondence from or to these officials were to be copied and sent to the Inspector. Whether intended or not, the system provided the capacity to insure that nothing could happen involving any federal official unbeknownst to the inspector and through him, to the president.

The centralist implications of the system were especially real in West Cameroon, deriving largely from the fact that district and subdistrict officers were defined by the decree as members of the system of federal administration. Nothing in the constitution, or as far as I know, even within the discussions preliminary to the establishment of the federation, anticipated such an arrangement.[15] Certainly the constitution did not prohibit it; the authority to establish an administrative organization is clearly vested in the federal authorities under Art. 6, the article listing "second stage federal powers." In fact, there was no explicit statement limiting this authority to federal administrative services. Nevertheless, it seems that the inclusion of state administrative officials within the federal structure was arbitrary, possibly reflecting the lack of personnel available for a separate federal administration in West Cameroon. It may have ap-

---

[15] Prime Minister Foncha is reported by highly placed West Cameroonian civil servants to have claimed privately that it violated his agreements with President Ahidja prior to reunification.

peared to eastern officials that utilization of West Cameroon administrators as the local agents of the federal administration constituted tolerance and a willingness to go slow in demanding West Cameroon's adjustment to its new status as part of a centralist federation. The effect of the provision was otherwise, however. District officers became the focal point of a dual federal-state chain of command. An expansion of federal responsibilities meant these former state administrators were correspondingly "federalized." They found it difficult to distinguish their federal and their state "selves." Health services, judicial matters, postal and telegraph and other informational services, and secondary and technical education gradually shifted from state to federal jurisdiction. Consequently an increasing amount of the administrator's time was spent on federal subjects, which were now subject to the supervision and coordination of the inspector, an easterner. The rules regulating these services were by and large eastern in origin or inspiration and generally unfamiliar to local officials. The local officials began to resolve doubt about jurisdiction or interpretation in the favor of federal authorities. Copies of their communications even with state bureaus, on matters within the domain of state powers, were often sent first to federal officials. The effect was to progressively deprive West Cameroon of autonomous administrative structure at the district or local level.

The federal administrative system clearly tied the states, as collectivities, closely to the federal machinery, even when functioning in areas within the states' own jurisdiction. The system did not reflect political values operative among West Cameroonians, a point to which I shall return in my discussion of the problem of enhancing the complementarity of the relationship. One would expect an effort in West Cameroon to change or circumvent the features of the system that threatened the integrity of the state's action. This came quickly in the form of a presidential directive, inspired by the prime minister, to all state officials whether or not also federal officials, to direct all communication with federal bureaus through the office of the prime minister.[16] Thus would the state regime screen out communications properly restricted to state personnel. The motivation was less a desire to curtail federal surveillance of the local regime than to protest the system and the manner in which it had been

[16] *Cameroon Times,* May 7, 1962. The directive was issued from the president's office in response to pressure from the West Cameroon regime. Another means the state government had to safeguard its jurisdiction over these officials was to continue to include a token salary for them in the state budget," so that their activities can be debated on the floor of the West Cameroon Assembly." *Estimates of West Cameroon, 1964–1965* (Buea: Government Press), Vol. 94, Item 52.

installed and to preserve some semblance of relevancy for the state apparatus. The prime minister rationalized the directive on the grounds that as vice president of the federation during the transitional period he outranked the federal inspector.[17] In recognition of the seriousness of the political issues involved, the inspector ultimately accepted the principle that his legitimate activities were limited to administrative matters concerning only federal operations in the state. In fact, however, his activities for many months after this episode resembled those of a political rather than administrative personage.

One controversial feature of the system was that it brought Yaounde too close not only to Buea, the state capital, but equally close to Kumba, Mamfe, Bamenda, and other principal administrative centers. The dangers in this were obvious to those interested in preserving a pattern of life in West Cameroon much as it had been before reunification, as Foncha had promised. As it turned out, not only was the state apparatus left porous and pitted, leeched of its life substance like laterite in the dry season, but old, indigenous structures were paralleled by new and foreign ones. This interpretation of the system was enhanced by the conduct of the inspector who often mentioned in his speeches that he was the "direct representative of the Federal President" in West Cameroon and that local administrative officers were directly responsible to him.[18] This alone was enough to cause many people to think the state government was no longer to be reckoned with. Such an impression could only be strengthened if one observed the inspector receiving petitions from the people for roads, schools, and other improvements, hearing local grievances, extolling the people to eschew corruption and violence and to work hard, and transmiting their greetings to the president.[19]

One can easily exaggerate the controversy over the localization of the federal government. Most citizens in both states seem to have desired this. Given the preponderant authority of the federal offices it was probably desirable to have the "real" government undergo the process. Most of

[17] The Inspector later countered with the assertion that if this were so, it would only be so during the time the prime minister was actually residing in the state and serving in his capacity as vice president, which was seldom, since there were few duties of the office he could carry out there.

[18] These assertions were made in a speech in Victoria in August 1962. During the colonial regime the district officers were the representatives of the colonial administration who were the most evident to the people—his office continued to be viewed as a symbol of the ultimate authority in the state.

[19] President's speech at Tombel, in *Cameroon Champion,* August 10, 1962. See also *Cameroon Champion,* August 17, 1962, January 8, 1963; and Federal Information Service, PR 1935, August 7, 1962.

the criticism voiced over this matter came from state government spokes-men. Despite the fact that it strengthened the potential of federal of-ficials to control local affairs, the process was popularly perceived as, and in fact represented, real decentralization. Federal positions in the local administration were filled by West Cameroonians, which brought the government into greater intimacy with the local people. This was espe-cially so following the creation of new administrative units at the subdis-trict level. Beginning with the 1963–1964 budget (July 1) eight new subdistricts were created within the six existing districts and each was placed under the direction of a district officer. This system, while fore-shadowed by the consolidated councils of native authorities, represented a change that aligned the system in West Cameroon with the pattern of administration in East Cameroon and resolved a conflict between the provisions of the presidential decree establishing it and the traditional practice of the West Cameroon civil service. It was an innovation in the West Cameroon system to equate the district officers with "Sous-préfets" in the east because these latter officials were subordinate to the "préfets," who headed more extensive units, including the same geographical areas. Senior district officers, the West Cameroon equivalent to *Préfet,* were se-nior only in experience and status, not in their relationship to regular dis-trict officers who headed completely separate districts of lesser impor-tance but of juridical equality.

Decentralization of administrative structures, represented by the pro-liferation of subdistricts or *sous-préfectures,* was also characteristic of the independence period in East Cameroon. Significant progress had been made in the decade prior to independence, stimulated by the rise of an urban-based and antitraditional group of young people pushing for modernization and democratization of local government structures, and stimulated claims of "under-administration" in a number of geographi-cally and economically critical areas. The greatest increment of admini-strative units occurred in the late 1950s as the UPC turned to violent re-bellion and terrorism. The government of independent Cameroon con-tinued to respond to such pressures.[20] Thus in the east, structures inter-

---

[20] The most important innovations have been in the "troubled areas." Bamileke Region, for example, was divided into five departments, each with its own *préfets;* each was later provided with additional sousdepartments (*souspréfectures*), totaling 15 by 1963. Similarly the areas of Catholic-based opposition around Yaounde, in the old department of *Nyong-et-Sanaga,* were split in 1964 into five new depart-ments. However, these areas lost one *souspréfecture* in the process. Sousdepart-ments usually correspond to traditional cultural areas or ethnic divisions. *Nyong-et-Sanaga* has not known widespread terrorism except in the capital. It remains an area

mediary between the administrative departments and the councils of village and municipal governments multiplied in an effort to link the governed with governors; but the marginal centralizing impact of such changes was less in the east than in the west. The change from a unitary to a federal system was less noticeable because, by and large, the same people did the same things before and after reunification. Administrators did not gain new functions outside their accustomed jurisdiction, such as supervising the police and security forces for the first time, as was the case with Western administrators. The territorial administration in the east was also initially a dual system, servicing both the federal and state government. But unlike western administrators, those in the east continued to operate within a single political situation. They took their cues from the same people as before, only these people now occupied federal offices. Only those antagonistic to the Ahidjo regime have much stake in protecting or expanding the domain of autonomous authority at the state level in East Cameroon. The fact is that throughout the life of the federation both the federal and state government of East Cameroon have been controlled by Ahidjo's party, the *Union Camerounaise*. Federalism has strengthened the control, but the administrative system has played a marginal role in this process because very few new local administrative jobs, patronage for loyal supporters, have resulted directly from the change.[21]

Juridically the states were not totally uninvolved in the control of their own administrations. *Préfets* and senior district officers and administrative officials down to the district level, all partially state officials, were appointed by the president, theoretically only "after consultation with the Prime Minister of the state concerned." In fact, however, the prime minister himself, at least of the eastern government, owed his position to his standing with the president and within his party. The appointment of the first Inspector of Federal Administration for West Cameroon was allegedly made without the president's "adequately" consulting Foncha. If the provisions for such consultation could be violated concerning West Cameroon, they were probably ignored altogether in the east.

of opposition, however, based on loyalty to the *Parti des Démocrates* rather than the UPC. Both the government and the local people may favor decentralization of this sort, the former because it enhances surveillance and control and the latter because it provides easier access to government services and a certain recognition of their ethnic or religious distinctiveness.

[21] I have already mentioned that the new system eliminated the constitutional provision for elected councils at the subdepartmental, departmental, and inspectorate (provincial) levels, which had a significant centralizing effect.

The administrative system was used to consolidate the control not only of the federal government, but more precisely that of the president. One important change for East Cameroon was the subordination of the administrators directly to the president, whereas before independence they were responsible to the prime minister, which practice, together with other provisions of the Republic's constitution already discussed,[22] enhanced his leverage vis-à-vis the President. It appears that the old *Inspection des Affaires administratives* continued to operate at the state level in East Cameroon and was free to conduct its own investigations into the operations of state bureaus, but had none of the operational powers given to the new federal inspectors.[23] More important, modifications were introduced in 1962 making the federal inspectors themselves subject to inspection. A *Service d'Inspection et du Contrôle,* akin to that mentioned above, was instituted in 1962 at the federal level, to carry out the same surveillance functions with respect to federal officials, including the inspectors.[24] The Service was empowered to conduct studies or make inquiries into the operation of any federal service or administrative body, to control the use of state credits, and to supervise the implementation of laws and executive regulations. It was to have free access to all administrative documents and records of all public and semipublic treasuries. Unlike the Federal Inspectors or administrative officials, the Service was not authorized to make its own decisions or to commandeer armed forces. Rather it was to receive its instructions from the minister delegates to the president in charge of territorial administration. These provisions were probably never activated. Instead, two years later a third mechanism was put into operation—the *Direction Générale du Contrôle*—to perform many of the same functions. Under the direction of a formerly close associate of the president, but one who may have lost favor, this office was slow to begin to carry out its assigned functions.[25]

[22] See the discussion of constitutional proposals compared with the constitution of the First Republic, in Chap. 8.

[23] Note sur le Champ d'action et les attributions respectifs de la direction générale du controle et de l'inspection des Affairs administratives," Tobie Kouh, *Direction Générale du Contrôle,* Yaounde, July 1965.

[24] Decree 62-DF-287 of July 26, 1962.

[25] The control office was established by Decree 64/DF/248 of June 30, 1964 and regulated by instruction No. 19/CAB/PR of September 25, 1964. I interviewed the director of the bureau in question in the summer of 1965, when the office had not yet carried out a specific study or control function it was willing to report about. Its activities did not appear to be important to the workings of the federal apparatus. On the other hand, the jurisdiction of the office is impressively broad. In addition to investigation and controlling federal services, it is charged with protect-

ONE of the most surprising aspects of federal infusion of state structures, surprising to West Cameroonians and a source of more than a little consternation to them, was the fact that institutions of local government did not remain immune from the process. The fullness of federal power vis-à-vis the states per se was only slowly revealed; but it did appear, at first, that state sovereignty unquestionably resided in the prerogatives of village and municipal authorities. The West Cameroon House of Chiefs and the Native Authority courts, which reflected the strength of the traditional local government structures in the West, were expressly guaranteed by the federal constitution.[26] None of the staff of the native authorities was incorporated into the federal administrative service. Any effort to do so would surely have tested the loyalty of the general citizenry. It was not as a result of these more or less technical provisions of the federation that westerners misperceived the relevance of federal power to local institutions. It was rather because the federal government was considered Big Government, an instrument and prefiguration of modernization. Most people think it the job of central government to instigate big development projects and to conduct the complicated new business of the emergent cities, not anything one is likely to find in the bush towns where old men rule and where most people still live. To most Africans the bustling new capital cities, extremely artificial though they are, are regarded by the new elite as its own special haunt. As the French colonial administrator Delavignette noted, the African village "is still a living entity." [27] Whether understaffed but imperious colonial or African central administrations realized it or not, the village always had only one chief. "In spite of appearances, it is the *village* chief who retains the ancient, intrinsically African authority." [28]

It is widely presumed that these comments are relevant only to African areas formerly under British rule. The "indirect rule" of the French is supposed to have penetrated deeply into the hinterland and destroyed the traditional basis of authority for chiefs. It is certainly not illogical to

ing the national wealth, and may thus supervise all organizations receiving public funds as well as participating in price control operations. The office was also to propose measures to reform the administrative services with a view to lowering their costs. Finally, the services claimed wider powers than those of the state inspectors, in that it could suspend personnel in the services investigated and question requisitions from administrators and the military.

[26] Members of the West Cameroon House of Chiefs are given the same stipends and allowances as the elected members of the House of Assembly.

[27] R. Delavignette, *Freedom and Authority in French West Africa* (London: Oxford University Press, 1957), p. 75.

[28] *Ibid.*

think that 75 years of European rule left its stamp on every aspect of African society. The distinctive styles and goals of various European regimes in Africa did engender local differences. The British colonial officer was generally more concerned with promoting his tenure than his tenets. They bothered less than the French to replace local life styles with their own or to modify systems of rule, particularly if they were strongly entrenched. But in eastern Nigeria (including much of present-day West Cameroon), where traditional rule seldom extended beyond the village level, they often found it necessary to intervene directly to establish "traditional African authorities" through which they could then rule "indirectly." [29] On the French side, in Delavignette's words "Assimilation and Association, the two formulas are often combined; the dosage of each varies with the practitioner's dexterity and the temperature of events." [30] There is little distinction to be made between British and French rule; both applied direct and indirect methods because on both sides of the Mungo River there were traditional rulers so strong that the colonial power found it expedient to consider their authority and regulation its own.[31]

Institutions of local government differed only slightly between the two states. Certainly the similarities were more striking than the differences, given the disparities in colonial backgrounds involved. In both areas those ruling in the villages tended to be the persons custom would have prescribed before the white man came.[32] Except in the Moslem areas to the north, this person was thought to be more independent of the state

[29] During the interwar period a system of "warrant chiefs" was instituted, authorities presumed to have customary legitimacy who were listed in the official gazette as chiefs. The system proved unsatisfactory. Seldom was the customary authority extensive enough for the operation of an effective local government. In 1943 a Native Authority system was established, modeled on the English county system. Preliminary to its application in Cameroon a complete survey of traditional structures was made (cf. Annual Report to the United Nations, UK, 1948). New structures had to be created which often had little basis in local tradition. The system was revised again in 1948 after a full review by the Eastern Nigeria House of Assembly. See L. G. Cowan, *Local Government in West Africa* (New York: Columbia University Press, 1958).

[30] Delavignette, *Freedom and Authority*, p. 49.

[31] As in Northern Nigeria the Fulani-dominated Moslem Emirate system was not much disturbed; one, Rei Bouba, was technically autonomous of French rule. It submitted to national rule only with Cameroon independence.

[32] Under the Native Authority system the governor of Nigeria, and later the commissioner of Cameroons, was empowered to appoint whomever he pleased as Native Authorities, but in fact he normally appointed the person indicated by local custom.

215

administration in West Cameroon than in East Cameroon.[33] Caught in the crossfire of westernizing warriors—cocoa and coffee, clergy and catechists, and cash—even a proper chief often appeared to his people to be a supernumerary, and in this all the more so if it were French rather than English that baffled him. At higher levels conciliar institutions of recent origin, with members elected from new occupational strata, set the pattern in both states.[34]

One way in which institutions of local government operated differently in the two states, however, was that these institutions were the agents of tax collection in West Cameroon. It was a simple difference, but of fundamental importance to the strength of local government. The income and poll taxes levied by the state assembly, a right preserved for it by the

[33] Officially the local chiefs in French Cameroon were part of the administration; even in British areas they came to depend on the backing of the colonial state to preserve their power. See K. Busia, The Modern Predicament of the African Chief, (London: International African Institute by Oxford University Press, 1951).

[34] Serious efforts to democratize and update the Native Authority councils did not get underway until 1954. Since then many small local N.A. areas have been regrouped into larger units capable of sustaining more impressive budgets. The ballot for election to the councils dates from 1954, first only in Mamfe and Kumba divisions, and followed the next year by Victoria. On the French side, members of the new representative institutions often voiced the view that African chiefs should be auxiliaries of the government but not its direct agents, less their authority be destroyed. The chiefs themselves usually pressed for greater backing from the administration. The French administrative reports calling for local government reforms from 1950 on, in greater intensity, spoke of the need to secure a position for the traditional system; "not to re-establish [chiefs] in a social structure that is dying, but to establish them in a modern Africa that is being born," as stated by Delavignette. The Chiefly institution was maintained in French Cameroon, but the administration "hedged it round with regulations." (See Preamble to the draft law on status of traditional chiefs, Report of UN Visiting Mission, 1949, T/798, p. 47.) In an effort to bring administration closer to the areas under the rule of the chiefs, posts lower than *chefs de sous-division* were created, 17 of them by the end of 1955. The towns of Douala and Yaounde were made *communes mixtes* in 1941 (where council and administrator appointed) and were given full powers in 1955, when the number of *communes mixtes urbaines* were expanded and given elected councils of from 9 to 15 members, with 2 appointed chiefs. Three years earlier, on August 21, 1952, *communes mixtes* were created in the "bush," with elected councils based on a constituency coinciding with the *sous-divisions* (12 in 1952, but generalized in 1955), with about 60 councils, some at the level of chieftaincies, among the Bamoun. Many of the mayors were French, but 10 were African in 1955, and the system was steadily Africanized during the years leading up to independence. Many Africans got experience as deputy mayors in these *communes*. Village councils, Councils of Notables, or councils at the level of sections of *communes* had existed in some cases since 1925, and were greatly expanded in 1949. The powers of most were limited to deliberating on the budgets, but they could also plan programs of public works and services in their local areas. See *Rapport Annuel, a l'ONU, Cameroun sous l'Administration Française*, 1956.

federal constitution, as well as fees and penalty payments enacted by each Native Authority, were initially collected by the local Native Authorities and put into either their own or consolidated treasuries comprising a number of local N.A. areas. One-half of the collections was then pressed on to the state government, and certain varying percentages to the area or town councils of the Native Authorities at the department or municipal level. While many councils scarcely raised enough revenue to pay their own staffs, a number carried on impressive operations, and all enjoyed the power, independence, and vested interest that comes in being a tax collector. The system in East Cameroon was the opposite of that in the west; rather than the state being dependent on the efficiency, goodwill, and honesty of the local government officials for its revenues, the local officials were dependent on the state. Official collections of any kind, whether head, herd, hut, or "hustle," were sent directly into agencies of the state treasury and then appropriate refunds were made to the local authorities. With the creation of a federal treasury, all the eastern state's funds were kept in federal institutions.[35] West Cameroon was exempted from the provisions governing the banking of state funds until 1965 when Ahidjo abruptly federalized the state treasuries.[36] The controlling elements of local government, which heretofore had been little influenced by the transformations occasioned by federation, felt the greatest impact of the change. They were now drained of an attractive instrument for local influence and perceived themselves, many for the first time, to be linked to a new system of power no longer centered in Buea.[37]

[35] It appears that for the first two years, though the federal treasury served both the eastern and federal governments, the accounting services remained under the jurisdiction of the state government. The Department of Public Accounts was a state service, carried only in the state budget, but responsible to the minister delegate to the federal president.

[36] *Cameroon Times,* June 16, 1965.

[37] Western officials expressed concern about this to me during a visit in mid-1965. They saw the change as signifying the loss of nearly all autonomous powers of the state. Many of the same officials were critical of the way in which the Native Authorities carried out their responsibilities for revenue collection, however. Corruption and inefficiency cost the state a great deal. Federalization of the treasuries did not mean an immediate change in the institutions for revenue collection—this would have to await the installation of federal agents at the local level or of the expansion of the administrative machinery to that level. The capacity to do this was enhanced the year before by the creation of the Local Government Service Commission in August 1964. At the time the treasury shifted to federal auspices, the state officials were discussing the establishment of a consolidated service in the Ministry of Finance (state level) to handle all collections. Interview with Mr. W. C. Épalé, Permanent Secretary, Ministry of Finance, Buea, August 1965.

THEORETICALLY federal prerogatives in fiscal, financial, and economic planning and control were nearly unlimited.[38] However, fundamental disparities between the two systems, limited familiarity with the British-based system among eastern officials, and the many pressures and demands associated with the transition itself precluded early, neat separation of responsibility in these matters. Consequently there was confusion about the efforts to deal with the economic life of the federal government, the states, and their people. There was little room for dogmatism and doctrinaire approaches. Ministries concerned with finance, commerce, and industry and planning for economic development existed at both the state and federal levels, for example. These were called *Ministères de Conception* at the federal level, ones which were *"à cheval sur les deux gouvernments, fédéral et fédéré."* [39] Dual responsibility reflected pragmatism and the ad hoc way in which leaders at all levels had to tackle the most difficult aspects of integration. Western officials initially had wanted to retain ample influence in these areas. At the Foumban conference Prime Minister Foncha proposed that "Federal Taxation and Customs" and "Development Planning and the Direction of Economic Policy," even the item, "Federal Budget," be placed in the list of "second stage federal powers." General policies relating to the domestic economy, other than planning, should have become state responsibilities, according to the Buea officials. No doubt, they considered that each of these matters were deeply rooted in local traditions and intricately interrelated with many other state institutions and practices, and thus could not easily submit to control from Yaounde even if handled by West Cameroonians. Uncertainty about placing such matters under federal control existed among East Cameroon state officials as well. They presumed that standardization of regulations and practices in these fields would entail disruption of economic life in East Cameroon. Prime Minister Assale stated the reason for the pragmatic approach taken: "It was necessary to take time to see how things would work out . . . [we] inherited institutions of a foreign formation. We must see if these services can work in a [common] Cameroon context, we must see if they render satisfaction. This is one technical problem, but added to this is the separation between

[38] The only limits to federal authority in the fiscal field derive from the constitutional restriction (Art. 5) of federal activity to the raising of revenue for federal expenditures. The monetary system itself, all credit policies, and general guidance of the economy and development planning were exclusively within federal jurisdiction, though state officials did continue to work in these fields for several years.

[39] Prime Minister Charles Assale, interview, Yaounde, June 14, 1963.

the federal and state levels." [40] All sides were prepared, therefore, to proceed cautiously and experimentally.

As a result of the approach adopted, the constitution lacked a fixed formula of revenue allocation between the federal and state governments,[41] which proved to be of considerable importance. There was shared participation in the allocation process, but this did not guarantee equality. Ultimate authority in matters affecting the financial plight of the states resided squarely in federal institutions. Through its prerogatives to regulate all external economic relations, the federal government acquired direct control of the customs regime, the principal traditional source of state revenue. Thus, budgeting for state operations and capital projects was made dependent on subsidies from the federal government and the size of such subsidies was made subject to political relations between and among the state and federal political elites, or was determined simply according to arbitrary rules.[42]

There were some important differences between the two federated

[40] Assale interview.

[41] Western officials compared the situation to that in the Nigerian Federation, and pressed for the inauguration of a system similar to it. The constitution (1963) of the Federal Republic of Nigeria provided for the redistribution to the four regional governments of fixed percentages of a "Distributable Pool." This fund was raised from 30 percent of the proceeds of import duties on certain products and excise taxes. Other revenues were allocated to the regions on the basis of proportionate share of imports. See Chapters 137–141 of the Nigerian Constitution, 1963.

[42] The secretary of finance and ex-prime minister, A. Jua, has stated that the lack of a fixed formula for such allocations "makes forward planning of expenditure a highly hazardous affair, since the State Government is not usually apprised in advance of the amount of the subvention that the Federal Government would be ready or able to grant." See Claude R. Welch, Jr., "Cameroon Since Reunification: 3, The Finances of Federation," *West Africa*, November 2, 1963.

Interviews conducted in mid-1965 by myself with officials in federal and West Cameroon ministries of finance indicate that the federal subsidies are usually fixed on an ad hoc basis in response to the requests made by each state government. When state budgets are initially drawn up there may have been few if any preliminary discussions about subsidies with federal authorities. After the federal government determines what amount is available for each subsidy (i.e. what is not required for federal projects) the sum is divided between the two states. No fixed formula has been used to determine the balance between the two states, although provision is made for a certain escalation of previous budget figures in response to inflation. Modifications of requested subsidies are subject to negotiation. Federal officials have attempted to avoid deciding which specific state projects would have to be cut, but this could seldom be avoided altogether. Ultimately the amount and nature of the pressure the states can bring to bear on federal authorities determined more than anything else the size of the subsidies. This makes the process essentially a political one, an aspect of the problem that will be discussed below.

219

states in terms of their financial relations to the federal government, but the confusion that marked the relations in the case of West Cameroon also existed in the east. It was harder to distinguish between federal and state services and officials in the east. As the Prime Minister stated in an attempt to underscore the continued importance of his government under the federation: "In speaking of East Cameroon . . . as between the Minister of Finance [federal] and the Secretary of State for Finance who belongs to my government, there is hardly any difference as yet, because the director of public accounting is the same for both budgets." [43] Assale further claimed that nearly all financial departments serviced both the federal and eastern governments, such as the office of the director of the budget, the department of public accounts, and the treasury. In this he revealed the confusion inherent in the system of "guiding" federal ministries. Despite the fact that the Treasury and Department of Public Accounts served both governments, as the prime minister stated, they did not "belong" to both. At that time the former was wholly financed by the federal budget and the latter wholly by the state budget.[44] Thus the eastern state subsidized at least one federal service, and in fact also subsidized the federal accountant's office in West Cameroon. Additional evidence of the ad hoc character of many of these arrangements is the fact that the Western governmental budget continued to carry some of the cost of some services, such as the Treasury and the Auditor's Department, after the federal budget had subsumed such costs in the east. In the case of the Treasury an arrangement for continued state contributions to such facilities reflects the concern of western officials that state responsibility in this area not dissipate by default.[45]

Initially the federal-state repartition of revenue resources seemed clear. In time the clarity of these arrangements gave way to confusion, sometimes to the enhancement and prolongation of state prerogative. It seemed federal authorities would control and federal coffers would re-

[43] Interview with Assale.

[44] See Budget de l'exercice 1963–1964, *Cameroun Oriental,* Chapters 111, 102, 201, 202, 203; and *Budget,* Cameroon Federal Republic, 1963–1964, Chapters 14, 102, 105, 202. The Treasury provisions of the latter show a department headquarters and a central office of the Treasury, with five regional offices in the east, a regional headquarters and five agencies in the west. The eastern budget provides for only attachés to four of the regional offices. Both provide for a *"Direction du Budget,"* however.

[45] In his budget speech of July 9, 1962, the secretary of state for finance noted that provision for a token state payment for the Treasury, despite the inclusion of this service in the federal budget, "is intended to demonstrate the Treasury's dual role as it will function both for the Federal and State Governments."

ceive all revenue from customs and revenue from all taxes and charges which the federal government established to meet federal expenditures. The constitution did not guarantee, but also apparently did not prohibit, an independent state-level capacity to levy taxes and other charges to meet its own revenue needs; eventually such a capacity became questionable.

There were two reasons for the charge. One resulted from the continuation in force of fiscal and customs laws in West Cameroon, supported by the maintenance of the customs barrier between the two states, which had inspired so many complaints during the mandate and trusteeship period and which the partisans of reunification presumably desired to remove. This was required by the disparities in wages and prices between the two states, which necessitated a slow and considered approach to the integration of the two economies. Given the continuation of the previous fiscal arrangements, however, Westerners were exempted from paying certain federal taxes levied in the east (a transaction tax particularly), while they continued to pay some state charges which easterners did not.[46] However, the system favored the westerners; the total weight of taxes on West Cameroonians in 1962 was only 10.6 percent of gross revenue, while it was 24 percent in the east. The persistence of prefederation tax schedules obscured the clear juridical authority of the federal government to drive the state out of certain fiscal domains by levying its own taxes and generating popular pressure to lower or eliminate duplicate state taxes.

The second reason was the fact that Cameroon's membership in the *Union douanière et économique de l'Afrique centrale* required the meshing of customs and fiscal policies throughout the federation.[47] Thus for several reasons it became increasingly difficult to determine juridically what taxing power remained with the state authorities. State officials

[46] The transaction tax, a charge of 9 percent of value on imports and 5 percent of "value added" for locally manufactured industrial goods, was instituted in June 1963 but was not applied to West Cameroon until 1965. This was the most important disparity in the fiscal laws of the two states, but others included significant disparities in personal income tax (higher in West Cameroon but compensated a bit in the "noncompany taxes") and company taxes (higher in the west). On the whole, business and financial activity was more heavily taxed in the east and personal income and business profits in the west. While some of the taxes levied in the east derived from state statutes, they were limited; in any case, they were determined by the top political leaders who concerned themselves with state *and* federal policy.

[47] The consequences of this change are discussed in some detail in Chap. 13. Cameroon joined the Union as an associate member in June 1959, when it was called the *Union douaniere equatoriale* (Chad, Central African Republic, Congo-Brazzaville, and Gabon), and instituted a common external tariff with these states in 1962. West Cameroon was exempted from the tariff provisions until 1966.

charged with financial planning responsibilities in West Cameroon found it ever more difficult to predict the level of state revenues, especially those which the state could raise on its own authority.[48]

State officials were also unsure of their prerogatives in the field of foreign aid despite the clear constitutional allocation of responsibility for such matters to the federal executive. The ambiguity worked to the advantage of state officials by permitting them greater latitude in initiating and pursuing contacts with representatives of potential foreign lenders and foreign aid sources. The reasons for this extrajuridical latitude related to the incapacity of the federal authorities to move quickly and efficiently into this domain of activity. West Cameroon needs in terms of external assistance were not clearly known even to Western officials because no sophisticated survey of the state's resources existed, unlike the case in her sister state. Thus Yaounde was obliged to take a back seat to local authorities on matters regarding foreign assistance to development projects in the West.[49] A Federal Ministry of the Plan was established among the first of the federal institutions as a holdover from the First Republic. However, no special department was established within this ministry to handle the problems of West Cameroon (other than the Inspector of Administration), nor were any West Cameroonians placed in high positions in the bureau. Rather than federal initiative being exercised, the state secretary for finance continued to formulate plans for capital development projects, as he had always done; and he continued to approach the diplomatic representatives of foreign governments resident in Buea (at the consular level) or passing through, regarding development projects.[50] This is not to say that state officials could conclude agreements with foreign powers or that Yaounde remained outside the discussions, but the latter's role was often peripheral during the first five years. Something like a five-year plan was drawn up by Western officials, for example, aided by officials of the United States AID mission. Once the preliminary discussions had terminated and a general program had been out-

[48] In order to bolster state revenues West Cameroon established a lottery in June 1963. In addition to the goal of providing the state government with another source of internal revenue, the change was also designed to arrest an outflow of foreign exchange to foreign, mostly Nigerian and European lotteries.

[49] The Stanford Research Institute has produced an eight-volume survey of West Cameroon resources and a cost effectiveness determination of rational development priorities. See *The Economic Potential of West Cameroon—Priorities for Development* (Menlo Park, Calif., June 1965). A survey of East Cameroon's industrial potential was published under M. A. Mercier, *Rapport sur les Possibilites du Developpement industriel du Cameroun* (Paris: Société d'études pour le developpement économique et sociale, 1960).

[50] Agustin Jua, Secretary of State for Finance, interview, Buea, April 4, 1963.

lined, federal officials were involved who later formally and officially placed requests for supporting funds with the U.S. government. West Cameroon development projects did figure in the federal reports of the first Five Year Development Plan, but their determination did not involve joint planning, if it involved any planning at all. The funding of such projects from the foreign aid or other resources available to the federal budget was determined in much the same way as the federal subsidies to the recurrent budget, by state officials pruning down initially desired projects to the point when they could be accommodated by the funds set aside for the purpose, a figure that was usually arbitrary.[51]

The structures established to elaborate a second Five Year Development Plan marked a diversion from the pattern established for the first. It devised a single plan for the whole federation, taking combined needs, resources, and priorities into balanced consideration. National planning boards were established in eight areas, from finance and credit to health and social affairs, with a ninth board to concern itself with synthesis and the general economy.[52] West Cameroon was underrepresented on several boards, but had technically qualified and appropriate representatives on each. The planning covered the entire federation, though few of the members were equipped to consider planning projects and establish priorities from a truly national perspective. If this fact faults the plan, it is primarily because it was made by human beings who like all others, especially so among African planners, necessarily hold a parochial point of view—which made the problem of coherence difficult even if one considers East Cameroon apart. Coherence and the consolidation of reunification were specific objectives of the plan.[53] Considerable energy went

[51] The secretary of state for finance stated in 1963 that he could not recall any case where federal authorities had altered the terms of agreements worked out between his office and representatives of foreign governments or organizations; but with respect to development projects financed by federal subsidies to the capital budgets, these programs had to be harmonized with the eastern programs, and a selection made of the most essential projects. He claimed that, "At the moment there is no federal development program. We are picking projects haphazardly from West Cameroon and East Cameroon development programs." They were then working on drawing up a detailed and rational program for the west—the Stanford Research Institute study.

[52] The boards were (1) Synthesis and General Economy, (2) Finance and Credits, (3) Structure-Information, (4) Education, Vocational Training, and Employment, (5) Rural Economy, (6) Industry, Power, Mining, and Artisan Activities, (7) Trade, Services and Tourism, (8) Infrastructure, Transport, Telecomm. Building, Town Planning, Municipal Administration, and Housing, and (9) Health and Social Affairs.

[53] D. B. Masuke, "L'elaboration du Premier Plan fédéral de developpement," *Europe France-Outre-mer* (May 1966).

223

into planning, so that all regions of the country, especially the two states, could fully participate in the national priorities. An intergovernmental committee met in 1963, two and a half years before the second plan. Later regional commissions of planning were established in each administrative region. West Cameroonian planners participated in each phase. Meanwhile, a detailed survey of West Cameroon was conducted, which contributed substantially to the plan's development. Overall, the second plan consisted of two if not three frameworks. One was for West Cameroon, based on the survey by experts; another was for East Cameroon, and was essentially a continuation of a development program begun at independence. One might consider as a third framework the development of a transportation and communications infrastructure, as exemplified by the Trans-Cameroon Railway and the development and improvement of road and rail links between the two states, which not only sought to provide an integrated national system, but to improve the connections between the north of East Cameroon and the southern coastal areas. General guidance and supervision of implementation became more tangible with the Second Plan; federal authorities were better equipped to oversee the program.

The structures used to establish and implement policies for developmental planning and the allocation of foreign assistance generally were redistributive in effect. Jurisdiction, defined as central jurisdiction, continued to be exercised decentrally—which was not intended. Considerable efforts were made to place authority over these matters clearly in Yaounde and to insure their coordination among federal officials and agencies. But coordination proved difficult; the Ministries of Finance and of National Economy had responsibility for directing private investment, for example. Soon after reunification the Economic and Fiscal Commission (EFC) was established on an interministerial basis to consider the problems of coordinating efforts relating to public services, customs, direct and indirect taxation, finance and the treasury, foreign trade, exchange and currency.[54] The commission was placed under the direction of the Minister of National Economy; it included representatives from both states. Though its various subcommissions met several times, the commission failed to achieve the desired integration of economic development and fiscal policies throughout the federation.[55] Even less success was achieved in coordinating foreign investment. Several months after

[54] Decree 62-DF-28 of January 4, 1962.
[55] There is no record of the third subcommission, concerned with customs and taxes, ever meeting.

the establishment of the EFC the president saw fit to issue an acerbic directive to all federal and state agencies reminding them of the primacy of the Ministry of National Economy in matters concerning the financial and economic orientation of the federation.[56] The structures could not be made to conform to the idealized ones contained in the constitution and the presidential decrees and circulars, however. The command structures in these fields failed to mesh adequately with the local counterparts; confusion resulted, to be sure, and the frustration one would expect among local officials, unsure of their prerogatives, was plainly evident. On the other hand, this situation was not without its benefits. The very obfuscation that caused these problems prolonged the possibility for local initiative and participation in the areas of economic and development policy-making and financial allocation. This might not have happened had central structures existed which were endowed with the capacity for tight command. I can suggest that the facts promoted integration because they hid from the view of westerners the extent of potential federal privilege in policy-making, and because they hid from the view of easterners at state

[56] Circular No. 29/CAB/PRF July 30, 1962. The directive merits extensive quotation:

Firstly, certain initiatives have been taken recently regarding studies concerning either the creation of various enterprises or industries or concerning private investment generally throughout the Federation. These initiatives have introduced confusion not only into your [ministers and secretaries of state] services as concerns their respective areas of competence, but also into the minds of the investors with respect to [determining] the Departments to which they are supposed to address themselves in order to realize their operations.

I know that the technical competence of certain ministries might predispose them to examine this or that project particularly relevant to this competence. It appears equally necessary to them, for obvious psychological reasons to immediately welcome all investment projects which would be useful to the country, even if, out of ignorance on the part of its promoters, it was presented to some department other than the one which should first examine it.

However, it remains . . . true that [certain] fundamental texts, assured of wide publicity outside the country, have been instituted respecting this subject and the lack of their observation risks jeopardizing the coordination which these texts wished to establish in a particularly important domain of our economic policy, whose general aims cannot succeed in an atmosphere of confusion or through divergent initiatives taken by our officials.

The Investment Code, notably, stipulates that every new investment dossier must be submitted initially to the Ministry of National Economy which will study it in liaison with the Ministry of the Plan and with the different technical departments concerned.

This dossier will then be transmitted to the Ministry of the Plan which, presiding over the *Commission des Investissements,* will receive once again, in commission, the advice of the Ministers and Technicians of the other ministries.

and local levels the extent of western privilege in the allocation of foreign aid and development resources.

I HAVE traced the major patterns of jurisdiction in the Cameroon Federation and the distribution of formal prerogative. Let us now consider the distribution of personnel within the governmental apparatus. I am concerned with what Etzioni calls the "degree of elitism," [57] not strictly with regard to the number of elite units throughout the federation—which I have already discussed, in part in my treatment of the allocation of formal jurisdiction and which I will consider again in discussing the political relations among Cameroonians—but in terms of the balance of representation (formal and informal) between east and west, north and south in the administrative positions of the federal government. Despite the fact that the federal government has the major share of formal prerogatives and certain distinct interests it pursues directly, it is not monolithic. Their personal perception and defense of federal interests notwithstanding, none of the federal officials is a neutral man when parochial interests and identifications are concerned and broad regional interests of West Cameroon and northern and southern East Cameroon complement and compete with those deriving from village and clan affiliations. These influences modify the pattern of "elitism" which might otherwise be ascribed to the federation, given the concentration of power in federal offices.

Membership in the federal elite could unite as well as divide, confronting regionalized subelites with each other, linking them but often exposing the disparities of their outlooks and interests in the process, while setting these same officials apart from their own former collaborators at the state and regional level. An intricate set of cross-cutting cleavages resulted, which could be made to inhibit the centrifugal forces of parochialism (or of geographically localized grievances), and to moderate the centripetal forces of federal dominance. To the extent that intrastate processes of integration parallel those involved in unions between states, such circumstances render doubtful the proposition that "we [can] expect a monoelite union to be more successful than any multielite pattern. . . ." [58] Multiple elites might form antagonistic factions; but this need not in itself nullify stability; reducing the potentially disruptive or corrosive impact of factions or cleavages by setting them in counterpositions

[57] Etzioni, *Political Unification*, pp. 68ff.
[58] Etzioni, *Political Unification*, p. 69.

has figured in democratic theory for a long time.[59] I am less concerned here with the emergence of a democratic order in Cameroon than with an integrated one, though the result is the same where levels of political participation are high and political aspirations moderately diverse. An assessment of the ways in which, and extent to which, social and geographically based cleavages were politicized in Cameroon must await analysis of the politics of integration. Our capacity to undertake such an analysis, however, is increased by a description of the broad patterns of regional representation in the structures of the federal government; let us prorogue for the moment the question of their political salience.

The most important cleavage in the distribution of personnel in federal structures was that which distinguished East and West Cameroonians among the holders of appointments in federal ministries. This is surprising, since so much prefederation controversy concerning what would be an appropriate relation between the representational strength of the two states had focused on the legislature. The impotence of the federal legislature, which was based on constitutional and supportive texts as well as the practice of federal politics, was not at first clear to West Cameroon leaders. For some time they expected their contingent of 10 deputies in the Federal Assembly—one-fifth of its membership representing their share of the federation's population—to serve as the first and principal defenders of the state's interests.

The list of West Cameroon deputies to the first, interim, Federal Assembly does not reveal the extent to which the Buea leadership appreciated the power centers at the federal level. Some of their top people were included in the list, but the great bulk of the talent in the KNDP remained in Buea and Victoria to run the state government. A number of deputies were only recent recruits to the KNDP, and were given their federal appointments as a reward for "crossing the carpet" from the opposition benches.[60] Fully half the contingent were young politicians who had recently participanted in party politics.[61] Of the 10 only two (Muna and

[59] See James Madison's *Essay No. 10* in *The Federalist Papers;* also S. M. Lipset, *Political Man: The Social Bases of Politics* (Garden City, N.J.: Doubleday, 1960), pp. 70–79, esp. 77, and *passim.*

[60] This is true of Martin Fusi, John Nsame, and Simon Ncha, the first of whom won his seat in the January 1959 elections as an independent and the other two as members of the CPNC.

[61] True of Z. Abendong who returned from university studies in the United States shortly before becoming a candidate (unopposed) in the December 1961 elections. Other new M.P.'s were John Sona Eyumbi, Nzo Ekhah-Nghaky, and Lifio Carr. The remaining members, Sam Moffor, Solomon Muna, Simon Nji, were party stalwarts, though the last mentioned was new to Parliament.

Ncha) had held parliamentary seats before the KNDP victory of January 1959, and the parliamentary skills of one had been little improved by the experience. It is evident that, despite the inclusion of a few experienced and highly talented people, the western delegation to the Federal Assembly was relatively weak. This is not surprising, considering the fact that the more powerful voices in the party, already holding down ministerial or parliamentary secretary positions at the state level, would not readily give them up for lower-paying positions whatever their illusions about the prestige and power of the federal representative posts.[62]

Also, representation of the western point of view in Assembly deliberations at the federal level was hampered by the fact that the most experienced or skillful of their delegates also held executive positions. I shall return to the question of the strength of the west in the federal executive; my object here is to note the consequences of dual federal roles of the abler deputies for western participation in the Federal Assembly. Because of East Cameroon tradition, derived from French tutelage, of conducting substantive legislative discussions only in commissions, rather than in plenary sessions of the legislature, proportional membership in that legislature for West Cameroon resulted in something less than proportional representation in the legislative process, especially when the ministers were too busy to participate (which was very often). The Western contingent continually found it difficult, if not impossible, to place a member in each of the four commissions, and filling its quota of three for each commission was nearly always beyond consideration. Certainly they could not achieve a balanced allocation of experience among the commissions, and often failed to participate effectively in any of them as a result of shifting the more active people back and forth, trying to visit them all.

North-south regionalism was also important in the federal allocation of power, but by omission insofar as the legislature was concerned. Northern delegates to the Federal Assembly did not group themselves into a block any more than they did in the eastern Assembly. All eastern deputies were members of the ruling UC, just as all western deputies were members of the ruling KNDP. It is important to note, however, that the eastern regime strictly observed the rules of balance between north and south in choosing their federal delegation. Only 19 of the 40 eastern

---

[62] Salaries were not unimportant in allocating personnel among the positions available. State secretaries (ministers) received 1,535,000 CFA francs a year, and federal M.P.'s only 824,400 CFA francs. Members of the state House of Assembly, with no other responsibilities, received an allowance of only 271,600 CFA francs.

deputies were from northern or Moslem constituencies (6 of the 10 West Cameroon deputies in 1961 were from the grassfields). On the other hand, as we shall see in the discussion of the broader patterns of federal politics, there was greater cohesiveness among the northern deputies, a result of their stronger voices and longer standing in the party. A few of the federal posts given to the southern deputies went as a reward to those who had deserted opposition parties fairly recently,[63] but most of the deputies from the south were converts to the UC during the period of its rapid consolidation of power following independence. The prominent names were those like Charles Assale, who continued to serve as prime minister of the eastern government while also a deputy; Ekwabi Ewane; and Hans Dissake; former members of the old *Forces Vivres de l'Opposition,* and Daniel Kemadjou (all had opposed the rules of Mbida and Ahidjo); Manga Mado, who gave the UC its base among the Kaka peoples east of Yaounde; and She Onana Paul, who provided a link with the Fang groups around Kribi, not to mention the five Bamileke deputies who had provided the first crucial UC strength in the south. The most important political payoffs came in allocating the new federal ministerial positions, which in turn made it possible to award state level posts to others who contributed to the consolidation of UC power in the south.[64]

Among the appointments to high posts in the federal executive, where the real power to initiate and command rested, West Cameroonians were strongly represented. At the level of minister or deputy minister their numerical strength was stronger than their share of the federation's population.[65] More important, those assigned to these posts were to the man capable of defending the legitimate particular interests of the west and making lasting contributions to the evolution of a distinctive and effective Cameroonian system.[66] The positions they occupied, even those at the deputy minister level, were substantive, and were concentrated in the

[63] Henri Effa and Gabriel Atangana were former *Démocrates* from the important Ewando area, who declared for the UC in 1960, the first of their party to do so.

[64] I consider these factors in detail in Chap. 12.

[65] There were 10 full ministries; of these West Cameroon had one. But they had three deputy ministers, making 30 percent of the ministerial posts. In addition, the vice president was the western prime minister (until the posts were separated in 1965), when Foncha dropped the prime minister's job and took on ministerial duties as vice president.

[66] There was initially some confusion in the designation of western officials for these posts, and A. Jua was briefly included among them as Deputy Minister of Health. He was quickly shifted to the more substantial job of Deputy Premier of the West; a much less capable person was given his federal post, who did not distinguish himself in the job.

areas requiring intimate knowledge of West Cameroon needs, leaders, peoples, and traditions. The Deputy Ministries of Justice, Foreign Affairs, and Health tended to monopolize the federal operations or concerns in these areas with respect to West Cameroon, and to participate in the broader pan-Cameroon operations as well. The mechanism of a deputy ministry permitted the early federalization of services and powers intricately linked to West Cameroon's daily life and which involved distinctively British-inspired procedures and/or institutions.[67] It would have been impossible for East Cameroonians to run or even closely guide their functioning, or to achieve standardization in their procedures. Appointing westerners to these posts provided the west with a substantial voice and presence in the federal executive, but still permitted the president to bring these activities within the orbit of federal authority, and thereby his own effective control. In the sense that this approach enhanced rapid federalization of government prerogatives, perhaps it was dysfunctional to western interests, viewed narrowly.

On the other hand, those holding the posts were not excluded from the inner councils of the government or isolated from its broader concerns. The Deputy Minister of Foreign Affairs, a position added five months after the inauguration of the other bureaus, found himself preoccupied with negotiations with the British government over the question of continuing Commonwealth preferences on important West Cameroon exports, especially bananas; but he was also concerned with the whole range of British-Cameroon relations. He must also have had a heavy hand in the negotiations with Nigeria in an attempt to restore normal relations following Cameroon's bitter dispute with that country (including a challenge in the International Court of Justice) concerning the plebiscite in Northern (ex-British) Cameroons. Included in these negotiations was the problem of fixing adequate compensation for the fixed capital Nigeria had invested in Southern Cameroons and had lost upon its separation in 1960. His assignment as head of a diplomatic mission to Asian and Middle Eastern countries in February of 1963 indicates that the Deputy Minister of Foreign Affairs was not restricted to problems affecting only West Cameroon.[68] The full ministry, held by the able Solomon

[67] It should be recalled that western constitutional proposals had envisioned continued state responsibility in each of these fields, particularly Health and Justice, and certain aspects of foreign affairs.

[68] *L'Unité*, No. 124 (January 26, 1963). Nineteen agreements were signed with six countries in Asia and the Middle East during this tour, providing for commercial, economic technical, and/or cultural cooperation. The Deputy Minister of Health dealt only with operations in West Cameroon, however. That of Justice had little to

T. Muna, a close associate of Prime Minister Foncha, was important. Transport, Postal Service, and Telecommunications were services which would play a key role in integrating not only the west and the east but the north and south, to say nothing of the many isolated localities throughout the still undeveloped north.[69] When in 1965 a new Ministry of Labor was added to the federal list, representing the last major area of prerogative to be federalized, it too was given to a West Cameroonian, Nzo Ekhah-Nghaky, who had previously served as Deputy Minister of Foreign Affairs and as Minister of Health.[70]

Representation in the list of the top positions in the executive branch in numbers proportional to regional population strength does not appear to have mattered much to the northern leaders. President Ahidjo has never attempted to balance north-south representation among holders of ministerial level positions, either in terms of absolute numerical preponderance or of relative population. In his first government after independence there were five northerners, besides himself, among 19 cabinet members. Northern strength has hovered around the level of one-third to one-fourth of the positions, before and after federation for the top positions, though federation increased northern strength in state level jobs and thus raised their percentage among all executive positions, federal and state.[71]

The most important position other than the presidency, that of Minister of Armed Forces, has always been held by a trusted northerner, but a number of other sensitive positions have been held by southerners, sometimes from regions hostile to the regime. Thus it is apparent that neither in terms of numerical strength nor strictly in terms of control of strategic positions has the president or the north emphasized regional or ethnic origin in allocating executive posts. The imperatives of politics, of consolidating control over authoritative structures, have affected the alloca-

do with the *operation* of the judicial system in East Cameroon, but a great deal to do with the difficult job of working out a harmonization of the two European legal legacies.

[69] This ministry was also assigned responsibility for mines, a peripheral resource in the Cameroon economy.

[70] The Deputy Ministry of Health was dropped in 1965, as health services became consolidated, and Ekhah-Nghaky, who had briefly occupied that full ministerial position, was shifted to Labor.

[71] The total number of positions at a ministerial level held by easterners has remained about the same from prefederal times. Since federation northerners have persistently held 5 out of 10 of the posts, and the prime minister has always been a southerner. If one combines federal and state ministers in the east, northerners hold and have usually held, slightly less than half the positions, 8 or 9 out of 19 to 21 positions.

231

tion of the most important strategic positions; generally the key power points in the system have been placed under the charge of close associates of the president, most of whom are northerners.

I conclude from the above observations that the allocation of formally representative positions and those of executive responsibility served to link all important regional areas into a common network of authority in a way that did not give any region per se preponderant strength or undue weakness. Though the federation was elitist, the federal elite was not structurally monolithic and did not sharpen geographical, cultural, or ethnic cleavages. Rather, the structural makeup of the federal elite reflected the main lines of cleavage within the state and local elites, which cut across those between east and west, and to some extent, north and south.

⚒ 10 ⚒

Conjunctive Structures of Political Activity: The Eastern System

CAMEROON has produced the form but not the substance of a single party state. There is no single pervasive network of people who have organized themselves into a stable hierarchy of influence and communication, who take orders from particular people and give them to certain others, and who all agree on the extralegal ground rules for the game of politics.

A formal organization exists, which embodies formal and informal hierarchies of power and which monopolizes the prerogatives of official political party activity. This organization is not cohesive, however; the differences between its factions and subgroupings are as important as the common ground of official party affiliation and loyalty they share. During the first five years of the federation the reputation and popularity of the ruling political parties of East and West Cameroon made mere token contributions to the legitimation of the federal state. As much as the achievement of the leaders, it was the ethic of modernism itself and the natural need for government, as well as the values associated with the campaign to achieve reunification of Cameroon, that legitimized the new federal state. As time went on and federal power became more evident and its costs more considerable, the marginal legitimizing influence of a single political party, if only a form, became more important.

The drive toward a comprehensive single party in Cameroon loyally followed the logic of this development throughout much of the rest of Africa, as analyzed by Zolberg;[1] it was a response to a felt need for an all-encompassing movement which was considered to be, in itself, a measure of the level of national integration achieved within the system. The rationale for this view of the single party is complex. In part, it holds that the party is to provide the masses of the people with a communications network and with an educational experience that can socialize them to the symbols, policies, and practices of the new national political order and thus stimulate the achievement of a more coherent political culture. This view is principally concerned with legitimizing the elite's composition and objectives for the masses. In Cameroon the legitimizing function of the single party was not as important as it has been in the political philosophy of other African regimes because the Cameroon regime has not se-

[1] Zolberg, *Creating Political Order.*

233

riously attempted to mobilize the masses on a grand scale. Indeed, since the potential disruptions and disintegrative pressures of massive social mobilization are great in fragmented societies,[2] the moderate approach taken to this objective in Cameroon may have made the party a more effective agent for legitimizing the regime than it has been in states where mass mobilization was a predominant theme of party activity, such as in Guinea or Ghana, and to some extent, Mali.[3] A more important motivation behind the push for a single party was the desire to legitimize the dominant factions of the elite in the eyes of other elite groups. What was thought to be crucial was the achievement of consensus among the powerful, not on all, or necessarily very many, policy matters, but on the minimal ground rules for politics—namely that all political factions would pursue their policy objectives and political interests from within a common organizational framework.

Whereas modern industrial states rely on the state apparatus to provide the common framework, most of the new states find the apparatus too delimited and weak to fulfill alone the function of providing the basis for common identity and commonly agreed on rules governing the competition for power. There are certain ground rules in Cameroon, as there are in the other new African states; though the great, and increasing, majority of the people abide by them they do so to avoid rather than express conviction. The states are not weaker than the parties, but in Cameroon the center of power is clearly the state apparatus. The legitimate rules of the state are not pervasive, though the state's means of enforcing them are becoming so. Early in independence the state and the parties enjoy a different though sometimes analogous legitimacy. Almost everyone in the new societies accepts the proposition that the state should exist, that it alone defines the national territory, regulates public life, and coerces in the name of the people. They do not accept the proposition that the state may regulate the intimacies of life, or may claim the enthusiasms and personal convictions of the people. For these peoples require a different kind of loyalty to each other, one more easily justified by the popular aspirations to collective dignity, harmony, importance, and/or vengeance —aspirations symbolized in the concept of a modern nation and organized into discrete programs by the party. The past legitimizes the state,

[2] Karl Deutsch discusses the disintegrative aspects of social mobilization in a number of his works. See especially his "Social Mobilization and Political Development," *American Political Science Review* (Washington, D.C.: September 1961), p. 501.

[3] The experience of the parties in each of these states is discussed in Coleman and Rosberg, *Political Parties.*

the future legitimizes the party which is the principal embodiment of government and seeks to join the two by serving as a "symbolic referent" and an "integration integer." [4] Thereby the party expands the range of claims the dominant groups can make against the rest, achieving voluntary compliance with demands the state cannot rightly assert or involuntary compliance with those the party cannot effectively enforce.

The targets of party appeals and punishments in Cameroon were to be found primarily among the elite groups, with certain notable exceptions in the north and west. The party served the function of aggregating elites rather than interests. Indeed, the propaganda put into the service of this function promised, sometimes explicitly, that less comprehensive organizations (political tendencies, ethnic and regional groups, factions) could continue to aggregate and articulate their own legitimate but particular interests so long as they did so from within rather than without and against the party—symbol and instrument of the incipient nation. Thus the national party was principally a mechanism of elite recruitment, communication, and socialization rather than general interest aggregation and articulation. Once established it progressively sought to disinterest subaggregates, to divest the factions of their particularistic programs and claims, and then to invest them with a more condensed and homogeneous version of the interests of the initially dominant leaders or groups. Little of this effort was issue- or policy-oriented. Form counted for a great deal. Powerful groups not willing to join the party were destroyed by state authority, and those that did join were often dissipated or reformed.

Though there were similar pressures in the two state, as well as in the federal governments, to consolidate the power of dominant factions through party mergers and absorptions, the party systems in these three contexts differed. The West Cameroon system was the most open and competitive, affording adequate opportunities for party formation and expression until it was dissolved in favor of a single national party at the

---

[4] Apter, *Politics of Modernization*, p. 241. By "symbolic referent" Apter means the mechanism for exemplifying the unity and potential of the nation in the personalities and programs of the present leadership. The role of the "integration integer" is one of defining roles, deciding on behavior models for each principal participant so as to maximize harmony and the achievement of shared values. The other core functions of government, according to Apter, are (1) "sanctional source," or the definition and enforcement of norms, which is a role filled more by the state apparatus than by the party as discussed here; and (2) "ethnic definition," or definition of the bases of identity or membership in the Nation. This role is not elaborated here, but is involved in the concept of nation as discussed here; it is a product of history, myth, and aspiration.

federal level. The system in East Cameroon was less open, though several parties have operated in the state, openly or under cover, up to this writing. The party system at the federal level was a compromise between the styles of the two systems. During the early phases of the federation the ruling state parties, the UC and the KNDP, combined into a single parliamentary group—the National Unity Group—but chose not to eliminate the particular identity of each state party or their expression of distinctly regional interests. Even after the creation of a single national party through the fusion of all active parties of East and West Cameroon (with the exception of the ephemeral structures of the *Travaillistes* and the UPC, members of these parties tended to operate as distinguishable factions within the new setting.

The meaning of the emergence of a single party structure for the whole of the country is more easily appreciated through consideration of the relations among the several parties which operated at the state level during the first four and a half years of the federation.

The East Cameroon Party System, 1958–1966

The relations among East Cameroon parties since the rise to power of Ahmadou Ahidjo and his UC party have been characterized by the consolidation of that power through the steady attrition of the leaders and members of other parties and their adhesion to the UC. By the time the federation was created Ahidjo's party had established irresistible dominance of the National Assembly, and by the time of the first general elections for the state legislature after federation it had eliminated all other rivals. This was no mean achievement considering the precarious base of power from which Ahidjo had led his country to independence.

Ahidjo was from the start of his political career dedicated to preserving the unity of at least French Cameroon. It is asserted that he refrained from demanding the prime ministership in 1957, despite the fact that his parliamentary grouping (of 31 deputies) was the largest in the Assembly, because he feared that such a move might split the country.[5] When Ahidjo did come to power just six months later nearly all of Prime Minister Mbida's support had evaporated and Ahidjo was elected unanimously on a program of national unity, independence, and reunification.[6] Though he was attacked by the UPC and other southern "nationalist" leaders as being a prisoner of the reactionary feudal *lamibé*, Prime Minister Ahidjo strengthened the cause of national unity rather than weak-

[5] Moussa Yaya, interview, Yaounde, June 1963.
[6] Mbida's party, the *Parti des Démocrates*, abstained.

ened it. On the eve of the 1960 elections his achievement was noted by *Le Monde,* which asserted, however, that though Ahidjo had succeeded in avoiding a "secession" of the north, no Cameroonian politician appeared equal to the task of establishing an equilibrium between north and south without a major regroupment of political forces. "If the local leaders do not achieve union, not only will they condemn the Cameroon to balkanization, but they will [thereby] prove that they have always fought more for the conquest of power than for independence," stated *Le Monde.*

The government Ahidjo headed on January 1, 1960 was as insecure as any African government has been at independence. What he lacked was a firm political, not juridical, base for his regime. Scarcely two months before independence he had been voted full legislative powers by the Legislative Assembly, which effectively made him the sole authority in the government. However, the Assembly had not renewed its popular mandate since December 1956; in those elections not only had the UC marshaled only 34 percent of the total vote, or 31 of the 70 seats, but the principal opposition party, the UPC, was excluded from the elections, and consequently had organized a boycott effective enough to restrict voting levels to 14 percent of the electorate in one district and less than 25 percent in another.[7] Initially Ahidjo's party was nothing more than the strongest of several important parties. The others could easily have formed a coalition government had they been willing or able to bury their differences in a common program.

Several efforts have been made to organize such a coalition of southern-based, allegedly "progressive," parties in order to preempt control of the government by northern politicians accused of being reactionary defenders of a political order perceived as backward, traditional, and semifeudal. Such efforts always shattered on the jagged edges of personal or tribal animosities and an unwillingness to share power once it was achieved. In June 1956 Soppo Priso organized the first and most promising of such efforts in the *Courant d'Union Nationale* (CUN), which drew from all the major southern parties and movements, but which fell apart in November when UPC militants decided that the French Administration's refusal to legally rehabilitate UPC activities and declare an unconditional amnesty would deprive the nationalists of any real power. Despite the fact that the unity movement had arisen out of general opposition to the reforms of the French *loi-cadre* of June 1956, and that its demands regarding the UPC (for an amnesty and guarantees for com-

[7] The overall level of participation was low—55 percent—but this was due as much to apathy in the north as to the boycott in southern coastal districts.

pletely free elections) had not been met, most of the moderate politicians found the attractions of even a marginal power position in the new Assembly too compelling to permit them to follow the UPC along a course of violence against the system. The reforms of the *loi-cadre* promised the creation of a government with some responsibility. Thus the stakes had become too high for southern politicians to dismiss lightly the prospects for an elected post. Southern control of such a government required effective unity among the various nationalist forces of the south, something the colonial administration sought to avoid and the politicians concerned seemed incapable of achieving.

The most serious threat to Ahidjo's rule came in the spring of 1959 during the special "Cameroons Session" of the Thirteenth General Assembly, reconvened after the adjournment of the regular session to consider an exclusively Cameroons agenda.[8] Isolated and desperate, the exiled (mostly Bamileke) wing of the UPC leadership had shifted its focus to the United Nations following the death of Um Nyobe, and the massive rallying to legal life (*ralliément*) of his Bassa followers. The UPC hoped that the UN would insist on an honest and general amnesty and new elections before approving Cameroon's accession to independence which Ahidjo and the French authorities had scheduled for January 1st of the following year. The Ahidjo regime approached the challenge of the General Assembly debate with several powerful argumentative weapons: the *ralliément* and subsequent quiescence, a new amnesty law, a new statute granting internal autonomy and scheduling independence (subject to Trusteeship and General Assembly approval), and a generally laudatory report from the Fourth UN Visiting Mission to tour the Territory.[9] The Mission had recommended approval of the request for independence and had disclaimed any need for new elections or for a plebiscite in French Cameroon concerning reunification or the modalities to terminate Trusteeship. On the other hand, Ahidjo's opponents were not without their own strengths. Some 18 petitioners spoke in opposition to the government or its position; 15 expressed some support for the position taken by the UPC. The radical African states represented in the United Nations attempted to achieve an African solution by arranging a compromise directly between the UPC's exiled presidents, Moumié and Ahidjo. The discussions failed, and efforts by the delegations, supported by the

[8] The events leading to and the development and results of the Thirteenth Assembly's resumed "special" session are discussed in some detail by Le Vine in his *Cameroons.*

[9] UN Document T/1441.

238

Soviet bloc states, came too late in the session for a united front of anti-colonialists. India and other excolonial states broke ranks to give their support to the Trusteeship Council's recommendation approving independence without new elections.[10] The anticolonialist states faced genuine dilemmas. On one hand a militant African nationalist party, which had suffered severely for its direct opposition to French colonial policy, was branding the Cameroon government a front for French maneuver, and demanding the opportunity through new elections to demonstrate its supposed popular appeal. On the other hand, it had been that maligned government which had negotiated an agreement with France that achieved internal autonomy and a promise of independence in one year's time. The UN Mission had noted the irony of the UN calling into question the representative character of a government that had just won a commitment to independence. Later President Ahidjo smugly ridiculed the actions of the UPC supporters: "France having been once and for all placed in the ranks of the so-called colonialist nations . . . [the] group of so-called anti-colonialist nations . . . had to oppose the demands of France and my government whatever their tenor. Thus, one was able to witness the curious spectacle of the so-called anti-colonialist nations voting against the Cameroun's independence.[11]

The anticolonial states, though sympathetic to the UPC, were faced with the untoward prospect of having to oppose a resolution whose 12 sponsors included prestigious India, a resolution which would usher in the fifth country of black Africans, the third in this century, into the prerogatives of independent statehood and membership in the United Nations. Either that, or they would have to give a vote of confidence to a government they had just vehemently castigated. Rather than doing either of these, 23 pro-UPC delegations abstained; the resolution carried 56-0.[12] The UPC failed even to win a demand that it be legalized.

There followed a frantic last-chance effort by the exiled UPC in the form of a resort to violence and terror in an attempt to force France and/or the Ahidjo regime to negotiate the UPC's return to legal political influence.[13]

The rallied forces, as well as other contingents of the opposition, then offered the UPC what seemed its last hope of achieving a measure of

[10] Eight African and Asian states initially supported delaying independence until new elections were held.

[11] *La Presse du Cameroun,* April 12, 1959, p. 1.

[12] United Nations Resolution 1349 (xiii). In the Fourth Committee debates the day before, the nine members of the Soviet bloc had opposed the resolution.

[13] I discuss this and other campaigns of violence by the UPC in Chap. 14.

239

power. The rallied UPC, the leader of the moderate nationalists, Soppo Priso, and members of the Démocrates called for a series of "roundtable" conferences of all factions aimed at achieving a general détente. The call was also supported by André Marie Mbida who had joined his ex-enemy Moumié in Conakry following Mbida's fall from power. Supporters of this idea argued that it was the only way national unity and internal peace could be restored. Privately many of them hoped it would isolate the Moumié wing of the UPC by removing any reason for continued subversion. The proposed purpose of the conference was to construct a government of national union, presumably including members of the UPC, and to draft a constitution and organize new elections for a government which could lead the country to sovereignty in peace. Moumié had no valid alternative in the face of the professed support for the idea, although he proclaimed his acceptance in terms Ahidjo would or could not accept. Though an August date had been demanded by Moumié, and elections before the end of Trusteeship, Ahidjo did not establish a committee to organize the roundtable conference until November and then excluded both the *ralliés* and the *Démocrates* from membership on it.

Ahidjo emerged virtually unbruised from the severe UPC attacks on his authority, both at the United Nations and in the latest UPC-directed campaign of rebellion which Ahidjo's armed forces had contained reasonably well by the fall of 1959. One might consider it evidence of self-confidence and strength rather than weakness and fear when in late October 1959 Ahidjo demanded full powers from the Assembly. The opposition voiced to this demand was as vehement as any had ever been from the forces of opposition in the country. The sessions in which the measure was debated and finally approved were as tumultuous as any Cameroon legislative assembly has been before or since, and the militant nationalists in opposition to the Ahidjo regime more united.[14] Perhaps none was aware of it at the time, but this expression of opposition to Ahidjo's approach, if not his control, was the last serious threat posed to either.

Ahidjo made good use of his powers to legislate by decree and to determine the constitutional proposals and election laws according to which the representative institutions would be filled. I have already discussed the structures inaugurated for the federation.[15] My wish here is to note their impact on the conduct of party politics. The prospects for the UC were strengthened in several ways, the most important of which was the enlargement of the Legislative Assembly from 70 to 100 seats. The sig-

---

[14] The session is described by Le Vine, *Cameroons,* pp. 185–88. The measure was approved by a vote of 50-12, with one abstention.

[15] See Chap. 8.

nificance of the increase was not in an alteration of the balance between districts in terms of the number of representatives, because the proportional distribution of seats remained much the same.[16] It was of considerable importance, however, that the UC was able to capture every one of the 14 additional seats in the north, while the increments of the other regions were often split between opposition parties. In fact, the UC was able to win seven seats outside the north in the elections of 1960, whereas it had been unable to capture one seat in 1956.

A second and very important instrument used to consolidate the power of the UC was the electoral law established for the 1960 elections to the National Assembly. The elections were run on the basis of party lists in each constituency; that is, parties were obliged to run a list of candidates covering all the seats in the constituency, and the party receiving a plurality of votes captured all the seats for that district. The effect of these provisions was modified in some districts, however, to the disadvantage of Ahidjo's opposition. Districts alleged to contain "minorities" or to have more than 400 thousand voters were divided. It seemed that only southern districts with strong opposition groups contained minorities— Wouri and Mungo districts were each divided into four separate single-member constituencies, for example. This forced popular Soppo Priso to oppose for the first time in either man's political career the Douala nobleman and doyen Cameroon politician Prince Douala Manga Bell, who eliminated Soppo Priso from politics. The Bamileke and Nyong-et-Sanaga regions were divided into 5 and 10 constituencies respectively, which effectively eliminated the list system in these regions, for no party was strong enough to win a plurality in all constituencies of either region. The electoral procedures encouraged political expression along tribal lines and made it more difficult for the UPC or *Démocrates* to realize their full voting potential.

The controversies surrounding the provisions of the new constitution and the procedures to govern the first general elections in independent Cameroon stimulated the eight opposition members of the Assembly to renew their efforts to achieve a united front of southern-based parties.[17] A

[16] The north gained 14 seats, but this represented an increase of only 1 percent in its percentage of the total number of seats, from 43 to 44 percent. The Bamileke districts gained about 2 percent of the total seats, but until the deputies actually shifted their allegiance to the UC the increment was a disadvantage for the UC.

[17] The members of the opposition called themselves the "Groupe des Huits." They were Charles Assale, M. Belhe Gaston, Betote Akwa, Ekwabi Ewane, Hans Dissake, François Obam, Aloys Ntonga, and Soppo Priso. Assale and Ekwabi broke ranks with the opposition, however, in order to accept ministerial positions in Ahidjo's preindependence government.

new movement was launched by Soppo Priso and Marcel Beybey Eyidi, called the *Forces Vives de l'Opposition,* which held several meetings to elaborate a common platform among leaders of most of the southern parties, of both moderate and liberal persuasion.[18] The group opposed the exiled UPC leadership's stand on the constitution by encouraging participation in the elections but rejection of the constitutional proposals. Following the constitutional referendum the *Forces* called public attention to the many disorders the UPC had stimulated and the harsh and punitive measures the government had used to restrict the opposition.[19] At a large meeting held March 6 and 7, a diverse group passed a resolution that stated in part: "Considering that any electoral consultation in the seven departments deeply troubled . . . can only result in passionate contests and protestations by all those who because of circumstances would not have had the opportunity either to present themselves [as candidates] nor to vote freely; in order to avoid such criticism . . . there is reason to have, before the elections, a total and unconditional amnesty so as to proceed to holding of a 'round table' [conference]." [20]

Electoral procedures were criticized at the meeting. The claim was that they would deprive the elections of their political meaning by instituting two different balloting systems, a list system in the north and single-member constituencies in the south. Consequently those attending the meeting implored the government to establish an electoral committee composed of all political tendencies, to unify the electoral regime, to order and insure the withdrawal of all French troops, and to conduct a new census before the elections. A delegation was selected to present the demands to Ahidjo who received them cordially but refused to meet any of the demands. The group succeeded in agreeing on collective endorsement of a number of lists of candidates, but was not able to agree on such lists for each southern constituency, nor were they able to eliminate al-

[18] Meetings were held on November 29, 1959, February 6 and 14 and March 6 and 7, 1960. Participants in the last and largest of these included key spokesmen from Eyidi's *Regroupement des Forces Nationales,* Soppo Priso's MANC, Mbida's *Démocrates,* from the rallied UPC and the UPC women, student, and labor affiliate organizations, from the militant labor federation and from a number of tribal associations.

[19] They singled out "arrests, house arrests, the interdiction of [certain] journals and of meetings, bloody incidents, and the exclusiveness of propaganda and propaganda media which the government reserved to itself." *La Presse du Cameroun,* March 8, 1960.

[20] *La Presse du Cameroun,* March 8, 1960 (my translation). Members of the delegation were: Soppo Priso, Mbong Silas (representing Mayi Matip), Bebey Eyidi, Nthep (of UPC), Etame Ebenezer (of the CGKT), Zogo Massi, Kohn Emile (of the UGTC), and Madame Ngapeth (the women's affiliate of UPC).

ternative lists of candidates. In the face of disciplined solidarity in the northern constituencies, reflected in the fact that no northern seat was contested by more than one candidate, over 400 candidates vied for the 56 southern seats.

The severe competition for the southern seats was a result of more than the continuing fragmentation of the southern political arena; there was also the value of the stakes involved. Since the elections of 1956 it had become increasingly clear to leaders and followers that lack of participation in elections resulted only in the exclusion of these groups from the benefits of the real resources and power embodied in the new institutions of government. Consequently the internal wing of the UPC and other non-UPC dissidents split with the exiled leadership over the question of participation in the 1960 elections. The former had been willing to support demands for a roundtable conference and a provisional government representing all tendencies, even the demand to delay the elections and to insure the necessary conditions for a completely free and open campaign and balloting. But the nationalists inside the country refused to boycott the elections, and once again refused to leave the political arena open to the play of forces they disliked.

Ahidjo had helped to consolidate the split by abruptly re-legalizing the banned UPC and affiliate organizations scarcely six weeks prior to the election. By doing so he rather gratuitously boosted his own prestige. Only the *rallié* wing of the party was willing or able to fully profit from the opportunity thus created. The Bassa elements of the UPC were in the most favored position because they had begun to rally in massive numbers in 1958, and by 1960 had succeeded in electing six deputies to the Assembly in special by-elections which Ahidjo had granted in return for the collaboration of Mayi Matip and his followers. In 1959 Kamdem Ninyim had also led a significant *ralliément* among his Bamileke followers though they were unwilling to join ranks with the Bassa wing of the party. In the constitutional referendum both groups had counseled participation, though the Bamileke supported the constitution, whereas the Bassa and most other southern dissident groups opposed it. The two groups of former rebels successfully ran lists of candidates in their own respective areas, against the vehement criticism of the exiled UPC leadership.

From Conakry and Accra the exiled leadership cautiously countered Ahidjo's initiative in legalizing the party by reiterating several old and some new demands: liberation of all political prisoners and the declaration of an unconditional amnesty; withdrawal of all foreign troops; the complete restoration of public liberties, including those of the press; and United Nations supervision of the elections.[21] Following a week-long meeting of the exiled leadership in Accra, they apparently decided that neither the elections nor a return to legal political activity offered any real promise of winning power in the country. Despite their earlier failure to win support in the United Nations or to stimulate a rebellion strong enough to oust the Ahidjo regime or force it to compromise, the exiled UPC once again called for revolutionary war and a boycott of the elections. They declared the *ralliés* and any others posing their candidacy to be "agents of Franco-American imperialism," to be considered as "traitors" and dealt with accordingly when the truly revolutionary forces won power.[22] The group announced that its program was now aimed at establishing a revolutionary administration-in-exile until they could establish internal administrations in the zones of liberation.[23] Rather than leading to increased power for the rebel UPC, its continued unwillingness to return to the country and peacefully pursue support endowed Ahidjo's action of legalizing the internal UPC with an image of sincerity and moderation which facts perhaps did not justify.

The exiled leadership feared that Ahidjo's promise of amnesty did not include them, fears which were not altogether unfounded. Several months before independence Ahidjo had announced to the Legislative Assembly his intention to declare a general and unconditional amnesty, but had not done so; he had advanced the excuse that such an act awaited the end to terrorism and a return to peace. In Ahidjo's view the amnesty UPC leaders demanded amounted to an armistice and the abdication by the government of its responsibilities. This he refused to do; he promised rather that even without a declaration a de facto amnesty was being offered to those who did rally to legal life and withheld from those who continued to reject reason and to perpetrate acts of violence. His government would use every available resource, including the foreign troops, to crush the terrorist movement.

The *rallié* elements of the UPC emerged from the April elections strengthened by the success of their candidates. It was the Bassa and Douala elements who profited from the UPC name, however, since the Bamileke candidates, though in many instances popularly identified with

[21] *La Presse du Cameroun*, March 1, 1960.

[22] See *La Presse du Cameroun*, March 19, 20, 1960.

[23] This aspect of the UPC campaign of violence is discussed in Chapter 14. The claim was falsely made at this time that the whole of the Bamileke and most of the Mungo regions had already been liberated. In fact, the exiled leadership had lost control of many of the rebel bands in those districts.

the party, chose to identify themselves by personalities or by other organizational names. Eight candidates were elected under the UPC banner, and at least five more former adherents (those in the list headed by Kamdem Ninyim) won seats in the Bamileke districts. The campaigns for the constitutional referendum and then for the elections had crystallized even more starkly the differences between the Bassa and Bamileke factions of the internal UPC, and of course had severed nearly every connection between either of the two groups and the exiled leadership. The success of the Bamileke deputies who had repudiated the exiled group, and their refusal to use the UPC's name, indicate an estrangement between the great majority of the Bamileke people and the party. Six of the old anti-UPC leaders who had grouped themselves into the *Paysans Indépendents* under the leadership of Mathias Djoumessi were also rejected. Only one incumbent Bamileke deputy was successful.

The old-guard nationalist leadership in other parties also suffered severe losses, in part due to the electoral procedures already discussed and in part as a result of popular rejection. Four members of the *Groupe des Huits* made unsuccessful bids for reelection.[24] The *Démocrates* also lost popularity; 10 Démocrate incumbents were defeated.[25] The new Assembly was made up of young men, most of whom were newcomers to parliamentary politics. Fifty-nine of the 100 deputies had not served in the Assembly before.[26]

The UC emerged from the elections considerably strengthened. None of its candidates lost, though nine of the former deputies retired from politics, and the party captured 51 seats, a majority of the new Assembly. For the first time, it won seats—seven of them—outside the predominantly Moslem districts.[27] It had garnered 45 percent of the total vote, which no other party came close to. The UPC had the next largest bloc of voters, about 25 percent of that of the UC, but only about 14 percent of the seats in the Assembly.

The victory of the UC was not so overwhelming that all chance for a southern-based coalition to gain control of the government was eliminated. On the basis of his party's own strength, Ahidjo's majority was by

[24] The most notable defeat was that of Soppo Priso who, as noted, was the unfortunate victim of the election laws. Others who lost their seats were Betote Akwa, M. Belhe, and Ntonga Aloys.

[25] Eyinga, "Les Elections."

[26] *Ibid.*

[27] UC gains were achieved primarily in the eastern districts of Haut Nyong, Lom-Kadei, and Boumba-Ngoko. Four of these new adherents were former *Démocrates*, one a former MANC (Ekwabi); two were new to politics.

only one vote. Opposition members were encouraged to make another effort to achieve unity, but the effort was led by André Mbida whose many abrupt changes of policy and affiliation inspired accusations of opportunism and suspicions of perfidy. Nevertheless, 38 deputies-elect came to a roundtable conference Mbida hosted in his Yaounde home for "all deputies from areas south of Adamawa." [28] The purpose of the meeting, according to Mbida's invitational telegram, was "to save the higher interests of the Cameroun." It resulted in a four-point "Minimum Common National Program," which called for (a) an unconditional amnesty; (b) formation of a provisional coalition government charged with the tasks, first and most important, of assuring the departure of French administrative department heads and bureau chiefs wherever possible, second, the redrafting of a constitution, and finally, the repudiation of the Franco-Camerounian secret agreements of December 25, 1959, permitting French military bases and troops in the country; (c) the complete withdrawal of French troops following an expansion of the Cameroonian ranks in the army; and (d) reunification of Cameroon through the creation of an ad hoc commission in the National Assembly and the establishment of all the practical measures necessary to realize the objective.[29]

The movement did not achieve any of its objectives, primarily because a number of the participants, especially those from the Bamileke areas, considered Mbida's approach (excluding the UC deputies) extremely dangerous to the territorial integrity of the country. They supported the program elaborated at the meeting only on the condition that the resolutions passed not be made public until all the other deputies were consulted. This was a promise Mbida did not keep, however; as the meeting closed the 18 Bamileke deputies withdrew and organized their own parliamentary grouping, the *Front Populaire pour l'Unité et la Paix* (FPUP). These deputies enacted their own resolution, which reiterated most of the substantive points agreed on in the larger meeting, but which took note of the special problems of the Bamileke districts wherein, according to them, "hundreds of Bamileke fall almost daily from the blows of machetes as well as bullets." The resolution complained of discrimination against Bamileke in both the public and private sectors, and maintained that the loss of lives and property was concentrated in their departments. They appealed to their countrymen to lay down their arms and cease their

---

[28] *La Presse du Cameroun*, May 4, 1960. Those from the south who did not attend were mostly *Progressistes* (Ndounokong, Zock Remy, Charles Okala, Akoa, Obam, Assale, Aboya) and Tonpoba Youta, Djuato of the Bamileke deputies, as well as the seven southern deputies affiliated with the UC.

[29] *Ibid.*, May 4, 1960.

quarrels and divisions, and pledged all their efforts to achieving a return to peace, an unconditional amnesty, and the replacement of French troops with Cameroonians. The Bamileke criticism of Mbida was joined vociferously by Beybey Eyidid and Douala Manga Bell, as well as the Bassa *"Upécistes"* (adherents of the UPC). "We did not want a meeting of southern deputies," stated Eyidi. "If the Cameroonian deputies offer the spectacle of division, what will the people think? We are putting the fire to the powder." Matip joined in the attack, claiming that their work must be national in scope, not something exclusive.

The failure of Mbida's roundtable conference meant that the southern deputies were unwilling or incapable of forming a united front against the UC. It is doubtful that they would have been able to capture the government even had they done so, because Ahidjo quickly won Assale's support and that of two others from his *Mouvement d'Action Nationale* party. Collaboration between the two leaders and their followers predated independence. Assale had been named Minister of Finance in Ahidjo's first government, and Assale's associate, Gaston Behle, was named Minister of Labor and Social Welfare. These two members of the *Groupe des Huits* incurred the wrath of the others when they supported Ahidjo's demand for full powers, and refused to honor the demands of the party for them to resign their ministries. Since that time, Assale and Behle had led the Bulu contingent of the movement (known variously as the *"Group des Huits"* in the Assembly, *Courant d'Action Nationale* in Douala, and MANC in the Bulu areas) into ever closer collaboration with the UC. In the constitutional referendum the MANC split again, with Behle and Assale campaigning for an affirmative vote and most of the other leaders campaigning against "Ahidjo's Constitution." When it came time to elect the president during the first session of the National Assembly, two Bulu deputies from the MANC, Obam and Akoa, were among the 20 deputies who nominated Ahidjo. With his election a certainty no one else felt strong enough to even pose their candidacy; most of the deputies jumped on the bandwagon and Ahidjo was elected, 89 votes for and 10 abstaining.[30] The abstentions came from the UPC deputies, joined by Eyidi and Douala Manga Bell, who had called for the ceremonial election of the defunct Reuben Um Nyobé as First President. Following the election of Ahidjo, Mayi Matip proposed the official rehabilitation of UmNyobé's name and the construction of a national monument to him, but the motion was tabled until a later session and was never revived.

Ahidjo moved quickly to consolidate his expanded support among

---

[30] *La Presse du Cameroun,* May 6, 1960. There were only 99 deputies present in this session. Owona Mimba, a UPC deputy, was in Conakry at the time.

formerly critical southern political groups by appointing a number of their spokesmen as ministers in his greatly enlarged government. Assale's support was handsomely rewarded with the position of prime minister. Four of the new Bamileke deputies, including Kamdem Ninyim Pierre, the former head of one of the guerrilla campaigns, were given government posts. Ekwabi Ewabi's defection from the opposition even before the constitutional referendum was rewarded with the Ministry of National Education. The *Démocrates* received three ministries, and two former *Démocrates* who had run this time as members of the UC, received ministerial posts. Ahidjo had offered ministerial positions to André Marie Mbida, Mayi Matip, and Beybey Eyidi, but they turned them down. The 14 ministers and 5 secretaries of state in the first government, who represented every major party with the exception of the Bassa-UPC, came close to constituting the *"gouvernement national intertendance"* Ahidjo's opposition had so often demanded.

Ahidjo made various efforts to reconcile the southern parties to his government. He legalized the UPC, was willing to include ex-UPC terrorists and representatives from the *Démocrates,* the *Progressistes,* and other dissident groups in his government, but all his efforts failed to solidify a national coalition or eliminate violence, rebellion, and factionalism from the political life of the south. In fact, the ranks of the opposition began to solidify and speak with a more determined voice. Though acts of subversion and terrorism continued sporadically in areas influenced by the exiled UPC leadership, the center of Ahidjo's opposition shifted to the south-central districts controlled by Matip's UPC and Mbida's Démocrates. The doyen of the Assembly, *Démocrate* Mballa Barnabé, set the tone of the opposition's attack. The aftermath of his bitter speech foreshadowed the regime's resolve to eliminate parochial, dissident power blocs and expand the ruling party into a universal and unchallenged framework for political expression.[31] Mballa complained that the country lived in a "perpetual state of anguish" due not only to the terrorism but to the odious, brutal, and bloody repression which he claimed characterized the government's state of emergency. It made one wonder if the country were really independent, he said, and reminded one of the situation in France in 1789. Mballa lashed out bitterly at the continued presence of French troops and military bases. He considered French influence to be evident in the government, and charged that the north was dominated by *lamibé* in an obsolete feudalism which seemingly no one there recognized to be obsolete.

[31] *Discours du Doyen d'Age, Assemblée Nationale,* October 1960.

Predictably Ahidjo and his closest supporters were so angered by the speech that they requested the *Démocrates* in the government to repudiate it; upon Mballa's refusal to do so, the *Démocrates* were promptly dismissed from their posts. Ahidjo thought the language used by Mballa to resemble that of his erstwhile colleague-become-bitter-enemy, Mbida.[32] Henceforth the *Démocrates* became special targets of the regime's wrath.

Ahidjo's willingness to participate in coalition politics with relative little quid for the quo he gave changed into insistence on new rules of the political game. These rules required allies to adhere to the ruling party, and were designed to effectuate the gradual attrition of other political structures. The first party to switch to the new rules was the MANC, which made the formal decision to declare its adherence to the UC on January 30, 1961 in an extraordinary session of the party's national congress.[33] Party leaders recalled that they had met in a special session in Yaounde in early October to discuss Ahidjo's appeal for national unity, and had initiated at that time an appeal for a MANC–UC merger, in order to create a large national party grouping leaders of all tendencies who desired to end the troubles and strife that had plagued the country. The formal merger of the two parties was to represent the realization of this stated desire. Rather than demanding a fusion of parties, however, as some of the MANC delegates insisted on, the congress simply voted to declare its allegiance to the UC, which in effect dissolved the MANC.

The Bamileke deputies got the message. Soon after Kamdem Ninyim officially quit the FRUP and declared his affiliation with the UC, a number of other deputies bolted, until in June the rest of the group officially dissolved it, claiming that its purpose had been served, and declared for the UC.[34]

These party switches were reinforced by similar changes in the voter preferences as revealed by the success of UC-invested-candidates in the June 11 by-elections in constituencies in Kribi: She Onana, an inconspicuous schoolteacher, narrowly defeated well-known Jean Bikanda who

[32] In an editorial in the party's newspaper, *L'Unité*, the UC let it be known whom they regarded as the instigator behind Mballa: "The Director of this scenario rubbed his hands together. He had pulled off a beautiful exploit: to lead his sheep to the pen; now, Mr. Mbida, for it was certainly he, will accept no diminutive situation: either he is in power and commands or [he is] in the opposition and directs." *L'Unité*, October 28, 1960.

[33] *Deuxième Congres du Mouvement d'Action Nationale du Cameroun*, Azem, January 27–30, 1961.

[34] *La Presse du Cameroun*, June 8, 1961.

had also expected UC support.[35] Two former deputies—one from the UPC and one from MANC, Ngué Ngué Elie and Ntonga Aloys—were roundly defeated in the election. Six months later another former deputy, Médou Gaston, an old rival of Assale's, did receive UC support and won another parliamentary seat for Ahidjo.[36] The UC considered the Kribi victory to be a significant breakthrough. The victory was achieved on different terrain than the other UC victories. "It is a question of the South, worked up by malevolent opinions on the *Union Camerounaise*. It was the democratic South, indeed, the anarchistic South, where Occidental individualism had found favorable ground. . . . Thus the *Union Camerounaise,* born on the banks of the Benoué, was falsely considered to be a party imported by foreigners and usurpers." [37] For the UC leadership this was not interpreted as a personal victory, but as a party victory, demonstrating to its followers that what is important "is to conform to its prescriptions, to submit to its decisions."

The UC was indeed beginning to work out a rationale and a method for achieving party discipline, organization, and support on a national scale. At the Second National Congress, held at Ngoundere in July 1959, and the Third National Congress at Maroua in September of 1960, party leaders discussed transforming the party into a national organization. Secretary General Moussa Yaya articulated the principles that would later be used: ". . . we must have our men everywhere at all times. . . . The role of these men is first to propagandize by every means, taking care to adapt their arguments to the milieu where they find themselves. . . . Propaganda is polymorphic and possesses almost indefinite resources. . . . The true propagandist, the man who desires to convince [others] applies all sorts of recipes according to the nature of the idea and those of his audience, but first he excites through the contagion of his own faith, by his own qualities of sympathy and statement. In a phrase it is a question of creating cohesion among ourselves and disorder and fear among our enemies." [38]

---

[35] Bikanda was expected to receive the party's investiture, and the UC itself claimed that many voters gave their support to him while ignorant of the fact that Onana had been the one endorsed. Bikanda was later made director of the Commission for Information.

[36] These seats had been vacated forcibly, by the Assembly's invalidation of the election of the Kribi deputy (Ngué Elie) and the arrest and imprisonment of the Dja-et-Loba deputy (Owona Mimba). Both were UPC members. Democrate Tsoungie Elie was also imprisoned.

[37] *L'Unité,* No. 49, June 23, 1961.

[38] *Rapport du Secrétaire Général du Comité Directeur, IIIe Congres du Parti Politique de l'Union Camerounaise,* Maroua, September 22–25, 1960.

The following summer, when the UC became earnestly preoccupied with the problem of building a strong and vigorous national party organization, some of these themes were elaborated on until Ahidjo was careful to distinguish the party he had in mind from a "single party regime" such as many people deemed to have evolved in other African states. The *"parti unique"* had already been defined by his own theoreticians in terms that would make it unacceptable: "The single party regime entails a concentration of power in the most classic sense of the term. All the governing organs, the edifice of government, are factitious, and the reality of power in all its forms rests in the hands of the leaders of the party." [39] What Ahidjo sought to build, instead, was a "regime du partie unifié," in the words of Senegalese President Leopold S. Senghor. Ahidjo was to speak on these themes many times, with little variation from his statement to the Fourth National Congress of the party which met the following summer at Ebolowa: "By *parti unifié* we mean a party having a single theme, a single objective. In the current Cameroonian situation, the work of national construction constitutes this theme, this objective to which can gravitate all points of view, all marginal ideologies whether it concerns economic social or diplomatic action." However, at Ebolowa he added something previous speeches did not contain: ". . . The Union Camerounaise is . . . the only political party endowing East Cameroon with a veritable national character. . . . There can be no question, for us, of a unified national party outside the framework which we offer."

The last point was made in distinction to what Ahidjo claimed had been his earlier outlook when people had talked of "roundtables" among diverse parties. He said he had offered in his November 1961 press conference to discuss with other parties the means for regrouping the Cameroonian people around the theme of national construction, but this appeal had found no authentic echo among the leaders of the dissident parties.

Whether Ahidjo's view of the route to national unity, as one that passed through the adherence of other parties to the UC, came before or after the refusal of others to respond to his call is not clear, but that is the view the principal leaders of the opposition parties feared from the start.

These fears seemed confirmed to many people when in January 1962 the national congress of the UPC, the first held since its rehabilitation and the third since its founding, was broken up and its participants dis-

[39] Kamé, "l'U.C. Droit-elle être vu parti de masse ou un parti d'élite?" *Première stage de Formation des Responsables de l'Union Camerounaise, Yaounde: de 1ᵉʳ ou 6 aout* (Yaounde: Government Printer, 1961).

persed by armed soldiers. The government's suppression of the congress was all the more surprising to its participants because the congress came after a long period of bitter dissension between the rallied elements in the party and the exiled leadership. Because the leadership had repudiated all efforts to reorganize the party internally, the holding of the Congress represented the victory and consolidation of the internal faction. Even the speeches of the congress leaders reflected the hostility between the internal and external wings of the party, and the character of the participation reflected some of the split between the Bamileke and Bassa factions. The congress leadership was almost solidly Bassa and Douala.[40] Its provisional chairman, Emma Otu, accused the exiles of being completely misinformed about the situation of the country; he asserted that it was false to claim that the pseudo-Army of National Liberation controlled any territory, labeled the terrorists still active as bandits, not patriots, called for an end to all foreign support to the terrorists, and in effect apologized for the rebellion. After the congress was broken up by force government spokesmen claimed that its 700 participants "could not furnish any motif of hope for the cessation of the bloody troubles." They claimed that the course of the congress disclosed that the UPC "had publicly bailed out the rebellion"; far from calling for an objective appreciation of the situation, certain delegates revealed "an attitude that bodes ill for the higher interest of the nation." [41]

During the spring of 1962 opposition leaders Mayi Matip, André Marie Mbida, Charles Okala (who had lost his ministerial post just prior to federation), and Beybey Eyidi, who had just formed a new party (the *Parti Travailliste Camerounaise*), decided to group themselves into a common opposition front called the *Front National Unifié*. They soon put to rest all speculation that a merger of parties might be achieved according to Ahidjo's terms. They published a joint open letter to the UC, in which they accused Ahidjo of seeking the totalitarian single party system he had warned the country against the previous November.[42] His call for a *parti unifié* was merely a call for the *parti unique* under a different name. For the purposes of highlighting and defining the dangers of the single party, as well as the dangers to free expression and organization which they perceived in the UC doctrines, they found ample material in

[40] The officers were: Emmah Otu (1st Sec.); Nonga Yomb (Sec. Ext. Rel.); Ntoula Albert (Fin. Sec.); Emile Kohn (Treas.); Jacque Ngom (Sec. Econ. Aff.); Mayi Matip (Sec. Educ.); J. P. Sende (Sec. Info.); Endangte, Ngue Eli, P. Tchamba, and Paul Tonye as Sec. Organisation.

[41] *La Presse du Cameroun,* January 23, 1962.

[42] Translation of the open letter is mine.

the speeches to the UC *Stage de Formation* of the year before. After quoting from those speeches, they mused: "What [good] does national independence serve if it is to create a neo-totalitarianism with a view to replacing foreign colonialism with a colonialism from within. [This is] the dictatorship of the single party. . . . For the undersigned, national unity requires the establishment of a new situation where there will be neither conquerors nor conquered, but rather where the majority will be united with the minority in order to find solutions to the concrete problems of the country. . . ." Pledging their support to the ideal of true national unity they nevertheless affirmed their intention to "conserve their political personality," neither out of a desire for power nor any kind of love of self, but as a result of their attachment to the principles of democracy.

The opposition's open letter caused the biggest stir the country had known in many months, but not as large as the one that followed a week later with their publication of a manifesto.[43] Like the previous letter the Manifesto was a small booklet of accusations and protestations. It affirmed, among other points, that:

> National Unity such as it is defined by certain people is a myth, and this myth borders on utopia. If we were really animated, all of us, by a desire for unity one would employ a different language than the one we are used to hearing from Radio Yaounde and the officials. As for ourselves, we believe that unity supposes first a minimum of courtesy towards those that one wants to unite; but we observe, to our great regret, that this unity will come about only when the holders of power have reduced the other Cameroonians to the rank of slaves. . . .
>
> National Unity with effective competition and activity among all the political and spiritual families of Cameroon. Yes!
>
> National Unity in the uniformization of the single party which will lead inexorably to dictatorship. No!

Within two weeks the signers of the letter and manifesto were in the custody of the police, charged with subversive and unlawful acts liable to cause public disorder.[44] A search was then made of their homes, and it was alleged that a number of weapons were discovered.[45] On July 11 they

[43] Translations from the manifesto are mine.

[44] Federal Information Service Press Bulletin No. 1895, July 4, 1963. It was charged that the manifesto incited hatred for the government and administration, expressed opposition to ethnic and religious bodies, and spread news liable to be harmful to public authority.

[45] It was claimed that in Mr. Okala's home there were found 6 pistols, 12 chargers, 1 carbine, and 168 cartridges. In Mbida's home it was alleged that 1 carbine, 2 rifles, and 11 cartridges were found. Press Bulletin No. 1895.

were tried, convicted, and sentenced to two and a half years in prison, a heavy fine, and loss of political rights. The official news agency noted that it was evident from the dispatch with which the government had acted that it had decided to carry on a radical and definitive struggle against all subversive activities in the country.[46]

Lesser politicians considered the imprisonment of the most powerful opposition leaders an unmistakable indication of the direction in which the political winds were blowing; many altered their stand in order to move with rather than against these winds. Throughout the next six months five UPC deputies, two socialists, and three *Démocrates*— including Mballa Barnabé himself, whose biting speech had started the UC crackdown—declared themselves members of the ruling party. Many other nondeputies, but important names in the opposition parties —Nguèlé Mathieu (former president of the *Démocrates*), Jacque Ngom, Emma Otu, Tina Bonfils, Mballa Benoit, to name a few, as well as some tribal associations such as the Ngondo, and the *Union Tribale d'Ntem et Kribi*—followed the lead of the deputies. Some were promised houses; others were given government positions; some were simply frightened into their new party affiliations. By early 1963 the ranks of the opposition in the Assembly had been reduced to six *Démocrates* and one UPC.[47] Since the rules of procedure in the Assembly assigned positions in the working commissions to parliamentary blocs having seven or more deputies only, neither opposition party was represented in the work of the Assembly until they joined in a common opposition front the fall of 1963.

The misfortunes that befell opponents of the single party were not limited to the top leaders of dissident parties; many secondary leaders and even the rank and file came to know them, and with a special intimacy in the case of the *Démocrates*. Not only was it hard to keep the loyalty of their existing deputies in the face of the varied pressures to change party affiliation, but it became particularly difficult to get any elected. The party officials claimed that they faced obstacles which their opponents in the ruling UC did not. Administrative officials to whom declarations of candidacy had to be made allegedly suddenly closed their offices when the agent of the *Démocrates* appeared, or these officials sent them to the

[46] *Bulletin Quotidienne*, No. 158, July 12, 1962. Six months later the four appealed their cases and had their sentences extended by six months and their fines doubled. *Bulletin Quotidienne*, No. 281 (December 6, 1962).

[47] The six Démocrates were Amougou Nguèlé Paul, Akono Claude, Manga Bilé, Nogo Eugene, Tsalla Mekongo, and Zezo'o Salomon. The lone UPC member was Schamba Njitam Jean.

wrong bureaus or simply refused to accept their applications and supportive documents.[48] If the procedures for declaring candidacy were successfully dealt with, the party leaders assert that they faced repeated harassment and administrative difficulties during the conduct of the campaign, including the opening of voting booths before official hours. It is quite certain that government and administrative persons openly campaigned for candidates backed by the UC. If all else failed, they alleged, the results of the voting were simply altered in favor of the UC candidate.[49] The whole range of difficulties allegedly was placed in the path of the PDC candidate for the Assembly seat of Djoungolo (Yaounde) during the by-elections of December 1961. Even so, the PDC claimed that its candidate, Bnounoungou Antoine, had really won the election although the administration installed the UC candidate, Fouda Gallus, in the post.[50]

The *Démocrates* claimed to have faced similar obstacles during the elections for the municipal councils of Yaounde and Douala a year later. By this time all other parties had been so intimidated that they even refrained from attempting to propose a list of candidates, the *Démocrates* claimed. Their own courage did them little good, however. Allegedly the *Démocrates'* leaders, particularly Akono Claude, head of the parliamentary wing, approached the mayor of Yaounde with his party's list, but met with evasions and subterfuge until it was declared too late to present declarations of candidacy.[51] The UC attached particular importance to the elections because they were the first to occur at the local level in six years, and presented the UC with an opportunity to demonstrate its popular strength in the heart of the areas traditionally opposed to it. It campaigned hard for extensive participation in support of the only list of

[48] Personal interview with former officials of the Democrat party, Yaounde, November 1963.

[49] One example of state action subject to the interpretation of being discriminatory against a particular candidate is that contained in Arrêté Préfectoral No. 305 of 14 December 1961 in Dja-et-lobo during the by-elections of 24 December 1961, which, after citing decrees fixing the circumscription, laws regulating public order, regulations proclaiming a state of alert in the district, and the ordinance governing the by-elections, noted that, "The candidate Ebo [Samson] [is] soliciting a public meeting this evening in the sports arena of 'Golgota,'" and declared ". . . Il est interdit . . . faute de moyens d'assurer le maintien d'ordre public."

[50] Declaration du Parti des Démocrates, December 28, 1961. André Marie Mbida. The party claimed that its candidate received 12,661 votes to Fouda's 5,982 and to the 4,650 that Mr. Fouda André received. The officially announced results were 13,254 for Fouda and 14,061 altogether for the other two.

[51] Personal interview with PDC officials, Yaounde, November 1963.

candidates—its own—and proudly publicized an 88.1 percent turnout in Yaounde, and a 79.1 percent in Douala as a smashing victory.[52]

The last true contest between the UC and an opposition party occurred during the elections for the federal National Assembly in April 1964. In a surprise gesture the regime established five constituencies in East Cameroon for the 40 seats, instead of a single constituency for the entire state, a system used with increasing frequency in other African states. This system permitted the *Démocrates* to run 10 candidates in its traditional areas of strength without having to amass superior support throughout the country. However, once again the *Démocrates* had intimidated voters to support its candidates.[53] Rather than sustain the sacrifices of running candidates against the UC in the state level general elections of 1965, the ranking officers of the *Démocrates* are reported to have approached Ahidjo with the proposition that all the opposition parties would declare for the UC if the latter would grant them 12 places on its list of candidates. Ahidjo allegedly professed interest in the proposition they all join the UC, but never gave an answer about the requested 12 seats. The *Démocrates* refrained from proposing a list of candidates; when the political party system of West Cameroon had fragmented to the point where all the Western factions were ready to dissolve their own organizations and join a single national structure, the *Démocrates,* along with the UPC, decided to join these ranks, even without any specific promise of places in the Assembly or the party executive.

Though it would take some time to acquire the formal trappings of a complete merger of dissident party organizations with the UC, the march toward a single party regime in East Cameroon was complete by the time of the 1965 elections. There remained only the task of achieving this in West Cameroon and then at the federal level.

[52] *L'Unité,* No. 121, December 16–23, 1962.

[53] The UC press organ, *L'Unité,* No. 180, May 9–16, 1964, complained of rock-throwing and attacks on voters.

ᛤ 11 ᛤ

Conjunctive Structures of Political Activity: The Western and Federal Systems

THE divergent characteristics of the reunification movements of East and West Cameroon, which became apparent during their latter stages before the UN plebiscite, were still in evidence after federation. Whereas in East Cameroon the initial spokesmen were excluded from power altogether and the latter-day reunificationists were able to progressively consolidate their political positions by supporting this theme, in the West all the political forces and nearly every person involved in the movement continued to exercise genuine power in the system. The political parties of West Cameroon became increasingly parochial in orientation and localized in support, and the party system progressively fragmented until it finally crumbled into a heap of factions, each of which was included in a single national party organized at the initiative of President Ahidjo and the *Union Camerounaise*.

The period of most severe fragmentation of the party system came in the mid-1950s when the reunification movement started the transition from its first phase, which was concerned with winning "home rule," to the later competition over which party or faction would control the new government. For a brief period there were recognizable factions grouped around Endeley in the KNC, Mbile in the KPP, Ntumazah and Mukong in the One Kamerun Movement, Moumie in the UPC, and Foncha and his KNDP. These factions coalesced and polarized into two main camps, initially over the question of secession from the Nigerian Federation, then over the issue of reunification with Cameroun or Nigeria. Favoring the Nigerian side were the Endeley and Mbile forces, which ultimately merged into the Cameroon Peoples National Convention (CPNC). The others favored "reunification," though prior to federation no single party included all of them. The UPC was expelled from the Territory and the OK, first a fragment of and later closely allied with the UPC, gradually dwindled away. Though politics in West Cameroon was often influenced by personal feuds and parochial interests, it did come to turn on principles and hard issues. Once the plebiscite was held and the question of reunification was decided, therefore, it would seem there was no basis for ideological differences. The two camps should have been able to unite in

257

a common statewide movement and to consolidate their position and edify the Cameroon personality. Instead, after initial important gains on the part of the ruling party, the party system drifted back toward its earlier factionalism, parochialism, and personality-oriented and dominated politics.

Once in control of the government, however tenuously, John Foncha was able to use the process of constitutional revision to the benefit of his own party, just as Ahidjo had been able to do in East Cameroon. Constitutional changes, which expanded the House of Assembly and democratized the elections for it, played a significant role in strengthening the KNDP through increasing the representation of the grassfields area, an area the KNDP dominated politically.

The Assembly was expanded in 1959 and again at the beginning of the Federation. In 1959 the KNDP gained 9 of the 13 additional seats, and the KNC-KPP alliance took the other 4. This change altered the balance of voting strength in the Assembly more than is suggested by the figures, because three of the four new KNC-KPP seats were filled by its supporters who had formerly held appointive seats in the Assembly.[1]

The federal constitution expanded the Western House of Assembly to 37 seats, an addition of 11 elected seats. In the new elections held on Christmas Eve 1961, just after federation, the KNDP again won nine of the newly created seats. Once again, its voting strength vis-à-vis the opposition, which had now merged to form the CPNC, was increased in larger measure than the increment in elected positions because it was also able to win seven seats formerly held by the opposition.

In both instances the proliferation of elected representative positions favored the northern, mostly grassfields, populations. Prior to 1957 the three northern districts—Bamenda, Nkambe, and Wum, which contained over 57 percent of the total population—controlled only about 55 percent of the elected seats. By 1961 the percentage of Assembly seats allocated to these peoples was about 60 percent. It is highly improbable that a comparative shift in population occurred in the interim; in any case no census was taken to determine if there had been. Moreover, a number of ostensibly southern "forest" seats were actually representative of the interests and orientation of immigrant grassfields communities resident in southern towns and plantation camps. Thus the northern populations came to be slightly overrepresented in the Assembly, an advantage that

[1] In the March 1957 elections the KNC was victorious only because four of the six appointed representatives of Native Authorities supported the KNC. The seats were replaced by elective ones in 1959.

was achieved through manipulation of the state apparatus which determined the size of the Assembly and the distribution of its seats.

The KNDP and the CPNC were more than regional parties. Both had supporters in all sections of the country and enclaves of strength in the forest and grassfields areas. Nevertheless, the dominant leadership in each party were either from the forest (CPNC) or the grassfields (KNDP); more important, since its inauguration in 1955 the KNDP had progressively concentrated its power in the grassfields, and the CPNC had been reduced to a forest basis of electoral strength. In the 1957 elections, for example, the KNDP had only one representative from the forest areas (Native Authority seats included) and the opposition (which four years earlier controlled all but one of the seats) had only three among grassfields constituencies. In 1959 the CPNC achieved impressive gains in the north, especially in Nkambe division, but was reduced to one northern Assemblyman in December 1961.[2]

Another indication that the growth of the KNDP reflected heightened parochialism among grassfields populations is the fact that the CPNC, whose member parties had formerly received their support, increasingly suffered defeat primarily in these areas. Had the two major party groupings been relatively free of regional identifications, increments in the number of elected positions should have benefited both parties, or have strengthened the CPNC, which had the longer history of political activity. In fact, the early strength of the Endeley party (KNC) throughout the country did not create durable traditions of support for it. The elections prior to those of 1953 had not been fought on a party basis; indeed, there had been relatively little campaigning. Only after the formation of the KNDP was there much opportunity to express regional aspirations through party affiliation. The CPNC leaders from the grassfields, as from the south, were mostly the first generation of politicians, men of eminence. But between 1957 and 1961 five party leaders of long-standing reputations were defeated in northern districts.[3] Only one such CPNC candidate, Motomby Woleta, was defeated in the south, and this because of the opposition of a significant immigrant population from grassfields areas.

Most of the top leadership of the KNDP were former leaders in the

---

[2] The CPNC controlled seven seats in the Assembly after the 1961 elections, and five of these represented constituencies in the single division of Kumba.

[3] They were: Rev. Kangsen, Mr. Lainjo, N. Y. Ndze, S. Ncha, A. Arrey (who had filled the seat of the late S. A. George, one of the most eminent of the early Southern Cameroons nationalists).

KNC who had broken away; [4] they were followed by a number of lesser figures. But this cluster of defections only strengthens the impression that the gains of the KNDP represented a closing of the ranks among grass-fielders. The old KNC stalwarts retained their positions in southern districts. In 1961, for example, 3 of the 10 CPNC representatives were among the first representatives elected to office in the Territory.[5] Only Foncha and Muna, among the 27 KNDP parliamentarians, could claim that distinction.

Despite the rapid growth of the KNDP within and without the House of Assembly, it is clear that the ranks of the opposition continued to be filled with skillful and respected men whose political future remained promising so long as free elections were held within localized constituencies. The KNDP leadership, particularly Foncha, lived in constant fear that some day the CPNC leaders, whom Foncha and others considered to be conniving and malicious, would cause them trouble. This was particularly so during the 10 months' interim between the UN plebiscite and the first state elections under the federal system. The first days of that period were filled with anxiety, caused by the CPNC's wild demands to have the state partitioned according to the plebiscite vote and the widespread fear that the rebellion underway in neighboring Bamileke areas would infuse the state.

To restore an atmosphere of popular confidence in peace and to make the most of the popular option expressed in the plebiscite and validated by the approval of the United Nations General Assembly, leaders from both parties met at the Fifteenth General Assembly and called on their followers to "forget the past and work together toward the achievement of a happy and prosperous Kamerun country." [6] Shortly after their return from the meeting they met again and expanded their pledge to cooperate by declaring a "truce" to their animosities and by calling on all citizens and organs of public opinion to "refrain from all provocative acts and utterances." The statement also announced that all parties would participate in the task of drafting constitutional proposals and that future meetings would be held between the KNDP and CPNC to "foster the general desire for cooperation and national unity." [7] The CPNC did not raise the issue of partition after these announcements nor did it criticize in public

[4] Foncha, Muna, and Jua.

[5] Endeley, Mbile, and Ajebe-Sone.

[6] Communiqué issued and signed by J. N. Foncha and E.M.L. Endeley at the Fifteenth General Assembly, New York, April 21, 1961.

[7] Communiqué signed by J. N. Foncha and E.M.L. Endeley, Buea, May 11, 1961.

or any excessive way the constitutional proposals which the government presented to the eastern delegation to the Foumban, proposals which it had helped to formulate.[8] Nothing more was said about party cooperation, however, until long after the KNDP victories in the December elections.

Ahidjo's appeal in November 1961 for the creation of a grand national unified party, coupled with the impressive gains by the KNDP in the elections, revitalized the discussion of party cooperation in West Cameroon. Significantly, however, the readiest response to Ahidjo's appeals came not from the ruling KNDP but from the opposition CPNC and certain other small dissident groups. It is not clear whether Ahidjo discussed his ideas for a single national party with Foncha before his November 11 speech, but it is certain that he discussed them with party leaders and the public the following January when he visited the state to open the House of Assembly.[9] Probably during that visit Ahidjo learned of the willingness, even eagerness, of the opposition party to join in a single national party.[10] On later trips to the West Ahidjo continued to call for unity and the creation of a combined national party.[11]

The discussion among West Cameroon parties about the creation of a single national party was carried on at three levels: (a) between the political leaders at the federal level; (b) among the parties at the state level; and (c) within the parties at the local and party congress level. Of course, the issues involved in creating party unity at the federal level are closely akin to the relations between parties at the state level. For much of the life of this discussion, however, it was the interparty relations at the state level that determined the course of events; it is convenient, therefore, to discuss this issue first as a matter of internal state politics. I will note those events at the federal level which directly affected the workings of the West Cameroon party system, but will reserve for a later more detailed discussion the development of the discussions and efforts to achieve a merger at the federal level between the two ruling parties.

The readiness of the West Cameroon opposition to accept a single national party has been rationalized in general terms that might apply to

[8] See the detailed discussion of the constitutional conferences, in Chap. 8.

[9] *L'Unité,* No. 78, January 12, 1962 refers to Ahidjo's leaving for Buea on 9 January and the *Cameroon Champion* of January 5, 1962 refers to his speech, which called for an end to past animosities and cooperation for harmonious advancement.

[10] Dr. Endeley affirmed in several personal interviews in April and July 1963 that he had talked directly with Ahidjo and made known to him his own preference for a single party.

[11] Ahidjo visited West Cameroon in January, May, June, and July 1962.

261

minority parties anywhere in Africa. The leaders of minority parties are constantly victimized, according to Dr. Endeley; they cannot express their views freely for fear of being accused of trying to bring down the government.[12] The government party views criticism as motivated by a desire to throw the party out of government immediately, and this is what lies at the bottom of the general attempt throughout Africa to muzzle the opposition and imprison its members. Endeley stated: "I believe that in spite of the fact that there will always be certain disagreement in any party system, if we are generally agreed, we can operate a one-party system which would certainly guarantee that everybody has the right to express opinions within the party. This would make the best use of the talent we have in the country, and we could evolve a system of agreement without engendering animosity." He also thought that the burdens of contesting elections on a national basis were too heavy for minority parties. Such parties could make a more effective contribution to the development of the country if relieved of such burdens through membership in a common party.

Dr. Endeley's views and those of his colleagues in the opposition were no doubt also rooted in the peculiar features of the Cameroon political situation, where the emergence of a single national party could come about through the clustering of all West Cameroon factions around the dominant power and organization of the UC, which had no local base in that state. Each minority party in West Cameroon could look on the UC as a neutral arbiter of local differences, thus its greatest promise for a return to influence and position.

This peculiar situation is probably what shaped the position of the government party as well, for it feared that the UC might not remain neutral, but rather would work out a deal with the opposition parties— either the CPNC or the One Kamerun—or simply serve as a route to power at the federal or even state level by circumventing the KNDP. When Ahidjo pressed for formalizing collaboration between the two parties, Foncha therefore responded by exacting a public announcement from Ahidjo that no branch of either party then existed in the other's state. Foncha's interpretation of this statement was that no such branch would be organized in the future; Ahidjo did not challenge the interpretation; thus it amounted to a pledge by each leader to keep hands off the internal political situation of the other. This agreement was of special importance to Foncha because he was obsessively fearful of the reemergence of Endeley, Mbile, and the other CPNC stalwarts. Foncha never

[12] Endeley, interview, Buea, April 1963.

seemed to fear losing his power and prerogatives to the federal government as much as losing it to his own opposition within the state.

Ahidjo also found the agreement satisfactory. He too had been fearful, without much cause, of a weakened political position as a result of an alliance between his own southern-based opposition, particularly that influenced by the UPC, and the reunificationists in Southern Cameroons. It will be recalled that it was the UPC that had first espoused the reunification theme in the French-speaking state, and had later set up a government in exile at Kumba. Moreover, there was the cultural affinity between the grassfields populations and the troubled, dissident Bamileke areas. Many of the southern opponents of the Ahidjo regime expected that reunification would strengthen the oppositional forces by adding to their votes at least those of the grassfielders if not all the voters in West Cameroon. It has also been reported that Foncha speculated publicly about posing his own candidacy for the federal presidency in the elections scheduled for 1965.[13] If Ahidjo ever harbored fears that Foncha posed a serious threat to his political position, these must have dissipated quickly as Foncha's own deep resentment of and animosity toward the UPC, which had once challenged him in his own constituency, became known. Foncha's demeanor in his prefederation contacts with Ahidjo never suggested any intention to pose such a threat; though Foncha and the grassfielders often spoke of "their brothers in the East," which included the Bamileke, their real ethnic and cultural ties were stronger with the pro-Ahidjo Bamoun areas than with the fragmented and often dissident Bamileke society.[14] Thus, though preferring to move rapidly toward the creation of a single party at the federal level, Ahidjo was willing to go slowly toward that objective so long as western politicians did not interfere with his own drive for a single party situation in the eastern state.

The UC–KNDP agreement of April 27, 1962 stopped short of merging the two parties, creating an alliance between them instead, in the form of a national unity group in the federal Assembly. A coordinating committee was established to work out the procedures for "harmonizing their relations and coordinating their actions."[15]

The West Cameroon opposition hailed the Ahidjo-Foncha agreement as a step in the right direction, but only a step. In an open letter to the KNDP, Dr. Endeley called for discussions of the merger of all parties in

[13] Foreign diplomatic representatives in Yaounde, questioned during personal interviews in 1963, spoke of hearing such speculation by Foncha.

[14] See Chap. 3.

[15] *Cameroon Champion,* May 4, 1962.

one single national party.[16] He thought that UC-KNDP alliance would achieve greater results if it included all parties and embraced those outside the orbit of the federal Assembly, as well as those in it. Endeley even suggested to Foncha that they merge their parties in West Cameroon: ". . . it might have been possible to effect an agreement between our parties of the same nature as you have now done with the *Union Camerounaise* and so prepare the way for the future all-country union. . . . I am sincerely appealing to you to reconsider the possibility of initiating discussion for a common understanding so that we could go forward together from here having resolved our domestic problems before we meet other parties in the East Cameroon to complete a National Party that will abolish once and for all the bane of multiple mushroom parties." [17]

For most West Cameroonians, however, the thought of a single-party system was disturbing. The *Cameroon Times,* normally biased toward the KNDP, carried editorials and private letters decrying any interpretation of the agreement as an endorsement of or attempt to create a single-party system, which they thought would lead invariably to dictatorship and a denial of free speech. Spokesmen for the KNDP stated privately that they feared the single party idea itself more than the rise of now diminished opposition leaders. Instead, their propaganda stressed their desire simply to build a "national party." [18]

At its annual congress in June 1962 the KNDP is reported to have rejected Endeley's call for discussions on a West Cameroon party merger, though Foncha asked the party to receive into the party's ranks those of the opposition who "had grasped the truth" and were willing to join the KNDP[19] The congress authorized the party leadership to consider any initiative by other parties toward reconciliation but required that no final decision be taken without approval of the national convention. Consequently a meeting of leaders from the KNDP and the CPNC was convened in the House of Assembly on July 17. According to the CPNC the meeting decided on four points:

[16] *Cameroon Times,* May 28, 1962. This issue also quotes an earlier press statement issued in Buea by Dr. Endeley.

[17] *Cameroon Champion,* May 15, 1962.

[18] Endeley stated in an interview that he failed to understand what the KNDP meant by "national party." Did they intend to permit other national parties? Would they permit many factions to express themselves within the party or not? He thought this a ruse motivated by their desire to keep the CPNC out.

[19] *Cameroon Times,* June 11, 1962. *Cameroon Champion,* August 24, 1962, reports that the party congress postponed discussion of UC-KNDP merger for one year.

1. That after unification there existed no major political ideological differences in Cameroon;
2. That there is a strong need for a National Party in Cameroon;
3. That any further delay will destroy the enthusiasm for unity which President A. Ahidjo's appeal has aroused;
4. That ways and means should be sought to implement this move for a National Party.[20]

Another meeting was scheduled for August 10th and 11th, but was never held, as it became clear that the KNDP was backing off from its agreement. To force the issue, the CPNC issued a statement noting the fact that the UC was the largest single party in the country and possessed the best framework for a national party, and proposed that both the KNDP and the CPNC should dissolve and declare membership in the UC, after which the president of the UC could call a national congress to revise the party constitution and formally launch the national party.

The KNDP response came quickly, in the form of a reassertion of the party's contribution to the achievement of reunification and its cooperation with the UC. It then invoked the April 27 UC-KNDP agreement in asserting that anyone from West Cameroon who wished to join the UC could and must do so by joining the KNDP. The KNDP leaders pledged not to discuss the issue of forming a national party with anyone but the members of the UC-KNDP Coordinating Committee, nor would they include any representatives from other parties in their delegation to the committee when doing so.[21] It was clear that the KNDP intended to push for a single-party system in West Cameroon before talking about one for the federation as a whole.

During the rest of the year these leaders constantly repeated the same themes and made no progress in resolving any of the outstanding issues, either between the KNDP and the CPNC or between the two parties in the federal government. Near the end of the year, shortly before a return visit to West Cameroon by President Ahidjo, the opposition forces began to press their case again, more forcefully and with growing sympathy from Yaounde. The *Cameroon Champion* published an ultimatum to the KNDP, calling on it to dissolve itself and join the UC by January 1, or

[20] Foncha continued to emphasize the need for the CPNC members to declare membership in the KNDP. He stated to the House of Chiefs: "only those of changed opinion and who are willing to cooperate will be accepted." Endeley thought Foncha desired simply to keep the CPNC leaders out of the party. "He wants the followers without the leaders." Interview, April 1963.

[21] KNDP, "The Path to a National Party: Steps and Principles," August 11, 1962.

265

else people would not take its policies seriously.[22] The intended threat was that impatient people would contact the UC on their own. During Ahidjo's visit the paper prominently displayed an editorial addressed directly to him: "Tribalism is at its peak [here]; nepotism in the civil service is a creed of a political party [KNDP]; political warfare and rivalry is the order of the day; malice, hatred, and enmity the pinnacle of sectional desires. Nationalism has been annihilated. But those anomalies are the things you have dedicated your life to eradicate. . . . Please come to our aid. . . . You have to issue directives as to the form our contribution will take." [23] Dr. Endeley held private talks with Ahidjo to reaffirm his commitment to the idea of a single party and his desire to play a constructive and loyal role in the political life of the country. It is thought that Ahidjo appreciated the CPNC's declared good faith; he began to voice assurances that "no one need be considered redundant" who sincerely wished to help build the nation.

The CPNC then brought the issue to the floor of the House of Assembly with a surprise motion which commended the leaders of the principal political parties for their efforts during the previous year to assure peace and unity, and approved "the appeal made in favor of the adoption of a single party for the whole of the Republic. . . ." It then requested that President Ahidjo "intervene in order that all persons interested take immediately the proper measures to insure the realization of a single party through the absorption of all existing parties in one single one." [24] The KNDP was embarrassed and could not reject the motion outright; so the party amended the motion to express acceptance of the principle of a national party and support for all measures taken in that direction.[25] Despite the moderation of the final version, the Tamfu resolution had served the purpose of gaining nationwide publicity for the opposition's desire for a single party and had led to increased pressure on the KNDP to move toward its realization.

Though the issue continued to be discussed, progressively in terms of the conditions the KNDP thought necessary to permit it to safely merge with the UC rather than those which would govern any affiliation with the CPNC, nothing changed the basic relationships among local parties until the spring of 1964, when the first public elections were held for seats in

[22] *Cameroon Champion,* December 7, 1962.

[23] *Cameroon Champion,* January 11, 1963. The editorial ended with the thought, "Often, the highest talents are wrapped in obscurity."

[24] Motion introduced by Representative Tamfu, February 1963.

[25] The amended version was passed by a vote of 20 to 7, strictly along party lines. Ten representatives did not participate or were absent.

the federal Assembly. The CPNC decided at the last minute—and to the KNDP's great surprise—to contest the elections. This decision amounted to an impressive display of confidence, because to contest the elections the party had to run a slate of 10 candidates and post $2,000 as a deposit. Endeley and Mbile put together the slate and raised the deposit in five days. Though their support was quite uneven throughout the country, the CPNC candidates attracted 24.7 percent of the vote, just short of the required 25 percent necessary to regain their deposit money. Party leaders claimed that this may have resulted from the government tampering with the results, and alleged many violations of electoral rules during the campaign and balloting.[26] Despite its loss the CPNC did demonstrate substantial support in the country, a fact specifically noted in the UC press.[27]

Radical changes in the relations among West Cameroon parties were in the offing, threatened not by the strengths of the opposition CPNC, which had suffered several defections and would continue to do so, but by growing fissions within the KNDP itself. The causes of division in the KNDP ranks were multiple—clashes of personalities and personal ambitions, resentment over the influence of tribal and regional loyalties in civil service and political appointments, a growing malaise about the changes occasioned by reunification, and disappointment with Foncha's defense of West Cameroon interests at the federal level. The single most important stimulus to division, however, was the prospect of succession to the prime minister's office created by the constitutionally required separation of that office from the vice presidency with the April 1965 presidential elections.

Foncha began to anticipate the political problems posed by this requirement in 1963.[28] If he chose to run for vice president he would no longer be able to completely control the prime minister's office, the main source of patronage and coercive power available to the party. In the vice president's office in Yaounde Foncha would be cut off from the main body of party underlings, from the major communications channels in the state, and isolated from his base of popular support. Over time this could cost him control of the party itself. On the other hand, if he chose to re-

[26] Endeley and Mbile, personal interviews, Buea, July 1965. They claimed that in Bamenda polling stations no boxes were provided for pro-CPNC ballots, that a number of their campaigners were harassed by police and *gendarmes,* and some supporters, or alleged supporters, were sacked from teaching and civil service jobs.

[27] See *L'Unité,* Nos. 180 and 181, May 1964. See Appendix B for election results.

[28] He apparently thought, mistakenly, that this separation had to be made in 1964 at the time of the federal assembly elections.

tain the prime minister's position he would lose the prestige of being the second highest federal official, the acting president during the latter's absence, and would not be able to oversee the interests of the western state as closely as he would like. Moreover, without an office in Yaounde Foncha might not be able to keep watch on other westerners who might try to effect an alliance with Ahidjo and other eastern leaders. To help him resolve some of these dilemmas he called a small meeting of associates at the coastal estate of Isongo shortly before the ninth annual national convention of the KNDP, which was held at Bamenda Hall in mid-August 1963. Foncha was reportedly advised to retain the prime ministership lest he lose his base of power,[29] but he refused to announce any hard decision on the matter, so camps began to develop around the two next most powerful men in the party, Solomon T. Muna and Agustin Jua.

The competition for the prime minister's post began at the ninth convention. It was the unspoken assumption of all factions at the meeting that whoever occupied the second spot in the party hierarchy, that of first vice president, would be the party's nominee to fill the prime minister's post should it become vacant.[30] This assumption was later contested by Muna's supporters after he lost an election for the post, and then was formally added as a part of the party's constitution.

The motivation of the two contenders was evident: it was a rewarding and prestigious post and each thought himself deserving of it. Each had considerable experience in public life, though Muna's was the more impressive.[31] Both men were named to federal ministerial appointments at the time of federation, though when Jua discovered that his post was only that of deputy minister he quickly resigned from it. Both men were long-time political associates of Foncha's, but Muna was also a personal friend. Though the position they sought had lost most of its governmental power, it paid better than any either had previously occupied and continued to be an important political command post.

The motives for the followers of each man were much more complex. Jua based his strength in the party's rank and file at the constituency or-

[29] The report of this meeting came from Dr. Endeley, and has been confirmed by Foncha aids.

[30] I was present at the convention meetings where this competition was the focus of most political discussions.

[31] Muna had been a minister for almost all his political career, having been made a minister without portfolio in the Eastern Nigeria government in 1951. Jua entered politics in 1953 and became a minister only when the KNDP took over in 1959. He had acquired considerable experience, however, as acting prime minister during Foncha's many absences from the state.

ganization level. He cultivated a number of important branch organizations so that their delegations to the national conventions were filled with his supporters. To the average man Jua was forceful, direct, shrewd, more complicated than Foncha but more likely to push hard against any opponent, even the federal government, to satisfy the needs of the state. To the more sophisticated party leaders, however, he was regarded as hotheaded and impetuous, less tribalistic than Foncha but likely to arouse fears and resistance in Yaounde. Muna enjoyed genuine popularity among the top leaders and the general populace, but was not as careful as Jua in organizing at the local level. Muna was respected as a talented and sophisticated man, but one who could stump the bush and turn a phrase as well in pidgin as in standard English. His longevity in political life unavoidably had given rise to an image of political meandering and opportunism since he had been a onetime ally of nearly every important personage and a leader of almost every party. Moreover, his Widekum tribe bridged the grassfields and forest areas, and though his people fought a war against the Bali and had lost large landholdings to them, Muna continued to maintain a farm in Bali country.

Muna attempted to capitalize on his longer experience and his knowledge of the workings of the federal government in his campaign. He could demonstrate the beginnings of a knowledge of the French language and a worthy record as the only West Cameroonian full minister in the federal government. But most importantly—and unfortunately as it turned out for him—he made one of his principal claims to the post the fact that he was the favorite of John N. Foncha. Foncha is known to have privately encouraged Muna, at least initially, and to have assisted his campaign financially.[32] The strength of this appeal lay in the parliamentary wing of the party, however. The constituency organizations, among which Foncha continued to enjoy significant popularity, had been neglected by Foncha and Muna alike and were more sensitive to the hardships resulting from federation than was the parliamentary wing. Muna's standing with the local party leaders was jeopardized even more by the fact that Foncha's principal organizing aide, Anthony Ngounjoh, joined his talents with the Jua cause. Foncha was not decisive in his support for Muna and refrained from campaigning for him among Foncha's own grassroots supporters.

Some of the support for Jua derived from dissatisfaction with Foncha's leadership not only on matters relative to the federation, but also con-

---

[32] Muna reportedly received 40,000 CFA francs from Foncha personally.

269

cerning affairs within the state. Dissatisfaction of the latter sort came to be acute among members of the civil service. In part it resulted from perceptions of discrimination in the appointment and promotion of civil servants according to tribal or former party affiliation. It was widely believed among people in the forest areas that they were disadvantaged during the Foncha administration, particularly if they had any history of association with opposition party members, whether by political affiliation, friendship, or even marriage. Occasionally people were dismissed from their posts, seemingly arbitrarily, on the basis of rumors of support to the opposition party or its affiliates.[33]

Ironically support for Muna often resulted from the same dissatisfaction with tribalistic practices of the Foncha regime. Many saw the succession as an opportunity for change, whoever won the post; as the competition developed, Foncha became more indecisive about his own preferences and consequently more isolated from each side. What was started by a fillip to ambitions became a defense of ego, a venting of personal vendettas, and a crude defense of principles of a sort.

At the 1963 national convention the competition was mostly a straightforward response to aroused ambitions. As one of the village delegates from Wum division put it: "I hear talk na somebody go wuk fo send Foncha fo outside so's somebody go get'um seat." Several leaders posed their candidacy—Peter Kemcha, the Secretary of State for Labor from Mamfe; Johanes Bokwe, the Secretary of State for Transport and Public Works from Kumba; and J. N. Lafon, the Secretary of State for Local Government from Nsaw. The field quickly narrowed to Muna and Jua, both of whom had bases of strength in the important grassfields constituencies. Foncha's support for Muna was generally known, and both Bokwe and Lafon are reported to have declined in his favor. Kemcha withdrew under pressures from Jua, and, as a result of a three-way split among his fellow Mamfe delegates, grouped around himself, E. Tabi Egbe, the federal Deputy Minister of Justice and a Muna associate, and Nzo Ekhah Ngahky, the federal Deputy Minister of Foreign Affairs and associate of Jua's. The latter two were young, skillful, highly educated,

[33] One notorious case concerned two Bakweri civil servants, Eric D. Quan and Peter M. Efange, both possessing University of London degrees, advanced study, and many years of satisfactory service, who were summarily dismissed without hearing or appeal apparently because someone had accused them of having given aid and support to the CPNC. The government then tried to deny them passports to permit them to seek employment elsewhere and prohibited the courts from considering a suit brought against itself in the matter. Ultimately one of them was taken into the bureau of Dr. Fonlon, a Foncha critic.

ambitious, and mutually antagonistic strategists for the two camps. They were drawn into the heart of the battle for the first vice presidency by each becoming one of the camp's candidates for the strategically important post of secretary general of the party.[34] The federal ministers in Yaounde neither needed nor wanted the post but were fearful it might fall into the hands of someone who would favor the other side. Although Egbe and Ngahky were closely associated with the candidates for the party's vice presidency, the association was not clearly perceived by many delegates, and the two contests were judged somewhat separately. The tactics of each man reflected the larger strategy of each camp, however. Egbe was the weaker of the two in constituency organization, so he attempted to circumvent the regular constituency organization, or at least what the convention recognized as the regular organization by bringing his own delegates to the meeting. They were given only observer status. Like Muna, Egbe also attempted to capitalize on Foncha's support, only to find it insufficient if not detrimental. Neither Ekhah Ngahky nor Jua depicted himself as an anti-federalist, though each cultivated an image of being determined to brook no nonsense on matters of West Cameroon interests in the federation. Ekhah made positive use of his fluency in French, his federal position, his former role in leftist student circles— all deemed as increasing his effectiveness in dealing with easterners. Jua and Ekhah won easily; Bokwe and Egbe were given minor posts.[35]

The Foncha-Muna camp demonstrated their political weakness at the local level in February 1965 during by-elections to fill the seats of those state assemblymen who had been elected the previous April to seats in the Federal Assembly. The constituency organization in Egbe's district nominated a man Foncha did not like, so Foncha encouraged his favorite to run as an independent. The candidate then pressed Foncha to give him the party's support, and Foncha personally authorized the candidate to use the party symbol. Many illiterate voters, not knowing this, mistakenly voted for the independent candidate thinking he had the endorsement of the local KNDP organization. Following his victory the branch organization successfully challenged the election in court. Jua made good propaganda use of the blunder by Foncha, and of the fact that Muna's hand-picked candidate for the latter's own former Assembly seat was defeated.

Muna remained convinced of his strength among the parliamentary

[34] The post of secretary general was vacated shortly before the convention by the sudden death of Z. Abendong, recently returned university student who, at 24, had been the youngest elected deputy in the State or Federal Assembly.

[35] Jua received 175 votes to Muna's 73. Ekhah Ngahky received 159 to Egbe's 95. Egbe was made legal adviser to the party and Bokwe second vice president.

wing of the party, however, and he therefore emphasized the constitutional right of the federal president on his own authority to nominate the state prime minister and of the majority of the House of Assembly (i.e. parliamentary wing of the majority party) to invest him. This was an obvious tactic to take advantage of Muna's strength, but it was turned into a highly confused debate on constitutional principles which a number of the involved apparently genuinely came to uphold. Egbe, the lawyer, legal adviser to the party, and Deputy Minister of Justice, argued that any attempt to preempt the president's or House of Assembly's responsibilities in the naming of the prime minister would amount to an attack on the constitutional order and threaten grave consequences. Ekhah, principal strategist for the Jua camp, accepted the legalistic argument but countered with an insistence on discipline within the party; surely the party convention, constitutionally the party's supreme body, had a right to require the parliamentary wing to abide by its decisions. Foncha felt himself caught in a dilemma: he believed the party juridically incapable of treating its selection of its own officers as an actual election of state officials and he desired not to have President Ahidjo nominate someone who might be rejected by the House. On the other hand, Foncha could not argue against the need for party discipline or the authority of the national convention over the political acts of party members. He wavered in his preference for Muna as the new prime minister.

In an attempt to strengthen the principle of parliamentary and presidential responsibility in the naming of the new prime minister, Egbe convinced Muna to withdraw his candidacy for the party post at the tenth national convention held in November 1964 in Kumba. However, Muna continued to believe that the parliamentarians would back him and perhaps that Ahidjo preferred him.[36] Foncha felt pushed to keep the Muna bid open by his own anger during the aftermath of the Bamenda convention, when many simple villagers asked the reason why he remained in the state: "Didn't we elect a new Prime Minister at Bamenda?" "Aren't you supposed to be moving to that other country in East Cameroon?" Egbe wondered if the convention wouldn't next attempt to designate all ministers.

The Jua forces attempted to consolidate his second victory for the

[36] There is no evidence that Ahidjo expressed any personal preference in this matter, but he did know and respect Muna and had relatively little knowledge of Jua. It is probable that Foncha expressed his own preferences to Ahidjo, and it was a widespread opinion in Yaounde that Foncha and Muna were easy men to deal with, whereas Jua could be difficult.

party's vice presidency, which was achieved at the 1964 Kumba convention, by amending the party constitution to insure that the holder of that position, in the absence of the president from the House of Assembly, would automatically be the party's nominee for prime minister.[37] This action nearly provoked violence between the factions at the convention.

Though Foncha opposed the amendment he now became fearful for Muna's standing with the members of the western House, so he personally consulted with each member of the Assembly to discover which of the two candidates might command a majority; that man was Jua. Muna was informed of this, as was President Ahidjo, but Muna refused to accept the consensus; because of their friendship and the obligations created by his previous support, Muna insisted that Foncha submit his name to Ahidjo, along with Jua's if need be. Flustered, Foncha convened a meeting on May 9, 1965 of the joint parliamentary delegations (state and federal), at which an open vote in the Assembly was demanded. Jua was shown to have the support of 23 of the party's 30 Assemblymen. Foncha then asked Muna to "step down," but Muna pointed out that he was not standing; he was not standing for any office in this body. Foncha accused him of challenging the party; Muna accused Foncha of being the party's "number one devil" and Ekhah Ngahky the number two devil. He claimed the president would nominate him anyway.

The power of the federal president to affect the course of politics, or even determine the political fate of West Cameroon politicians and in doing so spur the federation toward greater unity and integration or disruption and chaos, was never more real than at this juncture. Ahidjo could have nominated Muna despite the party's decisions, and by challenging the dominant power in the state, incur its utter hostility. Perhaps such a move would have spurred some Assemblymen to change their votes, but more likely it would have produced an impasse, with the president nominating and the Assembly failing to elect the candidate. Under such circumstances the president could then dissolve the Assembly and call for new elections, which might or might not have been honest ones, or perhaps declare a state of special emergency and establish a government under his own authority. In either case, Cameroon would have reproduced conditions similar to those that were leading to such great tragedy

[37] The amendment was vaguely worded. It is not clear that it would have accomplished what Jua and Ekhah intended to accomplish. It stated: "Where the leader of the KNDP is an elected member in the West Cameroon House of Assembly, he shall be the Party Leader of the Parliamentary Wing, and where the KNDP is the majority party he shall be recommended to become the Prime Minister." Whether Jua considered Foncha no longer to be the party leader is unclear.

in neighboring Nigeria. Rather than invite that, Ahidjo made his own reading of the political situation by consulting with not only every member of the House of Assembly but those of the House of Chiefs as well, all the Secretaries of State, the Federal Deputies, and Foncha. He named Jua as prime minister and the House quickly confirmed the nomination.

The day after Jua's appointment Foncha on his own authority suspended from the party Muna and all those who had supported him, including one who joined Muna's camp after the vote mentioned and one who had defied party discipline even before this case. This action was immediately validated by the Central Working Committee (an interim party executive), but was changed to expulsion by the executive committee of the party. In all, nine party leaders were expelled, among whom were three state ministers, two federal ministers, one ex-federal minister, several ex-federal deputies, and one director of a state agency.[38] Because Muna was absent from the country during the executive committee's "trial," action on his case was postponed and before another meeting could be held Muna resigned from the party.

Ahidjo was also in a position to determine the fate of the suspended leadership, because two of them, around whom the rest clustered, were his own appointees to federal ministries. Rather than bow to the angry demands of the victorious KNDP forces, Ahidjo demonstrated his independence from regional and personal pressures by keeping the men in their high-paying posts. Both sides were thus indebted to Ahidjo; both called some of his actions wise and fair.

But Foncha was isolated. He had lost control of his party and had incurred the wrath not only of Jua and his supporters but the Muna camp as well. The party executive had heard demands to strip him of his party membership, which seemed impossible to do since Foncha had been made "Life President." At the subsequent convention there was talk of removing the adjective from the title, but Foncha made sufficient amends with the Jua camp.

The expelled KNDP members and Muna organized a new party named the Cameroon United Congress, in a poorly disguised attempt to bring into being a "UC" in West Cameroon. They stumped the country earnestly for support and created a newspaper, which appeared only sporadically, a mimeographed newsletter, and the vague outlines of a platform that contained mostly complaints of injustice and a lack of democracy in the KNDP. Rather than project their party as a new movement expressing a new ideology, the CUC leaders emphasized that the

[38] Those suspended were S. T. Muna, E. T. Egbe, W.N.O. Effion, J. M. Bokwe, M. N. Ndoke, S. Mofor, L. I. Omenjoh, J.K.N. Tataw, B. T. Sakah, and M. Fusi.

party was created as a last resort in defense of long-held principles which presumably the KNDP had deserted. The CUC was formed by people who had not chosen to quit the KNDP (in fact, they asserted that it had been their conviction to work for change within the party), but by those who had been arbitrarily expelled from it, not because they "loved the Party less" but because they "loved the Federal Constitution more." [39] In their later propaganda they stressed their own desire to rapidly achieve a truly unified national party, and turned KNDP criticism, to the effect that it had dragged its feet on the unity question when members of the KNDP and had impeded the achievement of unity by creating another party, back on the KNDP by demanding to know how the KNDP could claim to be genuinely concerned about achieving unity in the society when it voluntarily, arbitrarily, and unjustly split its own ranks by expelling one-fourth of its parliamentarians. [40]

The propaganda, indeed the whole strategy of the CUC, seems to have been directed not so much at the average voter in West Cameroon but at President Ahidjo and the ruling circles of the UC. The quickest way back to prominence in the political life of the state, and the surest support for their tenuous hold to this at the federal level, was through the formation of a single national party bringing together all factions, something so often and for so long discussed. To stimulate the UC to move more forcibly toward this goal, and to demonstrate the complementarity of their motives and goals with those of the UC, Muna and his followers sometimes had to stress themes that embarrassed them at home. Support for the federal constitution is an example. The validity of the existence of an additional party is another. Credibility and influence demanded public support, however, so that the party leaders did have to organize a following or the semblance of one. Theirs was a short-run strategy, however; nothing would have jeopardized success for them more than either a prolonged or an early electoral competition with the KNDP or the CPNC.

The unity achieved among the leaders of the CUC would seem to have depended primarily on faith in this tactic. Most of the members of the group were among the weaker KNDP leaders with the electorate; they certainly were not the strongest, with the exception, perhaps, of Effiom and Muna himself.

Jua's route to power was an unusual one. He knew his hold on the

[39] Prior to their final expulsion the 10 drew up a "Charter on Party Democracy and Justice" and formed themselves into the "Defenders of the Constitution Group."

[40] See Cameroon United Congress Newsletters, esp. Vol. 1, No. 1, "Too Many Parties: Why Then the CUC?" by Tabi Egbe, March 1, 1966.

prime ministership to be none too secure, inasmuch as he confronted a strong opposition without and also within the party. The situation called for new alignments or a quick restoration of the former unity. The latter course was doubtful, not only because of the bitterness that had developed between the two camps—Jua having threatened at one point that if he succeeded he would fire any official who did not support him (which did much to consolidate the ranks of the Muna camp)—but also by Foncha's quick, personal action in suspending the dissident members from the party. This action suited Jua's purposes well, for it put the Muna camp on notice that it would have to rejoin the party on Jua's terms, but placed the onus for the final break, if and when it came, on Foncha instead of Jua.

At the same time that Foncha demanded the submission or the expulsion of the Muna camp, Jua extended the hand of friendship and a call for cooperation to the opposition party, Dr. Endeley's CPNC. In his inaugural speech Jua stated: ". . . the Opposition is respected and is respectable. . . . Mr. Speaker, I shall like to see both the Government and Opposition on the floor of this House cooperate as never before so that the West Cameroon electorate may reap maximum benefit from the efforts of the State Parliament. My Government will, therefore, stretch a right hand of fellowship to the Opposition and to its supporters outside this House. . . ." [41] Jua let it be known that a new day had dawned in West Cameroon politics.[42] He sought to distinguish his policies and approach from those preceding them. When the expulsion of the Muna camp became final Jua began to talk in specific terms about government and opposition party collaboration, privately holding out the possibility of ministerial positions. At the same time, he appealed to specific members of the opposition party and enticed two of its prominent members, E. E. Ngone and F. N. Ajebe-Sone of Kumba division, to cross the carpet. As a reward, Ajebe-Sone was given the post of Secretary of State for Finance. Jua had also profited from another CPNC defection, that of Tamfu, who had earlier introduced the resolution calling for the creation of a single national party. Tamfu was made Secretary of State attached to the Prime Minister's office.

Despite the defections from their party, Endeley and Mbile's position grew stronger as the breach in the KNDP led to the formation of a new party and made the prospect of reconciliation and reunion more remote.

---

[41] Speech by the Honourable Agustin N. Jua, West Cameroon House of Assembly, May 11, 1965.

[42] Speech adjourning the House of Assembly session, July 7, 1965.

276

Both sides began to court the CPNC leadership. The CPNC were cautious but attentive; Mbile remarked, "this is no time for a politician to be sleeping." Muna had little to offer the CPNC, however; indeed, he would have trouble holding his own retinue together for very long, without patronage to hand out. Jua continued to hint about governmental positions, something neither beyond nor below the interest of Endeley and Mbile, but the KNDP continued to talk officially about opposition members coming into their party. Foncha also made things difficult by issuing statements castigating the members of the opposition while Jua was publicly expounding the opportunities for their cooperation. For the CPNC, therefore, as for the expelled members of the KNDP, the key judgment to make concerned the probabilities of an early move by Ahidjo or Jua to carry out their announced intentions to fuse into a single party. Were this to come before the next State Assembly elections, scheduled for December 1966, a year and a half away, each party could claim strength sufficient to demand inclusion within the new party on terms more favorable than perhaps it could claim after a serious defeat in the elections. In fact, no party felt confident of its chances in an open general election. Each had an interest in moving quickly to the creation of the single party. Jua's KNDP would gain the most from an alliance with the opposition however; so early in 1966 he agreed to accept the CPNC leadership in a coalition government without demanding the destruction of the CPNC. Mbile took the post of Secretary of State for Public Works and Transport (the ministry he directed in his first ministerial post in the Endeley government). Endeley sought to maintain his prestige as one of the preeminent West Cameroon politicians by demanding a position on a higher level than secretary of state. A special post was created for the purpose, that of Leader of Government Business.[43]

It was clear that each faction was now prepared to accept a single national party, which came into being not long thereafter. It was also becoming increasingly clear that the government party stood on shaky ground. In February 1966 the mismanagement of the state-supported Cameroon Bank and large-scale default and delinquency on repayment of loans by important government and KNDP officials became public knowledge. Over the course of the next year the Bank scandal grew, and an additional one concerning other state corporations focused public dis-

[43] *Cameroon News Bulletin,* FRC Embassy, Washington, D.C. Special Issue (1966), p. 12. The functions of the post are not clear, but its protocol position is suggested by the fact that in colonial times this was the designation for the post just below the governor. The post became that of Prime Minister after independence.

277

content on the KNDP faction as the ruling circle. Added to this source of criticism was increased concern with Jua's seeming preference for grass-fielders and his continued harassment of nonsupporters among civil servants.

Ironically the ex-KNDP faction grouped around Jua found itself at a disadvantage in constituting the government as the faction prepared for the general elections to the West Cameroon House of Assembly to be held in late 1967 (the elections had been postponed a year). It was the scapegoat for critics within the state and it had few close connections with the national party leadership from the East. How far Jua had slipped was made evident when the 29-member Provisional Steering Committee of the Cameroon National Union selected a list of 37 candidates for the Assembly, which included every one of the expelled KNDP supporters of Muna (with but one exception who had since deserted the Muna forces to rejoin the KNDP).[44] Two members of Jua's government were excluded from the list of candidates, along with eight of his other supporters. Voting for the single list of 37 candidates took place on December 31, 1967; on January 11, 1968 President Ahidjo nominated Solomon Tandeng Muna as prime minister. The newly elected Assembly quickly confirmed Muna, dramatically reversing the course of the previous five years. Muna established a government containing many new faces and streamlined its organization.[45] His close friend and supporter, W.N.O. Effiom, was elected Speaker of the House of Assembly, and Dr. Fonlon took the federal post of Minister of Transport, Post and Telegraph. Though J. N. Foncha remained vice president he and his faction had been eclipsed. His active critics were in firm control of all the important centers of power occupied by West Cameroonians, at the state and federal levels.

The Emergence of a National Party

The timing of the emergence of a single party at the federal level in Cameroon was determined by the relationships that existed among the

---

[44] John Tataw was excluded from the list. His candidacy had been opposed by members of the local constituency organizations, which remained active under the single-party regime. Several constituencies took part in the designation of the single list of candidates. In Bangwa, for example, there was active opposition to Secretary of State Peter Kemcha who was replaced. Similarly, opposition was expressed to Tataw; a civil servant was selected in his place. This was the first election in West Cameroon in which civil servants were permitted to run for political office without jeopardy to their status and pensions, etc.; three were elected.

[45] Two ministries were merged with others and all positions of parliamentary secretary were abolished.

various parties at the state level on both sides of the Mungo River. Discussions about the nature of such a party preceded its achievement, however, and contributed to determining the moment of its appearance. All the while the KNDP was maneuvering to delimit if not destroy the opposition party, it also sought to better its position vis-à-vis the UC so that it could enter a national party under the most favorable circumstances possible. The KNDP had thus to approach the matter on several separate levels, approaches which were not always parallel or even logically compatible.

President Ahidjo did not expect or desire to move immediately to a complete fusion of the two ruling parties when in April 1962 he announced the creation of the Coordination Committee between them. Foncha was even less anxious to do so. The move was of symbolic importance, however, in that it signaled the direction in which the two leaders thought progress lay. It also represented an additional structural connection between the two communities and indicated the freedom of the two political organizations to press forward with their own efforts to consolidate their power without fearing that the other might interfere. On the other hand, each party knew it would have to give tangible evidence of its commitment to the stated objective lest the oppositional forces gain an advantage, by arguing the official line more eloquently than did the official party, as might happen in West Cameroon, or by taking the lack of such evidence as a sign of a slackening determination to absorb all other political forces, as might happen in East Cameroon. Ahidjo knew, and Foncha probably suspected, that ultimately one power structure would come to parallel the one bureaucratic state structure which had already taken shape in the country. Neither side was in any particular hurry to bring this about, so long as the primary interests of each, the preservation of their power base, were protected and trends carried them in the right direction.

The first meeting of the Coordination Committee did not take place until six months after its formation, at which time officers were elected and the commitment to the goal of a grand party at the national level was renewed.[46] In the interval between the formation of the committee in April 1962 and its first meeting in October, President Ahidjo continually emphasized this goal, but always stated that the process of its realization should commence with the fusion of all parties in each state.[47] The goal

[46] *Bullétin Hebdomadaire d'Information*, No. 22, October 15, 1962.

[47] *Cameroon Times*, June 1, 1962, referring to Ahidjo's speeches during a six-day tour of West Cameroon.

had been substantially reached in the east by the time the committee met; indeed, this fact may have influenced the decision to convoke it, but the discussions of party unity between the KNDP and CPNC during the summer had broken down and the KNDP party leaders were uncertain about, if not outright opposed to, the single-party system. Foncha had even denied that the agreement with the UC constituted an alliance between them.[48] Nevertheless, KNDP leaders began to prepare the foundations for a party merger. The KNDP Executive Committee met a month after the meeting of the Coordination Committee, and again in March, to confirm its acceptance of the principle of a national party. The party's leaders were authorized to carry out the necessary preliminary studies and, in turn, to instruct the Coordination Committee to set the process in motion.[49] This done, the Executive Committee would be ready to convoke a special national convention to study and ratify any acceptable agreement leading to this end. The Executive Committee, like the eighth annual convention before it, and the one to follow six months later, insisted that no positive step toward real merger be taken without a full discussion in the national convention. The purpose of the statements was to affirm in a dilatory manner a commitment to progress toward party unity.

The single-party system, as it has developed in Africa, has been rationalized in numerous ways. To some it is the post-independence embodiment of the pre-independence singularity of national purpose achieved in the anti-colonial struggle. To others it is the natural projection onto a larger scale of the political patterns exhibited on a diminutive scale in the tribe. Sometimes it is said to recapture the primordial unities of ancient Africa; other times it is avowed to be the necessary instrument of the modernizing revolution. If it is any or all of these things, it is also always a mechanism by which ambitious people or groups seek to acquire or maintain political power. None of the rationales expressed for or against this system predominate over the power interests of those concerned. At one time or another every Cameroonian political party argued for or against the single-party system in ideological terms. But whatever the ideological position taken, each party sought it or fought it according to whether its power would thereby expand or expire. In the dulling

[48] Minutes of Eighth Annual Convention UNDP, Victoria, June 1962. Jua also affirmed that the agreement meant only collaboration, and assuaged fears by remarking, ". . . the burnt child fears the fire . . ." (p. 4).

[49] Federal Press Release No. 2111, November 1962; *Cameroon Champion,* November 20, December 7, 1962; and *Bullétin Quotidienne d'Information,* No. 262, November 14, 1962.

280

euphoric aftermath of reunification, during the excitement of the launching of federal institutions, when the KNDP was in the strongest position ever relative to other *West Cameroon* parties, it seemed the natural thing to do to talk of unity of the two ruling parties. Neither ruling party found anything particularly threatening about it. In fact, it forced the issue of unity among all the state level parties on terms favorable to the dominant ones. But as the structures of the federal state became more real, muscular, and evident, the question of power relations between the two regimes became commensurately relevant—which caused the leaders of the KNDP to consider more carefully the implications of a UC-KNDP merger. In consequence, the rhetoric of the KNDP's argument changed, at least in informal and private discussion. Rather than refer to their collaboration with the UC as directed toward either a *single* or a *unified* party, they called it a quest for a "national party." As one party spokesman put it: ". . . a national party is a political body which embodies all the sections of the nation. At the moment we have only sectional parties: when the KNDP and UC merge together they will form a National Party and not a one-party system. [The] One Party System . . . means the establishment of dictatorship by law. This is contrary to the fundamental human rights provided in our Federal Constitution and also in the Constitutions of the KNDP and the UC." [50] The KNDP leadership expressed their willingness to achieve common, or linked, structures which would permit a pooling of the federation's manpower, but they strongly insisted that the character, internal structures, and especially the name of their own party be preserved. As noted earlier, their purpose was to avoid creating opportunities for the West Cameroon opposition leaders to circumvent the KNDP structure and acquire local or federal influence on their own. What the KNDP sought was the creation of a single-party system at the state level, the very thing it refused to accept at the federal level. In discussing the means of achieving working unity between the KNDP and the UC, the KNDP's arguments echoed those advanced by its own local opposition.

[50] Z. A. Abendong, Secretary General of the KNDP, Notes for Radio Summary of Abendong Tour of Bamenda and Sections of East Cameroon, March 4, 1963. About a year earlier, Foncha, speaking before the House of Chiefs, stated: "The present sitting of this Honorable House without opposition has proved the falsehood of the doctrine that a one-party government is undemocratic." He claimed that such a system manned by deceitful people might produce dictatorship, but that Cameroonians had learned their lesson about deceitful parties and intended to get rid of them. Federal Information Service Press Release, No. 1897, July 6, 1962.

INITIALLY the UC's leadership was tolerant of the KNDP desire to go slow on achieving party unity. What the UC feared most was that local dissidents on each side would attempt to stir up confusion and trouble, perhaps stimulate additional terrorism, around the symbols of the ruling party from the sister state. They were quite satisfied to pledge abstinence from any attempt to form an opposition to the government party in West Cameroon, in return for a similar pledge from the KNDP respecting the UC. But, following the success of the UC in eliminating the principal opposition spokesmen from the political scene, thereby stimulating a realignment of party affiliation among many of their followers, the UC became impatient with the KNDP approach. As the ninth annual convention of the KNDP approached, the UC leadership privately expressed its disagreement with the idea that the creation of a national party must await the achievement of single-party systems in each state. Such an approach, in their estimation, might make it more difficult to achieve genuine unity on a national basis; the more natural approach would be to form the party from all those of goodwill.[51] The UC therefore convened the Committee of Coordination to attempt to produce a clear and precise commitment to a quick merger of the parties. It is unofficially reported that this meeting, which took place in June 1963, actually did arrive at agreement among the party delegations and clear recommendations to the two executive committees.[52] The recommendations reportedly included:

1. The two parties were to proceed to a full merger.
2. The new party would have a new name, probably a combination of the two existing ones [though no decision was reached as to what it would be].
3. The two party presidents had to approve any decisions of the Committee of Coordination before these were made public.

The controversial issue was that concerning the name—which is related to the structure of any new party as well. The decision for a new name that combined the existing two was a compromise on the part of the UC; the party expected to provide the framework for unity, and implied that it would be willing to allow the KNDP to preserve its existing structure in West Cameroon. Though structures were not elaborated, one approach

[51] Mussa Yaya, interview, Yaounde, June 20, 1963.

[52] This report was made by an aide to one of the members of the committee. The meeting lasted three days and included the chairman, Tabi Egbe, J. N. Lafon, and D. A. Nangah of West Cameroon. The East Cameroon delegation was composed of Moussa Yaya, Hayatou Amadou, Onana Awana, Eteki Mboumoua, and Happi Kemayou.

considered was to invest the existing coordination committee with executive functions, especially with respect to the selection of party candidates for the scheduled April 1964 elections for the federal Assembly.

The West Cameroon participants in the Committee of Coordination took the recommendations back to the KNDP executive, which referred the matter to the political commission of the annual convention meeting a few weeks later. It was probably Foncha's intention and that of his associates to push for a full endorsement of the committee's decisions. In his opening address Foncha stated:

> To lay the foundation of peace and stable government, the KNDP and the UC have decided to operate as a single political party in the whole Federation. . . .
>
> The leaders . . . continued . . . [to seek] a lasting means of consolidating the ties between the two Parties. They then suggested the formation of a National Party.
>
> When the National Executive Committee met in March of this year [1963] it debated the recommendations of the Coordination Committee and authorized the leaders of the UC and KNDP to proceed with the formation of the National Party. . . .
>
> The KNDP is therefore set towards a National Party, and hopes that those of good will will join it voluntarily. . . .

These remarks met with some resistance on the floor of the convention, as many delegates generally accepted the proposal of union with the UC but wanted nothing to be done without a full discussion of it in the convention and even among the population at large. The delegates seemed to have feared that the UC-KNDP union would benefit the CPNC in some way (especially since the CPNC had openly supported union). It was also at this convention that the Foncha-Muna-Egbe camp, now identified with the merger proposals (Egbe had chaired the meeting of the coordination committee and was made the chairman of the convention committee discussing the issue), met the first of several defeats in a bid to move Muna into the prime minister's office. It would appear, therefore, that the refusal of the convention committee charged with this matter to make any recommendation to the convention was a last-minute reversal by Egbe and Muna, to avoid having the onus of this not yet understood cause fall on themselves.[53] The matter was thrown back to the coordination committee and postponed until the next annual convention.

[53] This is not to suggest that Jua had not put himself on record in favor of union. Speaking in Yaounde just a month before the convention, he expressed support for the venture, but in vague terms of achieving national unity. "Since the militants of

Despite repeated pledges by Ahidjo and Foncha to merge their parties, no more steps were taken until three years later, when the West Cameroon party system was fragmented into three strong factions, each of which had come to expect a greater measure of political security, or at least no loss of it through such a union. In the interim, the discussions between the KNDP and UC leadership had shifted to a consideration of a broader range of problems relating to the general character and quality of West Cameroon participation in the life of the federation. (See the next chapter.)

President Ahidjo took the initiative to end the procrastination concerning the creation of a single national party. On June 11, 1966, fully a year after the KNDP crisis, he summoned the leaders of the three West Cameroon parties, together with the prime ministers of the two states, to his presidential palace in Yaounde. There he proclaimed the futility of continuing the indulgence in strife, conflict, and bitterness which the multiparty system, in his estimation, had occasioned in Cameroon. He urged the leaders to decide the matter on the spot, and during the next two days each of them agreed to dissolve their organizations and create a new one, to be called the Cameroon National Union. This party was to be inaugurated before the end of August; to arrange the details the leaders set up a 30-member steering committee to oversee the transition and a working committee of 12 to draft the new party's statutes. Representation on the steering committee reflected the leadership of the UC in the initiative, as well as the weakened position of the KNDP. The UC was given 22 positions, the KNDP 4; the two minority parties were given 2 each. The working committee provided an early indication of the boost in prestige and influence the new party would afford the minority leaders, as each received a post on it. For the CUC there was Tabi Egbe, who turned out to be the chairman of the drafting committee. For the CPNC, Dr. Endeley's distinguished brother, the noted barrister Samuel M. L. Endeley, was the representative. Dr. Bernard Fonlon and Nzo Ekhah Ngahky represented the KNDP. It is notable that every member of the committee was a young, more militantly progressive political figure, and to the man, a critic of J. N. Foncha. The draft of the party statutes was approved by the steering committee on July 23rd. Two weeks later the CUC held the first of a succession of extraordinary party conventions to dissolve itself and will its

the two parties have confidence in their leaders, these leaders must show they have confidence in each other," he said. (Federal Information Service Press Release, No. 2553, July 19, 1963.) Jua was not forceful on the issue, however, and made no attempt to identify himself with it.

assets and membership to the new party. Dr. Endeley noted the significance of this gesture by the UC, which was certainly strong enough to have successfully demanded the outright adherence of the other parties to the UC: "His Excellency the President of the Federal Republic with his usual generosity, candor and love of fair play, has come one step towards us warring West Cameroonians and volunteered to dissolve his large and well established Party, the UC, so that we may meet him half-way and together build up the CNU on a stable basis of equality with no advantage or privilege to anyone, big or small." [54] The equity for themselves and their whole state, which Endeley, and no doubt the leaders of other factions in West Cameroon, expected and found in the new order, is epitomized by the provisional executive committee established to lead the new party. Foncha secured his place behind Ahidjo as one of the vice presidents of the party, the other being the East Cameroon prime minister, Dr. Simon P. Tchoungui. As assistant secretaries general, both Egbe and Ekhah Ngahky balanced the formidable East Cameroon team of Moussa Yaya as assistant and Samuel Kamé (of *Second U.C. Institute de Formation* fame) as general secretary. Jua and Endeley, as well as Dr. Fonlon and Henry Elangwe were included as general members.

THOUGH the burdens of change would again be heaviest on the western political groups, the creation of a new super party structure was meant to be more than fictive even for the UC. Not long after the launching of the new party, for example, both the *Parti des Démocrates* and the *Socialistes* officially dissolved and joined the Cameroon National Union. Ahidjo also attempted to emphasize that more than structure was involved, noting that ideological mergers and the integration of diverse political traditions have always been hazardous operations. He said:

> To the militant members of the *Union Camerounaise* I recommend modesty, tolerance, and an open-minded attitude towards others and the intellectual flexibility needed for the avoidance of any sort of "party patriotism."
>
> The essential point is not so much new organizational formulas and new statutes but rather a radical change in the mentality of party members.[55]

[54] *Cameroon Times*, September 1, 1966.
[55] Speech to the Special Congress of *Union Camerounaise*, August 1966, quoted in *Cameroon Times*, September 1, 1966.

⚥ 12 ⚥

Complementary Rewards of Political Activity

COMPLEMENTARITY in the product of political activity is the single most important integrative factor in a political system. Political systems may persist for a time on the basis of high levels of coercion, where different political actors are linked together by bonds of interaction which are not mutually beneficial, or they may persist on the basis of low levels of interaction so that potential conflicts are avoided and potential benefits forfeited. But historians record few political systems—ones within which significant numbers of people are politically mobilized—that lasted very long, where the rewards of politics were not rather evenly spread among important groups or where they did not tend to progressively become so. Fundamental change in a political system is usually reflected in a significant change in the distribution of political rewards or the definition of such rewards, or both. Complementarity in terms of the outputs of political activity within the context of the modern ethic which stresses equality so much, means achieving coherence not only with respect to the distribution of rewards but also their nature.

The political rewards of Cameroon reunification were incoherent. Each state elite derived different benefits from the achievement of reunification; the western leaders derived significant emotional benefits from having realized a longstanding popular claim and having emerged the victors in a risky competition, thus preserving their popularity. The eastern leaders improved their image among local and foreign adversaries, and thus increased *their* popularity. Both sets of leaders thereby consolidated their control of governmental power. As the Federation was established, the rewards continued to be imbalanced between East and West Cameroon elites, between the elites and the masses, and between regional factions within the states. The increasing conjunctivity of political action in the Federation only made the imbalances more evident. Thus integrative advance in one sense, that of increasing the number and range of connections between the political actors in the system, led to strains and stresses that threatened integration in another sense, that concerning the mutuality of benefits. One of the important aspects of the Cameroon experience with political union is that the dominant leadership within the system recognized the imbalances and the strains they had placed on the

286

system as dangers to integrative advance, and made real progress in alleviating them.

Concern over eliminating imbalance in the rewards of politics in the Cameroon Federation was expressed principally in terms of two general pursuits by members of the elite groups: (1) the quest for a common purpose and direction and (2) a quest for equality of influence and participation.

ONE ironic aspect of Cameroon independence—indeed, of the achievement of political independence by almost every African state—is that it tended to destroy rather than create the clear sense of collective purpose we usually associate with nationalism. Most observers of African nationalism have been struck by the intensity and singularity of purpose exhibited by the groups constituting the movements for independence in the African colonies. The immediate pre-independence period is often described as being one dominated by strong-willed, well-organized movements led by charismatic figures. There was very definitely a euphoric sense of unity and purposefulness at the time of independence. Some have suggested that this singleminded, concerted action continued in many African states into a post-independence concern for rapid economic advance, something which allegedly was viewed as "the consummation of freedom." In Cameroon there was not this clarity of purpose and unity of action after independence, perhaps because Cameroon failed to achieve a unified nationalist movement before independence. The general reordering of the system involved in the creation of a federation complicated matters and hampered the achievement of coherent political purpose and action. A more important truth about the change seems to be that it gave more evident expression to the differences and divergences that already existed. What was true in Cameroon may have also been true, though perhaps less clearly evident, elsewhere in newly independent Africa.

The post-federation goals of the dominant political leadership in Cameroon, in both states and at the federal level, tended to be ontological rather than teleological in character. The leaders were concerned with the "what" of nation-building rather than the "why," with form and structure and mundane short-run goals rather than consummatory or long-run "moral" ones. They quickly started to elaborate the instrumentalities of government, but the more fundamental objectives in the service of which the instruments would be put remained vague, and subconscious impulses only occasionally and with difficulty caught the leaders'

287

attention. This is not surprising, given the rudimentary nature of the state apparatus and the artificiality and short life of the governmental procedures and traditions which the African elites in Cameroon inherited from the colonial rulers. Independence confronted the leaders with myriad details of government, many of which were related to activities the colonial regimes had ignored or not confronted. The clear purpose of gaining self-government could not become transformed into clearly purposeful governing of self because the initial victory had constantly to be renewed lest the existing structures disintegrate, those that needed to be created not be created, and the many new enterprises and undertakings the ex-colonial masters and other foreigners seemed suddenly so interested in pursuing proceed uncontrolled by indigenous institutions. Such was the plight of every new African elite; it was especially true of the elite in Cameroon because of the transformations brought on by federalism. The resulting increase in the burden on the political systems diverted Cameroon's leaders from many local and state-level needs and slowed down the process of elaborating a clear and rational plan of national enterprise in each state. Since the major decisions for the Federation were taken by eastern leaders, the consequent confusion in the political life of East Cameroon constituted a sacrifice by easterners on behalf of federalism and political integration.

Among the top leadership of the Federation, especially those from the east, the desire to achieve a coherent purpose and direction was real but not obvious. The leaders' daily preoccupations obscured their commitment to this end. The commitment was shared by many younger people in each of the three governments, which is not to say that they all sensed themselves to be partners in a common cause. There were numerous divergent views about what long-run goals the country should pursue. However, the more militant young administrators and professional people more often criticized the leadership for lacking clear and fundamental goals than for pursuing the wrong ones.

Reunification was a theme which in itself focused the attention and energies of West Cameroonians, but it was also perceived to be the route to independence. In fact, the theme served as a substitute for the goal of independence and generated many of the same emotions and ambitions independence generated in other states. For the easterners a desire for domestic peace and order was the unifying goal in the immediate post-independence years.

President Ahidjo had no difficulty in stating national goals which could and would be pursued once internal rebellion was put down. His speeches contained all the rhetorical elements of the African Revolution: the birth and development of a Cameroon nation; the need for hard work and sacrifice in order to realize economic and technological advance, social change, and cultural enrichment; and the necessity for unity. But for a long while he mapped out no special route to the achievement of these objectives.

Most Cameroon leaders even failed to emphasize the one truly distinctive mission the country could embark on—an effort to project the Cameroon experiment with political union and political integration of disparate cultural legacies as a laboratory for African unity on a broader scale. Leaders from both states took their work of making a success of federation very seriously, but in the president's speeches to domestic audiences, especially in the east, and to foreign audiences at African interstate meetings, Cameroon's distinctive task of bridging cultures and synthesizing systems curiously was played down. Even at the inaugural meeting of the Organization of African Unity in May 1963, only a year and a half after the emergence of the Cameroon Federation where Ahidjo pleaded that "we accept each other, each of us, as we are" and where he affirmed the equality of states regardless of the composition or size of their populations, he failed to devote a single word to promoting the model of unity the Cameroon itself had afforded to a divided and diverse Africa.[1]

One of the reasons why Ahidjo refrained from referring to Cameroon as a model of African unity was that to do so might have suggested the idea of full political union between the African states, which he rejected outright.[2] Equally as important, perhaps, is the fact that at home Ahidjo did not want to encourage particularism by interpreting the country's integrative tasks in terms that would legitimize the cultural differences between the two states. Probably Ahidjo personally did not think of the task as one of cultural accommodation between different but legitimately durable traditions, but rather as one of cultural assimilation or perhaps of cultural synthesis and dynamism by which a new and different culture

[1] *Discours Prononcé par S. E. Ahmadou Ahidjo au Sommet de l'O.A.U. a Addis Abéba du 22 au 25 Mai, 1963.* A year and a half later, at the Cairo conference of nonaligned states, Ahidjo did refer to the Cameroon experiment as something of a model: ". . . the Federal Republic of Cameroon, composed of two states formerly under two different foreign dominations is a concrete case which demonstrates that arbitrary divisions can disappear if it is left to the peoples and nations concerned the latitude to freely decide their own destiny."

[2] At the Addis Ababa meeting Ahidjo stated that, "At present every rigid institutional form [of political union] seems to us to be premature. Thus, for the moment [we want] neither federation nor confederation."

would emerge from all the traditions that interacted in Cameroon. Even in terms of governmental structures Ahidjo gave no evidence of viewing Cameroon as a true federation with several separate and coordinate governments.[3] It may be that Cameroon leaders at the federal level did not propagandize their federal experiment as a model for African unity because they initially did not conceive of it as such. Recall that Ahidjo had stated explicitly during the elaboration of the constitution that he considered the union not to create a new political and moral organization but to fulfill an old one. The task of achieving national unity, which was stressed in nearly every presidential speech, was usually expressed simply in terms of achieving a single party and eliminating strife and opposition.

As time went on, however, and as the erosions of their power and authority became more evident to West Cameroon officials, they began to emphasize not only the supposed commitment to federalism but also to cultural pluralism. This represented less a backing away from pre-reunification attitudes than an increasing awareness of the specific problems and forms of integration. At the Foumban constitutional conference Foncha had declared his expectation that the various discrete cultural forms among the Cameroonian peoples would gradually be transformed: "The form of government is one thing, while culture is another. While we will keep the form of government now envisaged, the foreign cultures will have to take care of themselves, and I hope, by the process of evolution, to be replaced by an indigenous one." Though these sentiments were widely shared in both states, and most public officials spoke of their expectation to see an authentically Cameroonian culture evolved, the easterners never seemed willing to specify which of their own traditions they might give up; and Westerners came increasingly to ask themselves, "what single one of our practices or customs has been adopted in East Cameroon?" The many new procedures and usages that had come into daily western life from the eastern state were visible to everybody.

Foncha and the top leaders of the KNDP were under growing pressure from their followers and West Cameroon intellectuals to define a set of goals not only for the West Cameroon regime, but for the whole of the

---

[3] One French diplomatic official who worked closely with the Cameroon government for a number of years and was reputed to know its leaders better than almost any other foreign official, stated to me that not only were Ahidjo and his associates from East Cameroon not federalists, but that federalism was almost incomprehensible to "the French mind." "They accept the federal arrangement only as marking a period of transition," he stated; "their real aim and expectation is to assimilate the West into the patterns of government being developed in East Cameroon." Jean Marie Bonnier, interview, Yaounde, January 1963.

country, especially regarding the question of cultural interaction. They wanted a program that could be articulated in federal circles and could lead to a greater measure of duality in the cultural interchange between the two communities. Letters to the editors of local newspapers, private conversations, and meetings of the inner circle of party leadership all mediated such sentiments.

The most articulate spokesman for westerners who were dissatisfied with the seeming lack of direction and influence of the Buea regime in national politics was Dr. Bernard Fonlon, the most highly educated West Cameroonian and an author of international reputation. Fonlon did not seek to entrench English customs in the cultural life of the country. Though it is possible that his many years of seminary and doctoral studies had developed a sense of intimacy and proprietorship of British culture equal to his own mastery of it, it is important to note that Fonlon was also intimately familiar with the French language and culture. He was the most accomplished Cameroonian in the two cultures.[4] For this reason, Fonlon had proved invaluable to President Ahidjo as chief of mission in Ahidjo's office.

It was Dr. Fonlon more than any other person who put the Cameroon experience with federalism in terms that linked it to the broader issues of African unity and held out the promise of a truly distinctive mission for the country. Through the bilingual cultural journal *Abbia,* which he helped found, he propounded his argument: "When President Ahidjo says that this country is a pilot state, he is not bragging, nor is he using a phrase void of meaning. It is precisely the historic opportunity to effect an integration of these three cultures [African, English, French] that has invested Cameroon with the singular, enviable mission to pilot the rest of Africa into continental unity. It would be a curious lack of a sense of history to be indifferent to an enterprise of these dimensions."[5] Fonlon claimed that what he sought was the emergence of a new and truly African culture, for "the union of a people is not complete until they have forged for themselves a soul, that principle of life and continuity, that unity of thought and feeling that only a common culture can give." The one way to achieve this, he said, "is to create a new culture thoughtfully, methodically, diligently, from those which are met on the continent today." In effect, however, Fonlon's argument bolstered the legitimacy

---

[4] Fonlon initially studied for the seminary in Eastern Nigeria. He received a Ph.D. from the University of Ireland, studied for two years at the Sorbonne, and received a Master's in Education from Oxford University.

[5] Fonlon, "Will We Make or Mar," in *Abbia,* No. 5 (March 1964).

and augmented the role of the British heritage in Cameroon, because the real danger to cultural synthesis came from intolerance by French influences in the country for any other. The mere existence of two states, and the juxtaposition of their officials in the institutions of the Federation, was an inadequate guarantee of the cultural and moral equality of the two communities, because French influence in the commercial, administrative, and cultural life of East Cameroon was too overwhelming and the East too dominant in the affairs of the Federation to secure such equality. In Fonlon's words:

> Therefore, unless the East Cameroon leader and intellectual, in whose hands cultural initiative lies, is prepared to share this authority with his brother from West of the Mungo, unless he is prepared to make the giant effort necessary to break loose from the strait-jacket of his French education, unless he will show proof of his intellectual probity and admit candidly that there are things in the Anglo-Saxon way of life that can do this country good, there is little chance of survival, neither for English influence, nor even for African values in the Federal Republic of Cameroon.
>
> With African culture moribund, with John Bullism weak and in danger of being smothered, we will all be French in two generations or three! [6]

For one of the cultures in Cameroon to oust the rest in this fashion would be, in Fonlon's view, "to mar an historic chance, to wreck the noble mission that Cameroon had been called upon to fulfill in the name of all Africa."

For true cultural synthesis to come about in Cameroon, one must first recognize the equality of each cultural community in terms of opportunities to contribute to the cultural development of the country, and then carefully and thoughtfully to select for preservation and development those features of each most suitable to the needs of the whole country. This selection would have to be made largely from the heritage that was rooted in the work of the European powers in Africa. Dr. Fonlon believed that the kind of planned cultural change that could produce African unity amounts to a job of grafting and pruning, but on a tree whose trunk must be African, rooted deep in the black soil of the African cultural heritage, "so that the sap that enlivens the whole and confers oneness on the entire organism, should be African." On the other hand, he also believed that

[6] *Ibid.*

292

the cultural initiative necessary for this work "lies exclusively in the hands of the westernized few." "The African tradition, today, is largely a dormant culture," he stated, "because it is not the vehicle and instrument of modern progress; and, as we know, it is the power to promote scientific thought and technical know-how that endows a culture with dynamism." Thus the real point is that the promise of cultural melange in Cameroon depends on the fate of at least the *two* colonial cultures. In this Fonlon reflected the conflicting imperatives that motivate the African quest for unity—the desire for Africa to achieve a secure and influential place among technologically advanced States, and to reassert the dignity of the indigenous African culture and explode the myth that Africans are without "a history of their own."

To Fonlon, "the point to establish and ram down is that, in this federation, these two cultures stand on the same footing of equality." One might expect cold objectivity among Cameroonians regarding the place of these grafts from foreign cultures, but, alas, Fonlon noted: ". . . in this country, the elite, especially, has become so imbued with these outside cultures that this emotional detachment is not to be taken for granted. There is a real danger that, called upon, in the general interest, to part with an element of the foreign culture in which we have been bred, some of us would take up arms in a blind and headstrong crusade, in the wrong-headed belief that the surrender of such a use or institution is a defeat and humiliation. . . ."

The answer, the only answer, to this conundrum is to recognize the cultural diversity of the country as an opportunity and to take biculturalism at least, and ultimately triculturalism, seriously, despite the evident inequalities in the size and resources of the communities concerned. "Cultural equality and equal participation" would have to become the guiding principles of the Federation if political integration is to be fully realized.

Dr. Fonlon and the many West Cameroonian intellectuals and young people whom he influenced focused on two specific institutional domains within which cultural equality and equal participation would have to be secured in order to give real cultural mélange a chance in the Federation: the official languages and the educational system.

Language became a focal element in the discussion concerning national purpose and the role of the two federated communities in its definition and pursuit. Several issues were involved. Was the country to evolve an integrated culture or not? And if so, could this be achieved on the basis of bilingualism or would it be desirable or necessary to have a genuine *lingua franca,* a single national language, spoken throughout the country? If one language was to become a *lingua franca,* which language, one of the two official "European" ones or one of the vernaculars?

On the French-speaking side, commitment to the French language ran deep, partly because of the reverence for the language that French culture had encouraged, even among its African colonial subjects. In the Cameroon case, this commitment also resulted from the numerical superiority of East Cameroonians, plus the fact that many more of them were well trained in French. Many articulate easterners make no effort to hide their own conviction that general knowledge of standard English in the west is so rudimentary and the numbers who know it well so small that, in effect, its western citizens would have to achieve monolingualism before the country could preserve bilingualism. Considering the extent to which the West Cameroon school system lags behind that of East Cameroon, and the supposed extent to which pidgin English interferes with the popular acquisition of standard English, many people considered the pursuit of a bilingual state to be a waste of time and resources. Prime Minister Assale is alleged to have once thought it preferable to rebuild the whole educational system of West Cameroon along the lines of the one in the east, since so few schools would be involved, than to seriously try to harmonize the systems. Many French-speaking officials in the federal government exhibited a certain imperiousness by refusing to learn or speak English, even though most of them had had some schooling in it. In 1965, four years after federation, western citizens still complained of federal communications and notices sent from Yaounde in only a French version.

West Cameroonians did not have to be particularly sensitive to be alarmed about the future status of English, a concern that went beyond mere pride in linguistic accomplishment or demands for personal courtesies. The stakes for West Cameroon leaders included the political stability of their regime, the prestige of its leaders, their relative claim to national resources and power, for all these were linked to the place accorded the "European" language they used for official purposes. Something more than the juxtaposition at the federal level of the two official languages seemed to be required in order to insure that the severely outnumbered speakers of English would maintain a viable role in the cultural and political development of their own state if not the whole of the country.

Again Dr. Fonlon was the most forceful and articulate spokesman for

294

the western interests in the language question.[7] He argued that the only policy worthy of the country's high mission as a pilot for African unity —and this was one reason for his formulating such a mission—was the most thoroughgoing bilingualism possible; (in reality trilingualism because he believed African languages should remain the native tongues) —not simply at the level of the government, but of each individual citizen. Perhaps only a tenth of the population could really be expected to master both official languages along with their native one, but most could master one and learn the other well enough for normal use.

Language is a fundamental element of a culture, a proposition subscribed to by people on all sides of the language debate in Cameroon, indeed, as it is wherever language policy is debated in Africa. Fonlon shared this view; he considered language to be "the very warp and woof of our mental life." To him it enshrines the common experience, it is the instrument of intellectual development, it forges a sense of intimate union among those who hold it in common. However, to argue, as he did, that the official languages must be thoroughly mastered by as many as possible and taught well to all Africans is to suggest that the cultural complexes they embody are central, not peripheral, to the civilization Africans wish to build. This gave a new twist to the language issue in Africa, for it suggests that the world language is as legitimate and durable a vehicle for the expression of the African culture and personality as indigenous African languages.

The idea of general bi- or trilingualism was opposed in Cameroon by a wide variety of people. One person who attempted to counter Dr. Fonlon's argument seems to have been equally as concerned as the latter that the official languages not be learned in a slipshod fashion. Instead of putting so much effort into teaching both world languages, Dr. Pierre Ngijol, of the Cameroon University faculty and an *agrégé de grammaire,* argued that one or more of the vernacular languages should be developed into a national language. The idea of the use of vernaculars as national languages has wide currency in Africa; many of its proponents share Dr. Ngijol's conviction that language is more than merely the means of expressing a civilization—"c'est la civilisation même." Can Africans adopt someone else's language without also adopting his civilization, was his question, "Eh bien, non!" his answer. But Ngijol seems to have been

[7] He expressed most of his views on the subject in his article, "A Case for Early Bilingualism," in *Abbia,* No. 4 (December 1963); it appeared in a French version in No. 7, October 1964.

less concerned about forfeiting the authentic African personality or civilization than with being deprived of any civilization at all. It is "a brilliant illusion," he argues, that knowledge of the official languages is widespread or substantial; no more than a twentieth of the population speaks these languages, which constantly deteriorate under the siege of the official languages, pidgin English, and the "half assimilated." [8] "Our civilization dissolves with no counterpart to take its place," he argued, and predicted that if existing trends continued, Africans would eventually emerge from their schools speaking "un créole affreux propre à nous."

Some who also desire a linguistic vehicle for greater unity are less embarrassed by or fearful of the prospect of a "créole affreux." One such person, Mr. Jack Kisob, then the assistant to the federal vice president, argued in the pages of *Abbia* that pidgin English, which he called "a living language," should be made an official language or at least taught and emphasized as a *lingua franca* among the masses and middle classes of the country. It is certain that pidgin English is widely spoken, especially in the border areas between the two states, but no more than a handful of Cameroonians acquire it as a native language. Consequently, in the words of Dr. Pierre Alexandre, "it has to be learned, thus taught." Alexandre and others would regard any effort formally to teach pidgin English as a waste of energy and resources; one might as well teach standard English or the vernaculars.

What the advocates of indigenous national languages fail to clarify, however, is the specific vernacular languages which are widespread or politically and ethnically neutral enough to peaceably serve the purpose of national integration. Africa includes nearly 1,500 languages, and none is extensive geographically or demographically. The most extensive non-alien languages are Arabic, which has penetrated black Africa only superficially, Swahili, spoken by perhaps 25 million people in east and southeast Africa but which links the majority of the people of only one country (Tanzania), Hausa, spoken by perhaps 20 million or so mostly in Northern Nigeria, Yoruba, and Ibo, spoken by less than 12 million in southern Nigeria. Not one of the latter languages could unite even Nigeria; in fact, any attempt to spread any of the languages would only intensify the deep divisions and animosities already violently expressed in that country.

In Cameroon there is no vernacular that is truly widespread in terms of

---

[8] In fact, the vernaculars may be growing much faster than the official languages, due to the rapid population growth which often outstrips the expansion of the school systems.

population, although *Fulfuldé* (Fulani) is known in most parts of the north. It is rumored that the schools of East Cameroon may one day soon begin instruction in vernaculars, in which case "unified *Beti*" (Ewondo, Bulu, Fang), Bassa and Douala would be the likely candidates alongside Foulbé in East Cameroon. In West Cameroon Douala and Bali were developed and widely used by the Germans and by many missionary schools in subsequent times, but this practice engendered opposition, and a number of other more limited vernaculars are now used.

Neither Dr. Ngijol, who has openly advocated the adoption of an indigenous national language, nor Dr. Fonlon, who accepts the idea on a long-term basis, can point to any widely agreed on candidate. The very assertion of intimacy between language and culture would seem only to strengthen primordial language loyalties. The logic of this argument justifies fears among every tribal group that it must guard its language in order to preserve its identity and its culture. In this respect the defense of the world languages involves the same considerations.

Fonlon argued the case for genuine bilingualism in terms of a specific program for the schools which he considered to be the principal instrument for forming the Cameroon culture: "My present contention is that if the importance of bilingualism in our national life has become so primordial we must begin it early enough to bear it through successfully; in other words, the teaching of English and French together, here in Cameroon, should start right from the very first day that the child takes his seat in the infant school." He wanted the primary schools to concentrate on language education and to include a program promoting bilingualism in English and French. Dr. Fonlon was as concerned as almost any other African that too early an emphasis on the official world languages not leave African children deracinated and ignorant of their authentic African heritage, so he suggested that the first language of instruction should be African. This process should not last unduly long, he thought, because no African language was yet "developed enough to offer itself as an effective all-round instrument of modern technical progress." For practical reasons, however, and to permit initial instruction in the native languages, Dr. Fonlon compromised his proposals for early and complete bilingualism in several ways: by delaying the introduction of either world language until after some literacy and instruction in the vernacular, and by making the language of instruction the dominant language in each state, with the second language introduced and following along a year later at each level. The study of both languages would be intensified at the secondary level, though the dominant language of each state would continue

297

to be the language of instruction in its schools on through the higher school. Students taking a specialty would pursue intense study of the second language in the field of specialization. At the university level students should be prepared to undertake their studies with indifference as to the language of instruction, and the staff of the university, as well as its curriculum, should be equally rich in their coverage of the culture, institutions, and usages of the two systems.

The most vocal advocates for a thoroughgoing bilingualism were the West Cameroonians, for whom Dr. Fonlon was the most articulate and effective spokesman. Despite this, the eastern regime evidenced a commitment to this ideal equally if not more sincerely than the west. Legislation to make the study of both official languages in the secondary schools and teacher training colleges compulsory took effect in January 1963, which was a greater innovation if not a greater task for the school system of West Cameroon than that of the East Cameroon. English had been taught in many secondary schools of the Cameroun Republic for a number of years; thus for the eastern state the curriculum change required only that the practice be made universal. To be sure, with the greater number of schools being in the east, their offering competent English instruction in every secondary school would be no mean achievement. In the west very few students had the opportunity to study French; thus for almost every school it meant expanding language courses. West Cameroon found itself incapable of carrying out the legislation; moreover, many of its educators feared that the already rudimentary knowledge of English among West Cameroon "school-leavers" might deteriorate still further. The state minister of education announced in July 1963 that "French should not be taught to those who do not have a solid foundation of English," lest they be diverted, learn neither, and have pidgin English become the *lingua franca*.[9] Despite Fonlon's prodding, and in fact in contribution to it, the western regime's policy was to strive not for individual bilingualism at any early date, but for the juxtaposition of the two languages in the public affairs of the Federation.

Even the eastern regime worried about its school system's capacity to teach both languages. The teaching of English improved considerably over several years, aided by the work of the Peace Corps, the U.S.A.I.D. and UNESCO-supported programs of English instruction and linguistic study; but at the same time it is reported that the quality of French teach-

[9] L. M. Ndamukong, Secretary of State for Education, quoted in *Cameroon Times*, July 26, 1963.

ing has been going down at an alarming rate.[10] This is cited as one reason for vernaculars being considered for the first grades of the eastern primary schools.

A significant step toward achieving the competence to produce numbers of Cameroonians, particularly teachers, with a firm knowledge of the two languages was the establishment in September 1963 of the federal bilingual school at Man-O-War Bay, West Cameroon. This school is considered by some education experts to be the best grammar school in the country. Its enrollment remains small, however. Another step the federal government took to encourage its officials to acquire a working knowledge of both official languages was to grant working time off for these officials to take the English courses offered by the U.S.A.I.D. program. During the first few months of the Federation a significant number of Easterners in both the federal and East Cameroon governments did so, but gradually participation dropped off. Eventually the federal government considered it necessary to offer salary bonuses to those officials who were or had become competent in both languages.[11]

Although for various reasons none of the three Cameroon governments has been able to fully implement its policy commitment to bilingualism, it is clear that the assertion that it should be a fundamental part of the national purpose of the country to instill in each citizen a respect for, knowledge, and blend of each of the major cultures, has been accepted. As concerns the role of the language in this process, President Ahidjo has taken as pragmatic an approach as anyone. He does not rule out the eventual possibility of adopting an indigenous language as the "national language" in order to give fuller expression to the African cultural base, but he has announced that until such time as the Cameroon and other scholars concerned about the problem come up with a language

[10] Pierre Alexandre, ed., *Cahiers d'Etudes Africaines,* personal correspondence, June 1966. This is a more general problem, of course, although the greatest concern has been expressed on behalf of the vernaculars. The report of a conference on language problems in Africa, published as *Language in Africa* (London, 1963), carries an article by the linguist John Spencer, who argues that in most bilingual situations each language is most efficiently used where there is a complementary context; otherwise one of them is likely to suffer. A study of bilingualism in Yorubaland, by E. C. Rowlands and published in *African Language Studies* (London, 1963), noted that Yoruba was being distorted by borrowings from English and that "this is not a bilingual situation which can continue for any length of time in equilibrium. . . ." The major threat to the world language derives from the poor qualifications of the teachers in many of the schools.

[11] Mr. J. Kisob, Cameroon civil servant in the service of the United Nations Secretariat, interview, New York, May 1967.

which meets the needs of the country, he intends to speak French as well as he can.[12] It is thought that Ahidjo has worked diligently but privately to learn English. In any case, he has committed the federation to the policy of an early and intensive program of bilingual instruction in the schools. In doing so he expressed this caveat: "When we consider the English language and culture and the French language and culture, we must regard them not as the property of such and such a race but as an acquirement of the universal civilisation to which we belong."

HOPES for a give-and-take between the two Cameroon systems ran higher; perhaps disappointment among at least West Cameroonians was more profound concerning the field of education than any other. It was not because the difference between the two educational systems were less severe, but because education was seen as the keystone of nearly all the rest of the cultural superstructure of each state. Any sincere commitment to cultural synthesis ought to reflect itself in the educational system.

The allocation of federal and state prerogatives in education reflects the same disparities in the values and approach of the two political elites that have been confronted in other domains. Perhaps President Ahidjo thought the educational system would strengthen regional loyalties and cultural distinctiveness if left under the control of the state elites. He insisted that all education above the primary school level be under federal control. As a spokesman for regional interests, Prime Minister Foncha pressed during the constitutional discussions for state control of all local educational institutions, except perhaps a federally run and supported university. As we have seen, the president's view prevailed. Federal officials moved quickly to supervise the secondary and technical schools in West Cameroon, but due to personnel shortages these federal officials, who were seconded from the state ministry of education, continued for a time to supervise the primary and teacher training operations as well.[13] Naturally this approach slowed down the impact of federalization on the West Cameroon educational system. Eventually the disparities between

---

[12] This statement was recalled by the U.S. ambassador, H. E. Leland Barrows, from a press conference Ahidjo gave around the time of federation. The press version of the conference allegedly added the words "and Foulbé" after "French."

[13] A West Cameroon official in the state ministry of education, Mr. Ako Mengot, was appointed to the federal position of Cultural Delegate in Charge of Education in July 1962. The federal budget did not carry all the expenses of the post-primary school system until July of 1963, however. He continued until that time to supervise primary and teacher training and in terms of these responsibilities reported to the state secretary of state for education.

the two systems, most striking in terms of a timetable but more important in terms of curriculum and conception, demanded tighter coordination and adjustment.

Adjustments were made and still more are planned, but in general the pattern of such adjustments is to remodel the system of education in West Cameroon along the lines of its eastern counterpart. One of the first changes effected in the system harmonized the timetable on the basis of, first, a seven-year primary program for West Cameroon, and later, a six-year program in each state. Proposed reforms called for up to seven years of secondary training in two cycles of unequal length in each state.

Examinations and certificates continued to follow their colonial models, but the courses of study faced important reforms. Decolonization of education was a central theme of the reforms in each state. Although the effort derived primarily from the achievement of independence, reunification of the country gave an impetus in the west that it might otherwise have lacked. History and geography, especially, acquired an African and Cameroonian framework. Vocational and more general and limited terminal secondary programs were added, facilitated by a dual-cycle secondary program. Thereby, the French mid-secondary exams (*brevet*) were eliminated. The diversification envisioned with these reforms began in East Cameroon at the primary level. Here, too, a dual cycle was introduced, permitting vocational training for terminal secondary school students, some with a rural orientation. Students who pursue a full general secondary education receive a Cameroon degree, which replaced the old baccalaureate or "General Certificate of Education, Advanced Level."

These reforms, based primarily on East Cameroon patterns, required a significantly greater coordination of the two educational systems. A first step was a plan for standardizing the entrance examinations to the first cycle of secondary school throughout the federation. The exams, alike in content, but given in either French or English, replaced the West African School Certificate formerly used throughout formerly British Africa. These common qualifying examinations for secondary schools undoubtedly increased the pressure for closer coordination; if not full standardization, of primary school programs, as well as the secondary programs.

One of the chief differences between the two states in the pattern of primary school education is the role played by private, especially missionary, institutions. About 85 percent of the students attend such schools in the west. The private schools are heavily supported by state subventions in West Cameroon. French-speaking educational officials, on the other hand, are used to a system which historically, even during

301

the colonial period, placed the greatest responsibility for education on the government. They sometimes describe the system that exists in former British Cameroon as one with "a free enterprise spirit," leading to a situation of "semi-anarchy." The place for private schools, especially secular ones (often called general colleges), has steadily shrunk in the east. The government closely inspects and monitors their activities and seems to be intent on eliminating them altogether. Only in the church-supported schools in the east is religious instruction permitted, and there it is left to the unfettered control of the sponsor. The secular curriculum of all schools, government or missionary, is carefully prescribed and rigidly supervised. In West Cameroon the role of religious instruction has been and continues to be different. Until 1965 religious instruction has been a part of the instructional program of nearly every school, because so many of the schools were founded and continue to be supported by missionary organizations. In the west the secular program is less rigidly supervised. Missionary officials are fearful, however, that the general intensification of governmental supervision being carried out at the federal level and in East Cameroon endangers religious instruction in West Cameroon. Indeed, recently, perhaps overzealous western officials serving in the federal ministry of education called for its elimination throughout the system. Any threat to the deep-rooted tradition of religious instruction in the schools considerably endangers popular and especially official enthusiasm for the Federation among westerners.

Many officials in both states desire to reform the educational systems of the Federation and have worked diligently toward that end. One who was especially effective in this regard was the Cultural Delegate in Charge of Education in West Cameroon, Ako Mengot. Though a westerner, Mengot did not believe that educational reform and harmonization of the systems should exempt the West Cameroon system from significant change.[14] He believed that the division of federal-state authority between the primary and secondary schools was dysfunctional to rational educational planning and development. Either all pre-university education should be under federal control or it should be under state control, in his view, though he understood as well as anyone why the division had been made. The College of Arts and Science was cited as a case in point, where

[14] Most of the reforms enacted in the West Cameroon educational system were the results of plans developed by Mengot. He was able to develop a scheme of free primary education and put the staffing of schools on a more rational basis. His general views on educational reform were expounded in various personal interviews, in Buea and Yaounde in 1963, and Cambridge, Massachusetts in 1965–1967.

302

the division in authority over aspects of education caused serious confusion and held back development. The college was ostensibly under federal control, since it was a higher school offering technical subjects; but there was also a proposal to add an "agricultural terminal component" (i.e. a vocational school) which many thought should be under state jurisdiction. The controversy inhibited the rapid development of the college, but was eventually resolved in favor of federal control.[15] Authority to grant scholarships for higher studies was also confused by this division of control. No one questioned the right of the federal government to grant such scholarships and to control those offered by foreign countries, but many did question the assumption that this right excluded the state governments from granting such scholarships. On the other hand, frequent interference by the state in granting scholarships to students at home and abroad, purely for political reasons, caused much consternation in federal institutions even among West Cameroonians. Finally all officials dealing with government scholarships of any kind were put under federal authority.

Mengot was also concerned about the possible negative impact on competence in English if the West Cameroon schools, even at the secondary level, took seriously their legal obligation to give each student a full knowledge of French. In an effort to protect English in the schools western leaders created their own educational council and attempted to elaborate an educational policy of their own. This led to the announcement by the secretary of state referred to earlier, to the effect that French would be given only to those students well grounded in English. It is reported that the West Cameroon also requested at this time (early 1963) that the secondary schools be left under the control of the state government. Eventually there was also established an education council at the federal level, which the president himself chaired until the westerners, primarily Dr. Fonlon, persisted in demanding so many changes in the educational system that Ahidjo turned the job of running the council over to Vice President Foncha.

Fonlon's ideas for educational reform went far beyond his demands for early and complete bilingualism. Besides having the primary schools concentrate on language instruction, his plans called for an earlier introduction to specialized studies, and provision for such specialized studies to be accompanied by intensive study of the second official language in

[15] Federal-state interests and jurisdictions were also involved in choosing the site of the college. The federal authorities preferred a location at Kumba, and certain state officials wanted it in Bambui, in the grassfields; the latter won.

303

that specialty. Underdeveloped countries cannot make do with Jacks-of-all-trades, Fonlon argued; thus their school systems should be geared to producing specialists in every field: "That is why I am firmly of the view that the sixth form [corresponding to the West Cameroon higher school or the College of Arts and Science] should be given a choice place in our national educational system. As this institution does not exist in East Cameroon, it should be introduced." [16]

Fonlon was especially anxious to see the Cameroon University become a unique and serious experiment in bicultural, bilingual studies:

> Normally, a bilingual university is one in which any student can follow whatever course he pleases in any of the two languages. Such a bilingual university is in fact a double university with a double faculty for every branch of knowledge that is cultivated there, as is the case with the Belgian university of Louvain, where Dutch and French are the languages of instruction. I can imagine that this type of bilingual university would be very expensive to set up.
>
> The great advantage of the type of bilingual education system that I propose is that it makes this costly type of bilingual university unnecessary.
>
> Since the lower stages of the system make the student bilingual, and since the higher school prepares him for his special field in both languages, it would be enough for our bilingual university that lectures can be given in it in either language, and that provision be made for both languages to be adequately represented on the staff.
>
> Furthermore—and this is very important—none of the two languages should be given an official position of privilege over the other in the university. . . . We should keep a sharp eye against this type of thing in every Federal institution in the Republic, lest, instead of bringing off successfully this lofty experiment for cultural integration in Cameroon, we end by turning the country into a cultural battleground.[17]

Despite professions of intent to create a university close to the image Dr. Fonlon projected for it,[18] very little progress has been made toward that end to date. The start was to be made with the establishment of a chair in English, but the first appointment to the chair was a Frenchman,

[16] Fonlon, "Case for Early Bi-lingualism."

[17] *Ibid.*

[18] The Higher Education Council of the Federation decided in early August 1964 to commit the University officially to a policy of bilingual instruction and a bicultural curriculum. *Cameroon Times*, August 11, 1964.

which West Cameroonians protested so strongly that eventually an Englishman was found for the post. Some of the federal minister of education's personal advisers, including Frenchmen, pressed for an experiment perhaps even more original than the one Fonlon envisioned, where the university would be a true hybrid of the standard French version and the best English universities. According to this scheme, English professors would have French-speaking assistants and vice-versa, so that the burden of teaching courses bilingually would be on the university instead of the student. The scheme, in general, allegedly was bitterly opposed by British advisers to the West Cameroon government, as well as by a number of French technical advisers to the federal government. The only genuine progress toward bilingualism was the appointment of two professors with an adequate competence in both languages.

Little was done to make the university bicultural as well as bilingual, however. The law faculty and program of the university exemplifies the problems faced and the approach taken. A number of West Cameroon students had been recruited to the law school in 1963, who expected to be able to pursue studies in English devoted to British Common Law and the legal system in operation in West Cameroon. Upon arrival in Yaounde not only did they discover that almost nothing was taught about the legal system and traditions of their own state, but that all courses were taught in French. After some months of their stumbling along trying to follow the courses in French, they were all sent to Paris for intensive instruction in French. Most did surprisingly well both in the language and the legal studies. A few, those with extraordinary drive and enterprise, took correspondence courses in British law while finishing their studies in Cameroon in the French system. The prospects for a truly bilingual, bicultural, and comparative legal studies program have improved with the inclusion of courses on aspects of the British system, but the eventual success of the program remains uncertain.

Harmonization of the more technical and operative aspects of the legal systems was a goal of those who sought to commit the country to the cause of cultural integration. There has been greater give-and-take in this than in most others. Discussions continue as of the date of this writing on many aspects of the effort. Federal laws have been passed that cover procedures for the supreme court of the Federation, harmonize the rules governing the qualifications and recruitment procedures of judicial and other legal personnel, outline procedures to be followed by the courts in civil and criminal cases, and create common civil and criminal codes. In each area the federal system incorporates some elements of each of the systems formerly operative in the two states, but the basic framework of the new system seems to remain French, with relatively few innovations for the legal system in East Cameroon.[19]

The task of rationally constructing a new, essentially Cameroonian legal system out of the materials of the previous ones, a goal eloquently argued by Cameroonians from each state, was complicated by the fact that the rapid pace of political change in West Cameroon made it difficult to determine just what its laws really were. Nigerian legislation was carried over into the federal period along with certain parts of British common law. New state and federal legislation superseded some of this legal heritage, but no one knew for sure and in much detail which part. Informed discussion of a unified federal system required a codification of West Cameroon law. Overworked western officials and legal advisers have undertaken the task, but its significance and their morale diminishes with each indication that the eastern system may become the national one, largely intact.[20]

A malaise about the place of long-range goals and conscious planning in the priorities of the regime existed among a number of French-speaking officials in the eastern and the federal government and involved issues other than those associated with the integration of the cultural systems of East and West Cameroon. Discontent was evident among students, certainly those outside the country, but it was also to be found among the leftist, ex-student leaders Ahidjo had recruited into his government in hopes of demonstrating his willingness to forget the past and

[19] Harmonizing the criminal codes entailed relatively few difficulties, because both systems contained similar or compatible definitions of crimes. Greater difficulty arose over court procedures in criminal cases, including the definition of and admission of evidence, the nature of penalties, protective rights for the accused, and the procedures for preliminary hearings. These must be taken as preliminary observations, based on interviews with the members of the legal commission established to elaborate a common civil and criminal code. It is not my purpose here to undertake a detailed examination of the nature and problems of legal synthesis in Cameroon.

[20] The balance of federal-state authority affects this issue as well. Pressures for a balanced synthesis of the two systems would be greater if the states were more autonomous or retained more of their own traditional precepts and procedures. In fact, however, very little of "the law" is within the jurisdiction of state governments. It was suggested at one time, for example, that state legislation might not be permitted to provide for penalties in case of its infraction because "criminal law" is one of the federal powers. (This was suggested in a memorandum from the Ministry of Justice to the West Cameroon government in 1965 with reference to a state "antiquities bill.") Though the issue was not pushed to any definitive conclusion, it suggests that the states are potentially without any legal means of enforcing their own rules.

work with all elements who returned the favor. Several of these officials, a few of whom had held high level posts, complained privately of finding themselves isolated from the real centers of decision-making, not consulted on major policy questions, essentially unused to consolidate the popularity of the administration or to aid the administration elaborate a well thought out, coherent, and practical program of development activity over the long haul. One such official who had quit his post in frustration stated that "in over two and one half years of serving in the government not once was I able to have a political discussion with the political leaders of the country." He said that part of the reason the younger progressive (and formerly dissident) elements were not consulted on fundamental long-run policy questions was that very little thinking was devoted to such questions by anyone: "In no domain is there any thinking about tomorrow."

There was little opportunity for subordinates to initiate discussions or organize any effort on their own to elaborate programs or policy papers of this type for fear of being imprisoned, or otherwise punished under suspicion of subversion. This was true for those outside the ruling UC. None of the opposition leaders was able for very long to attempt to organize public opinion against the regime, as the previous discussion of the emergence of a single party has indicated. In truth, however, the parties or leaders did not formulate their protests or appeals to public opinion in terms of long-range goals and program objectives; they were necessarily preoccupied with the question of interparty relations per se, for on that rested the issue of party survival. The import of the criticisms referred to above, however, is that it was also impossible to really criticize the regime or work to give it direction or change its direction from *within* the government party. The charge was, in effect, that there was no progressive wing of the party because none of the potentially progressive militant modernizers was given free enough rein to create one.

A statement of fundamental objectives and program was made by Dr. Fonlon, however. It is significant that the political situation, the existence in the Federation of essentially two political arenas, and the greater openness and freedom of the West Cameroon political atmosphere made possible critical statements and different policies from that quarter. The meager measure of federalism the country did enjoy preserved some air of open politics longer than perhaps would have been the case had the governmental and political party structures been consolidated from the start.

Dr. Fonlon's opportunities to critically discuss and suggest the funda-

307

mental issues of public policy and to lobby for particular principles both among the general populace and the inner councils of government and party structure were greater than those of any other Cameroonian intellectual. This resulted from several factors: A West Cameroonians in and out of government became increasingly frustrated with their lack of initiative and influence in the Federation and yearned for an articulate and forceful spokesman; as West Cameroon's most distinguished intellectual and a person who had not been tarnished by political infighting, Fonlon was respected in all quarters and was considered a potential defender of the legitimate interests of every faction and section of the state; as someone who had acquired sophistication in the French language and culture and who had rendered distinguished service in the president's office, he was respected by many of the top eastern political leaders.

Fonlon's criticism was directed as much against the West Cameroon regime, if not more so, than against the federal regime. He was particularly alarmed at the intensifying climate in West Cameroon of interregional and intertribal animosity and charges of nepotism and favoritism towards grassfielders and KNDP loyalists and of persecution against anyone identified with the opposition, charges which were directed increasingly against the Foncha regime. His influence derived largely from the clarity and force of his argument and from the pride all Cameroonians, especially from the West, could take in his obvious intellectual achievement. This influence was enhanced by his election in the spring of 1964 to the federal National Assembly and his subsequent appointment by Ahidjo to the post of deputy minister of foreign affairs.[21] He had become very critical of Foncha, but as a close friend of each of the parties concerned he refrained from involving himself in the Muna-Jua, Egbe-Nzo competition.

[21] Fonlon was persuaded to run for the National Assembly by the younger progressive elements of the KNDP, especially Muna and Egbe, but probably also Nzo Ekhah Ngahky who is also something of an intellectual and is fluent in French. Nzo entered politics much earlier than Fonlon and became a deputy minister in February 1962. Fonlon and Nzo were quite close intellectually. Fonlon did not desire to be thought of as a politician, however; so he refused to campaign for the post or request the nomination. His friends did this for him, pursuading B. T. Sakah, an ex-federal deputy minister, to give up his seat in the National Assembly. Fonlon's candidacy was not initiated from the constituency organization, but rather from the party's executive branch, which caused some tension, but most of the voters in Nsaw, Fonlon's home, seem to have been proud to have him serve in a representative post. Fonlon has continued to consider himself basically "above politics," however; thus he may in time either lose his political base or the purity of his image as a "philosopher." His rise in authority may not have been altogether accidental: he constantly invokes Plato—"kings must be philosophers or philosophers kings." The top members of the Eastern regime refer to him as "Monsieur le philosophe!"

It was from his base as a federal deputy and deputy minister that Fonlon pushed, with wide support among the younger members of the KNDP, for a direct confrontation and dialogue between the two ruling parties, with the aim of airing the complaints of West Cameroonians about their role in the development of the Federation, as well as the wider question of the general direction development ought to take. In September 1964 these efforts led to the holding of a two-day closed-door conference among the top leaders of the KNDP and the UC.[22] The KNDP's grievances were fundamental and the directness and boldness with which they were presented stunned the eastern leadership, but the latter listened carefully and discussed the points raised in some detail.

The major concern of the KNDP contingent was, of course, that of acquiring for West Cameroon a place of equality with the UC in the making of policy at the federal level, and of restructuring the federation to restore some of the authority the states lost to the federal government. (These concerns will be considered in some detail below.) Let us focus our attention now on what was a less urgent but nonetheless large issue, especially for Fonlon and those concerned with what they considered to be drift and thoughtlessness in the conduct of public affairs at the state and federal levels.

Nothing worthy could be built in Cameroon, in Fonlon's estimation, without a clear and widely agreed upon sense of purpose. The achievement of this required that both thinkers and doers be associated in the enterprise. Sometimes one finds these two qualities combined in the same man, but this was not the case in Cameroon, he argued. One of the unfortunate realities of the state of affairs in the country was that the intellectual and the political communities stood apart:

> And there is a danger that, instead of complementing each other as they should, these two may become suspicious partners, scheming rivals or even sworn enemies. A disaster to the state!
>
> But so necessary is the contribution of each that they must, at all costs, strive to work as united in this enterprise of national reconstruction as hand and eye are united in the same worker. . . .
>
> But since it is only the politician who has received a mandate from the people, it is principally with him that rests the responsibility to

[22] Attending the meeting for the UC were President Ahidjo, Moussa Yaya, Samuel Kame, Njoya Arouna, Marcel Marigoh. For the KNDP, Foncha, Nzo Ekhah Ngahky, Tabi Egbe, D. Nangah, Victor Mukete, Fonlon, J. Totah, S. T. Muna, Patrick Mua, P. M. Kemcha, and J. N. Lafon. Fonlon wrote and presented the major statement of the meeting, serving as the chief spokesman for the KNDP in doing so.

take all measures necessary to associate the intellectual closely with himself in the building of the state.

To do this is not merely sound wisdom . . . it is not the conferring of a favour that may be withheld or withdrawn at pleasure; it is a duty.

How the intellectual community was to be brought into collaboration with the political leadership Fonlon did not spell out, but he did explicitly suggest that the federal regime already relied too heavily on foreign intellectuals and experts. "This is an African nation," he stated; "its principal builders should be African."

In subsequent months Fonlon demonstrated the role of the intellectual by publishing long and closely read articles in the press which laid out the principles and goals he thought should guide the nation's leaders. His call was basically for the adoption of "democratic socialism." In his longest and most sweeping article (serialized over nearly two months in the *Cameroon Times*) Fonlon stated what he considered to be the essential principles of the democratic and socialist program he would have the country adopt.[23] The socialist component required that "the commanding heights of the economy, the major means of production, distribution and exchange, should be held by the State, should be exploited and administered for the common welfare." By democratic he meant a government of, by, and for the people, based on equality and respect for rights, freedom of speech, the rule of law, the separation of powers, and the supremacy of the judiciary over the executive. Both sets of principles were deemed compatible; both were sweeping the world, having an impact on the United States and the Soviet Union alike, and both presumably were far from being realized in Cameroon.

The top leadership, especially President Ahidjo, was probably influenced by Fonlon, but others had also pressed the regime toward similar objectives. In fact, Ahidjo himself had committed the country to the path of "democratic socialism," at least in terms of slogans and rhetoric, before Fonlon's articles began to appear in the press. Ahidjo's socialism differed from Fonlon's, however. Indeed, it may have been this difference that caused Fonlon to devote so much time and energy to the elaboration and propagation of his own views. At the fifth national congress of the UC, held in December 1965 in Bafoussam—for the first time in the heart of Bamileke country and of the former UPC directed rebellion—Ahidjo's presidential address revealed his enduring pragmatism. "There

[23] The articles appeared in the *Cameroon Times* from Vol. 5, No. 117, December 16, 1965 through Vol. 6, No. 13, February 3, 1966.

is no longer any absolute cleavage between the two formulas" (of Western capitalism and Marxist socialism), he stated. He recalled that at the fourth congress of the party, held in Ebolowa in the summer of 1962, he had declared his policy to be a socialist one, but an original, liberal kind of socialism similar to that of Senegal's Senghor.[24] Now it was time, he declared, to be more precise about their goals, directions, and principles, "to leave [behind] these dialectical ambiguities." "We wish," he said, "in a word, to lay the basis for a social democracy which rejects all idea of the alienation of man, even if this alienation carries the promise of a better life for our children and grandchildren. We are therefore for liberalism, a modern, planned liberalism, thus one tempered by the regulatory action of the State. Thus, we consider that private ownership of productive resources and their utilization for private profit is an element of progress. The collectivity can only benefit from the pecuniary stimulus which arouses groups and individuals to effort and which compensates their work. Thus, we are disposed to welcome foreign investments [something which is] absolutely indispensable at the present juncture."

The role of the state in Ahidjo's scheme would be to orient investments toward the areas of greatest social and economic need, to sometimes participate in the ownership and capitalization of important and needed industries, and even to buy out foreign investors and sell their shares to local investors who currently lacked the savings to undertake such ventures. The national plan would take its character from this philosophy, which admittedly did not have a revolutionary resonance, but which sought to assure the country a full economic blossoming in dignity, liberty, and justice.

THE higher national purpose of serving as a laboratory for cultural synthesis in the name of African unity, to which the West Cameroon leadership sought, somewhat successfully, to win over the ruling circles of the country, provided a rationalization for their more immediate and pressing objective of winning a measure of influence and participation in the governing of the country more nearly equal to that of the eastern leaders.

[24] The program Ahidjo proposed at Ebolowa represented a major effort on his part to win over the more militant leftist student, ex-UPC and sophisticated elements of the southern, urban population in Cameroon. Many of the components and much of the rhetoric of African socialism were incorporated into the speech. It marked Ahidjo's first effort to cast the UC and his own leadership in the mold of an ideological mass movement. Coupled with the elimination of the major opposition leaders, the speech led to a spate of new affiliations with the party and the beginning of a popular base for Ahidjo in the south.

West Cameroon never expected to be and never will be equally powerful or play as important a role in the Federation as East Cameroon. This fact did not cause much concern among westerners until about two years after federation because it did not become clear to them until that time just how much of their lives and fortunes would be affected by decisions taken at the federal level of government. However, they had expected to enjoy two kinds of equality with easterners in the federation: the equality of freedom to rule themselves, and a sense of the moral equality of the two states as the dual embodiment of the Cameroon nation. The latter was denied by President Ahidjo's approach to the procedures of constitution-making (the assertion of the "one Cameroon" slogan to maintain the continuity of East Cameroon's constitution), and the former was eliminated by the product of constitution-making (a highly centralized federal system). The higher national mission westerners promoted was supposed to legitimize their reasserting the moral equality of the two communities and thereby justify reopening the constitutional question.

The Foncha regime expected that there would be a general reexamination of the constitutional structure of the Federation around the end of the transitional period, but little was said of this at the start because Foncha's general approach was to attempt to demonstrate good faith and a desire not to add to the many practical problems of launching the new system, winning peace, and consolidating independence. Western officials often did explicitly refer to "the tumultuous seas" on which they knowingly had embarked and the "unsuspected rocks" and difficulties they confronted, but they counseled patience and goodwill among their followers. As time went on, however, their concern for a reconsideration of questions decided at Foumban against what they considered to be their own interests became acute enough to stimulate more direct demands for serious discussion of constitutional review.

It was not until the closed-door meeting during the first two days of September 1964 between the top leaders of the two ruling parties that definite demands along these lines were made. The demands were expressed by Dr. Fonlon in his general presentation of the arguments for the higher national mission already discussed. Fonlon made the western desire for equal standing in the policy-making process explicit; there were several realities about the task of building Cameroon that had to be recognized, according to Fonlon: that there were two sets of builders, "two communities, two political parties divided in background, mentality, methods," and the materials to be used had to be "the two historic-geographical entities, East and West Cameroon" and "the principal cultures that have met in this federation." This being so, and given the admitted fact that proper building requires a plan or purpose, then there must be true collaboration and agreement between them.

> Unless building is preceded by discussion and agreement, one of two things will happen. Either each party will try to work according to its own ideas and we will have the confusion of Babel reenacted once again or the stronger party will usurp the enterprise and reduce the weaker partner to a passive onlooker. . . . In fact, this second thing is what has happened and is happening. Since we came together, the KNDP has done hardly more than stand by and look on. For talking sincerely, can we name one single policy in any field—economics, education, internal affairs, external affairs—that has been worked out jointly by the two parties? Can we point a finger at one idea that took birth in the KNDP and was welcomed and implemented by this government?
>
> There has been disillusionment; discontent and frustration are sinking and spreading. . . . This desperation can become explosive.
>
> The KNDP demands to take a genuine part in the making of this country.

The Buea regime wanted a say about what positions in the federal government would be offered to westerners, and even on which easterners would be chosen for federal policy level posts. The parties should sit down together and define the general policy framework for the country; what was more important; a mechanism should be established to put the desired dialogue between them on a permanent basis. This was so important in the estimation of the Buea officials that they wanted it backed by the sanction of law. Six specific and fundamental demands were made:

1. A general framework policy covering all major fields of government activity, together with a specific plan for its implementation should be established through joint UC-KNDP efforts.
2. The KNDP should enjoy effective participation in the conception, elaboration, and implementation of all government policy.
3. Permanent committees of representatives from both parties should be established to elaborate government policy on a continuing basis.
4. The constitution should be revised, to provide, among other

313

things, that all government policy decisions be taken in a council of ministers.

5. Ad hoc committees should be established immediately to work out the details of these proposals.

6. These changes should be put into effect before the April 1965 presidential elections.

The six points and the discussion of them made it clear that the western leaders sought a position of strict equality with the UC leadership in the establishment of broad government policy, through equal representation on the various committees demanded for this purpose. Moreover, it was their conception that the joint party efforts should take precedence over, and guide, the governmental structures. The demands were strongly resisted by the eastern contingent. One of President Ahidjo's closest political associates, Moussa Yaya, explained that the UC rejected both the idea that representation on UC-KNDP policy committees should be on any basis other than proportional representation or that party discussion and agreements could in any way interfere with the constitutional freedom and responsibility of the president to decide executive policy and procedures.[25] The eastern position explicitly affirmed the primacy of the state over the party, indicative of its nonideological predilections and grassroots weakness.[26] In effect, Eastern policy was set by the principal political leadership of the ruling UC.

The western regime was insistent on the question of constitutionally reestablishing a council of ministers that would consent as a body to all executive rules and projects before their submission to the president for approval. This had been the practice in the First Cameroun Republic and was still the practice in West Cameroon. The eastern leaders pointed out that this was a feature appropriate to a parliamentary system but not to a presidential one, where the president and his government were responsible to the people directly, not to the parliament. The president bore the singular responsibility for the government's actions. His ministers would not necessarily have any popular mandate. Thus they refused to accept a legal commitment to take decisions in council. President Ahidjo did later

[25] Moussa Yaya, personal interview, Yaounde, July 1965.

[26] It may be that the eastern position on the issue inspired or confirmed Muna's and Egbe's later contention that the KNDP could not legitimately attempt to "decide" the successor to the premiership on the basis of party decisions, that the western parliamentary wing had the same constitutional right and responsibility to freely vote on the question of investiture as the president had in nominating a candidate.

314

return to the pre-federation practice of holding meetings of the ministers and discussion, though now without any formal power to veto, on pending projects and bills, but the meetings were infrequent.[27]

With respect to the general lines of criticism Fonlon expressed for the West Cameroon community at the September meeting, especially as he presented them in his later published articles, the eastern spokesmen were less accommodating. "The basis of their whole position is pride!" argued Moussa Yaya.[28] The eastern leaders were willing to discuss the fundamental questions of policy, though they did not believe it appropriate for the party officials to bother themselves with the details of government. But what concerned them most was what they considered to be Fonlon's willingness to publish his own personal thoughts as if they were public opinion or represented fact. They thought he unfairly ignored the many efforts the federal regime and the easterners generally had made on behalf of successful integration—and they cited the prodigious efforts to make bilingual instruction in the secondary schools a reality in East Cameroon, and bilingualism a reality in the public service. Too much in Fonlon's articles was simply assumed, in their view.[29] No doubt the eastern leaders also resented being blamed for the lack of initiative and vigor on the part of the Buea regime in promoting West Cameroon's ideas and interests.

Indeed, Fonlon's criticisms were just as often directed at just such faults of the KNDP leadership as they were at the supposed faults of the federal leaders. In his article, "Under the Sign of the Rising Sun" (referring to the symbol used by Ahidjo and Foncha during the 1965 presidential elections), which Fonlon had adorned with his likeness dressed in an Nkrumah-style waistcoat and reprinted for general distribution, his attack and appeals were directed almost exclusively at the KNDP:

> The burden of this article is that the time has come to give this party [KNDP] a new birth, to embue it with a new spirit, . . . to give to it, anew, an ideological, a moral and an effective youth and vigour worthy of the new era that has been born Under the Sign of the Rising Sun.
>
> . . . we must give it right from now, a well-defined doctrine; we must streamline its organization and strengthen its authority; we must foster unity and brotherhood among our party members in particular,

[27] The first of the meetings of the full complement of federal ministers was not held for nine months, however, in June 1965. At that meeting Ahidjo merely outlined his major domestic and external policies. *Cameroon Times,* June 19, 1965.

[28] Moussa Yaya, interview, Yaounde, July 1965.

[29] *Ibid.*

and among all Cameroonians in general; we must pronounce a severe and final anathema against such disruptive and hate-inciting practices as inordinate ambition, corruption, laxity of discipline, intolerance of criticism, spying and tale-bearing.

Foncha, who bore, or perceived himself to bear, the brunt of Fonlon's attack, responded in terms not unlike those used by the Eastern leaders: "Fonlon's articles were nonsense . . . why had he made no statement within the councils of the party, in the National Convention? . . . why did he publish his articles before telling me about his criticisms first? . . . Fonlon has never criticized the party to me directly . . . his criticisms were barbaric." [30]

Despite the coolness in some circles to Fonlon's criticisms, at least in response to the demand for the immediate creation of a UC-KNDP committee to implement the program of reform suggested at the September meeting, President Ahidjo and Foncha announced at the close of the meeting that a 17-member national working committee would be established, in order to "reinforce their collaboration and to better their methods of work, notably in the relationship between the two parties." The committee would be designated by the executive organs of the two parties and "would meet periodically to study fundamental problems." The first such meeting was held in October of the same year; but rather than deciding on procedures and timing of any constitutional review, which the western leaders hoped for, the meeting preoccupied itself with the problem of merging the two parties. This issue continued to usurp other issues among the West Cameroon leadership, as the Muna-Jua competition for the prime minister's office became more acute. Though Foncha and Jua expressed the hope in the summer of 1965 for a general constitutional review, no such review or revision has come about to the date of this writing. The emergence of a single political party grouping all West Cameroon factions and many of those in East Cameroon has created new opportunities for full participation in the work of national development by both states and minorities within them.

It would be an exaggeration to say that the quest for national purpose and for a sense of equal participation and influence in public policy making by all regions (especially the two states) and all major factions within them has been satisfied in federal Cameroon. It *is* fair to say that a new day dawned with the emergence of the single party, for the period of preoccupation with form and structure was at a close. Trends toward a com-

---

[30] Vice President J. N. Foncha, interview, Yaounde, August 1965.

mitment to cultural integration in pluralism, toward greater collaboration between Buea and Yaounde, toward a greater voice for the young
and the intellectuals in the party, and for a more independent and tightly
planned Federation-wide and African-oriented economic policy seemed
clear.

⚶ 13 ⚶

Complementary Allocations of Resources

AGGREGATE figures for economic and financial conditions in the Cameroon Federation reveal few spectacular changes in the years since reunification. These figures belie considerable turbulence and change in the economic plight of the states and of certain sectors of the economy, however. Economic and financial officials remained at sea throughout the period, riding out waves of prosperity and growth in some sectors while plunging into the troughs of decline and hardship in others. They lost or at least lacked a sense of control over the economy; some, especially from West Cameroon, also lacked a sense of participation in the process of selecting goals for the economy or planning its course. They enjoyed little security or anchorage in any firmly based authority. This situation gave many such officials an exaggerated sense of motion but little sense of advance.

Federal officials did adopt policies concerning development planning which clearly had a redistributive impact on the allocation of national resources, largely in favor of West Cameroon. This resulted from conscious policy, and reflected the political imperatives attendant to making the transition to federalism a smooth one.[1] Federal subsidies to West Cameroon, for example, rose steadily during the first five years of the Federation, from $5 million in 1962–1963 to $8 million in 1966–1967. The transfers represented on the average about two-thirds of the revenues for the regular West Cameroon budget, and in 1966–1967 accounted for nearly 70 percent of the total revenues of the state. The capital budget grew about 80 percent over pre-Federation levels as a result of increased foreign aid and growing federal subsidies. Subsidies to West Cameroon sometimes surpassed those that the federal budget granted to East Cameroon, four times larger in population and about three times larger in state government expenditures.[2] Though federal subsidies to West Cameroon initially surpassed customs collections in that

---

[1] I have already touched on the political imperatives for achieving a greater measure of mutuality and complementarity in the benefits of federation. See Chap. 12 esp.

[2] Table 5 indicates the amount of federal subsidies to the two states and the total revenue figures for each government since independence.

318

state, more recently they have not.[3] It should be noted, however, that at the time of reunification about 40 percent of the state government's expenditures went for services or costs which the Cameroon federal government had taken over. If the costs of the services have increased no more rapidly than have the costs of the services the state has continued to bear (apparently there has been no elimination of services), then the value of all government services provided in the state would amount to about $17.2 million. At that level the portion currently borne by the state's own resources would amount to only 20 percent of the total figure; at the time of federation, the state's share of the total burden of costs for government services (i.e. adding those previously provided from the Nigerian federal budget) was slightly more than 25 percent. West Cameroonians are at least five percent better off as a result of federation, having lowered by that amount their share of the costs for public services.[4]

Even if one ignores the expanded job opportunities and public services offered in the federal sector, as regards the revenues of the West Cameroon state government itself, there is evidence of moderate growth since federation. Total state revenues have increased by 37 percent from the first regular budget in 1962 to that of 1966–1967 (but only 12.4 percent from prefederal budgets). The improvement relieved the chronic problem of budget deficits because state recurrent expenditures for 1965–1966 were only six percent higher than those for 1961–1962. Moreover, there is some evidence that the state had a richer economic base to tap for purely locally generated revenues in 1966, for these revenues had increased by 66 percent over 1961 levels.

Any traveler of the state's highways and secondary roads is well aware of the development that has occurred in recent years in West Cameroon. Roads, perennially a source of embarrassment and inconvenience to Southern Cameroonians, bolster the pride and ease the burden of many present-day travelers, as United States AID equipment has transformed long sections of the principal routes throughout the country into well-graded and surfaced highways. In early 1966 the president inaugurated work on "Reunification Road," 35 miles of highway linking Douala with Victoria, the main commercial and port districts of the two states, which was officially opened in early 1969. Formerly travel between them required a 125-mile detour, or a trip by canoe through marshes and bogs.

[3] Data are not available which would permit a precise comparison between total revenues derived within and total benefits, including the costs of operating the federal departments within the state, returned to it.

[4] It should be noted also that these services increased in quality and in scope as well as in cost.

Bananas, coffee, and tea, as well as passengers, may now quickly reach eastern markets or ports via a rail extension from Kumba to the eastern Nkongsamba-Douala rail axis. But what westerners are most apt to mention as proof of the correctness of their vote for reunification is the improvement in the school system. In the first three years after federation the number of primary students jumped by 35 percent, and the number of primary schools by 29 percent. The expansion was paid for with foreign aid and local resources freed for concentration in primary education by the federal takeover of secondary and technical educational services. The three secondary schools of pre-Federation days had grown to 14 including two for girls, an experimental bilingual grammar school, and the first coeducational secondary school. The technical training center, which had been forced to close for lack of funds and personnel prior to reunification, was reopened and greatly expanded. There were seven new teacher training schools and one university preparatory institution. Important, and perhaps even more spectacular, gains were made in other domains as well, especially health services. Total expenditures on health services increased by over 130 percent from 1958 to 1964–1965; [5] the largest gains came as a result of expansion in government-sponsored (both federal and local) and corporation-sponsored services. The number of hospital beds increased from 1,123 to 1,617 (nearly 45 percent increase) in the same period, and maternity units more than tripled. Road mileage doubled (mostly subsidiary roads) between 1959 and 1964, and the number of vehicles registered in the state nearly tripled.[6] The number of telephone outlets increased by about 70 percent.[7]

Much of the development of West Cameroon was financed directly with foreign assistance. The United States contributed significant sums to the road development program, as well as to some agriculture and animal husbandry improvement programs. A large contingent of Peace Corpsmen taught each year in the West Cameroon (and some East Cameroon) schools or assisted in community development projects. During the first post-Federation regular budget U.S. assistance for roads amounted to over $1.5 million; and nearly $7 million in addition were given by the European Development Fund and the Fond d'Aide et de la Cooperation

[5] From *Report for the Year 1958,* HMG in the United Kingdom to the General Assembly of the United Nations; 1964–1965 figures from Stanford Research Institute, *The Economic Potential of West Cameroon,* Vol. III, Appendices C and D.

[6] *Ibid.,* Vol. IV, Tables 5 and 12. About 700 of these vehicles may have been previously registered in Nigeria. The total cumulative gain for 1959–1963 was 4,113.

[7] *Ibid.,* Table 39.

(FAC) for other programs. These figures do not reflect the significant contributions of aid received by the Cameroon government which are not itemized and measured monetarily.[8] Since 1962–1963 the amount of aid received by or pledged to West Cameroon has increased.

Of course, westerners might still look across the Mungo River at their new compatriots and consider themselves relatively deprived. The east started from a privileged position and grew more rapidly than the west. This is true with respect to growth in government revenues, not only for the eastern state, the revenue receipts of which were 7½ times those of West Cameroon and increased by 49 percent from 1962 to 1965, but more importantly for all revenues supporting expenditures in the east (which include significant levels of federal expenditure), which also increased by 49 percent.[9] The revenues of the West Cameroon government acquired the more modest increment of 31 percent over pre-Federation levels. However, if as little as 10 percent of federal expenditures (excluding the federal subsidies to the states) benefited westerners directly, then the latter realized a doubling of resources available for governmental services in their state. It also appears that the gap between the two states in gross domestic product has widened in favor of the east in the years since reunification.[10]

Despite the gap, perhaps a growing one, between the wealth and level of development of the East and West Cameroon, taken as collectivities, the elite and the masses alike among westerners were prone to continue to look still further west to Nigeria for a base for comparison. Their memories of the association with Nigeria were almost all disagreeable, especially in terms of their share of Nigeria's wealth and development resources. Comparisons between the experience of West Cameroon in the new Federation with what might have been had they remained in the old one can be only speculative; but that it has fared better is a fairly safe assumption, especially in terms of foreign assistance. The state's devel-

[8] Some of the aid received was in the form of personnel whose salaries and expenses were carried by the lending government. A number of federal operations also benefited from foreign assistance.

[9] These figures are calculated from those given in Table 5. Combined expenditures, 1965–1966, in the east are calculated by subtracting the sum of federal subsidies to all state budgets and then subtracting an additional 10 percent from the remaining federal figure, representing the estimated West Cameroon share of federal jobs and services, and adding the figures for East Cameroon. The difference between the resultant figure and total eastern revenues for 1961–1962 divided by the latter gives the percentage increase.

[10] R. H. Green, "The Economy of the Cameroon Federal Republic," mimeo. p. 13.

TABLE 5

Government Revenues for Recurrent and Capital Budgets, 1960-1961 through 1965-1966 (federal and state)
(billions of CFA) ($1 = 245 CFA)

	Federal				East Cameroon					West Cameroon				
Year	Recurrent (foreign subsidy)	Capital (foreign subsidy)	Sub. to states	Total	Total	Recurrent (federal subsidy)	Capital (federal subsidy)	% fed. subsidy	% Sub. state budget	Total	Recurrent (federal subsidy)	Capital (federal subsidy)	% fed. subsidy	% Sub. state budget
60/61	n.r.				14.2	(total for. aid 2.9)				n.a.				
61/62	n.r.				18.85	16. (1.89)	2.75 (1.93)		7.4	2.49	2.09 (.36)	.4 (.22)		8%
62/63	15.45 (1.85)	1.22 (.2)	1.73	16.67	6.51	6.06 (.30)	0.45 (.19)	28.4	7.5	2.02	1.71 (1.16)	.31 (.09)	72.6	62
63/64	16.33 (.67)*	1.06 (1.0)	2.54	17.39	7.10	6.70 (1.18)	0.40† (—)	47	17	2.38	1.98 (1.27)	.40 (.09)	54	57
64/65	18.55 (.65)	1.41 (0.5)	2.8	19.96	7.47	7.19 (1.41)	.28 (.271)‡	50	19	2.31	1.96 (1.4)	.35 (—)	50	60
65/66	19.91 (.61)	2.97 (—)	2.67**	22.88	9.72	8.84 (1.32)	.89 (—)	50	13.5	2.8	2.22 (1.35)	.578§ (2.2)	51	48
66/67	25.02	2.77	n.a.	28	n.a.					2.8	2.75 (1.95)	.20		70

n.r. = not relevant.

n.a. = data not available to this author.

* This figure is missing from some reports.

** Includes 2.2 for calculating machines in West Cameroon.

† Soulevement sur la caisse de reserve.

‡ Transferred from reserve.

§ Federal grant to West Cameroon for conversion of calculating and weighing machines.

Sources: *Budget, République Fédérale du Cameroun, Exercise* 1962/3, 1963/4, 1964/5, 1965/6, 1966/7; *Budget, Le Cameroun Orientale, Exercise* (same as above). Estimates, West Cameroon, years (same as above) plus Supplementary Estimates, 1961/2, 1962/3; *La Zone Franc-Comité Monétarie* 1965.

opment program receives far more attention than it would merit by any rational calculation were it an indistinguishable part of Cameroon or still a part of Nigeria. When one considers how poorly Nigeria has done in attracting foreign aid, the combined figures for all development budgets from all foreign sources for 1962–1963 amounted to only $27 million, the great bulk of which went directly into federal projects, it is apparent that tiny out-of-the-way West Cameroon would surely not have received significant sums from such sources.[11] Perhaps it could claim as much as one percent of the total capital expenditure for the Federation. At $190 million, the figure for that year, West Cameroon would have received only $2 million, a figure considerably lower than it has steadily received in development revenues as part of the Cameroon Federation.[12]

The West Cameroon political elite had a sense of economic benefit and progress from federation which the masses did not share; for the former were able to appreciate and personally profit from the improvements in the collective resources of the state. The average citizen, however, while taking considerable pride in the growing evidence of capital formation in the form of improved roads and communications facilities, experienced a sharp and painful decline in his standard of living. Every family— indeed every single participant in the market—felt the impact of the decline. While frantic efforts were made and continue to be made to change the situation (and the downward trend has clearly been reversed), only in 1966 did the real income of westerners begin to overtake its level at the time of reunification.[13] Clearly the most persistent and difficult integration problems the Federation faced were economic.

Replacement of the Nigerian currency with that of the Republic, the "CFA franc," heralded the first impingement of the union on the eco-

[11] Figures from *Progress Report 1964, National Development Plan,* Federal Ministry of Economic Development, Lagos, Table 2.2, p. 28.

[12] *Ibid.,* Table 2.6, p. 32. (Total resources available for capital projects in 1962–1963 is reported at $261.5 million, a figure made artificially high through accounting techniques. It is apparent, nonetheless, that not all funds available were spent.) For the two years 1962–1964, Nigeria received only $51.8 million in foreign assistance. One percent of that figure would fall considerably short of what West Cameroon received in foreign assistance during the same period. Total capital resources was $421 million and Cameroon's share of that would have also fallen short.

[13] Wage increases failed to keep up with price increases, even in government sectors, for West Cameroon. Employment levels fell in both states, since 1958 in the east and since 1960 in the west. Green, "Economy," Table III-A.5, shows slight growth in per capita GNP from 1959 to 1962–63, but census figures for the earlier period are questionable, and personal real income no doubt has not improved significantly (growth per capita GNP, 1959 prices, put at +.4% by Green, "Economy," Table III-A.1.

nomic life of the western villagers. Six months after federation, and for a period initially scheduled at two months and later extended to three, the CFA franc was made legal tender and was to be exchanged for Nigerian pounds at a rate of 692 francs to the pound. This rate, which reflected the government's calculation of official exchange rate equivalents then in existence, made the cost of Nigerian pounds appear artificially high to traders (mostly Nigerians seeking to repatriate earnings), or conversely, made the value of their sterling holdings appear unjustly cheap to the citizenry, given the fact that on open markets the going exchange rates between CFA and Nigerian sterling had been 800 francs to the pound.[14] A black market soon developed for sterling at about the latter rate. Illiterate market women struggled to master the conversion rates and to determine if the new prices reflected the old values. Cautious traders, particularly those from Nigeria who handled most of the small trade, consistently resolved uncertainties in their own favor; prices rose apace. Confidence in the new currency was not high. Neither the government, whose departments (e.g. PTT's, Health) compounded the inflationary pressures on the market and on private exchange rates by charging higher fees in CFA than was warranted by the old ones at official rate equivalents, nor the increasing number of French commercial firms, which refused to honor the single franc coins (a widespread practice in East Cameroon as well) helped overcome popular doubts about it.[15] Most people did not exchange their sterling holdings, or at least not most of it, in the period allowed. The government believed that over £4 million was in circulation prior to the conversion, but that only a million was brought in during the official exchange period.[16] The rest presumably was used to purchase smuggled goods from Nigeria or was remitted extralegally by Nigerian

[14] See *Cameroon Times,* June 18, 1962, which asserts that the exchange rates for CFA-Nigerian pound prior to reunification had been 800/£. Black market prices ranged from 800 to 1,000 CFA?/pounds during the year following the conversion. Process of conversion was planned by a commission of business experts (est. 62-DF-26 of 17 January 1962), nine persons, which included three people from West Cameroon (the Secretary of Finance, Jua, and the currency Adviser of the government who was the Bank of England representative, and treasurer of Cameroon Bank).

[15] *Cameroon Champion,* May 8, 1962 carries an article which gave the following table of CFA/pound equivalents actually offered on the market:

	actual	official		actual	official
/2d =	10	8	1/2d =	50	43
/6d =	20	17	2/6d =	100	90
1/ =	40	35	£1/7/ =	1000	945
			£7/ =	5000	4844

[16] R. C. Matheron, political officer, U.S. Embassy, Yaounde, interview, February 1963.

traders or by Cameroonians to relatives living in Nigeria. There were many victims of fraudulent exchange transactions. One widely circulated story held that a fast-talking slickster tricked an old man out of his life savings of £100 ($280) by convincing him that 100 CFA francs (40 cents) was its official equivalent. The story goes that when the old man discovered his predicament he committed suicide.

The conversion of currency was an extremely important feature of the integration of the two states, not simply because it united them into a single market, which entrained a number of benefits as well as costs, but because it dramatized the change the union represented and made it salient to every participant in the cash nexus. To be sure, the reaction to the change and its consequences was decidedly negative: "Dis money too light, I no fit buy proper t'ing self"; "Me, I no sabi dis money; too humbug." [17] Some of the anger was vented on Ibos traders, the "demons" who inspired so much of the desire for Cameroon reunification. They were accused of selling only to holders of sterling and of raising prices when sterling was not offered.[18] Shoppers complained, "you cannot make any purchases with francs in the local market, because it is unsteady." Government officials joined in the competition for sterling, making their own purchases at the best rates they could get, a competition that came to be referred to as "unification plague."

To standardize the system of weights and measures would be a logical sequel to the standardization of currency; the federal government attempted to quickly follow the money change with this one. It was thought that this might relieve the difficulties of the market women, who were prone to try to figure their purchases and sales first according to the old imperial system and then to translate to CFA equivalents. A metric system of measures would easily fit into prices calculated in a metric system. But federal officials had failed to appreciate the psychological significance of the currency conversion. Any rapid introduction of yet another system to learn would have strained not only the capacities but the patience and flexibility of the people. The government circulated complicated posters with almost no simple graphic presentation of the principles of transfer between the two systems which proclaimed: "After the franc C.F.A., West Cameroon welcomes the metric system . . . the most universal, simplest and practical system of weights and measures." Those who could read the posters probably read instead: "New equivalents to learn, more equipment to buy, higher prices to pay." The federal Inspec-

17 *Cameroon Times,* May 18, 1962.
18 *Cameroon Champion,* August 31, 1962.

tor of Administration realized the likely popular reaction to the change, and postponed it, first for three months and then for six; it was not completed until 1965.[19]

Perhaps the most important innovation in the commercial and economic life of West Cameroon that resulted from reunification, one which logically followed from the standardization of currencies but which derived from additional factors, was the termination of West Cameroon's tie to the Commonwealth of Nations and to the sterling bloc. Withdrawal from the Commonwealth had been among the preplebiscite promises of the reunificationists and had become an accepted though ill-considered part of the program.[20] As such, it was simply the counterpart of the aspiration among French-speaking Cameroonians to break the tie to the French Union, a tie perceived as an evil mechanism to deny the country its independence more or less permanently. It is questionable whether withdrawal from the sterling bloc was a necessary adjunct to termination of the Commonwealth tie or vice versa, but it appeared to everyone as concomitant to the switch to the CFA franc.[21]

The change affected both economies, but imposed more important and numerous disruptions on that of West Cameroon. Especially important was the resulting loss of "imperial preferences" offered certain exports of members to other Commonwealth countries, particularly to the U.K. The preferences are matched or surpassed for a few products in the EEC; but

[19] The switch was decreed by 62-DF-351 of 21 September, providing for a terminal date of 1 April 1963, which was extended by 63-DF-110 of April 2 for three months, and extended again by 63-DF-213 of July 5 until December 31, 1963. When the change was finally made, local merchants and others had to replace their old equipment, adapt it or export it, and acquire equipment calibrated in the metric system. A subsidy of 22 million CFA was granted West Cameroon in 1965 to cover the cost of replacing the equipment.

[20] The *Federal Constitution* by KNDP, circulated during the plebiscite campaign, referred to an agreement signed between Foncha and Ahidjo on October 17, 1960 which promised: "The unified territories of Cameroun [sic] should be a federal Sovereign State outside the British Commonwealth and the French Community." The independence of the states of the *Conseil de l'entente* in August 1960 made the Community irrelevant. It is not clear if any Cameroon leader ever anticipated breaking the tie with the Franc Zone; it is especially improbable that Ahidjo did.

[21] Provision for Nigeria to become an associated member of the EEC suggests that the technical problems of linking nonfranc economies to the Franc Zone are not insurmountable. Certainly British officials must deem such an association as possible because they contemplate membership in the EEC. West Cameroon might have continued using a sterling currency. Even with the currency change, the Commonwealth tie might have been maintained, though restricting such membership to West Cameroon would have been difficult.

for many products the loss was permanent; the preferences provided many West Cameroon producers, particularly the independent farmer, with the whole of their profit margin.[22] Those most threatened by the loss of preferences were the banana producers, for whose product the preference was a considerable £7/10s per ton. The largest producer, traditionally the Cameroon Development Corporation (CDC), which provided 41 percent of the state's banana exports in 1960, had a profit margin not much larger than the figure of the preference.[23] Independent farmers with slimmer profit margins, selling their product through cooperatives, found the threat of losing the preference so great that a number of them cut down their trees in anger and let the fruit rot. Withdrawal of the preferences was postponed several times in response to the pleadings of the western leadership, but they finally did occur at the beginning of 1964. The 1963 crop, marketed after the withdrawal of preferences, enjoyed a boom market, nonetheless, due to the elimination of important competitors in the Caribbean, hard hit by hurricanes. Those who had not despaired enough to destroy or ignore their crops, despite bonus earnings, were to have their own day of reckoning the following year. The total 1965 banana crop was the smallest in a decade, down two-thirds from peak production figures realized just prior to reunification.[24] Independent farmers continued to expand their proportionate *share* of total production, due to sharp reductions in the plantation efforts devoted to this crop. However, their total production fell off steadily in the years following federation; 1964 production was only about one-third that of 1960 which had been the peak year for independent farmers. East Cameroon production in bananas is also considerably lower than the peak year (1957) figures, when it accounted for 74 percent of CDC production; but it has steadily risen since 1959, following severe losses due to disease and weather damage. By 1965 the eastern crop had nearly regained peak production figures. The expanding external market for East Cameroon bananas was denied western producers on the grounds that the quotas es-

[22] Cameroon was undoubtedly the benefactor of the preference relationship with the U.K., although this was not true for all members of the Commonwealth. Cf. "The Commonwealth Preferences: A System in Need of Analysis," Harry Johnson, in *The Round Table* (October 1960).

[23] The corporation based its hopes of remaining competitive in the English markets despite a discriminatory tariff (the preference) only by considerable reforms in planting methods (move to intensive cultivation) and lower labor/production ratios. Alternative varieties, and close planting are additional innovations aimed at increased efficiency. Mr. Moss, assistant to the chairman, CDC interview, Bota, April 1963.

[24] Stanford Research Institute study, Vol. II, Table 14.

tablished on the French and certain other EEC markets were insufficient to exhaust eastern production. Completely new markets had to be found for West Cameroon's product, and hopes were raised with respect to the Italian market, but this seems to have fallen through.[25]

TABLE 6

External Trade, Federal East and West Cameroon, 1951–1965

	1951	1960	1961	1962		1964	1965
External Trade—East Cameroon (Value in millions CFA, $1 = 245 CFA)							
Total Imports	16,496	20,849	23,716	25,141	27,520* (26,727+)	33,080* (28,593+)	n.a.
Total Exports	11,372	23,951	24,203	25,516	30,878* (29,117+)	31,870* (30,037+)	n.a.

External Trade—Federal Cameroon (includes estimates for Southern Cameroons)

	1951	1960	1961	1962		1964	1965
Total Imports	18,800	27,450	30,000	30,150	31,850 (30,953+)	37,150*	38.163* †
Total Exports	14,200	29,650	29,700	31,080*	35,877* (29,950+)	36,798* (33,250+)	31.804* †

External Trade—West Cameroon

	1951	1960	1961	1962		1964	1965
Total Imports	n.a.	3,728	3,838	3,179	3,953	4,263	4,083
Total Exports	2,427	5,964	5,858	4,264	4,191	4,253	4,928

* These figures are reported for the fiscal year July 1–June 30 and thus include trade during the first six months of the year following the one under which they are listed.

† Principal items only.

n.a. = not available (plus figures taken from Europe-France-Outre Mer government sources).

Sources: Reginald H. Green, *The Economy of the Cameroon Federal Republic,* Table IV-C-1; and *Europe-France-Outre Mer,* No. 436; Stanford Research Institute, *General Report,* Table D-1, and Green, "Economy," Table IV-B-1. Import figures from French Embassy, Yaounde, Report on Commerce Exterieur du Cameroun Occidentale, 1964, January 24, 1956, Conseiller Commercial.

West Cameroon exports reveal sharp declines since the immediate pre-Federation period in a number of important items such as palm kernels and oil, and especially in timber (due to the exhaustion of accessible supplies of the most lucrative varieties and lack of roads giving access to additional resources of this sort). Only slight gains in production were made for a number of products; often the gains were nullified by a fall in the market price for such exports.[26] The state shared the predicament of most poor economies, of having to pay rising prices for its imports, especially those needed to spur development, while receiving less and less for its own products. East Cameroon was not exempted from this trend; it

[25] Budget speech, P. M. Kemcha, Secretary of State for Finance, July 1966.
[26] See Table 6.

suffered particularly acute disruptions both in general revenues and in the incomes of an important political sector of the population—the independent cocoa growers of the south and southwest.[27]

TABLE 7

Interstate Trade as Percentage of Total External Trade

	1960	1961	1962	1964
West Cameroon				
Imports	2.0	2.1	12.3	19.0
Exports	.01	.2	.35	1.0
East Cameroon				
Imports	.004	.05	.06	.15
Exports	.03	.33	1.5	2.7

Source: Figures from Table 2, plus *Service statistique générale, Ministère de l'Économie nationale*, 1960, 1961, 1962, 1964.

Cocoa is an important crop in both states, but especially so for the east. The steady decline in cocoa prices on the world market since 1959, and a precipitate falling off during the 1966 season turned a previously lucrative industry into a net drain on local and national resources, causing important political repercussions in the eastern state.[28] The impact of the precarious situation in the cocoa market was moderated by a perceptible rise in these prices toward the end of 1966; by year's end there was considerable optimism. However, rapid shifts from dire pessimism to impetuous optimism are nothing new to African producers of primary products. They follow, if somewhat out of phase, the frequent and abrupt fluctuations in world market prices for these products; which, in itself, is a source of difficulty for their economies, especially for planning officials. President Ahidjo displayed the frustration and anger of African officialdom over their predicament in vehemently imploring that "this rummage sale of our agricultural production must stop." [29]

[27] See Table 7.

[28] Cocoa prices have undergone severe fluctuations over the course of the last 15 years, reaching a peak in 1953–1954 and falling since then, with the exception of a slight rise in 1957–1958. In mid-1966 the price was 12 cents a pound, aften insufficient to meet shipping and handling costs.

[29] A. Ahidjo, speech to CEDIMON in Paris, quoted in *Afrique Express*, July 5, 1966. He pointed out the following disparities in the value of cocoa vis-á-vis important import items between 1960 and 1965. In the former year one ton of cocoa would buy:

cut cloth (pagne)	880 meters but only	300 m. in June 1965
crude cloth	2700 meters " "	800 m. " " "
corrugated aluminum roofing	1130 pieces " "	440 p. " " "
cement	1200 kilograms "	450 kg. " " "

Opportunities for trade in goods between the two states were not great at the time of federation, but did exist for some products. West Cameroon has no real industry. It has a number of "corn mill societies" which are cooperatives, both of producers and consumers, which own grinding mills for pressing corn and palm for oil products. Most of the palm oil produced in West Cameroon continues to be consumed locally. In the future one state might sell palm oil and other palm products to the other (we have already mentioned the case of the Bamileke) but this is not likely to develop to significant proportions because each side can produce these items in surplus of its needs.

East Cameroon produces a number of "industrial" products, several of which might find a market in West Cameroon. Table 8 indicates production figures for the most important industrial manufacturers of East Cameroon in 1962.[30]

TABLE 8

Industrial Production in East Cameroon, 1962

(Unless otherwise indicated, figures are in metric tons)

Acetylene	30,000	Cocoa Oil Cakes	3,900
Aluminum Household		Cotton Oil	1,200
Articles	254	Cotton seed Oil	
Aluminum Sheets	400,000	Cake	3,900
Beer	207,000 (hectolt)	Gold	25 (Kgrm)
Bicycles	11,800 (units)	Oxygen	115,000 (m³)
Clothing	1,600,000 (pieces)	Polyethelene	228
Cocoa Butter	3,580	Shoes & Sandals	670,000 (pairs)
		Cigarettes, Cigars	26*

* This figure is for 9 months' exportation in 1962, production for year probably 35 tons.

East Cameroon produces or assembles a number of items which might find a market in West Cameroon, especially items of personal consumption such as beer, bicycles, cigarettes, clothing, shoes, and the like. Some new industries were just starting production or were in the process of establishment at the time of reunification.[31] These—especially the company, "Les Grands Moulins du Cameroun" (millery for making flour from corn and millet), a match-making factory, a meat-processing and attached biscuit-making factory, and the refrigeration industry—should find a ready market for their products across the Mungo.

One of the factors that hindered interstate trade or led to hardship for West Cameroonians when such trade developed significantly was the dif-

[30] Chambre du Commerce, *Rapport Annuel*, 1962.
[31] *Europe France-Outre-Mer*, No. 298.

330

ference in the cost of living between the two states prior to reunification. The most widely accepted estimate of the magnitude of the difference is 100 percent (i.e. the cost of living in East Cameroon was twice that in West Cameroon for persons of similar social status). One corroborating index of this estimate is the difference that existed in wages for similar employment. There were widespread disparities in wage levels from region to region. East Cameroon was divided into four salary regions, the salary scales for which presumably corresponded to the level of the cost of living for a paid worker in that region. Two lists of minimum wage-salary scales were applied in East Cameroon, an agricultural and an industrial list. In both types of employment West Cameroon salaries and wages at the time of reunification ranged from one-half to three-fourths lower than the minimum levels in East Cameroon.[32]

Discriminatory tariffs applied in French-speaking Cameroon against non-EEC goods resulted in a near monopoly of the Republic's import market for the higher priced exports of France and the other Common Market countries. English-speaking Cameroonians bought in cheaper markets, especially Nigerian markets. Imports from Nigeria were admitted with little or no tariff duties and certainly lower duties than goods coming directly from Great Britain. A reunification of the customs regimes of the two states, assuming that the interests of the larger partner would dictate a continuation of her agreements with the EEC and the Franc Zone, could only result in *enchérissement* of import goods to West Cameroonians, and probably rapid inflation generally. The change was therefore delayed for several years.

Though the customs barrier between the two states was maintained until early 1966, certain parts of the tariff and license regime of French-speaking Cameroon were made applicable to West Cameroon commerce as early as mid-1962. One consequence for traders in the west was the obligation to place import orders much more in advance than had previously been the case.[33] This disrupted Western commerce consider-

[32] *Documentation Française,* No. 2, 756, Table 4, Annex No. 1.

[33] Decree No. 62 DF-9 of February 23, established regulations for foreign exchange and trade control, and Decree No. 62-DF-98 of March 31, 1962, extended to West Cameroon those general provisions regulating external trade and foreign exchange. This system was for the most part put into effect on July 1, 1962, though the common external tariffs were exempted in West Cameroon for some time, especially for British goods. The licensing requirements appeared to western importers as cumbersome, requiring applications by September for the importation of specific classes of items *throughout* the following year. Applications for foreign exchange were also due well in advance, for the whole of the following year. This had the effect of obliging importers to predict their market a year in advance of sale.

ably, because the local markets were seldom sufficiently predictable to permit such a system to work smoothly, even for the large expatriate (British) firms. The many small traders, mostly Nigerians, found these procedures impossible and either retired from the trade or pursued it illegally. As the goods they habitually supplied became more and more scarce, inflation advanced. The federal government was quickly forced to modify its regulations insofar as Nigerian traders were concerned, permitting them easier access to foreign exchange for short-term import programs.[34] Many of the largest firms found it easier to switch to French and other European Common Market goods, to which discriminatory tariffs were not applied and which did not require special licenses or foreign exchange allotments.[35] Given the generally higher prices for French and EEC imports, however, prices continued to rise. Federal officials frantically attempted to contain inflationary pressures in the west, first by claiming they did not exist and then by exempting Nigerian small traders from all license and foreign exchange regulations; but the large firms, particularly the British ones, continued to suffer. Britain's share of the West Cameroon market steadily declined,[36] and was replaced by a westward flow of products from French firms in East Cameroon. A number of British firms pulled out of the Cameroon market entirely—for example, the Union Trading Company, with respect to retail trade, and Kingsway, which sold its sizable network to the French Chain of *Printania*.[37]

Some of the French import and marketing firms in Douala and Yaounde devised grand plans for developing the western markets, initially from their own somewhat overstocked shelves of goods already in

[34] See Federal Press Release, No. 1,956 of August 23, 1962. The traders had to register with the district office. Imports from Nigeria were exempted from license if ordered prior to July 1962, but required proof to this effect.

[35] The federal tariff applied a discriminatory tariff of 4 to 30 percent of value to goods coming from other than l'Union douaniere et économique de l'Afrique centrale or EEC countries. There was also an import tax and, following July 1, 1962, an across-the-board federal tax of 17 percent (for which West Cameroon received an exemption for a year), calculated after other charges had been paid (constituting an additional discriminatory levy). Ordinance 61/OF/8 of October 14, 1961 ended all import preferences previously applied in the west.

[36] The British share of West Cameroon imports have declined since 1951 (77 percent) to about 45 percent at the time of federation. It had fallen to less than 20 percent by 1964, though the Sterling Zone collectively continued to supply about 43 percent of West Cameroons' imports.

[37] It should be noted that the owner of Kingsway, the United Africa Company (UAC), itself a subsidiary of Unilever, is also the owner of CAMAG which runs Printania. The transfer made a difference, however, since the Paris-based company withdrew from the Kingsway line of retail trade and stopped purchasing produce. The wholesale trade of these companies was not much affected.

the country.[38] There were a few tentative steps in the opposite direction by enterprising East Indian merchants and by R. W. King Ltd., which had operated for years in both states, and in both English- and French-speaking African countries.

Trade developed rapidly between East and West Cameroon, in both directions, although the trade flow from east to west was many times that of the reverse direction.[39] The mere indication of impending union, in the form of the favorable plebiscite vote, stimulated a sharp advance in trade between the two areas. By late 1961 eastern exports to West Cameroon rose over 900 percent (value) over the level of the previous year. Westerners spent nearly four times as much on eastern products in 1962, during the first full year of reunification, than they had the year of the plebiscite, and doubled this latter amount by the end of 1964, at which time westerners were spending on East Cameroon goods over 100 times the amount they had spent in 1960, the year before the plebiscite. To be sure, westerners also sold considerably more to their newfound compatriots, but the rate of increase in the trade in this direction was only about half that in the reverse direction. In 1964 they sold roughly 60 times the value of goods sold to East Cameroonians in 1960.

Despite the rapid growth in interstate trade it is apparent that relative to total external trade of the two states, interstate trade was never very important for East Cameroon. The Western market absorbed only about three percent of East Cameroon's total exports in 1964, but East Cameroon represented a significant share of West Cameroon's import supply. That year western buyers spent nearly one-fifth of their expenditures for imported items on eastern products or products supplied by eastern merchants. The market that eastern buyers represented for western producers or merchant houses never achieved great magnitude; they absorbed only about one percent of western exports in 1964. The lopsided character of interstate trade prior to the removal of the internal customs barrier was important. The customs barrier moderated the economic impact of reunification on West Cameroon. One consequence of the arrangements was

[38] Firms establishing in the west, in addition to Printania, included: S.H.O. (Societé de Haut-Ogooué), along with its auto and tractor distributors; S.C.O.A. (Societé Commerciale de l'Ouest Africain), which handled industrial imports as well as local products and household items, furniture, and construction materials; Cie FAC (Compagnie Française pour l'Afrique Occidentale), in tractors, trucks, and autos; and SONAC (Societé National Camerounaise)—government-connected, which set up agencies in four West Cameroon towns to handle retail and wholesale merchandise.

[39] See Table 7.

that the benefits of customs unions, postulated by the classical literature as a shift in the sources of supply, usually to bolster local infant industries and to enhance the attractiveness of the local markets to potential capital investors—these benefited Eastern enterprises only. The shift in the sources of supply was to higher priced ones. The Cameroon became analogous to the "wrong kind of customs union" that Jacob Viner describes in the case of East Africa, where Cameroon created a protected market for the produce and products of expatriate interests in only one of the regions.[40]

The impact of the creation of the modified common market with artificial trade monopolies was not limited to the considerable inflationary pressure it placed on West Cameroon markets; it also included the more psychological problem, of no mean political significance, of upending or frustrating traditional tastes and purchasing habits. New trade flows brought new and unfamiliar goods, many of which were ultimately unable to gain a stable place in the baskets of shoppers in Victoria and Kumba, Mamfe and Bamenda. French sugar would not dissolve in tea quite as thoroughly as the British product had. French brands of rice tasted peculiar to palates accustomed to English varieties. French flour would not produce dough that would pound and knead as easily, or make the bread westerners liked. Not even "standard VI" graduates could read the labels on cans of *haricots* or *farine,* and none of the French stores seemed to be familiar with baking powder (many incredulous French women insist that even if it is possible, which they doubt, it is still quite uncivilized to make a cake with less than four eggs).

The union did permit the few complementarities in the economies of the two states to affect their markets. Industrial products made or assembled in East Cameroon found important new markets, items like aluminum roofing, household utensils, and small tools, and footwear of all types. At least in terms of the percentage increase in trade figures, if not in terms of their absolute magnitude, significant levels of trade occurred in industrial products—electrical goods of all kinds, industrial chemicals and chemical products (including perfumes and toiletries), products of iron and aluminum for infrastructure and construction, and initially trucks, autos, and tractors. They were among the leading items of growth during the first two years of reunification. As time went on, however, it became clear that the most important items, in both absolute and persistent growth terms, were items of personal consumption of the type which

[40] Mentioned by Nye, *Pan-Africanism and East African Integration,* p. 142, n. 25.

figure in the list of initial local manufactures in most of the new states of Africa—clothing and footwear, yard and leather goods of all kinds, tobacco, and products of tanneries, breweries and bottling companies. Though initially there were slight gains in the value of eastern sales of food, livestock, agricultural products, and fats and oils, these soon dissipated, and trade in them fell off significantly during the years following reunification—an ironic circumstance, since traditional trade relationships in precisely such products had figured centrally in the arguments used to justify the demand for reunification.

Whatever British colonial officials failed to achieve in 35 years of administration in Cameroon, they did succeed in implanting a taste for British goods. Against this the hopes and plans of a number of East Cameroon entrepreneurs, most of them French, splintered. The initially high and growing figures for interstate trade were misleading. Many French firms developed overstocked shelves and warehouses in both states. Some firms chose to switch back to the brands and varieties familiar to shoppers in West Cameroon towns, but in doing so they created new problems for themselves, for now they needed to request foreign exchange, and procedures regarding import licenses were more complicated. They faced problems akin to those of the firms they had replaced. As a net creditor to the Franc Zone, Cameroon had no fundamental problem in acquiring foreign exchange because members of the Zone, even perennial debtors, seldom have had any problem drawing on foreign exchange holdings in Paris. It was the Cameroon government itself which made it difficult for some large importers by establishing exchange quotas.

The system of exchange quotas during the first five years of federation had the effect of favoring the growth of indigenous African import firms. The many small and still largely inefficient African firms did not in any case receive quotas as large as those established for the expatriate giants; but their inclusion limited the share of the total supply which could be granted to each.[41] Several of the largest expatriate firms claimed that

[41] Import firms were divided into three categories for purposes of assigning exchange quotas. These were based on size of operations, the first being for firms doing 250 million CFA or more a year, the second for those realizing a turnover of between 50 and 250 million CFA, and the third for those whose turnover is less than 50 million a year (with 5 million established as the minimum necessary to justify an import license and inclusion on the list of authorized recipients of foreign exchange). Some exceptions were apparently made for West Cameroon firms. Federal Press Release No. 2,727 of October 9, 1963 stated that applicants for import licenses in West Cameroon had to have "business capital" amounting to one million CFA. No mention was made of requirement of 5 million CFA turnover.) The quotas established for each category were such that those firms in the first category received four

these procedures resulted in quotas for them which were far below their real and traditional trade capacity and arbitrarily restricted the size of their operations. One by-product of the system, they claimed, was a restriction on the African work force they could support, and likewise, the contribution they could make to governmental revenues through taxes. The indisputable fact was that during 1964 and 1965 there was an appreciable shrinkage in the size of the retail trade of a number of important European firms, a reduction estimated at about eight percent of their former turnover.[42] The profit margins for European firms in general commerce fell steadily during the years following independence of East Cameroon until in 1965 it was only about two or three percent for even the largest, presumably most efficient, firms.[43] There were undoubtedly multiple causes for this trend, but most of the expatriate businessmen blamed it primarily on the proliferation of small, what they called inefficient, perhaps dishonest African merchants and importers,[44] and on the continuation of the internal customs barrier, which was a factor closely related to the first one mentioned. Despite the flexibility in the total sums of foreign exchange available each year, the supply was not unlimited, and the proliferation of firms stiffened competition for that which was available. This fact alone tended to reduce the amount of exchange allotted to the small and the large import houses alike since their one-seventh or four-sevenths of the total, as the case may be, would be a

times and members of the second received two times the maximum sum made available to those in the third category. The large import houses were quick to point out that "the system permits four little importers, realizing a turnover of five million [CFA] to obtain an allocation [of foreign exchange] equal to that attributed to the most important enterprise in Cameroon." Specialists, those firms importing in a particular limited field, were automatically assigned to the first category. The sums of exchange actually granted did reflect the disparities of need among middle and large firms, because they tended to request only what they needed, or to at least use all they were granted. Many of the small firms enjoyed surplus exchange-drawing authorization. This factor was modified by virtue of the fact that import licenses required application in advance (nearly a year), were granted according to each of the 21 rubrics of the import schedules and three regions of the country. (Northern and southern East Cameroon were two separate regions which required separate licenses even if the enterprise operated in both places, and the West Cameroon importers constituted a third category. Import licenses were also differentiated according to the origin of the products, namely EEC and non-EEC products.)

[42] J. Rhomer, Director, S.H.O., interview, Douala, July 1965. The reduction was in the gross figures for general commerce.

[43] *Ibid.*

[44] Syndicat des Commercants-Importateurs, Exportateurs du Cameroun, Notes for Commission No. 7 (Commerce, Services, Tourism) subcommission on internal commerce, minutes of meeting in Douala, July 1, 1965. The transaction tax was also cited by participants as a cause for the degradation of general commerce.

larger sum were there to be only, say, 100 firms in the competition, instead of the nearly 250 actually inscribed on the official list of holders of import licenses for East Cameroon in 1965.[45] It seems that only about 60 to 100 of the import firms were African-owned; of these only six or so were large enough to be inscribed under the second category of firms doing between 50 and 250 million CFA worth of business a year.[46]

Africans in increasingly large numbers found it possible to enter the field of general and import commerce, in part because some of the largest European firms were constrained to a somewhat artificially low level of import activity due to the allocation of exchange. But this was not the only reason; perhaps it was not even a significant reason why some African firms could become reasonably important. The continuation of the internal customs barrier seems to have given them an assist, making it possible for a number of large and small African firms to organize a significant illegal trade across the ill-guarded border. No real attempt was made by the government to police the customs barrier.[47] Thus it was an easy matter for African business firms to smuggle goods across the border. The fact that imports brought in from non-EEC countries through Victoria were exempted from paying the discriminatory tariffs established by the UDEAC and EEC Association agreements meant they could undersell competitors in the east. This provided adequate incentive to such merchants to seize the opportunity. There were various license and accounting measures designed to prohibit such an illicit traffic, but they were relatively ineffective with the small African firms whose books were disorderly and whose activities were not so exposed to public or official scrutiny.[48] Several African import firms from East Cameroon

[45] Liste des Importateurs Inscrits au CTRI (Comite Technique de Repartition des Importations), Ministère des Affaires Économiques et du Plan, Direction des Rélations économiques exterieurs, service du commerce exterieur, Décember 1964–November 1965.

[46] I am indebted to the staff of the Cameroon Chamber of Commerce, especially to M. Fohem, its secretary, for indicating 58 names on their own list of principal importers which he recognized as being African. The official list of importers, referred to in note 45, is somewhat longer. It would appear that about 100 of the names listed are African. No African names appear in the list of regular First Category importers (the largest), nor among the Specialized Importers enjoying the same share of exchange.

[47] There were only six customs stations along the 225-mile border between East and West Cameroon. Stations were located at the following points: Mboya, Moundame, Pamja, Loum, Bamenda, and Banjouen; a seventh station at Bamajou was burned by terrorists. No troops were stationed between these customs stations.

[48] Ordinance No. 61/OF/3 of October 1, 1961 regulated the customs barrier and the goods that were permitted passage free of customs charges. Transfers between states of other items required the normal licenses and taxes, receipts, and other records that were checked by the treasury and accounting offices.

began to operate in the west, and many of the western ones participated in the trade.

Despite the special arrangements for stimulating the growth of African business in the north, such as the separate allocation of exchange and licenses for importers operating in the north, neither the illegal trade nor the general economic expansion seems to have benefited northern enterprises. At least through 1965 no import licenses and no foreign exchange allocations were granted to African importers in the north.[49]

Government officials and some African businessmen denied having ignored the illegal trade. The fact was, however, that the trade became quite important (even automobiles figured in it), and African firms did begin to impinge on the large expatriate firms. For the first time in the country, especially on the French-speaking side, a group of African businessmen (they have not yet emerged as a class) were finding it possible to gain a foothold in the theretofore expatriate-controlled markets. Despite the cries and threats from these European merchants, and despite some loss to the governmental coffers through unreported transactions and income, African officials could regard such a situation as favorable to the long-run interests of the country. That this might benefit the country was also recognized by some of the important European businessmen.

Several of the largest expatriate firms bowed somewhat to the inevitability of a growing African commercial class. They tended to revise their operations to emphasize industrial and other heavy equipment where profits were more substantial and growth potential higher. Most of the transplanted eastern firms conducting general merchandizing operations in West Cameroon resolved to hang on in the hope that eventually fiscal, tariff, and licensing procedures would be harmonized and all firms could compete on the basis of strict procedural (but not de facto) equality.[50] Many European businessmen—in fact, most of them—responded to the stiffened competition from African firms and to the general falling off of their sales by joining to put pressure on the federal government.

The expatriate businessmen had several instrumentalities by which to articulate their interest and press their claims against the government. One of the most important was the long-established *Groupement interprofessionnel pour l'étude et la coordination des intérêts économiques du*

[49] Only eight firms (CFAO, King, SONAC, CCHA, SOCONORD, SHO, CRC, CGA) were given import licenses and exchange allocations to operate in the north in 1965. Though there were a number of African firms with North Cameroon names, these all received their allocations to import into South Cameroon.

[50] M. Leauté, Secretaire, GICAM, interview, Douala, July 1965.

Cameroun (GICAM). As the name implies, this group drew from all commercial and productive sectors and was devoted in part to research concerning the potential benefit to its members in the general economic and financial sectors. On the basis of what appear to be grossly distorted figures for the patterns of trade between the two states, provided in a special presentation by the president of the *Syndicat des Commerçants Importateurs et Exportateurs du Cameroun* (SCIEC), another of the powerful voices of the commercial interests, the group charged in July 1964 that the illegal trade between the two states was conducted on an important scale and in a systematic manner.[51] Privately GICAM officials estimated that over 40 percent of all West Cameroon imports illegally ended up in East Cameroon. In the opinion of the group the only solution was to make the customs and fiscal regimes of the two areas completely uniform. Shortly before, the meeting of GICAM the SCIEC had also discussed the matter of the dual customs and fiscal regimes and had called for quick and decisive governmental action. Despite the fact that, in the view of the SCIEC merchants, for over two years the illicit trade had "distorted traditional commercial circuits, partially destroyed the equilibrium of the market . . . and [produced] the retreat of certain merchants who could not assure their turnover . . . ," it seemed that the various economic commissions convened by the government to deal with economic reunification had failed to consider the commercial aspects of it. The merchants called on all concerned to give the matter the attention it deserved.

Oddly enough, the expatriate large businessmen of East Cameroon were joined by many citizens of West Cameroon in demanding removal of the customs barrier. Western officials felt pressed enough on this issue to mention it often in their speeches, promising that the barrier would be removed as soon as possible.[52] It was clear to most officials in both states

[51] M. Benard, president of SCIEC, stated to the 27th session of the general assembly of GICAM that whereas eastern exports to West Cameroon went from 71 to 565 million CFA in 1961–1963, the reverse trade actually declined from 11 to 9 million. Official statistics indicate the east-west trade was 81 million in 1961. 1963 figures are not available, but the 1964 east-west level was 813 million. Benard is probably correct about the 565 million figure. 1961 west to east figures were 12.2 million, however; and 1964 figures were 44 million. It appears that Benard used quantity instead of value figures for the 1963 west to east trade.

[52] Foncha and his top officials, particularly the Secretary for Finance and the Secretary for Commerce and Industry, repeatedly spoke of the barrier as "unfortunate," and promised its removal when "an agreement form of collecting revenue" was established, and wage-price differences were not so great. Foncha stated to a Kumba audience in September 1962: "It will not be long [before the customs barrier

that the matter involved many technical problems: the standard of living in the west was much lower than in the east, and eastern prices were much higher, patterns of trade were not harmonious, etc. Various technical committees were established to work out plans for harmonizing fiscal policies, which began to happen in 1962, and ultimately to create a completely unified economy.[53] But by mid-1965 it was apparent that the issue was no longer a technical one; it had become primarily political.[54] Under heavy pressure from its major commercial houses the federal government pressed West Cameroon to agree to end the custom barrier as of January 1, 1965.[55] Western officials resisted the move, however, although they publicly affirmed the eventual desirability of such a move. They pointed to the severe inflation the consumers of the state had already suffered, and the incapacity of the government and major employers to afford sharp wage increases. The Buea regime would require some compensatory resources to accomplish the desired transition. However, it became virtually impossible for West Cameroon to impede the harmonization process once the treaty obligations of a common tariff among all five states of the *Union douanière et économique d'Afrique centrale* (UDEAC) went into force in January 1966. The expatriate firms had featured this prospect in their own propaganda.

During the Christmas season of 1965 Prime Minister Jua was called to Yaounde to confer with President Ahidjo, following Ahidjo's return from a meeting of the five heads of state. It was made clear that the UDEAC tariffs would go into effect at the first of the year and that special provisions for West Cameroon could not be maintained long after that.[56] The immediate and expected popular response was strong protest (the real benefits of the barrier had by then become a matter of public knowledge) over the prospect of rising prices. This concern was justified, for with the very mention of the change many merchants raised their prices. The Buea government had to threaten severe action against such practices, and

is removed] . . . we all know that unification and the subsequent introduction of a new currency were, like any other change, bound to bring along a certain amount of hardship." Federal Press Release No. 2,000, September 25, 1962.

[53] In April 1962 an exchange office and external exchange bureau was established, which attempted to resolve the problems of extending portions of the federal tariff regime into the west. Several special meetings were held in July 1962 between Federal Minister of Economy Victor Kanga and State Secretary Peter Kembha. General price controls were introduced as part of this effort.

[54] Even officials in the East Cameroon government viewed the barrier question as a political one, and several discussed it in this light during personal interviews in Yaounde in July 1965.

[55] W. C. Epale, Permanent Secretary for Finance, interview, Buea, August 1965.

[56] *Cameroon Times,* December 21, 1965.

quickly moved, not only to establish price controls but to study the feasibility of wage increases. Jua also succeeded in obtaining some "special concessions" to ease the transition to an integrated economy: (1) a further period of up to six months during which the new tariffs and taxes would gradually be introduced; (2) continued exemption during this time of a 10 per cent turnover tax and partial exemption of a six percent transaction tax for West Cameroon firms; and (3) exemption from all new import tariffs and taxes for goods ordered the previous year. One effect of the provisions was to preserve the custom barrier between the two states, symbolizing the duality of the customs regime, until July of 1966. Federation stimulated more than a flow of goods and services between the two states; it also stimulated a flow of people, although the flow remained light, and declined after a few years.

There was a general impression in Douala shortly after reunification that quite a number of westerners visited the city, many apparently looking for jobs, but perhaps simply to inspect the source and sample the sophisticated atmosphere of the bright glow that residents of Victoria and Tiko could see at night off to the southeast. One corroborating indication of the influx was the United States Information Agency library in Douala, the only major source of literature in English in Douala. It was the estimation of the African librarian that in 1965 about one in ten of the users of English language books were from West Cameroon. A check of membership cards in the library of a sample of 73 people using English books indicated that 33, about 45 percent, had names local members recognized to be West Cameroon names.[57] Additional samples of library members using books in English who joined the library in 1963 and in 1965 indicated that in the earlier year about 16 percent of them had names thought to be West Cameroonian, whereas in 1965 the percentage had dropped to about eight. This general decline in the percentage of West Cameroonians among the users of English books is made even more significant by the fact that the percentage of all USIA library books in Douala used which were in English declined from 21 percent in 1963 to 14 percent in 1964 and 16 percent for the first half-year of 1965.[58]

[57] This check was made by this author from among the readers of books about Afro-Americans, American Government, and Economics. There was very close agreement among three African staff members of the Library about the East or West Cameroon origin of the names. Moreover, most of the names from West Cameroon, and most of those reading English material were Bamileke, with large contingents from Mamfe (Banyang) and Bakossi. Few were Bakweri, a people related to the Douala.

[58] Membership and circulation records, U.S. Information Agency Library, Douala, August 1965.

In mid-1966, as the time approached to remove all vestiges of protection for the West Cameroon economy, the Trade Union Congress demanded the harmonization of wage and salary scales between the two states, along with an adequate minimum wage law. The congress threatened a general strike if the demands were not met. The demands came in the aftermath of a government initiative in early March to stave off the mounting criticism and popular malaise over wages. Jua and Foncha announced to the KNDP convention that all government workers would receive at least a 10-percent wage increase; those lowest on the scale would get a 15-percent increase retroactive to the first of the year. However, the TUC convention that followed deemed the increases insufficient; more importantly, it sought to obtain a general wage increase that would protect all workers, particularly in the all-important Cameroon Development Corporation.[59] A major strike by 3,000 workers of the local government councils added credibility to the threat of a general strike. The general strike was averted when the Federal Inspector of Administration stepped in to mediate between the TUC and all involved employer organizations.[60] During these negotiations the leaders of the West Cameroon TUC maintained limited contact with their trade union counterparts in the east, but it is significant that no collaborative action was taken on the matter. The eastern unions had already been subjected to control by the UC. Moreover, a westerner, Nzo Ekhah Ngahky, was made Federal Minister of Labor, one of the most sensitive positions in the government, insofar as East-West Cameroon relations were concerned. Much of the potential state-federal conflict over the question was avoided by serious and sincere efforts to elaborate a program technically adequate to provide the resources needed to bring wage and salary scales in the two states closer together. Western leaders found it more efficacious to use their leverage within the federal government than to work for strong bonds between the labor movements of the two states. Indeed, one of the evident differences between the two areas was the persisting freedom of the labor unions in West Cameroon, their autonomy from the political parties, in the face of effective, if indirect, political control over the labor movement in the east. Finally it should be noted that eastern labor leaders had little hard interest in harmonizing either the customs, fiscal, or wage systems. The illegal trade aided the workers who were the poorer consumers in the east, and wages were generally much higher in the east, so harmonization would either mean lowering eastern wages or providing some sort of sub-

[59] *Cameroon Times,* June 21, 1966.
[60] *Cameroon Times,* June 30, 1966.

sidy to western businesses. The source of the subsidies would likely be the federal government, i.e. East Cameroon resources.

The employer organizations also established contact with each other during the course of the difficulties over harmonization, but real collaboration never materialized. The interests of these groups were more disparate than those of the workers. It was clear to western employers, including transplanted eastern firms, that they enjoyed an advantage which harmonization would destroy. Once the internal differences are eliminated, however, it is reasonable to expect that both employer and employee organizations will find it in their interests to organize at the federal level in collaborative efforts to manipulate the federal institutions or spell out their interests to them.

President Ahidjo and his principal associates have been more concerned with reallocating the benefits of economic growth and development within East Cameroon than between the two states. Northern East Cameroon has remained as impoverished in modern economic and social development as the West Cameroon regions, if not more so. To correct the situation Ahidjo pressed hard and early for a long-talked-of railway connection between the existing Douala-Yaounde line and the large cities of the north.[61] Thirty-three million dollars in loans and grants were secured in 1961 to begin work on the first section of the line, which would go as far as the town of Goyum, near where flatbush and the scrubby hills of the southeast give way to the rising savannah of the central plateau of Adamawa region and the north. The second section will link this line to Ngaoundere, the principal center of the Adamawa region and a major northern city of Cameroon. Nearly $74 million must be raised, 60 of it from foreign sources to realize this portion of the project. From Ngaoundere later, a line will be extended to the Chad Republic's city of Moundou.

Extension of the Transcam Railway to Ngaoundere will drastically alter economic conditions in the northern part of the country. An important benefit will be the profitable exploitation of bauxite deposits in the town of Martap, about 50 miles southwest of Ngaoundere. The deposits

[61] The existing rail lines in the country were planned and surveyed by the Germans, who lost control of the country before they could complete all sections of it. The German plans called for an extensive, 3,000-kilometer network that would have covered all sections of the country. The French extended the rail lines from Eseka to Yaounde and Mbalmayo and surveyed a route north, which they were unable to realize. Ahidjo took up the plan soon after his election as prime minister; it became his first and foremost large development project for discussion with other states after Cameroon independence.

are among the most promising in Africa; their exploitation will permit the smelters which now process imported ores at Edea to place Cameroon among the prime suppliers of finished aluminum products to Africa. The railroad will expand commercial activity, human mobility, and export industry generally in the north. The predicted traffic for 1970 between Ngaoundere and Yaounde is 188 million ton-kilometers in the down direction and 169 in the up direction (toward Ngaoundere), traffic about as heavy in each direction as the combined traffic in both directions for the entire rail network of Cameroon in 1965–1966.[62] By 1980 total traffic figures are expected to be 60 percent larger than those predicted for 1970.

THE years of Ahidjo rule have already occasioned marked growth in the economy of the north. No doubt some of the growth has resulted from the anticipations connected with the new railway; road development has been extensive in the north, for example. The most significant road development is that which affects national Highway 1, the major road from Douala through Yaounde to the north. More than $6.5 million has gone into the work, the greater part on the portion north of Yaounde.[63] A major bridge is planned to cross the Benoue River at Garoua, which the FED will finance, and major feeder roads and extensions are planned for the far northern part, for which, with minor exceptions, financing had not been obtained by the end of the first five-year plan (1963). An additional $2 million worth of secondary roads were constructed in northern areas under the first plan. The size of the fleet of private and commercial vehicles in the north was only just beginning to reflect the improved transportation network by 1964 when about 450 new vehicles were registered in the six northern regions.[64] This figure is about the average annual number of new registrants for West Cameroon during the years 1960–1964, but is less than a fourth of the total number of newly registered vehicles for East Cameroon that year.

The north has also realized substantial gains in several other areas of

[62] Traffic predictions are taken from *Le Chemin de fer transcamerounais,* Commissariat general a l'information, Yaounde, p. 24. The total freight traffic for 1965–1966 is put at 175 million ton-kilometers by *Entreprise* (Paris), *Supplement No. 602,* March 23, 1967, p. 23.

[63] Rapport General sur l'Execution du Premier Plan quinquennal. Ministere des Finances et du Plan, Yaounde, 1963, p. 32.

[64] From *Parq automobile du Cameroun Oriental, and . . . Occidentale, Service de la Statistiques, Ministère des Affaires Economiques Nationale,* Yaounde, 1964.

344

production; this is particularly true of cotton. Cotton was first introduced in the country in 1950 when the Compagnie française pour le Développement des Fibres Textiles (CFDT) began to establish experimental stations and farms. Since then, 150 thousand families have been drawn into this activity in the north, aided by the CFDT, which provides seeds, gives training, organizes the farmers, and purchases and markets the crop. Cotton production rose 24 percent a year from 1959 to 1963, until by 1965 cotton was Cameroon's third largest export crop, although it lagged far behind coffee and cocoa. The cocoa farmers continue to earn much more, on the average ($177 a year) than do the cotton farmers ($100). Production of ginned fiber reached 22,500 tons in 1966–1967; raw production in 1965–1966 was nearly triple what it had been the year prior to independence and earned the Cameroon over $9 million, about 60 percent of which accrued directly to the peasant farmers involved in cotton production.[65] Six ginning factories and two cotton seed oil pressing plants have also been constructed in recent years. In 1966 a large processing plant was built at Garoua, capable of producing 7 million meters of cloth a year. Groundnut production is another important and fast-growing northern industry. Production increased by 40 percent between 1959 and 1963, achieving annual growth rates of nearly 15 percent from 1961 to 1965. But these rates permitted the country merely to regain the high position in exports it had achieved in 1958. Also, there are important herds of cattle, goats, sheep, hogs, and poultry; in 1967 there were over two million head of cattle, for example. Even with recent growth all along the line in northern products, the region still lags far behind the south. In 1962 production in the north was only about a quarter that of East Cameroon. The rate of growth, in an absolute sense or on a per capita basis, is not available, but it is unlikely that it surpasses that planned for or achieved in the southern districts. The first five-year plan concentrated on internal projects such as the railway and road projects already mentioned (much of which helped the north) and industrial growth centered mainly in the south. Growth in the latter was 16 percent from 1959 to 1963, and upwards to 25 percent between 1962 and 1965.[66] Moreover, to the extent that the new Central African Economic Union concentrates Cameroon's

[65] The growers' share of earnings is estimated on the basis of 1963 figures, where total export earnings were 2 billion CFA and 1.2 billion CFA. CFA was put directly into circulation in the north from these earnings. *Entreprise, Supplement No. 602,* p. 14.

[66] Figures include processing, thus represent growth in value-added as well as production.

benefits primarily in the industrial sector, the concentration will favor the south.[67]

One important difference between the character of economic growth in the two sectors is that because it involves industrial products and a greater percentage of social overhead gains, the southern development has a more negligible impact on individuals and families than the growth in the north which is bringing many people into the cash nexus and export economy for the first time. In any case, the political speeches of the president and his northern associates always signal the gains of the north, which, in Ahidjo's words, "was formerly justified in considering itself forsaken." He proudly refers to the Transcam Railway as the project that will give a veritable whiplash to the economy of the entire country, especially the north, and "will consolidate its unity and make of it a homogenous nation." He states his objective as one of satisfying the "thirst for economic equity," and affirms that "we desire that the inequalities which were born of geography and history should be corrected, whenever economic realities permit it, and that development should not be the privilege of some regions to the detriment of others." [68]

IT IS clear that despite overall economic gains in gross national product, from domestic and foreign sources, and gains in governmental revenues, federation caused severe disruptions in the financial life of the governments and the economic lives of the general populace. Most importantly, the burden of change and adjustment fell disproportionately on westerners, but easterners, even large expatriate interests, were not exempt from their effects. Governmental decisions acquired a stronger role in directing the economy. The relationship of the political system to the economy became extractive but remained responsive as well. There were also important shifts in trade patterns as East Cameroon firms and goods displaced Nigerian and British ones. Interstate trade rose sharply and became an important factor in Western imports, though it remained unimportant to the eastern economy.

---

[67] Ahidjo has also announced his intention to promote the industrialization of the north through the encouragement of animal and fish meat-processing plants, transportation and communication development, and construction industries. There is also under study plans for the development of water and hydroelectric potential in the area as part of a larger effort to develop the Chad Lake basin. Indeed, the four basin states—Niger, Nigeria, Cameroon, and Chad—have formed the Chad Basin States Organization to promote development.

[68] A. Ahidjo, Speech given at the inauguration of a cotton-processing plant at Garoua, February 5, 1965.

Important gains have been realized in northern East Cameroon in terms of expanding cash crop production. The most significant development venture, the Transcam Railway, is designed to open up the north to full participation in the world economy and to more nearly equalize its share of national economic resources and growth. It will require several years more and considerable foreign aid before these plans, initiated with the first section of the railway, can be realized.

The consequence of the changes resulting from federation was to redistribute collective wealth in favor of the west but to make individual westerners worse off. Most of the changes in economic patterns were evident ones to westerners and hidden to their compatriots. This situation contributed to a profound realization among westerners that their decision to become full-fledged Cameroonians had ushered them into a new world. It was a world not without its own special appeal, based on the excitement of innovation itself, if nothing else, but a world that affirmed the reality of the plebiscite decision precisely by denying, in a rather stark and brutal way, all the conscious motives and visions which had inspired it. The advent of federalism quickened the pace and disrupted the patterns of administrative, and to some extent, of social and economic life in the east, and to that degree relieved the lackluster character of public affairs following independence and the suppression of the UPC rebellion. But what was fundamentally different in East Cameroon after federation did not touch the private lives and material resources of the average man quite the same way it did west of the Mungo, nor did it alter much the established patterns of power and resource allocation, except to cloud them over. Thus easterners generally had a sense of life going on pretty much as before, perhaps only more so. The result was to tie the behavior of everybody, especially westerners, in public and private life, to larger circuits and to effectively subject them to the constraints of the larger system. Only in rare cases, however, could these linkages be described as complementary in the sense of being mutually supportive and balanced in terms both of the distribution of costs and the relation of costs to benefits.

☆ 14 ☆

The Control of Dissidence

CAMEROON's experience is an exception to the general pattern of decolonization, in that it involved violent and protracted conflict between militant nationalists and the colonial authority. It is a commonplace observation that in nearly every newly independent black African state only a minimum of struggle was required to achieve independence. No other nationalist movements, until the crisis in the former Belgian Congo, involved a sustained war effort. The purpose of most movements was to organize public opinion or create a broad and vociferous front of groups which would demand accelerated progress toward the realization of goals already established or rather easily accepted by the colonial powers. The will and mutual confidence of the leaders in these countries were untested; the weak, self-serving and/or less efficient leaders were not identified as such. The costs of dissidence and strife had not been clearly demonstrated to the people. No Thirty Years' War, Hundred Years' War, Great Revolution, or Grand March had brought about a coherent and efficient political leadership or had joined the military establishment to the leadership. Consequently the nation remains inchoate in most of the new states of Africa; its will to exist is as much the result of the achievement of independence as its cause.

Has the difference in experience made for any difference in the post-independence development of Cameroon? Did national integration proceed at a faster or slower pace than in the other countries of Africa that did not experience rebellion and intensive internecine strife? In what respects does rebellion have a positive impact on political integration?

Certainly the nature of the strife and the context in which it occurs affects its impact on the subsequent development of the country. The degree to which it is controlled to serve particular ends, and the nature and context of the ends determine whether national integration is made more or less easy. To appreciate these possibilities one must first consider the development of the rebellion.

It is convenient to date the rebellion in Cameroon from April 22, 1955. On that date the leader of the UPC and several other UPC-affiliated organizations issued a "Joint Proclamation" declaring that the Trusteeship Agreement was terminated. The UPC also demanded: (a) general elections for a constituent assembly, to be held before the end of 1955; and

348

(b) the immediate installation of a United Nations commission to supervise the establishment of an African executive committee, the purpose of which would be to serve as a provisional government.[1]

The declaration came on the heels of a series of hurried but large public meetings throughout the larger towns of southern Cameroun, at which the leadership of the UPC (Reuben Um Nyobé, Felix Roland Moumié, Ernest Ouandié, and Abel Kingué) whipped up strong popular protest to the newly appointed commissioner, Roland Pré, and repeated longstanding claims for reunification of all the territory of the former German Kamerun and its full independence. A series of poorly organized strikes followed the meetings, which was the work of the UPC and the French CGT-affiliated USCC. During early May of that year the public meetings of UPC sympathizers grew larger and the demands of their spokesmen more violent.

Speaking with elation but premature confidence, UPC president Moumié announced that he no longer had to deal with the French commissioner. He declared himself open to discussions with the French Ministry of Foreign Affairs. He also announced that, like Mao Tse Tung and Ho Chi Minh, Reuben Um Nyobé had already taken to the *"maquis."* [2] The revolution was in full swing.

The UPC and its affiliated youth, women, and trade union groups stepped up their program of mass meetings and wildcat strikes throughout the southern towns. A general strike was scheduled for mid-May 1955, but it failed. Finally the UPC launched a series of riots and mass demonstrations in the capital, the major port city of Douala and a number of towns throughout regions of the country settled by the Bamileke, Mungo, Douala, and Bassa peoples. One of the leaders shouted to an assembly of UPC faithful: "You are authorized to stop all foreigners, commissioners of police, and *gendarmes*. Kill them! I am responsible." [3] Armed with nail-studded clubs, machetes, axes, and some guns, rioters in Douala burned down houses, attacked Europeans and Africans on the streets, overturned cars and set several on fire, attacked the radio stations, and blocked major roads.[4] Similar occurrences wracked the other large cities. After 10 days of this activity the government succeeded in

[1] See Owona, *Le Mouvement d'Inspiration Marxiste;* and Le Vine, *Cameroons,* p. 154. The organizations were the Jeunesse Démocratique (JDC), the Union Démocratique des Femmes Camerounaises (UDEFC), Union des Syndicats Confédérés du Cameroun (USCC), along with the UPC.

[2] Owana, *Le Mouvement.*

[3] *Ibid.*

[4] See Le Vine, *Cameroons,* p. 156.

pacifying the areas. Twenty-six lost their lives and nearly 200 were officially declared wounded; thousands were homeless. Several weeks later the administration banned the UPC and its youth and women's organizations, the JDC and the UDEFEC.

The great popular uprising which the UPC leaders expected to follow the forceful suppression of the riots failed to materialize. But there is little question that the UPC leaders acquired a vast following as a reward for bearing the brunt of the administration's opposition to nationalist aspirations.

Within two months most top leaders of the UPC had fled to the sanctuary of Kumba, across the border in southern British Cameroons. Soon thereafter, Reuben Um Nyobé, the executive secretary, and his close associate and head of the youth wing, Theodore Mayi Matip, initiated a guerilla-type campaign in Nyong-et-Kélé division among their fellow Bassa.[5] Over the next three years, until late 1958, bands of mostly Bassa *"maquisards,"* taking their orders from Um Nyobé, committed arson, murder, terrorism, and sabotage. The bands operated in a fairly delimited stretch of territory, in what the government called the *"Zone de Pacification"* (zopac), north of Douala through Ngambé to the capital, Yaounde, and south to Eséka. Occasionally the Bamileke and Mungo districts along the border with British Cameroons would fall victim to rebel attacks from across the border. No doubt these were directed by the exiled UPC leaders in Kumba.

Among the most violent and widespread terrorist campaigns was that waged in late 1956 and early 1957 to discourage participation in the general elections for a new legislative assembly. The assembly was established under the provisions of the *loi cadre* passed by the French National Assembly in June 1956. Militant UPC sympathizers, led by the Moumié wing of the party, rejected the reforms promised in the law, and organized a boycott of the elections.[6] In the course of the campaign two of the

---

[5] The initial uprising was actually stirred up by the Bamileke UPC leader, Abel Kingué, working among Bassa-related groups in the Sanaga Maritime division.

[6] The UPC leadership was canvassed about the elections by Um Nyobé over a period of some weeks or perhaps months in early 1956, to determine if a boycott was to be conducted. Those in the *maquis* with Um Nyobé were probably in favor of the boycott, although moderate nationalists like Soppo Priso apparently convened various meetings supposedly attended by *Upécistes,* but who were either former adherents or nonparticipants in the clandestine activities. Moumié and his group of UPC officials were canvassed by written dispatch to their headquarters in Kumba, British Cameroons; their decision to boycott the elections settled the matter. To develop some popular sentiment for participation, Soppo Priso launched the movement *Courant d'Union nationale* in late 1956, and conducted a meeting in Ebolowa December 2 and 3. The meeting failed to achieve solid support for participation, however, and the *Courant* died shortly thereafter.

candidates were assassinated. One report states that the UPC made good on its threat to eliminate "les valets des colonialistes" in 90 instances.[7] Trains were derailed, telegraph wires cut, houses burned, roads blocked, polling stations burned or disrupted, and voters intimidated. The voter turnout was markedly reduced in only two districts, however—in Wouri (containing the city of Douala) and the Sanaga Maritime division (Bassa country).[8]

The region was relatively quiet for nearly a year after that, until the short dry season in the final months of 1957. Thereafter, for about a year, the Sanaga Maritime and Nyong-et-Kélé divisions were terrorized by *maquisards* and government armed forces alike. In mid-September 1958 a phase of the rebellion ended when a military patrol surprised and killed Um Nyobé in his hiding place near his home at Boumnyébel.

Mayi Matip, who escaped detection despite being with Um Nyobé at the time of the ambush, soon turned himself in to the authorities and sent an appeal to his fellow rebels to do the same. During the next three months, with Matip and other Bassa UPC leaders aiding the government, the *ralliément* (return to legal life) campaign succeeded in enticing about 1,300 rebels out of the forest. The *ralliément* campaign organized by the government and army had already produced about 800 defectors since its inception.[9] Despite condemnation and threatened assault by the exiled UPC leadership in Cairo (soon to relocate in Accra and Conakry), Matip had continued an impressive success with the *ralliément.* By April 1959 the *rallié* UPC was strong enough to successfully run six candidates in by-elections throughout the troubled areas.

By this time the first African government in Cameroon, with André Marie Mbida as prime minister, had fallen in disarray, its support having disintegrated because of Mbida's adoption of an unpopular program (that of renouncing early independence and reunification) and his imperious style of leadership. His successor, Ahidjo, pressed for realization of the two principal planks of the original UPC program. Ahidjo proceeded to negotiate an agreement with the French, setting January 1, 1960 as the date for Cameroon independence. With its hero, Um Nyobé, dead, his most devoted followers among the Bassa *rallié,* and its program usurped, the exiled UPC was desperate. It turned once more to familiar tactics

[7] Lamberton, "La Pacification du Sanaga Maritime—December 1957 a Janvier 1959," Etude 3760 (Paris: Centre des Hautes Etudes d'Afrique moderne).

[8] See Le Vine, *Cameroons,* p. 161 and Appendix B; see also Marcel Nguini, *La Valeur Politique de la Tutelle Française* Nguini, Marcel. *La Valeur politique de la Tutelle Francaise.* Ph.D. dissertation. D'Aix-en-Provence: University d'Aix-Marseille, Faculté de Droit, 1956.

[9] Gardinier, *Cameroon,* p. 87, states that 2,500 had rallied by the end of 1958.

and initiated a new wave of terrorism and sabotage. This final stage of the rebellion centered in the Bamileke areas or neighboring divisions heavily settled by Bamileke such as Wouri, Mungo, Mkam, and Mbam.

The attacks, initially concerted, dwindled in number, brutality, and degree of coordination, but fairly frequent outbursts continued throughout 1961. The incidence of the attacks was high and concentrated on the eve of and immediately following independence.

The exiled leaders no doubt feared that the amnesty Ahidjo had announced in early 1960 was not intended for them, so they continued to encourage and support those terrorists who remained active in the countryside. In Accra they attempted to establish a revolutionary government in Cameroon and to stir up a general revolt back home. In addition to more frequent assaults on the towns and workers' camps in the Bamileke, Mungo, and Douala areas, the rebellion turned to a scorched-earth policy by hacking down banana and coffee trees and burning crops.

Atrocities by government troops and police seem to have stimulated some continued rebel activity, but the general revolt the Accra faction had hoped for never materialized. The influx of diplomatic personnel and businessmen, the ceremonies connected with the handing over of power, the subsequent dispatch of Cameroon diplomats to the UN and other foreign capitals all made the charge that Cameroon independence was fictitious less and less tenable, despite the continued presence of French troops and advisers in the troubled areas.

The tangible costs of six years of intensive violence in Cameroon were considerable. No official estimate of the loss of life or property has been issued, so it is impossible to measure the cost accurately.

Le Vine gives various figures for the number of persons killed by rebels or government forces or by accident. He suggests that the number might be between 6,000 and 15,000, and arbitrarily suggests 10,000 as a reasonable estimate.[10] Published estimates from those with access to government documents and/or personal experience in the area at the time suggest that the most accurate number is closer to Le Vine's minimum.[11]

[10] "The Course of Political Violence," in Lewis, ed., *French-Speaking Africa,* and Appendix II. See also Le Vine, "Insurgency and Counterinsurgency in the Cameroun, 1955–1962."

[11] Owona, "Le Mouvement," states that the Sanaga Maritime *maquis* took 1,000 lives in 1956–1959. On the other hand, Professor G. Horner, "Togo and Cameroon," *Current History,* Vol. xxxiv (February 1958), 84–90, suggests the figure of 2,000 for the period December 1956 to March 1957. The Bamileke *maquis,* in the three months prior to and following independence, may have killed another 1,000.

More precise figures are available on the destruction of public services and property attributable to the rebellion *in the Bamileke areas*. The Fond D'Aide et de la Coopération (FAC) took an inventory of the damage caused by the rebellion in the areas in order to determine the costs of a rebuilding program.[12] The report states that 74 public schools (116 classroom buildings and an equal number of teacher lodgings) were destroyed. Also destroyed were three hospitals, 46 dispensaries, about 40 bridges, and 12 agricultural stations. Over 750 kilometers of road were made impassable and several hundred kilometers of telegraph line pulled down. While the water pipelines were not systematically destroyed, they were a source of piping with which the rebels manufactured guns. The estimate of the damage to missionary schools, churches, and health facilities was put at 1.6 billion CFA francs, or about $6.4 million.

The degree to which open and armed resistance or challenge to governmental authority is controlled for particular objectives is an aspect of rebellion central to its significance to the country.[13] Violence may arise from generalized, diffuse grievances about the general allocation of values and the pattern of social and political stratification, or quite specific grievances about a regime's performance, or one's personal or group situation. Those supporting the rebellion may seek to alter the status or leadership of the entire territory or only a portion of it. Each motive tends to affect the course of violence in a peculiar way, with a distinctive impact on the political life of the country.

The Cameroon experience involved elements of each of the above-mentioned motives, and more. The result was that the rebellion lacked effective control, which in turn, while making it more difficult for the central government to stop the violence, ultimately discredited the rebellion and strengthened the hand of the government.

The most important deficiency of control in the rebellion was on the part of the organization that initiated the rebellion and attempted to di-

Newspaper accounts of the violence during the first three months of independence report the deaths of about 540, including government military casualties. (*La Presse du Cameroun*, January 1–April 25, 1960.) Violence by rebels then tapered off, but casualties in government operations increased. Two thousand are (unreliably) reported killed in one operation at Lowé in December 1961. *Cameroon Times*, December 22, 1961.

12 See "Les Regroupements en Pays Bamilekes," FAC and Ministry of Cooperation, Republic of France, October 1962–January 1963.

13 See Nathan Leites and Charles Wold, Jr., *Rebellion and Authority: Myths and Realities Reconsidered* (Los Angeles: RAND Corporation). See also Lucian W. Pye, "The Roots of Insurgency and the Commencement of Rebellions," in J. Eckstein, ed., *Internal War* (Glencoe, Ill.: Free Press, 1964).

rect it. During the period of the rebellion the UPC was rent into at least two factions which functioned with little coordination and cooperation.

The split with the UPC involved but was not limited to a difference of opinion on whether the rules and structures provided by the administering authority could ultimately accommodate nationalist objectives, or whether they required a violent showdown with the regime. The executive secretary of the party, Reuben Um Nyobé, and a number of close associates may well have abstained from the decision to incite the riots and demonstrations of May 1955. Um Nyobé was not among the UPC officials who appeared publicly, for some mysterious reason.[14]

The split in meetings of the *Courant d'Union Nationale* and the UPC in Ebolowa in December 1956 reflects such differences. Um Noybé is said to have favored participation in the elections, but bowed to the greater numbers in supporting the position taken by Moumié, Ouandié, and Kingué.

It should be evident by now that the division in the UPC had something of an ethnic base, or coincided with ethnic differences. Those who argued within party ranks for an increasing use of violence after 1955 were almost all Bamileke. One of the ironic facts about the UPC, and a factor that seriously affected its impact, was that despite the universal nature of its objectives—reunification, independence, modernization—the party was quite particularistic in its organizational base. Though its appeal reached beyond, its structure and leaders came from the Bamileke, Douala, and Bassa peoples almost exclusively, and it was these groups that tended to reflect distinct tendencies within the party.

Um Nyobé, unlike the exiled UPC, was not especially interested in stirring up general chaos in the Bamileke areas. Even before the *maquis* was organized, Um Nyobé had implored party branches to put good organization ahead of polemics concerning the "great problems of the hour." "We know by experience that all political problems can be resolved with a good organization," he wrote in a letter to the Éséka UPC

---

[14] Franz Ansprenger notes that during the 10-day May disturbances, Um Nyobé was in Nigeria, but he does not say how long he had been there, how long he stayed, or what his purpose was in going. Ansprenger, *Politik Im Schwartzen Afrika* (Köln: Westdeutscher Verlag, 1961), p. 200; Le Vine, *Cameroons*, p. 156, merely repeats Ansprenger. No direct mention of Um Nyobé's presence in Kumba following the dissolution of the UPC has come to my attention, although many reports mention his *return* from there to establish the *maquis*. The 1958 UN Visiting Mission says, Document T/1441, p. 11, that he "withdrew into the forest" following the events of May 1955. It is probable that Um never went into exile at all, but, rather, immediately set about organizing the Bassa.

bureau, "whereas, all sorts of failures and even catastrophies are possible in a poorly organized movement." [15] The extent of his control over the *maquis,* the support for them among the people, his personal displeasure with unnecessary bloodshed, and his understanding of who the enemy was are reflected in the fact that contact with the military was avoided and the general level of terrorism was relatively low. Sabotage of government facilities, intimidation of would-be voters, and attacks on Europeans were commonplace, however. "It is less a question of overthrowing legitimate authority than of leading it imperceptibly to disinterest itself in Bassa problems, which should be resolved among Bassa." Pursuing this logic, Um Nyobé after January 1957 instructed his forces "to avoid all contact with the military and the guards in order to pursue the organizational effort without being disturbed."

The external wing of the UPC provided little effective help to the Bassa *maquis.* The various bands of *maquisards,* most of which seemed to have contained less than 55 men, often had only a dozen guns. Many of their weapons were of their own making, and much of their supplies was stolen from the military or provided by well-placed sympathizers in the government. Very little of their supplies, and apparently very little money, came through the exiled contingent.[16]

The autonomy of the Bassa element of the UPC from the exiled group, and the effectiveness of its leaders' control over the rebels, is most dramatically indicated by the quick success of the *ralliément* campaign, and their victory at the polls in the elections of April 1960.

The Bassa leaders of the UPC, for whom reunification, and especially independence, was an important goal, seem to have pursued different objectives from those of the exiled leaders. Their rejection of participation in the legal structures was first inspired by their disbelief that the structures would give Cameroonians genuine power or would permit them to gain independence. When the Mbida government was installed they had ample proof that their own objectives were not those animating Mbida's government. Yet there was always a certain measure of faith in the popularity of the UPC and the possibility of the system to respect that popularity. With the advent of the Ahidjo government, the coming to

[15] Quoted in Lamberton, *La Pacification,* p. 5.
[16] Brzezinski, in his *Africa and the Communist World* (Stanford: Stanford University Press, 1963), suggests that communist aid did not become substantial until Moumié moved to Conakry and contacted the Chinese, probably in mid-1959. Gardinier, *Cameroon,* indicates that it was in May 1959 that modern weapons and supplies began arriving for the Bamileke rebels (p. 93).

power of de Gaulle in France, and a new status for Cameroon, Um Nyobé wearied of the *maquis* and questioned its efficacy. He is known to have sounded out colleagues and friends in Douala shortly before his death about terminating the rebellion; he was advised to continue the struggle. It is not beyond possibility that the location of his headquarters was made known to the authorities by more extremist "friends" with the party.

The progress and nature of the rebellion in the areas settled by Bamileke differed greatly from that just discussed, with the exception of the fact that both rebellions were profoundly affected by the traditional societies in which they occurred.[17] The grievances of a young deposed Bamileke chief provided the exiled leaders of the UPC with its first opportunity to stir up widespread violence in the Bamileke region. Kamdem-Ninyim Pierre, a young militant nationalist student in Paris and a member of the pro-UPC student group (*Union Nationale des Etudiants Kamerunaises,* the UNEK), inherited the throne of the Chief of Baham in 1954. He then joined a UPC study group and began to organize a *comités de base* for the party. His pro-UPC attitudes led the French to depose him a year or two later. The UPC leaders encouraged Pierre to organize a terrorist campaign against the new chief. After the UPC was banned, Kamdem-Ninyim established a front organization—the *Courant d'Action Nationale.* It was the leaders of this group (Tchoumba Isaac, Singap Martin, Peze Marcel) who established the first Bamileke *maquis.* Kamdem-Ninyim's activities were soon discovered; in November 1956 he was imprisoned and the CAN was suppressed. In connection with the exiled UPC leaders, however, Singap and Tchoumba continued the rebellion.

The termination of Bassa activities in late 1958 and early 1959, along with Moumié's move to Conakry, was followed by increased terrorist attacks in the areas settled by Bamileke and among a number of holdovers from the earlier Sanaga Maritime operations. But here again the UPC was unable to achieve effective coordination. The *Armée de Liberation Nationale du Kamerun* (ALNK) was established to direct the operations, which were placed under the leadership of Singap Martin. Soon another *maquis* sprang up under Momo Paul, another of Kamdem-Ninyim's colleagues and one who remained loyal to him. It became known to the officials that Momo was not taking his orders from Moumié,[18] although he

[17] See Chap. 7.
[18] President Ahidjo reported this in a speech January 19, 1960. *New York Times,* January 20, 1960.

continued to propagandize himself as the real head of the ALNK. Momo was repudiated by the exiled leaders, along with Kamdem-Ninyim.[19]

The various separate *maquis* units, organized into districts, and then broken up into rebel bands (typical names: Algeria, Morocco, Cuba, Accra), often felt the strain of conflicting ambitions; many split up. Conflict among the local *maquis* leaders became so bitter that on several occasions some of them had to be pulled out of the field for a meeting with the leaders. An example of the depth of the bitterness occurred between Tankou Noé, head of the Douala district, and Tomo Henri, sent out from Conakry to assist in the Douala campaign. Tankou accused Tomo of having diverted arms due for Tankou's men and of spreading false rumors that he was pocketing $40 a month for each rebel in his command. Tankou later claimed he never received any money from the exiled UPC. This dispute occasioned the establishment of a bureau of liaison in Kumba to facilitate communication with Accra and Conakry and to provide aid in resolving conflicts. The bureau did not succeed, however, for occasionally special meetings had to be held, such as the one that met in Conakry July 14, 1960, to clarify the attributions of the ALNK and designate Tankou Noé as one of the commanders.[20]

Many of the local districts were poorly coordinated, if at all. Tankou Noé never succeeded in establishing a general staff, for example, because the head of the liaison bureau never gave him the necessary confirmation of his nominations. Though the Yabassi district was supposed to be under Tankou's command, he never had any contact with the rebel groups in the area. The equipment he received from Conakry was hardly sufficient to support his operations: 8 Czech pistols. The very few 12-gauge shotguns in their possession they either stole in Douala or got through customs officials. Their money was raised through periodic "dues" from well-placed sympathizers, a number of highly placed government people among them.[21]

Contact between the exiled leaders and the marauding bands of terrorists who remained active in the areas of the old Bassa *maquis* was infrequent. Control of the groups, commanding perhaps 500, was almost nonexistent, as was their equipment.[22] Control over, if not contact with,

[19] Interviews with Kingué and other exiled leaders, Accra, December 1963.

[20] Jugement No. 85, Tribunal Militaire Temporaire de Douala, September 6–9, 1963.

[21] *Ibid.*

[22] Reverend Bijeck, former prisoner of Bassa *maquisards,* in an interview in Obolowa in June 1963, claimed that when he fled from the *maquisards* about 500 were in a camp near Ngambé. Official and other estimates suggest this number for

the groups operating in the Bamileke areas was nearly as rudimentary. The principal division was that between the exiled group and Kamdem-Ninyim and those who gave him support, such as onetime member of the UPC *comité directeur,* Tagne Mathieu, both of whom "turned traitor" and not only rallied but joined the Ahidjo government. Kamdem-Ninyim was made Minister of Health, but while occupying the post he continued to direct guerilla forces in the Bamileke districts. In this, he seems to have been joined by other members of the *rallié* UPC list who later regrouped with all the Bamileke deputies into the *"Front Populaire pour l'Unité et la Paix."* These leaders were accused by the exiled group of organizing their own *maquis.*[23]

Clearly, from the turmoil and competition among UPC sympathizers in the Bamileke areas and from the significantly greater number of casualties and property damage there, objectives were less specific and impersonal than in the earlier Bassa rebellion. While the rebellion was used as a cover for the violent settlement of many personal disputes in both areas, this aspect seems to have been central to the Bamileke case. The targets of the violence were only remotely related to the sources of strength of the central government; in fact, it was just the reverse. The extensive destruction of public welfare services and the limited number of Europeans attacked suggests a campaign intended simply to intimidate local residents.

WITH the sequential development, the organizational and motivational aspects of the rebellion in mind, we can return to the initial questions regarding the significance of the experience already described. Has the net effect of those years of turmoil and strife been enhancement or hindrance of Cameroon's potential to achieve a politically integrated society?

THE Cameroon experience with insurgency resulted in certain gains with respect to development of conjunctive and compatible, if not fully complementary, political action. Of course we must keep in mind the frightful costs of any such gains in terms of lives lost (perhaps 10,000) and property and capital destroyed (about $8 million). It is not my intention to imply that these represent *net* gains when measured against such costs; I know of no way such measurements can be made.

all rebels, Bamileke and otherwise, at the end of 1960. The cumulative figure is probably conservative.

[23] Interview with Kingué and others, Accra, December 1963.

The government's response to the rebellion in the Bamileke districts was not only to make heavy use of repressive means, but also to initiate a large development and social reorganization program. Termed the *"Regroupement en pays Bamiléké,"* the scheme had a predecessor on a smaller scale among the Bassa, but it was actually more akin to the effort among Kikuyu in Kenya during the Mau Mau campaign. It sought to relocate the widely scattered Bamileke homesteads into villages which could then be policed and protected. These settlements could also more easily profit from health and educational services than could the scattered communities. Most important in terms of reducing the level of conflict among the people is the fact that the regrouping constituted an effort to establish administration and government on a new basis among the Bamileke. As one young Bamileke official put it, "The regroupments have also permitted a break with not only the traditional isolation [of families] but also with the encroaching hold of the chiefs." [24] The expectation was that these measures would reduce the conflict between traditional authorities and the youth.

One of the recognized functions of internal conflict is to strengthen cohesiveness within if not between conflicting groups.[25] The Cameroon rebellion(s) resulted in some important gains in this respect. Though the conflict that gave rise to, and resulted from, the rebellion divided some groups it united others and was thus functional in the process of integration, at least at certain important subsocietal levels.

The consolidation of Bassa solidarity was notable. The CNO's use of the moribund secret societies, the intense loyalty to Um Nyobé that developed among the Bassa, all gave an organizational coherence to Bassa public life that it had not known for many years. Though there was initially some resistance to UPC claims, and considerable vengeance in long-standing feuds, the Bassa came to act pretty much as a group. The Bassa UPC leaders were able to turn the rebellion on and then off again with remarkable effectiveness. Once rallied, these ex-"terrorists" were able to command the overwhelming support of the Bassa electorate. The payoffs of their relative loyalty to the state have been meager, however. The massive development program, which was finally launched in the Bamileke areas, was missing from the areas settled by the Bassa. No important

[24] Dina Lobé, "Mission dans la Region administrative de l'ouest, September 14–21, 1962, Ministry of Planning (Yaounde, 1962).
[25] Georg Simmel, *Conflict,* tr. K. H. Wolff and L. R. Bendix (Glencoe, Ill.: Free Press, 1955), pp. 13–55. See also chap. 2, and Lewis Coser, *The Functions of Social Conflict* (New York: Free Press, 1964).

Bassa have been high government officials in recent years.[26] Mayi Matip was once offered a cabinet post, but turned it down. It is hard to imagine that Bassa will long remain tranquil if their "good behavior" continues to go unrewarded.

There is nothing among the Bamileke even approaching the rudimentary level of organizational solidarity and collaborative political action that exists among the Bassa. No pan-Bamileke organization has emerged to coordinate and control the 90-odd chieftaincies. Still, there have been some gains among the group.

During the seminal period of Cameroon politics in the late 1940s, the UPC leadership did have some success in attaching itself to tradition-based structures that tended to span the breadth of Bamileke chiefdoms. One of the most important Bamileke chiefs, the first president of the UPC, Mathias Djoumessi, created or revitalized the *Kumze,* which he touted as the "traditional association" of the Bamileke, but which has doubtful historical justification. Though Djoumessi succeeded in planting the organization in most of the chiefdoms, he used it more to aggrandize his personal following than that of the UPC. As other Bamileke chiefs became fearful of a certain anti-traditional, anti-chief orientation among the UPC leadership, Djoumessi found it more convenient to break with the party. The *Kumze* did not survive the split and the subsequent conflicts on which the rebellion fed, although Djoumessi continued to head a loose parliamentary group of mostly Bamileke deputies, the *Paysans Indépendents.*

Bamileke representation in the central legislature has consolidated, however, in a way never before achieved among their elected leaders. This is a direct outcome of the rebellion, in that the rallied Bamileke UPC deputies and the rest who did not run on a UPC list but who tended to share the UPC suspicions of the Mbida and Ahidjo regimes, all grouped into the *"Front pour l'unité et la paix."*

WITHOUT extensive attitudinal surveys or other measures of the psychological orientations of important groups of Cameroonians, an assessment of the degree to which their actions and predispositions complement each other is hazardous. However, there is some evidence that suggests there is a growing body of shared values among formerly hostile political forces in the country, ones that seem to have been strengthened by the experience of the rebellion itself. The most important of these values is the

---

[26] The director of the Sûreté is Bassa, but has no personal political following among them.

value concerning the peaceful resolution of conflict. No public speech or publicly circulated pamphlet (and in fact no private conversations known to me) have contained any serious appeals to violence or forceful pursuit of political objectives since 1962. Even the manifesto and open letter of the United National Front, which led to the imprisonment of the principal opposition leaders, carefully eschewed the application of force in politics—especially on the part of the government.

Almost every political leader in Cameroon had pursued a course of action compatible with the objectives and programs of the ruling circles in the single party. No significant political leader, other than Victor Kanga, the former Minister of National Economy, has been in jail of late for an offense that is widely considered to be political in nature. Conflict of a violent sort, or even assertive competition, is at the lowest ebb since the late 1940s. This is due partly to a widespread weariness with factionalism, tribalism, and political dissidence, which has for over a decade drenched various parts of the country in blood. This is not to say that all political tendencies are harmonized and fused into an enthusiastic collaboration, but merely that none of them seems willing any longer to threaten a tired populace with any truly active pursuit of their own programs.

One of the UPC directors, Ernest Ouandié, was thought to be pursuing the guerilla campaign against the government of Ahidjo as late as 1968 although there has been no direct proof that this was so. The head of the rallied UPC, Theodore Mayi Matip, and the late Douala UPC sympathizer, Bebey Eyidi, refused to embrace the party of Ahidjo, but their organizations were solely themselves. These leaders, along with two others—André Marie Mbida, the former prime minister and head of the *Démocrates,* and Charles Okala, the former foreign minister and head of the Socialists—endured three years of detention on charges of subversive activities. Mbida and Okala then carried their organizations (only the former was substantial) into the ruling party. All the parties of West Cameroon, including a splinter of the KNDP, formed in 1966 have completely fused with the ruling UNC.

The acquiescence to the consolidation of power in the hands of formerly much aligned President Ahidjo only caps what has been an established tendency. Not only the rest of the southern population, but the Bamileke themselves, have perceived opposition to the government as a threat of violence. This has been so ever since the formation of the group of 18 Bamileke deputies into the *Union pour l'unité et la paix.* Bamileke leaders came to the point of expressing shame in the fact that their region was unique in its propensity to violence, although such an admission was long and difficult in coming.[27] Considerable resentment was generated just a few years ago when Bamileke were singled out as terrorists and when the "troubles" associated with the UPC seemed so only with respect to the Bamileke wing and not the Bassa wing of the party. Appeals to end the rebellion switched from pre-1960 themes stressing governmental reforms (such as the declaration of a complete amnesty, the conduct of a roundtable to establish a provisional government, the removal of foreign troops, and the holding of elections open to all factions) to straightforward and unadorned demands for an end to violence. Efforts of Bamileke sympathizers of the UPC to achieve a general roundtable of hostile Cameroon political factions changed to appeals for a roundtable *among* hostile Bamileke factions.[28]

Another value that has gained ground is that which legitimizes an independence which continues to involve large-scale aid from the former colonial country. Former Upécists, *maquisards* among them, have come to accept the fact that Cameroon is independent, at least as much as the other states of the former French Union. It must be mentioned that many are still dissatisfied with the extent of French influence in government circles, but most dissidents on this point seem to anticipate a gradual but steady loosening of these ties. Indeed, Ahidjo has become more forceful and autonomous over the years, and has incorporated a great many former opponents into the government. French troops have withdrawn and there are fewer French advisers. The major source of criticism of French influence in Cameroonian affairs now emanates from the English-speaking community, whose attachment to institutions and symbols associated with the former administering power, as among the Francophones, has deepened a bit since reunification.

I HAVE discussed some of the aspects of the integrative backlash the rebellion produced. Ultimately the regime the UPC(s) sought to destroy was strengthened. The consolidation of national identity was advanced as a result of this vivid demonstration of the costs of factionalism, tribalism, internal dissidence, and strife. The Ahidjo regime could claim with increasing effectiveness that it embodied the country's best hope for domestic justice, peace, and progress.

[27] Vice President Foncha, widely though incorrectly thought of as being Bamileke, waged a "cold war against terrorism," in which he repeatedly reminded the Bamileke that they stood alone in perpetrating terrorism (Press Release 2512, July 1963). Foncha was fired upon during this tour.

[28] See *La Presse du Cameroun*, January 18, 1963, appeal by a Bamileke deputy and Minister of Animal Husbandry.

15

Conclusions

SCHOLARSHIP on Africa is in turbulence, and not simply because African events are themselves unsettled. There has been so much new literature on Africa to appear in the last few years that there is no suitable way to keep up with it. The mixture that results is kept so ebullient by activity that there is as yet no settling of the worst, or a surfacing of the best of these works. Moreover, the larger body of general political and social analysis also knows a good deal of unsettledness. Theories rise and fall before they are subjected to adequate empirical tests, only to be replaced by new ones which suffer from the same deficiencies and are subject to the same fate. The only certainty in all of this is that the number of theories is increasing much faster than the number of theorists. In present circumstances it may seem to be folly, therefore, to venture any conclusions about the nature and the wider meaning of the Cameroon case examined in this book. Rather than accept the all-too-frequent and easy out of being satisfied if more questions have been raised than answered, let me attempt to peg my case to a number of ideas and theories that were circulating when I began writing this book, although they may long since have been abandoned, for no good reason, even by their originators, by the time the book is read.

The Cameroon experience with political integration calls into question a number of widely held theories about the process of integration. Perhaps the most important is the assertion that political integration means advance toward political community, that is, toward the emergence of a broad and coherent cluster of political values around national symbols of identity and authority. Such an achievement would represent a high level of integration, to be sure, because the complementarity it implies would be self-sustaining on the basis of rather unconsciously common orientations and interests. But Cameroon has made remarkable integrative advances without consolidating a sense of political community, and in several ways which do not involve that kind of development. Thus a range of advances toward greater complementary interactions can be identified which do not rest on the basis of common values or even common interests, but which can be made to serve the need for integration by conscious manipulation. To the extent that the idea of political community is joined to that of nation, we are able to differentiate

363

the mechanisms of political integration from those of nation-building on the same basis. Perhaps the latter subsumes the former (more empirical evidence is needed to prove this), but the reverse proposition is not necessarily true and is challenged by the evidence of the Cameroon case.

The Cameroon case reaffirms the intimacy between the processes of political integration and political development that Myron Weiner has described. It also adds new dimensions to that relation. Weiner described the relationship in essentially negative terms: "A high rate of social and economic change creates new demands and new tasks for government which are often malintegrative." [1] The Cameroon experience demonstrates a more positive connection. As the system overcomes the social disruptions occasioned by social and/or economic change, as it expands the range of social connections and the amount of meaningful complementarity, i.e. as it becomes more integrated, it becomes more developed, assuming no regression to less demanding goals. In the context of constant goals or increasingly challenging ones, political integration is a way of conceiving of political development.

A final general conclusion about the significance of this case concerns the problem of detecting and evaluating social change through integration analysis. It is evident that, regarding the emergence of new super political systems where none existed before, there may be little difference between integration (functional) and conflict-focused analysis. My treatment of the Cameroon experience is both at the same time. The new structures and processes came into being and began to function shrouded in controversy and tension, but patterns and continuities did develop. The meaning of both the continuities and the discontinuities could be fully understood only in relation to the general patterns of values, interest and activity which came to define the system. Thus not only could gross change be appreciated through focusing on the integration problem, in some ways such an appreciation required this. Equally as important, perhaps, is the fact that many subtle changes in the patterns of politics and the nature of the Cameroon political systems were also revealed through this analysis.

A NUMBER of interesting conclusions can be drawn with respect to less general propositions—having to do with the processes which bring about political unions between separate systems or those which consolidate them once in existence. It is also important, in order to fully justify my conclusions about the more general questions of meaning, to sum up

[1] Weiner, "Political Integration."

the character of the Cameroon political systems before and after federation. Let us turn to these more limited points and attempt to assess their more general meaning.

The political systems of the two merging Cameroon states and the basic value orientations of their elites were quite different. Moreover, until the time of the union, there had been no extensive experience of social, political, or economic interaction between the people or leaders of the two. The union was therefore highly artificial.

The political structures and traditions with which the two elite groups were familiar were also substantially different. The political system that existed in the independent Republic of Cameroun can appropriately be identified by David Apter's label "neo-mercantilist." [2] In this respect it was little changed from the terminal period of Trusteeship. French rule of the territory did not develop a truly open and impersonal pattern of government based on authoritative elected councils; thus the colonial regime was neither a representative nor a responsible one. In both colonial and independent French-speaking Cameroon, power was organized in a mildly hierarchical structure.

Power was much more diffuse throughout the territory and various social strata of Southern British Cameroons. Unlike the French Trust Territory or its successor Republic, the political system in the English-speaking territory until federation was a proper if still immature representation of what Apter labeled the "reconciliation system," a system he considered to be a model for the long-range development of the independent African states.

The style and structure of politics were disparate, although less so than the governments. The KNDP tended to pursue pragmatic goals in every field except that concerning separation from Nigeria. The desire to separate from Nigeria and the associated goal of achieving Cameroon reunification were the only pursuits endowed with anything like an ideological or consummatory fervor in Southern Cameroons. In certain circles, particularly among grassfielders, there was a passionate desire to overcome the economic and modern social development disparities between the grassfields and the southern forest areas; the instrument for this achievement was thought to be the assertion and consolidation of the political preeminence of the grasslands through the strengthening of the KNDP and the weakening if not destruction of the opposition CPNC. The style of the UC leaders was also largely pragmatic; they desired to regain a peaceful

[2] Apter, *Politics of Modernization.* See also the discussion in Chap. 2.

365

order, to realize tangible economic advance, to legitimize the regime and party in the dissident areas of the country torn so long by rebellion. The dominant elements of the UC also pursued a policy of north-south equilibration as the captives of these kinds of goals. But for the most part their efforts were directed at constructing utilitarian-based coalitions with southern factions. They also sought to prove Ahidjo's independence and effectiveness as a nationalist leader. A truly mass movement, based on a passionate assertion of solidarity and a militantly ideological commitment to social change, were unrealistic goals for these leaders. Indeed, only the UPC-affiliated organizations had ever sought to pursue such an objective, and they too lost sight of it in their quest for power. The quest, and the need to consolidate order which it generated in East Cameroon, led to a certain amount of rigidity and heavy-handedness in eastern politics. In the western state the commitment to free speech and assembly was stronger and the opportunities to realize them greater. There were many pressures from within as well as without the system to preserve and expand opportunities for both.

Despite the evident disparities of the two political systems and the value orientations and style of their leadership, there are some striking parallels in the development of the reunification movements that emerged in the two territories. In both cases the movement was initiated with the objective of winning a greater measure of home rule, that is, the devolution of authority onto truly representative institutions at the territorial level. The earliest leaders of the movements in both areas came from southern, better educated, economically privileged, and more westernized stock. In both areas the goal of reunification was made the instrument of an effort to disassociate the territories from larger political systems which dominated them and within which they could never hope to have a strong political voice. In the British sector the early reunificationists were able to use the myth of "the Kamerun Nation" to serve the interests of an affronted minority in general Nigerian politics; in the French sector they used it as an instrument to fragment the French Union, or at least to pry the territory loose from the Union.

In both territories genuine gains were made toward achieving the substance of home rule by about 1958, but as this happened competitive groups emerged in each sector to appropriate the slogans of the reunification movement. The process was similar in some respects in the two areas, but it also accentuated some of the existing differences. In both areas the latter-day reunificationists represented northern, less well-educated, less economically privileged, and less westernized populations.

Each group now used the appeals of the reunification idea not to win home rule but to determine who would rule at home. Each sought to gain power or consolidate power thereby. This competition had different effects in the two territories, however. In the British sector the initial supporters had been able to nearly monopolize the elected positions of political power accessible to Africans. In the French sector, however, the early spokesmen for reunification were unable to gain power. The issue did not contribute to a power base for its advocates. UPC leaders, for example, were caught in the dilemma of advocating themes too universal in scope to fully benefit from tribally based support (themes such as nationalism and pan-Africanism), but they worked too closely and were too much identified with particular ethnic groups to avoid the costs of tribalism, namely the hostility of the traditional antagonists to the tribes which supported the UPC. With the emergence of the latter-day reunificationists in the British sector, the slogans of the campaign ceased to promote territory-wide political groupings and became the hallmark of the spokesmen of regional interests. But the reverse happened in the French sector.

From what has been said it is evident that the motives behind the reunification campaign were complex. The campaign represented as much a negative goal—the repudiation of the existing ties between each of the two Cameroon Trust Territories and other colonially dominated political systems—as the positive one of affirming the desirability of creating or restoring direct and close ties between the two territories. But one must be prudent about assigning the motives for this repudiation, especially concerning Nigeria. It is too easy to ascribe this to widespread animosity among Southern Cameroonians for the Ibo from Eastern Nigeria. Undoubtedly many people harbored such animosity, some of which no doubt was inspired by the cultural and personality traits of that nationality (aggressiveness, ambitiousness, mobility, entrepreneurship). It is important to note, however, that this animosity had more to do with the general position of privilege and dominance which Nigerians generally (the most numerous of which were probably Ibo) occupied in the commercial and administrative life of the territory. The fact was, Nigerians occupied the position of the "dominant alien community" normally reserved for nationals of the European colonial power elsewhere in Africa.

We should also note that the idea of reunification was based on positive propositions, although not always ones with simple implications. First, the idea was supported for its own sake, inasmuch as its achievement would restore "ancient unities," i.e. the unity of those tribes which had

367

been divided by the border, and those supposed unities established under German rule. Second, it was supported as a means of achieving home rule, or even full independence, as I have described. Third, it was supported as a means of gaining or consolidating political power for a particular political party, representing the dominance of particular ethnic or regional groups. All three types of motives were positive ones, but only the first required the full realization of political union between the two states. The logic of the second motive actually worked against the realization of reunification, by propounding a course of political development that would probably be compromised, perhaps nullified, by it. The merger of the two systems would almost surely limit the political autonomy of one or both of the two elite groups. The dilemma involved in the second motive also pertained to the third, because what was true for the two elites was also true for factions within them. The dominant factions in each state felt somewhat threatened by the full implementation of the reunification program, because each faction feared that the others might be able to put together a political coalition from among its own local opponents that would be effective on a national level and thus jeopardize its power base in the state.

THE development of the political union movement in Cameroon may have some meaning for such movements elsewhere and for the growing body of theory relating to such unions. For one thing, it puts a new twist in the idea advanced by Ernst Haas that "upgrading common interests" is one of the most effective motives behind such movements.[3] In this case the common interests were common only in the sense of being parallel. There was little collaboration between the parallel interest groups in the two territories.

Despite this modification, the process involved in the Cameroon case remains compatible with Haas's view of it, inasmuch as it involved the autonomous powers of a mediating agency. An important difference, of course, is that Haas based his discussion of international integration on the example of regional organizations or unions which involve supranational agencies established solely by cooperating states. In Cameroon the external mediating agent was the United Nations in the narrow sense, coupled perhaps with the role of Great Britain as administering authority; in the more general sense it was the established international legal order. An important point to make about this process, which Haas ig-

[3] Haas, "International Integration: The European and the Universal Process" (Boston), World Peace Foundation, Vol. 15 (1961), 366–92.

nored or perhaps even rejected, is the fact that much of the efficacy of the mediator lies not in his powers of persuasion but in the internal commitments (to legal procedure, for example) of the parties themselves. In Haas's view even the procedure of upgrading common interest, while the nearest of all such processes between states to the patterns of conflict resolution that operate within sovereign states, nevertheless is a procedure of negotiation that does not involve coercive capacities. The Cameroon case points to the possibility for coercion in processes of interstate bargaining and negotiation.

On the other hand, I do not wish to make too much of the lessons for other union efforts that might be derived from the Cameroon case of interstate political union. So much of this experience was unique, or nearly so.[4] Few political union movements in recent times have involved only two states, and perhaps none which is likely to occur in the future involves any of the restraints, real or imagined, that operated in the trusteeship system.

As I have demonstrated, here and elsewhere,[5] and as Claude Welch has shown with respect to other West African unification movements,[6] the impetus to union derived from a nationalistic impulse for political and administrative self-rule, not from an ideological commitment to the larger unity implied by pan-Africanism. Thus the goals of the movement were incompatible with a full measure of political unification with any other system, even the new ones which these movements claimed to desire. This fact sets these cases apart from those in eastern Africa,[7] in Europe,[8] or in Latin America.[9]

The important lessons about political integration to be learned from the Cameroon case derive more from the patterns of activity directed to-

[4] There are many parallels between the Cameroon case and that of Togo, which shared the common history with it of German rule and division between British and French administrations under the mandate and trusteeship systems. See Welch, *Dream of Unity*, for a comparison of these two plus the Senegal-Gombia and Ghana-Guinea-Mali union efforts.

[5] See Johnson, "Cameroon Reunification."

[6] Welch, *Dream of Unity*.

[7] See Nye, *Pan-Africanism;* and Donald S. Rothchild, *Towards Unity in Africa* (Washington, D.C.: Public Affairs Press, 1960).

[8] See Ernst Haas, *The Uniting of Europe: Political, Social, and Economic Forces* (Stanford: Stanford University Press, 1968), among the many studies of the European unity movement.

[9] See Joseph S. Nye, "Central American Regional Integration," in *International Conciliation*, No. 572 (May 1967); and Ernst Haas and Philippe Schmitter, "The Politics of Economics in Latin American Regionalism," Monography Series, University of Denver, 1965.

ward consolidating the union rather than from those which preceded its establishment.

CLEARLY the political structures of the two states that formed the Federation were quite different. The political cultures animating them were also different, as represented by their spokesmen in the process of constitution-making for the Federation. The differences, along with the political situation and trends which obtained in the two states in the immediate pre-federal period, help to explain the differences in the conceptions the two elite groups had of the new federal order. As the spokesman of regional interests, Prime Minister Foncha seems to have sought a confederation of almost autonomous states. Ahidjo, on the other hand, apparently wanted a nonfederation, one so strong at the center as to approximate a unitary structure.

The contrasts between the positions of the two leaders reflects that between two larger schools of thought about the proper approach to political union, especially when the union sought is a premature one, i.e. when there has been no ongoing history of economic, social, and political intercourse between the potential partners. Foncha's approach suggests that one should begin with little more than functional cooperation and add on formal political (coercive) structures only very much later when the idea of a common identity has become considerably legitimate. The other approach, that of Ahidjo, suggests that one should commence with full political union and use the structures created thereby to build up a pattern of interaction and loyalty. The latter approach is that enunciated by Nkrumah in his famous doctrine: "Seek ye first the political kingdom." It is ironic that Ahidjo, so much maligned by Nkrumah's propaganda, should have been the first African unificationist to implement Nkrumah's views.

The new federal order in Cameroon differed significantly from the previous system of Southern Cameroons, and in fact, altered the structure of political life among the peoples of the Cameroon Republic as well. It structured power in a starkly centralized and hierarchical manner, not only within the federal domain but in its relationship with the states. It is clear that after its establishment the Cameroon Federation fit the "neo-mercantilist" type of political system as described by Apter. As I have described the French-speaking Republic from which it derived, it seems clear that that system, too, was a modified version of the same general type. Thus federalism did not fundamentally alter the character of the political system or the style of its operation for East Cameroonians.

370

Many important changes were introduced in the eastern state, but initially their import was to make the system more purely the same. The impact was quite different in West Cameroon. There, federalism altered the identity of the political system fundamentally, changing it from a working reconciliation system into a neo-mercantilist one, even at the state level, since so much of the state level functions have become extensions of federal activity.

Political forms and styles have not remained static in the new Federation. A process of gradual change seems to have been underway since reunification, which may alter the identity of the system at the federal level. These changes have been gradual enough, and based centrally enough on the patterns already established to permit some sense of their direction. It appears that the current regime desires or feels pushed to become more nearly a "mobilizationist" one. However, because the country has already suffered from the supermilitancy which the UPC rebellion promoted, Ahidjo has not sought to mobilize the masses. On the other hand, he has attempted to project himself in the image of a proper, if prudent, modernizationist. He has favored social change among the northern pagans, whose political emergence could threaten the Fulani-dominated Moslem emirates on which Ahidjo had initially based his party's strength. Perhaps in an effort to avoid too abrupt a change in the north he has also encouraged the Islamization of the pagan communities and their incorporation into the mainstream of the political party's life. In the south and west Ahidjo has sought to build a base of genuine if not frenzied support by capitalizing on the many rivalries and disunities among the southern political groups, by carefully playing the role of honest broker between them, and by displacing the older established leadership with younger and more technically oriented and competent people who owe their high position solely to Ahidjo's favor. Rather than stabilize his regime and secure its future on the basis of an élan, Ahidjo has attempted to dampen political militancy, especially in rebellion-weary southern and central areas. He has catered to the interests of neglected groups for a more equitable distribution of national wealth and growth in the hope that significant growth in the industrial sector and moderate improvement of the economy generally would mollify the dissident but comparatively privileged areas of the Central South.

The mechanisms by which integrative advance was realized in the Federation were essentially structural and manipulative, and potentially even coercive. The consolidation of power in the federal executive was deliberate but was not achieved in a way that threatened the political base of the West Cameroon leadership. This fact may have played a decisive role in legitimizing the federal order to West Cameroonians. No faction in West Cameroon was made to fear for the security of its own true following. In fact, ultimately each such faction came to seek allies at the federal level, and, of course, they each expected to find this through merger into a single national party. How different the Cameroon case was from the Nigerian one, where increasingly since 1962, the federal regime, dominated by northern leadership, interfered in local politics and denied power in the western region to the majority faction's initiating the troubles which led to the Biafran war. Here we have cause to modify Etzioni's hypothesis that mono-elite unions are likely to be more successful than multi-elite unions.[10] The semblance of dual or multiple elites may be important; in fact, it may enhance and satisfy the commitment to equalitarianism which, Etzioni agrees, is also likely to strengthen a political union. Thus, also, I offer a caveat about the role of good communication. When it is not counterbalanced with responsiveness, good communication between unequal partners may disrupt union.

This case may counsel some modification of Claude Ake's conclusion that integration is best advanced by an emphasis on common identity, to the extent he means by this a singular or monolithic identity.[11] Provision of a respected place for the distinctive identity and values of all major ethnic and cultural groups may be the key lesson Cameroon contains for other fragmented societies faced with a problem of integration. Integration in such circumstances cannot come cheaply, but is made considerably cheaper if based on the ideal of an honestly pluralistic identity. This may be as true for single countries as for unions of several. The problem is not unlike that posed by the multi-tribal and multi-nationality composition of almost every new African state. Here again Cameroon offers a model, for Ahidjo has claimed: "it is not by attacking the tribes that we will overcome tribalism."

Cameroon's capacity to use identitive power was considerably smaller than its capacity to satisfy the utilitarian interest of its various factions or to wield coercive power where necessary. West Cameroon paid a high cost in the transition to federalism, but the costs were borne mostly by the masses who had few means of effective protest. Most of the changes introduced into western life affected highly visible aspects of everyday life: currency, prices, the nature of imported goods, weights and measures, traffic regulations, relations with the police and security forces, and in

---

[10] Etzioni, *Political Unification,* proposition No. 1.
[11] Ake, *Theory of Political Integration,* pp. 3–5, 15.

some instances, language. The elite were usually rewarded: more jobs with higher pay, increased prestige as a result of independence, and being part of a distinctive system despite the sapping of the authority of their state government offices. Of course there were also some collective gains: great growth in the level and quality of public and welfare services, especially educational, health, and communications facilities. The monopoly of legal enforcement, administrative and coercive machinery was clearly in the hands of federal authorities. Thus, manipulative and coercive structures provided the main force behind the integrative advance. The strategy behind the establishment and use of these structures was to build up the union first, as Etzioni hypothesized, but it also involved some significant reallocation of powers and perquisites, in contradiction to the other half of that same hypothesis.[12] Also, rather than a deceleration of integration, as he suggests, its acceleration seems to have helped consolidate a premature union.[13]

It seems evident that the Cameroon union was strengthened by a good deal of what Ernst Haas has termed "spill-over," where new commitments to the central (union) structures and an expansion of their tasks is made necessary in order to fulfill the former commitments and tasks. Haas is borne out by this case in his postulate that the greatest amount of such spill-over is likely to occur in the economic sector. Most of the important changes introduced into the life of West Cameroon were rooted in the productive commercial sector, and engendered the need for ever more encompassing harmonization of the two economies until the customs barrier between the two states, symbolizing the persisting differences in the character and levels of their economies, was finally removed.

Etzioni and Ake postulated that the use of utilitarian power is less effective than the use of identitive power, and that in the long run coercive power is probably the least effective of all. The validity of these propositions would seem to depend on how one perceives identity and whether one perceives utility and coercion. The strategy followed in Cameroon has worked, at least until this writing, eight years after reunification. The strategy first concentrated on defining a full-grown political union juridically, so that it concentrated in the central executive the jurisdictional strength necessary to exercise forceful control; the strategy was then to quickly embellish that jurisdiction with working structures. Later there was a shift to a more relaxed and redistributive approach which would provide the lagging and neglected regions of the country with new eco-

[12] Etzioni, *Political Unification,* "proposition" No. 16.
[13] This proposition—No. 15—seems to contradict No. 16.

nomic resources and legitimize in that way the lack or loss of formal power they may have experienced in the process. The apparent lack of clear perception of trends by the West Cameroon leadership postponed strong challenges to the federal leadership, which probably enhanced the initial consolidation of the union. The failure of western leaders to clearly articulate their own interests may have actually attenuated some of the difficulties which the union faced, by delaying their consequences until it was stronger. There were many tensions in the relationship between the two elites, of course. Before long, however, it was clear that the tensions were manageable and that the major lines of cleavage in the system did not all reinforce each other. Those conflicts which pitted the Eastern against the Western leadership, such as the issue of balanced participation in the building of the system, were attenuated and modified by other issues which fragmented the two state elites, such as the issue of adopting a more zealous policy of modernization. Particularly in West Cameroon, minority or local factions could find needed allies at the federal level. Even the rebellion which had wracked the country for so long produced some positive integrative pressures on the system, as most people became acutely aware of the cost of militant opposition and strife and as the violent resolution of conflict consequently lost legitimacy.

Finally, the most evident lesson from the Cameroon case is that the integrative advance every African country desires to make is not limited solely to the road of nation-building in the limited consensus-building or common core-value and singular-identity sense of the term. It has revealed something of the difference between nation-building and state-building, as it were. While most new African countries desire and need both, few have attained either. Cameroon has been remarkably successful in consolidating the state. By doing so it has given itself an even chance for some day becoming the One Cameroon Nation.

Appendixes

Bibliography

Index

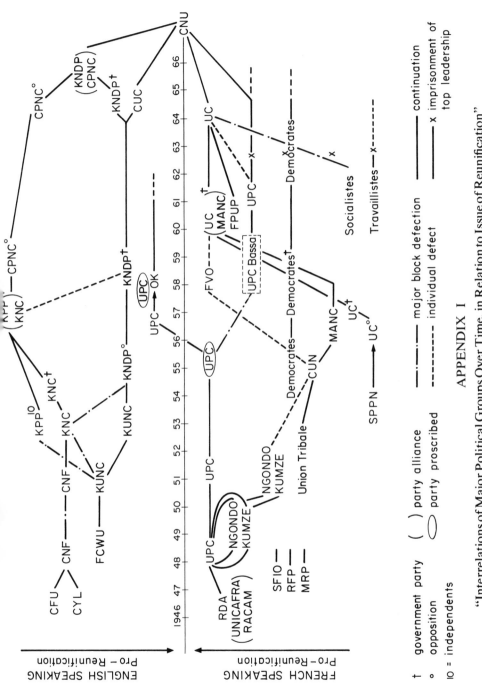

APPENDIX I

"Interrelations of Major Political Groups Over Time, in Relation to Issue of Reunification"

APPENDIX II

Election Results: East and West Cameroon, 1953–1967, by Party

	Dec '53 EHA	Dec '56 ATCAM	'57 SCHA	'59 SCHA	'59 by EC	'60 CNA	'61 WCHA	'61 EC by	'64 FNA	'64 EC by	'65 PRES	'65 ECLA	'67 WCHA
East													
Union Camerounaise													CNU+
candidates run		30				51			40	1	1	100	37
positions won						51			40	1	1	100	37
percent of vote		34%				45%			93.59%	41%	100%	100%	100%
Démocrates													
candidates run		20				21		1	10				
positions won						11							
percent of vote		21%				10%		14.3%	6.41%				
Movement d'Action Natl													
candidates run		8								1			
positions won													
percent of vote		6.5%								7%			
Union Populat Du Cam													
candidates run					6	n.a.		2		1			
positions won					6	8		0					
percent of vote						11%		20%		39%			
Front Popul Unité Paix													
candidates run						18							
positions won													
percent of vote						10.5%							
Groupe des Progressetes													
candidates run						10							
positions won													
percent of vote						4.5%							
West													
Kamerun Nat'l Congress													
candidates run			6(4)**	21*									
positions won													
percent of vote			45.4%										
Kam Natl Dem Party													
candidates run			2	25			35		10		1		
positions won				14			24		10		1		
percent of vote			22.6%	53%			55%		76%		100%		
Total seats available					6	100	37	2	50	1	2	100	37
Total vote (thousands)			83.			1,350	255	68	2,248	31.7	2,685	2,300	n.a.

	Dec '53 EHA	Dec '56 ATCAM	'57 SCHA	'59 SCHA	'59 by EC	'60 CNA	'61 WCHA	'61 EC by	'64 FNA	'64 EC	'65 PRES	'65 ECLA	'67 WCHA
Cam. People Natl Cong													
candidates run				27			22		10				
positions won				12			10						
percent of vote				37%			27%		24%				
Kam People Party													
candidates run				6†									
positions won													
percent of vote													
One Kamerun													
candidates run													
positions won													
percent of vote													
Cam United Cong													
candidates run													
positions won													
percent of vote													
Total seats available				26			37		50				37
Total vote (thousands)				137			255		2.3				n.a.

† Cameroon National Union, composed of UC, KNDP, CUC.   * See Cam. People National Congress.   ** Appointed seats.

Sources: V. Le Vine, *Cameroons*, pp. 151, 248–51; Le Vine, "Cameroun," in J.S. Coleman and C. T. Rosberg, eds., *Political Parties and National Integration in Tropical Africa*, p. 161; *La Press du Cameroun*, April 28, 1964, and occasional issues; *l'Unité*, Nos. 76, 176–80, plus other numbers; Welch, *Dream of Unity*, p. 196; UN Visiting Mission to West Africa, 1958, pp. 13–37 (Cameroon under U.K. administration).

Abbreviations:
EHA   Eastern (Nigeria) House of Assembly
ATCAM   Assemblee Territoriale du Cameroun
SCHA   Southern Cameroons House of Assembly
EC by   East Cameroon by-elections
CNA   Cameroon National Assembly (Assemblee Nationale du Cameroun)
PRES   Presidential and Vice Presidential elections
WCHA   West Cameroon House of Assembly
FNA   Federal National Assembly (Assemblee Nationale Federale)
ECLA   East Cameroon Legislative Assembly (Assemblee Legislative du Cameroun)

Bibliography

The bibliography does not repeat all the footnote listings. I have selected only the most helpful items on Cameroon and those works of theory on integration federalism and political development which have shaped the analytical framework for this study. I have excluded works bearing on African affairs more generally, however widely recognized.

A. BOOKS

Ake, Claude. *A theory of Political Integration.* Homewood, Ill.: Dorsey Press, 1967.

Alexandre, Pierre and J. Binet. *Le Groupe dit Pahouin.* Paris: Presse Universitaire de France, 1958.

Almond, G., and James S. Coleman. *Politics of the Developing Areas.* Princeton: Princeton University Press, 1960.

Almond, G., and G. Binghan Powell, Jr. *Comparative Politics: A Developmental Approach.* Boston: Little, Brown, 1966.

Ardener, E. O. *Coastal Bantu of the Cameroons.* Part XI of *Western African Ethnographic Survey of Africa.* Daryll Forde, ed. London: International African Institute, 1956.

Ardener, E. O., Shirley Ardener, and W. A. Warmington. *Plantation and Village in the Cameroons.* Nigerian Institute of Social and Economic Research. London: Oxford University Press, 1960.

Ansprenger, Franz. *Politik im Schwarzen Afrika.* Köln and Opladen: Westdeutschen Verlag for the Deutsche Afrika-Gesellschaft e.u. Bonn, 1961.

Apter, David. *The Politics of Modernization.* Chicago: University of Chicago Press, 1965.

Ashby, W. Ross. *Design for a Brain: The Origin of Adaptive Behavior.* New York: Barnes & Noble, 1966.

Aujoulat, L. P. *Aujourd'hui l'Afrique.* Paris: Casterman, 1958.

Baeschlin-Raspail, Beat C. *Ahmadou Ahidjo: Pionnier de l'Afrique moderne.* Monaco: Edition Paul Bory, 1968.

Bola, H., and R. Lagrave. *J'Aime Mon Pays: Le Cameroun.* 2nd ed. Yaounde: Federal Republic of Cameroon, Ministry of National Education, 1963.

Brezezinski, Zbigniew. *Africa and the Communist World.* Stanford: Stanford University Press, 1963.

380

Bridgeman, Jon, and David E. Clarke. *German Africa*. Stanford: The Hoover Institution on War, Revolution and Peace, 1965.

Buell, Raymond Leslie. *The Native Problem in Africa*. Vol. II. New York: Macmillan Co., 1928.

Carter, Gwendolyn M. *Five African States: Responses to Diversity*. Ithaca, New York: Cornell University Press, 1963.

Celarie, Andre. *Les Moyens d'Information au Cameroun*. Vols. I and II. Paris: Office de Cooperation radio phonique, 1965.

Chambre du Commerce du Cameroun. *Bilan économique de 1957–1960*. Douala: Chambre du Commerce, April 1964.

—————. *Le Cameroun Occidental—Pays Essentiellement Agricole*. Douala: Chambre du Commerce, December 1961.

Cohen, Sir Andrew. *British Policy in a Changing Africa*. No. 2. Northwestern University series *African Studies*. London: Routledge & Kegan Paul, 1959.

Coleman, James S. *Nigeria: Background to Nationalism*. Berkeley and Los Angeles: University of California Press, 1958.

Coleman, James S. and Carl G. Rosberg, Jr., eds. *Political Parties and National Integration in Tropical Africa*. Berkeley: University of California Press, 1964.

Cooley, John K. *East Wind Over Africa*. New York: Walker & Company, 1965.

Corret, A., J. Gorse, Y. Gillet, and F. Pattier. *Les Regroupements on Pays Bamiléké*. I. Yaounde: Imprimerie Nationale, January 1963.

Coser, Lewis. *The Functions of Social Conflict*. New York: Free Press of Glencoe, 1964.

Crowder, Michael. *West Africa under Colonial Rule*. Evanston, Ill.: Northwestern University Press, 1968.

Currie, David P. *Federalism and the New Nations of Africa*. Chicago: University of Chicago Press, 1964.

Dahrendorf, Ralph. *Class and Class Conflict in Industrial Society*. Stanford: Stanford University Press, 1959.

Delarozière, R. *Les Institutions politiques et sociales des populations dites Bamiléké*. Paris: Mémoires de l'Institut Français d'Afrique Noire, 1951.

Delavignette, Robert. *Freedom and Authority in French West Africa*. Oxford: Oxford University Press, 1957.

deReuck, A., ed. *Conflict in Society*. Boston: Little, Brown for the Ciba Foundation, 1966.

Deschamps, Hubert. *Les Methodes et doctrines de colonisation de la France*. Paris: Collection Armand Colin, 1953.

Deutsch, Karl. *Nationalism and Social Communication; An Inquiry into the Foundations of Nationality*. Cambridge, Mass.: M.I.T. Press, 1953.

―――. *The Nerves of Government: Models of Political Communication and Control*. Glencoe: Free Press, 1963.

Dubois, Marcel. *Systemes coloniaux et peuples colonisateurs*. Paris: G. Masson, 1895.

Dugast, I. *Inventaire ethnique de Sud Cameroun*. No. 1 in *Série: Populations*. Mémoires de l'IFAN. Yaounde: IFAN, Centre du Cameroun, 1949.

Easton, David. *A Systems Analysis of Political Life*. New York: Wiley, 1965.

Emerson, Rupert. *From Empire to Nation*. Cambridge, Mass.: Harvard University Press, 1960.

Enonchong, H. N. A. *Cameroon Constitutional Law: Federalism in a Mixed Common-law, Civil-law System*. Yaounde: Centre d'Edition et de Production de Manuels et d'Auxiliaires de l'enseignment, 1967.

Etzioni, Amitai. *Political Unification*. New York: Holt, Rinehart and Winston, 1965.

Ezera, Kalu. *Constitution Developments in Nigeria*. Cambridge, Eng.: Cambridge University Press, 1960.

Forde, Daryll, ed. *Ethnographic Survey of Africa*. In seven series. London: International African Institute, 1945 to present.

Froelich, J. C. *Cameroun-Togo*. Paris: Editions Berger-Levrault, 1956.

―――. *Les Musulmans d'Afrique Noire*. Paris: Editions de l'Orante, 1962.

Gardinier, David. *Cameroon: United Nations Challenge to French Policy*. London: Institute of Race Relations, 1963.

Groves, C. P. *The Planting of Christianity in Africa*. Vol. IV. London: E. G. K. Hewat, 1958.

Guernier, E., and Froment-Guieysse, G., eds. *Encyclopedie de l'Afrique française*. Vol. V. Paris: l'Union française, 1951.

Haas, Ernest B. *The Uniting of Europe*. Palo Alto: Stanford University Press, 1958.

Hanna, W. J., ed. *Independent Black Africa: The Politics of Freedom*. Chicago: Rand McNally, 1964.

Hardy, Georges. *Histoire social de la colonisation française*. Paris: Larose, 1953.

Hazlewood, Arthur, ed. *African Integration and Disintegration*. London: Oxford University Press, 1967.

Hicks, U. K. et al. *Federalism and Economic Growth*. Oxford: Oxford University Press, 1961.

Holt, Robert T., and John E. Turner. *The Political Basis of Economic Development: An Exploration in Comparative Political Analysis*. Princeton: Van Nostrand, 1966.

Houlet, Gilbert. *Les Guides Bleus: Afrique Centrale, Les Républiques d'expression Française*. Paris: Hachette, 1962.

Hurault, J. *La Structure sociale des Bamiléké*. Paris: La Haye-Mouton et Cie, 1962.

Jacob, Philip, Henry Teune and J. V. Toscano, eds. *The Integration of Political Communities*. Philadelphia: Lippincott, 1964.

Kaberry, Phyllis M. *Women of the Grassfields*. London: HMSO, 1952.

Kanga, Victor J. C. *Le Droit coutumier Bamiléké en contact avec des Droits européens*. Yaounde: Imprimerie du Gouvernement, 1959.

Kaplan, A., and H. Lasswell. *Power and Society*. New Haven: Yale University Press, 1950.

Ketchoua, Abbe Thomas. *Contribution a l'Histoire du Cameroun*. Yaounde: Imprimerie nationale du Cameroun, 1962.

Kilson, Martin L. *Political Change in a West African State*. Cambridge, Mass.: Harvard University Press, 1966.

Kirk-Greene, Antony H. M. *Adamawa, Past and Present*. Oxford: Oxford University Press, 1958.

Kluckhohn, Florence R., and Fred L. Strodtbeck. *Variations in Value Orientations*. Evanston, Ill.: Rowe, Peterson, 1961.

Kwayeb, Enoch. *Le Droit coutumier Bamiléké au contact des droits européens*. Yaounde: Imprimerie du gouvernement, 1959.

Labouret, Henri. *Colonisation, colonialisme, décolonisation*. Paris: Payot, 1952.

Lane, Robert E. *Political Ideology*. Glencoe: Free Press, 1962.

LaPalombara, Joseph and Myron Weiner. *Political Parties and Political Development*. Princeton: Princeton University Press, 1966.

Lecoq, R. *Les Bamiléké*. Paris: Presence Africaine, 1953.

Lembezat, Bertrand. *Le Cameroun*. 3rd ed. Paris: Editions Maritimes et Coloniales, 1954.

———. *Kirdi, les populations païennes du Nord-Cameroun*. No. 3 Série *Populations,* Mémoires de l'IFAN. Yaounde: IFAN, Centre du Cameroun, 1950.

———. *Les Populations Païennes du Nord-Cameroun et de l'Adamoua*. Paris: Presse Universitaires de France, 1961.

Le Vine, Victor. *Cameroon: Mandate to Independence.* Berkeley and Los Angeles: University of California Press, 1964.

Livingston, William S. *Federalism and Constitutional Change.* Oxford: The Clarendon Press, 1956.

Logan, Rayford. *The African Mandates in World Politics.* Washington: Public Affairs Press, 1948.

Mabileau, Albert. *Décolonisation et régimes politiques en Afrique noire.* Paris: A. Colin, 1967.

Mahiou, Ahmed. *L'avenement du parti unique en Afrique noire.* Paris, 1969.

Mamahon, A. W., ed. *Federalism, Mature and Emergent.* Garden City, New York: Doubleday, 1955.

McCloskey, R. G., ed. *Essays in Constitutional Law.* New York: Vintage, 1957.

McCullough, Merran, and I. Dugast et al. *Peoples of the Central Cameroons.* Part IX of *Western Africa, Ethnographic Survey of Africa.* Daryll Forde, ed. London: International African Institute, 1954.

Mercier, M. A. *Rapport sur les Possibilites du Developpement industriel du Cameroun.* Paris: Société d'études pour le développement économique et social, 1960.

Merton, Robert K. *Social Theory and Social Structure.* New York: Macmillan, 1957.

Middleton, John. *The Effects of Economic Development on Traditional Political Systems in Africa South of the Sahara.* The Hague: Mouton, 1966.

Moore, Wilbert. *Social Change.* New York: Prentice Hall, 1966.

Murdock, G. P. *Africa, Its Peoples and Their Culture History.* New York: McGraw-Hill, 1959.

Mveng, Engelbert. *Histoire du Cameroun.* Paris: Presence Africaine, 1963.

Nguini, Marcel. *La Valeur politique et sociale de la tutelle Française au Cameroun.* Aix en Provence: Faculté de Droit, 1956.

Njoya, Sultan Idrissou M. *Histoire et Coutumes des Bamoun.* Translated by Henri Martin, No. 5 of Série: *Populations,* Memoires de l'IFAN. Yaounde: IFAN, Centre du Cameroun, 1952.

Parsons, Talcott. *The Social System.* Glencoe: Free Press, 1951.

Parsons, Talcott, and Edward A. Shils. *Toward a General Theory of Action.* Cambridge, Mass.: Harvard University Press, 1951.

Perham, Margarie. *The Colonial Reckoning.* New York: Knopf, 1962.

Pye, Lucian, and Sydney Verba. *Political Culture and Political Development.* Princeton: Princeton University Press, 1965.

384

Rathery, Gilbert, ed. *Cameroun, terre d'avenir.* Chambre de Commerce du Cameroun, ed. Paris: Editions Diloutremer, 1960.

Riker, William. *Federalism: Nature, Origin, Significance.* Boston: Little, Brown, 1964.

Rivkin, Arnold, ed. *Colloquium on Institution Building and the African Development Process U.C.L.A.* Garden City: Anchor Books, 1968.

Roberts, Stephen H. *History of French Colonial Policy.* London: Shoe String Press, 1929.

Robinson, Kenneth. *The Dilemmas of Trusteeship.* London: Oxford University Press, 1965.

Robson, Peter. *Economic Integration in Africa.* Evanston, Ill.: Northwestern University Press, 1968.

Royal Institute of International Affairs. *Nigeria: The Political Background* (Sections on British Cameroons). London: Oxford University Press, 1960.

Rudin, Harry. *Germans in the Cameroons, 1884–1914.* New Haven: Yale University Press, 1938.

Schwartz, David. *Nigeria: The Tribe, the Nation or the Race.* Cambridge, Mass.: M.I.T. Press, 1966.

Simmel, Georg. *Conflict and the Web of Group-Affiliations.* (K. H. Wolff and L. R. Bendix, translators.) London: Free Press of Glencoe, 1955.

Sloan, Ruth and Associates. *The Educated Africa.* Helen Kitchen, ed. New York: Praeger, 1962.

Spencer, John, ed. *Language in Africa.* Papers of the Leverhulme conference, held at the University College, Ibadan. Cambridge, Eng.: Cambridge University Press, 1963.

Tardits, Claude. *Les Bamiléké de l'Ouest Cameroun.* Paris: Berger-Levrault, 1960.

Thompson, Virginia, and Richard Adloff. *French West Africa.* London: Allen & Unwin, 1958.

————. *The Emergent States of French Equatorial Africa.* Stanford: Stanford University Press, 1960.

Trimmingham, J. S. *Islam in West Africa.* Oxford: Clarendon Press, 1959.

Turner, Frank L. et al. *The Economic Potential of West Cameroon.* In 9 volumes. Palo Alto: Stanford Research Institute, 1965.

UNESCO. *The Use of Vernacular Languages in Education.* Monographs on Fundamental Education VIII. Paris: UNESCO, 1953.

Verba, S., and Lucian Pye, eds. *Political Culture and Political Development.* Princeton: Princeton University Press, 1965.

Vernon-Jackson, H. O. H. *Language, Schools, and Government in Cameroon.* New York: Teachers College Press, Columbia University, 1967.

Vesse, A. *Étude de l'Économie Camerounaise, en 1957.* 2 vol. Yaounde: Section de la Statistiques Générale, 1957.

Warmington, W. A. *A West African Trade Union.* For the Nigerian Institute of Social and Economic Research. London: Oxford University Press, 1960.

Welch, Claude E., ed. *Political Modernization.* Belmont, Calif.: Wadsworth, 1967.

Welch, Claude E., Jr. *Dream of Unity: Pan-Africanism and Political Unification in West Africa.* Ithaca, New York: Cornell University Press, 1966.

Wells, F. A. and W. A. Warmington. *Studies in Industrialization, Nigeria and the Cameroons.* Oxford: Oxford University Press, 1962.

Wheare, Kenneth. *Federal Government.* 3rd ed. London: Oxford University Press, 1953.

Wieschhoff, Hans. *Colonial Policy in Africa.* Philadelphia: University of Pennsylvania Press, 1944.

Williams, Roger. *American Society: A Sociological Interpretation.* New York: Knopf, 1960.

Zolberg, Aristide. *Creating Political Order: The Party-States of West Africa.* Chicago: Rand McNally, 1966.

B. ARTICLES AND PAMPHLETS

Aberle, D. F., A. K. Chen, A. K. Davis, M. J. Levy, Jr., and F. X. Sutton. "The Functional Prerequisites of a Society," *Ethics,* 60, January 1950, pp. 100–111.

Allen, R. L. "Integration in Less Developed Areas," *Kyklos,* Basel, Switzerland, 1961, pp. 315–336.

Andersen, Kjell. *Report on the Economic Aspects of Reunification.* Presidency, Republic of Cameroon. Yaounde: mimeographed. February, 1961.

Anjah, E. A. *Kamerun Reunification, A Discussion of Reality.* For Kamerun United Commoner's Party, Aba/Nigeria: Ofomata's Press, 1956.

Ardener, Edwin O. "Cautious Optimism in West Cameroon," *West Africa,* September 30, 1961.

Ardener, Edwin O. "Crisis of Confidence in the Cameroon," *West Africa,* August 12, 1961.

————. "The Kamerun Idea," *West Africa,* Nos. 2147, 2148. Liverpool: June, 1958.

————. "The Nature of the Reunification of Cameroon," A. Hazelwood, ed., *African Integration and Disintegration.* London: Oxford University Press, 1967.

————. "The Political History of Cameroon," *The World Today,* XVIII, 1962, pp. 341–350.

————. "Social and Demographic Problems of Southern Cameroons Plantation Area," *Social Change in Modern Africa,* Aidon Southall, ed. Oxford: Oxford University Press.

Bederman, Sanford H. "The Cameroons Development Corporation: A Unique Example of Government's Role in Commercial Tropical Agriculture," *Essays in International Relations.* Atlanta, Georgia, Spring 1967, pp. 8–19.

Berman, Paul. "Systems Theory and Political Development," Social Science Research Council Paper, M.I.T. Center for International Studies, Archives, September 1967.

Berrill, Dr. K. E. The Economy of Southern Cameroons. Lagos: Government Printer (?), 1960.

Bigart, Homer. "Cameroon Leader Ending His Exile," *New York Times,* February 28, 1960, p. 14.

————. "Hashish-Mad Rebels Kill 74 in Cameroon," *New York Times,* February 25, 1960, p. 1.

————. "A Test for Ahidjo," *New York Times,* February 23, 1960, p. 3.

————. "Crushing Issues Face Cameroon," *New York Times,* January 25, 1960, p. 4.

————. "Cameroon Terror Perils New State," *New York Times,* January 21, 1960, p. 1.

————. "Cameroon Chief Cites Terror Rise," *New York Times,* January 20, 1960, p. 1.

————. "Clashes Spread Over Cameroon," *New York Times,* January 3, 1960, p. 20.

Binet, Jacques. "Commandement Africain au Cameroun," *Receuil Général de Jurisprudence, de Doctrine et de Législation d'Outre-Mer.* No. 616, January 1954.

————. Sociologie urbaine au Cameroun. Yaounde: Institut de Recherche scientifique de Cameroun (IRCAM), 1956.

Bouchard, Joseph. "Histoire," *Cameroun, Togo* in *Encyclopedie de l'Afrique française,* pp. 51–56.

Boutillier, C. Tardit, and R. Diziain. *Étude sociologique et économique des Douala, Bamiléké, Bassa.* Office de la Recherche Scientifique et technique de la France Outre-Mer. Paris: 1957 (?).

"Britain in the Cameroons," *West Africa,* July 16, 1960, p. 795.

Brown, A. J. "Economic Separatism Versus a Common market in Developing Countries," *Yorkshire Bulletin of Economic and Social Research,* May and November, 1961.

Bulletin de l'Institut d'Émission de l'Afrique Equatoriale française et du Cameroun. Paris.

Cameroon National Union. First National Congress: General Policy Report. Presentation of A. Ahidjo, National President. Garoua: CNU, March 1969.

Cameroons Peoples National Convention. *Plebiscite Message to all Voters of the Cameroons.* Lagos: Times Press, February 1961.

"Cameroons on the Eve," *West Africa,* September 19, 1959, p. 1105.

"Cameroons under Strain," *The Economist,* Vol. 196: 175–6, July 9, 1960.

"Cameroons under United Kingdom Administration and Cameroons under French Administration," *International Organization,* Vol. 13, Spring 1959, pp. 302–305.

"Cameroons' Fulani Premier," *West Africa,* January 2, 1960, pp. 5–6.

"Le Cameroun a la veille de l'indépendence," *Europe-France Outremer,* No. 355, June 1959, pp. 24–51.

Cancian, Francesca. "Functional Analysis of Change," *American Sociological Review,* 25, 1960, pp. 818–827.

Centre des Hauts Études d'Afrique Moderne (CHEAM) Studies, Paris:
Alexandre, Pierre. *La Détribalisation.* January 18, 1957. Study 2822.

———. *Le Mouvement Fang au Regroupement Pahouin.* Study No. 2518, 1956.

Arnould, Maurice. *Musulmans et païen-Évolution Générale d'une subdivision du Nord-Cameroun, guider.* Study No. 2775, 1957.

———. *Transformation des structures traditionnelles du Nord-Cameroun.* Study No. 2877, 1957.

Binet, J. *Va Vie politique traditionnelle des Bamoun.* Study No. 2225, 1953.

Gauthier, Henri. *Nord et Sud Cameroun.* Study No. 3433, 1961.

Lamberton, Colonel. Les Bamiléké Camerounaise d'Aujourd'hui. Study No. 3761, March 16, 1960.

388

————. *La Pacification de la Sanaga Maritime.* Study No. 3760, February 18, 1960.

Merlo, J. R. P. *Le Proletariat à Douala.* Study No. 3263. February 1960.

N'Kamgang, Robert. *Les Chefferies traditionnelles dans l'organisation administrative du Cameroun.* Study No. 3266, 1959–60.

Vincent, J. *Évolution de la société dans le Sud Cameroun.* Study No. 3275. January 1960.

Cercle Culturel Camerounaise, "Débat contradictoire sur la Constitution," *Cahiers d'Éducation Divique,* 2 trimestre, 1960.

Chilver, E. M. and P. Kaberry. "From Tribute to Tax in a Tikar Chiefdom," *Africa,* Vol. XXX, No. 1, January 1960, pp. 1–19.

Coleman, J. S. "Current Political Movements in Africa," *The Annals for the American Academy of Political and Social Sciences,* March 1955, pp. 97–112.

Comte, Gilbert. "La Cooperation avec la France," *Europe France Outre-Mer,* No. 379. Paris.

————. "La réunification avec le Cameroun meridional," *Europe France Outre-mer,* No. 379, June 1961, pp. 24–26.

Cooper, C. A. and B. F. Massell. "Toward a General Theory of Customs Unions for Developing Countries, *Journal of Political Economy,* October, 1965.

"Dangerous Divisions in Africa," *West Africa,* November 12, 1960, p. 1267.

Delaroziere, R. "Camerou, inventaire ethnique et linguistique du Cameroun sous mandat français," *Le Journal de la Société des Africanistes,* Vol. IV, No. 2, 1954, pp. 203–208.

Deutsch, Karl. Political Community at the International Level: Foreign Policy Analysis Series No. 2. Princeton: Princeton University Press, September 1963.

Devernois, Guy. "Cameroons 1958–1959, from Trusteeship to Independence," *Civilisations.* Vol. IX, No. 2, 1959, pp. 229–234.

Diop, Alioune. "Political and Cultural Solidarity in Africa," *Présence Africaine,* XIII, 41, 1962, p. 69.

Dizain, R. "Les facteurs de l'expansion Bamiléké au Cameroun," *Bulletin de l'Association de Géographes Française,* No. 235, 1952, pp. 117–126.

"Doctor of Revolt," *Drum,* October 1959, pp. 27–28.

La Documentation Française, Notes et Études Documentaires. *La Republique du Cameroun,* Étude No. 2741. Paris, January 19, 1961.

————. *l'Organization économique et sociale de l'État fédéré du Cameroun occidentale* (Republique fédérale du Cameroun). Étude No. 2806. Paris, August 19, 1961.

————. Notes et Études Documentaires. *Le Cameroun sous tutelle britannique a l'heure du plebiscite.* Étude No. 2756. Paris, March 1, 1961.

Douala Manga Bell, Rene. "Contribution a l'histoire du Cameroun," *L'Effort Camerounais,* Nos. 210, 211, 212, 214–219, 222, 233, October 25, 1959 to January 24, 1960.

Ducat, Marc. "Du Mandat a l'Independance," *Marches Tropicaux et Mediterranéens,* No. 732, November 21, 1959, pp. 2547–2554.

————. "Les problemes politiques et les perspectives au Cameroun," *Marches Tropicaux et Mediterranéens,* No. 822, August 12, 1961.

Eisenstadt, S. N. "Institutionalization and Change," *American Sociological Review,* XXIX, April 2, 1964, pp. 235–247.

Endeley, Dr. E. M. L. Speech to Resumed Constitutional Conference. London, 1958. Mimeographed.

Etzioni, A. "The Dialectics of Supranational Unification," *American Political Science Review,* Vol. LVI, No. 4, pp. 927–935.

Eyinga, Abel. *Les Élections Camerounaise du 10 Avril 1960.* Thèse, Faculté de Droit et Science Économique, Université de Paris, 1960.

Farine, Avigdor. "Le Bilinguisme au Cameroun," *Canadian Jounal of African Studies,* Montreal, Spring 1968, pp. 7–12.

"Federal Constitution for Cameroons," *West Africa,* July 29, 1961.

————. *West Africa,* September 23, 1961, p. 1056.

Fonlon, Bernard. "The Case for Early Bi-lingualism," *Abbia,* Yaounde, December 1963.

Fonlon, Bernard. "Will We Make or Mar," *Abbia,* Yaounde, March 1964.

————. "Under the Sign of the Rising Sun," *The Cameroon Times,* Victoria, April 1965.

————. "The Language Problem in Cameroon: An Historical Perspective," *Comparative Education,* Oxford, February 1969, pp. 25–49.

"The French Cameroons Today," *West Africa,* May 18, 1958, p. 439.

Frodin, Reuben. "Flies in the Trusteeship Ointment," *American Universities Field Staff Reports,* No. RF-1-'61, February 25, 1961.

"The Future of the Trust Territories of Cameroons," *International Organization,* Vol. 14, Winter, 1960, pp. 152–155.

Gardinier, David. *The Movement to Reunify the Cameroons.* Paper presented to the Annual Conference of the African Studies Association, 1960.

George, Sampson A. *Kamerun (Unification)*. London, 1956.

Gonidec, P. F. "Les Institutions politiques de la République Fédérale du Cameroun," *Civilisations,* Vol. 11, No. 4, 1961 and Vol. 12, No. 1, 1962.

—————. "Questions internationales interessant la France: de la dépendance à l'autonomie-l'état sous tutelle du Cameroon," *Annuaire Français de Droit Internationals,* III, 1957. Paris, Centre National de la Recherche Scientique.

Green, Reginald H. "The Economy of the Cameroon Federal Republic." 1965. Mimeographed.

Green, Reginald H. and S. H. Hymer. "Cocoa in the Gold Coast: A Study in the Relations between African Farmers and Agricultural Experts," *Journal of Economic History,* XXVI, pp. 299–319.

Groupement Interprofessionnel pour l'étude et la coordination des interets économique du Cameroun. Proces-Verbal—27eme session de l'Assemblée Générale. Douala, June 29, 1964.

Gua-Nulla, Dr. and T. M. Ndumu. *The Kamerun Society and the Nigerian Constitutional Conference, and the Unification Question.* Victoria, The Kamerun Society, 1957, p. 9. Mimeographed.

Haas, Ernst B. "International Integration: The European and the Universal Process," *International Organization,* Vol. 15, pp. 366–392.

Haut Commisariat de la République Française au Cameroun, *Cameroon: From Trusteeship to Independence.* Paris, 1959.

Hodgkin, Thomas. "The French Cameroons. 2: The German Period," *West Africa,* November 27, 1954, p. 1109.

Hodgkin, Thomas and Ruth Schacter, "French Speaking Africa in Transition," *International Conciliation,* May 1960.

Horner, George R. "Togo and Cameroons," *Current History,* Vol. 34, No. 198, February 1958, pp. pp. 84–90.

—————. *The Response of Selected Cameroun Ethnic Groups to French Political Institutions.* Archives, Boston University Program of African Studies, November 1959.

"How Real Was Ahidjo's Victory," West Africa, April 23, 1960, p. 459.

"Issues Before the General Assembly," *International Conciliation,* Nos. 493 (8th); 504 (10th); 514 (11th); 519 (13th); 524 (14th); 529 (15th).

Johnson, Willard R. "African-Speaking Africa?" *Africa Forum,* New York: AMSAC, I, 2, 1965.

―――. "Political Instability, Political Disintegration and U.S. Policy Towards Africa," archives U.S. Department of State, Center for International Systems Research, Symposium on Great World Issues of the Next Decade, May 1966.

Kaberry, Phyllis M. Women of the Grassfields. London: Her Majesty's Stationery Office, 1952.

―――. "Traditional Politics in Nsaw," *Africa,* Vol. XXIX, October 1959, pp. 366–383.

―――. "Retainers and Royal Households in the Cameroons Grassfields," *Cahiers d'Études Africaines,* Vol. III, 1962–63, pp. 282–298.

Kamerun National Congress. *Manifesto: Elections.* March, 1957.

―――. *Statement by Leaders of the KNC and the KPP.* November 12, 1957 (forming an alliance of these parties).

―――. *Opening Speech* by the Hon. Dr. E. M. L. Endeley at the Nigeria Constitutional Conference, Lancaster House, London, September 1958.

―――. *Memorandum* presented by the KNC/KPP to Resumed Constitutional Conference, London, September 1958.

"Kamerun National Congress Convention," *West Africa,* May 14, 1955, p. 444.

Kamerun National Democratic Party (KNDP). *Newsletter,* July, 1958, and sporadic.

―――. *Presidential Address to the Annual Convention.* June 8, 1962, Victoria; August 9, 1963, Bamenda.

―――. *United Cameroons-Federal Constitution.* Victoria: Cameroons Printing and Publishing Co., Ltd.

Kamerun Society, "Economic and Financial Problems of the Cameroons," Victoria, 1957. Mimeographed.

Kanga, V. and C. Onana Awana. "Le Cameroun Fédéral," *Europe France Outremer,* No. 398, March 1963. Special number on Cameroon.

Kilson, Martin. "Authoritarian and Single-party Tendencies in Africa," *World Politics,* Vol. XV, No. 2, January 1963.

Lamberton, Colonel J. "Les Bamiléké." Paris, Centre des Hautes Études de l'Afrique moderne, No. 3761.

Larin, V. "The Cameroons Fight for Unity and Independence," *International Affairs,* No. 10, 1955, pp. 90–98.

Le Vine, Victor T. "P-Day in Cameroon," *West Africa,* March 4, 1961, p. 236.

—————. "Calm Before the Storm in Cameroon?" *Africa Report,* May 1961, pp. 3–4.

—————. "The Cameroun Federal Republic," in G. Carter, ed., *Five African States: Responses to Diversity.* Ithaca: Cornell University Press, 1963.

—————. "Cameroon Political Parties," in J. S. Coleman and C. Rosberg, eds. *Political Parties and National Integration in Tropical Africa.* Berkeley: University of California Press, 1964.

—————. "The Course of Political Violence in Africa," paper presented at the Congress on French Speaking Africa, Georgetown University, August 21–27, 1964.

—————. "The Politics of Partition in Africa," *Journal of International Affairs.* New York: Columbia University, Spring, 1964.

"London Log," *West Africa,* November 19, 1960, p. 1321.

"Malgré la victoire du référendum—l'avenir du Cameroun reste charge des nuages," *Marches Tropicaux et Mediterranéens,* No. 747, March 5, 1960.

Mengot, Ako. "Pressures and Constraints on the Development of Education in the West Cameroon," *Africa Today,* Denver, Colorado, XIV-2, 1967, pp. 18–20.

Migeod, Frederich W. H. "The British Cameroons, its Tribes and Natural Features," *Journal of the African Society,* Vol. 23, No. 91, April 1934, pp. 176–187.

Mouvement d'Action National du Cameroun, *Rapport de Politique Générale et Résolutions Adoptées.* 2nd Congress, January 27–30, 1961.

Mukoko-Mokeba, Magnus P. "Cameroon Reunification: A Case Study in the Process of Political Integration," Master's Thesis for Graduate School of Public and International Affairs. University of Pittsburgh, 1966.

"Muted Triumph for Premier Ahidjo," *West Africa,* February 27, 1960, p. 235.

North, E. C., H. E. Koch Jr., and D. A. Zinnes. "The Integrative Functions of Conflict," in *Conflict Resolution.* Chicago, September, 1960.

Okotie Eboh, F. Speech to Nigerian House of Representatives, Lagos, February 17, 1959.

One Kamerun Movement (OK). *Our Federal Constitution Exposed.* Lagos: T.O.C. Press, 1961.

393

————. Ntumazah, Ndeh. *Statement Circulated at the Conference of African Freedom Fighters, June 4, 1962.* Accra: The Guinea Press Ltd. (and reduced).

Organisation Africaine et Malgache de la Cooperation Économique. *Revue Trimestrielle.*

Owona, Adalbert. "Le Traite protectoral Germano-Douala, 1884," *Revue Camerounaise,* No. 8, March–April 1959. Paris: Cercle Culturel des Étudiants Kamerunais.

————. Le Movement d'inspiration marxiste: UPC (unpublished paper).

————. *Le Nationalisme Camerounais.* No. 5 of Série: No. II Étude de divers types de nationalisme. Paper presented to Table Ronde, May 25–26, 1962. Association Française de Science Politique, Paris.

Pavec, Albert. "l'Idée de rérunification des Cameroun," Paris, Institut Nationale des Hautes Études d'Outre-Mer, unpublished study No. 126, 1958.

Philipe, Antoine. "L'essor des partis politiques au Cameroun," *Latitude,* No. 3, 1958.

Philippson, Sir Sydney. *Report on the Financial, Economic and Administrative Consequences to Southern Cameroons of Separation from the Federation of Nigeria.* Prime Minister's Office, Southern Cameroons, 1959.

Piquemal, Marcel. "Le Problèmes des Unions d'états en Afrique Noire," *Revue Juridique et Politique d'Outre-Mer,* No. 1, Janvier-Mars 1962, pp. 21–58.

Radcliffe-Brown, A. F. "On the Concept of Function in Social Science," *American Anthropologist,* Vol. 37, July–September 1935.

Rapoport, Anatol. "What is a Viable System?" *ETC: A Review of General Semantics.* San Francisco, XXIII, December 4, 1966, pp. 463–74.

"Le référendum du 11 Fev. et les aléas de la réunification des Camerouns," *Marches Tropicaux et Mediterranéens.* No. 795, February 4, 1961, p. 318.

Retif, Andre. "Apropos de l'Union des Populations du Cameroun: Communisme et religion au Cameroun," *L'Afrique et l'Asie,* No. 33, November 1955.

"Reunification in the Cameroons," *West Africa,* November 26, 1955, p. 1116.

Ritzenthaler, Robert E. "Anlu: A Women's Uprising in the British Cameroons," *African Studies,* XIX, 1960, pp. 151–156.

394

Rivlin, Benjamin. "Self-Determination and Dependent Areas," *International Conciliation,* No. 501, January 1955.

Roberts, Margaret. "Cameroons on the Eve," *West Africa,* December 19, 1959, p. 1105.

—————. "Political Prospects for the Cameroun," *The World Today,* Vol. 16, July 1960, pp. 305–312.

Robinson, Kenneth. "The Public Law of Overseas France since the War," *The Journal of Comparative Legislation,* 3rd series, Vol. XXXII, 1950 (or as No. 1 of Oxford University Institute of Colonial Studies, Reprint Series).

—————. "Constitutional Reform in French Tropical Africa," *Political Studies,* Vol. 6, February 1958, pp. 45–69.

Southern Cameroons (West Cameroon) Bar Association. *Analytical Review of Constitutional Proposals,* Buea, 1961. Mimeographed.

—————. Minutes of the Emergency Meeting, July 12, 1961. Buea, 1961. Mimeographed.

Syndicat des Commerçants Importateurs, Exportateurs du Cameroun. Note présentée pour la Commission No. 7, Douala, July 1, 1965. Mimeographed.

Um Nyobe, Reuben. "Cameroun, Naissance du mouvement national," *Cahiers Internationaux,* Vol. 6, No. 52, January 1954.

—————. "Cameroun, Objectifs immediats du mouvement national," *Cahiers Internationaux,* Vol. 6, No. 53, February 1954, p. 75.

—————. "Cameroun, Où en est le nationalisme camerounaise?" *Cahiers Internationaux,* Vol. 7, No. 64, March 1955, p. 81.

—————. "Pour la dénouement de la crise-Kamerunaise," Lettre a M. Mbida, in *Revue Camerounaise,* No. 5, September–October 1958. Paris: Cercle Culturel des Étudiants Kamerunais.

l'Union Camerounaise, Parti de *Statuts. Premier Stage de Formation des Responsables de l'Union Camerounaise,* August 1–6, 1961. Yaounde: 1961.

—————. (Report) Congres, du Parti Politique de l'Union Camerounaise, Iᵉ, 1958, Garouia; IIᵉ 1959, Ngaoundere; IIIᵉ 1960, Maroua; IVᵉ 1962, Ebolowa.

—————. *Bulletin Mensuel de Liaison.* Monthly 1960 on.

Union des Population du Cameroun. *La révolution kamerunaise, ses objectifs, sa signification et ses repercussions dans le continent africain.* Cairo, February, 1960.

—————. Abdou Mfonzie. *Les Yankees en Afrique ou l'Amitié du Loup et de la Brebis.* Probably Accra: 1963.

———. Moumie, F. R. *Intervention de M. Felix Roland Moumie, chef de la délégation Kamerunaise,* Second Conference, Afro-Asian Peoples, Conakry, April 11–15, 1960. Conakry: Comité Directeur de l'UPC. April, 1960.

———. ———. *Rape of the Cameroons.* London: Committee of African Organizations, November, 1959.

———. Moumie, F. R. and Njiawue, N. *La révolution Kamerunaise et la lutte des peuples africaine,* Conakry, September 1959.

———. Mme. Veuve F. R. Moumie. *Dr. Felix-Roland Moumie, My Memories on his Life.* Conakry: 1960.

———. Bureau National Provisoire (legal UPC), *La Ligne d'action de l'UPC.* Secretariat National. Yaounde: June 16, 1962.

———. *Ce Que veut le peuple Kamerunais.* Comité Directeur, 1952.

———. *Le Kamerun sous un régime de dictature fasciste.* Probably Accra: Comité Directeur, 1960 (?)

———. *L'Oppression française au Kamerun.* Probably Accra: Comité Directeur de l'UPC, 1963.

———. *La révolution kamerunaise, ses objectifs, sa signification et ses recherches dans le continent africain.* Cairo, February 1960.

———. *Unification Immediate du Cameroun.* Comité Directeur, 1952.

———. *Unification Immediate du Cameroon.* Paris: Imprimerie speciale des Étudiants Camerounais, 1953.

———. *Unité Africaine ou Neo-Colonialisme?* La Délégation de l'UPC a la Conference des Organization nationalists. Accra, May 1962.

Union Nationale des Étudiants Kamerunais. *Compte Rendu des Travaux de la Conference Pan-Camerounais des Étudiants.* Yaounde, August 1959.

Vaughan, James H., Jr. "Culture, History, and Grass Roots Politics in a Northern Cameroons Kingdom," *American Anthropologist,* LXVI (1964), pp. 1078–1095.

Warmington, W. A. "The Cameroons and the Fiscal Commission," *West Africa,* No. 2143, May 10, 1958, p. 443.

Weiner, Myron. "Political Integration and Political Development," *The Annals,* March 1965, pp. 52–64.

Welch, Claude E. Jr. "Cameroons Since Reunification," *West Africa* in 4 parts, October 19, October 26, November 2 and November 9, 1963.

Zang-Atangana, J. M. "Les Partis Politiques Camerounaise," *Recueil Penant,* No. 684, December 1960, pp. 681–708.

————. "Les forces politiques camerounais," mémoire submitted to the Faculté de Droit de Paris, 1961.

Zoa, Abbe Jean. *Pour un Nationalisme Chrétien au Cameroun.* Yaounde: Imprimerie Saint-Paul, 1957.

C. JOURNALS AND NEWSPAPERS

Abbia. Yaounde.

Africa. Journal of the International African Institute, London.

Africa Digest. Africa Publications Trust, London.

Africa Report. (formerly Africa Special Report), African American Institute, Washington, D.C.

l'Afrique et l'Asie. CHEAM, Paris.

Afrique Nouvelle. Dakar.

American Sociological Review. 1960, New York.

The Annals of the American Academy of Political and Social Science. Philadelphia, 1965.

Annuaire Francaise de Droit International. Centre National de la Recherche Scientifique. Paris.

British Journal of Sociology. London, VII, No. 2, 1956.

Bulletin de l'Afrique Noire. Ediafric, Paris.

Bulletin de l'Association pour l'Étude des Problèmes d'Outre-Mer. (formerly . . . des problèms de l'Union of française).

Bulletin. de l'Institute Française d'Afrique Noire. Dakar.

Bulletin mensuel de la statistique d'outre-mer. Plus supplement.

Bulletin. United States Department of State, Washington, D.C.

Cahiers Internationaux de Sociologie. Paris, July–December 1961.

Cameroon Campion. 1959-February. 1963 Biweekly. Victoria: Motomby Woleta, Pub.

Documentation Française. Secrétariat Général du Gouvernment de la France. Paris.

The Economist. London.

E'effort Camerounais. 1955-present. Yaounde: (Pere Fertin ed. until 1960). Catholic weekly.

Ethnographic Survey of Africa. London: International African Institute, 1954.

Études Camerounaise. Institute de Recherche Camerounaise, Yaounde (formerly of the IFAN, Centre au Cameroun).

Europe France Outremer. Paris.

Industrie et Travaux d'Outre-Mer. La Société René Moreaux, Paris.

Les Institutions d'Afrique Noire. série 17, État du Cameroun, weekly. Ediafric, Paris.

Interafrique Presse. (Bulletin Hebdomadaire). Paris.

The Journal of Conflict Resolution. Chicago, September 1960.

Marches Tropicaux et Mediterraneens. Paris.

Le Monde. Paris.

Neues Afrika. Afrika-Verein eV. Bonn: monthly.

The New York Times. New York.

Nsaw Africa. London: International Institute of African Languages and Cultures.

Perspectives Africaines. Ediafric, Paris.

La Presse du Cameroun. 1965-present daily. Douala: Havas Afrique, Agent.

Receuil Penant. Paris.

Revue française de la science politique. La Foundation Nationale des Science Politiques, et l'Association Française de Science Politique, Paris.

Revue juridique et politique de l'Union francaise. Paris.

The Times. Lagos.

The Times. London.

L'Unité. 1958-present. Yaounde: Union Camerounaise.

La Voix du Kamerun. 1951–1955 (?) Douala (?) UPC paper.

La Voix du Peuple. 1959–1960. Eseka: T. Mayi-Matip and J. P. Sende, UPC.

West Africa. Liverpool, June 7, and June 14, 1958.

West Africa. West Africa Publishing Company, London.

West African Review. West Africa Publishing Company. London.

World Today. Royal Institute of International Affairs, London.

D. OFFICIAL DOCUMENTS

Cameroon, Federal Republic of. l'Assemblée Nationale Fédérale, Journal Officiel des Débats de. Annual sessions Yaounde: Imprimerie Nationale, 1961.

———. Chambre de Commerce. *Bulletin Mensuel,* Douala.

———. ———. *Rapport Annuel,* each year.

———. Chamber of Commerce and Industry. *Exposé sur la situation Économique du Cameroun au Ier Janvier, 1960.* Douala, February, 1960.

———. Commissariat général a l'information, *Le Chemin de fer trans-camerounais.*

————. Commissariat a l'Information, *Bulletin Quotidien d'Information.* (Continued from the Republic, formerly Bulletin Mensuel d'Information.)

————. ————. *Annuaire National,* 1963, 1965, 1967.

————. *Constitution,* October 1, 1961.

————. Institute of Education, *Cameroon Review of Education* (Yaounde).

————. *Journal Officiel-Official Gazette,* October 1, 1961 to present. Yaounde: Imprimerie nationale.

————. Ministère des Affaires Économiques et du Plan, Relations économiques exterieures, Comité technique de Repartition des Importations Procès-Verbal (especially February 17, 1965).

————. Ministère des Affaires Étrangères, *Bulletin d'Information.* (Continued from the Republic.) Daily.

————. Ministère de Cooperation, *Économie et Plan de Dévelopement,* July 1962.

————. Ministère de l'Économie Nationale, Service de la Statistiques, *Annuaire statistique du commerce exterieur du Cameroon Oriental* Imprimerie Nationale. Yearly.

————. Ministère de l'Économie Nationale, Service de la Statistiques. *Supplement au Bulletin de la Statistique Générale.* Yaounde: Imprimerie Nationale. (Continued from the Republic).

————. ————. *Bulletin Mensuel.* Yaounde: Service de la Statistique Générale, mimeographed. (Continued from the Republic.)

————. ————. *Enquête Démographique Contre et Est,* 1963. Yaounde: Imprimerie Nationale, May, 1963.

————. ————. *Enquête Démographique Nord-Cameroun.* 1962 (?) Yaounde: Imprimerie Nationale.

————. ————. *Note Trimestrielle sur la Situation Économique.* Yaounde: La Service de la Statistique Générale.

————. ————. *La Population de Yaounde, 1962.* Yaounde: Mairie de Yaounde, Imprimerie Nationale.

————. Ministère des Finances, Direction du Budget, *Budget de l'Exercice.* (July 1–June 30 for each year). Yaounde: Imprimerie Nationale. (Continued from the Republic).

Cameroon, Federated State of West Cameroon, *Official Gazette,* Buea: Government Printer.

————. Land and Survey Department. *West Cameroon Tribal Boundaries* (map No. M260 from data supplied by E. O. Ardener). Buea: November 1959.

————. *Record*. AIL Party Conference on the Constitutional Future of the Southern Cameroons, Bamenda, June 26–28, 1961. Buea, Government Printer.

————. *Record*. Conference on the Constitutional Future of the Southern Cameroons, Foumban, July 17–21, 1961. Buea: Government Printer.

————. Secretary of State for Finance, *Estimates* (for each fiscal year).

————. ————. *Budget Speech* (by the Hon. A. Jua, M.H.A.) July 9, 1962. Buea: Government Printer.

————. *Quarters List and Directory*. Buea: Government Printer (quarterly).

Cameroon, Republic of. *Constitution*. February 21, 1960. Yaounde: Imprimerie Nationale.

————. Ministere des Affairs Etrangeres. *La Position de la République du Cameroun a la suite du Plebiscite des 11 et 12 Février 1961 dans la partie septentrionale du Territoire du Cameroun sous Administration du Royaume-Uni de Grande-Bretagne et d'Irland du Nord*. Paris: Éditions Diloutremer 1961, p. 77.

————. Ministère du Plan. *Plan de développement économique et sociale, travaux préparatoires*. 3 Vols. Yaounde: 1960.

————. ————. *Rapport sur les possibilites de développement industriel du Cameroun*. (Prepared by Société d'Études pour le Développement Économique et Social.) Paris: 1960.

————. La Présidence. *Report on the Economic Aspects of Reunification*. By Kjell Andersen. Yaounde: February 18, 1961. Mimeographed.

Cameroons under French Trusteeship. Assemblée (Territoriale) du Cameroun, Session Budgetaire de Mars–Avril 1957, *Analyse des enseignements tires du bilan d'ensemble des premiers plans quadriennaux et solutions proposées*, fait par A. Mandon (President de la commission des Grands Travaux et du Plan).

————. Chambre de Commerce et d'Industrie. *Bulletin Mansuel*. Douala, beg. January 1959.

————. Direction of Foreign Relations. *Cameroun, 1946 from Trusteeship to Independence 1960*. Paris, 1959 (pam.).

————. État du Cameroun Assemblée, *Journal Officiel du l'Assemblée Représentative du Cameroun*. Procès-verbaux des Séances. From March 31, 1949–December 31, 1959. (Later Assemblée Legislative.)

————. ————. Service d'Information du Gouvernement Camerounais. *Discourse prononce par M. Le Gouverneur P. Messmer, Haut-*

Commissaire de la République, a l'Ouverture de la Session Budge-taire de 1957 l'Assemblée territoriale du Cameroun. Yaounde, March 25, 1957.

————. ————. Service d'Information du Gouvernement Cameroun-ais. *Discours d'Investitute prononce* par M. Andre-Marie Mbida, Premier Ministre, Chef du Gouvernement Camerounais, 15 Mai 1957, devant l'Assemblée legislative du Cameroun.

————. ————. ————. *Discourse prononce le 9 Novembre 1957, a Boumnyebel* (Subdivision d'Eseka) par M. Andre-Marie Mbida, Pre-mier Ministre, Chef du Gouvernement Camerounais.

Cameroons under French Trusteeship. État du Cameroun Assemblée, Service d'Information du Gouvernement Camerounais. *Discours d'investiture prononce par M. Ahmadou Ahidjo, Premier Ministre de l'État du Cameroun le 18 Février devant l'Assemblée Legislative du Cameroun.* 1958.

————. ————, ————. *Communication de M. Ahidjo Ahmadou. Premier Ministre de l'État du Cameroun le 18 Octobre 1958 a l'Assemblée Legislative du Cameroun.*

————. ————, ————. *Communication de M. Ahidjo Ahmadou. Premier Ministre de l'État du Cameroun le 6 Mai 1959 à l'Assemblée Legislative du Cameroun.* Yaounde: Imprimerie du Gouvernement.

————. *Guide Économique de Cameroun 1959.* Yaounde, 1959.

————. Information Service. *Cameroons 10 Years of Investments and Progress under the Leadership of France.* Paris: Diloutremer, 1958.

————. Ministère des affaires économiques. Service de la Statistique Générale. *Annuaire Demographique du Cameroun. Edition Provi-soire 1946–1956.* Yaounde: Imprimerie du Gouvernement, 1956.

————. ————. ————. *Resultats du Recensement de la ville de Douala 1955–56. Population Autochtone.* Fascicule 2 Resultats d'ensemble. Yaounde: Imprimerie du Gouvernement, 1957.

————. ————. ————. *Resultats du Recensement de la Subdivision de Mbalmeye, 1956, Population Autochtone.* Yaounde: Imprimerie du Gouvernement, 1957.

Cameroons under French Trusteeship. Ministère des affairs économiques. Service de la Statistique Générale. *Resultats du re-censement de la ville de Yaounde 1957. Population autochtone.* Yaounde: Imprimerie du Gouvernement, 1958.

————. ————. ————. *Resultats du recensement de la ville*

401

d'Ebolowa, 1958. Population autochtone. Fasc. 1. Yaounde: Imprimerie du Gouvernement, 1959.

―――. Présidence du Gouvernement Camerounais service de la section d'Information. Info-Cameroun, *Bulletin Mansuel Information du Gouvernement Camerounais* (monthly). Yaounde: Imprimerie du Gouvernement. Nos. 1–7 (Janv.-July 1959).

―――. Service des Douanes. *La Commerce Exterieur du Cameroun. Année 1958.* Yaounde: Chambre de Commerce et d'Industrie, ed. 1958.

Cameroun, État Fédéré Orientale. *Journal Officiel,* October 1, 1961 to present. Yaounde: Imprimerie Nationale.

―――. Secrétariat d'État aux Finance, Direction du Budget, *Budget de l'Exercise.*'(July 1–June 30).

France. Agence Économique des colonies autonomes. *Cameroun,* magazine trimestriel. 1926–January 1937. (Colonial Ministry).

―――. Caisse Centrale de la France d'outre-mer (Paris). *Graphiques de l'Evolution économique du Cameroun: population, prix, budget ordinaire, investissements.* Paris: 1953.

―――. Comité Monétaire de la zone Franc. Secrétariat Général. *La zone Franc en 1957. Cinquième Rapport Annuel du Comité Monétaire de la zone Franc.* Paris: 1958.

France. Institut d'Émission de l'Afrique Équatoriale Française et du Cameroun. *Rapport Annuel du Gouvernement Français sur l'administration du Cameroun sous Mandat.* (1921–1938).

―――. ―――. *Rapport d'Activité, Exercice,* 1958, Paris 1959.

―――. Ministry of Overseas France (Ministère de la France d'Outre-Mer.) *Documentation Française. Notes et Études Documentaires,* "L'évolution récente des Institutions Politiques dans les Territoires d'Outre-Mer," No. 1847, March 11, 1954.

―――. Ministry of Overseas France (Ministère de la France d'Outre-Mer and Ministère des Affaires Étrangères), *Rapport Annuel du Gouvernement Français a l'Assemblée Générale des Nations Unies sur l'administration du Cameroun place sous la tutelle de la France.* (from 1947 to 1959).

Great Britain. Colonial Office. *Annual Report of H.M. Government to the Assembly of the United Nations on the Cameroons under United Kingdom Administration.* 1946 to 1960.

―――. Foreign Office. Historical Section. *Cameroon.* Peace Handbooks, # 111. London, HMSO, 1920.

―――. ―――. *Draft Mandates,* 1921. Cmd. 1350. London: HMSO, 1922.

402

————. ————. Nigeria, *Report of the Fiscal Commissioner (A. L. Chick) on the Financial Effects of the Proposed New Constitutional Arrangement.* Cmd. 9828. London: HMSO, 1953.

————. ————. *Report by the Conference on the Nigerian Constitution, London, July–August 1953.* Cmd. 8934. London: HMSO, 1953.

Great Britain. Foreign Office. *Report by the Resumed Conference on the Nigerian Constitution. Lagos, January–February 1954.* Cmd. 9059. London: HMSO, 1954.

————. Secretary of State for Colonies. *Report of the Nigeria Constitutional Conference 1957.* Cmd. #207. London: HMSO, 1957.

————. ————. *Report by the Resumed Nigeria Constitutional Conference 1958.* Lagos, Federal Government Printer.

Nigeria, Federation of. Federal Information Service, Lagos, for Southern Cameroons Information Service. *A statement of Policy by Dr. E. M. L. Endeley.* Lagos: 1958.

————. *First Progress Report of the Economic Programme.* Sessional Paper No. 2 of 1957. Lagos: Federal Government Printer, 1957.

————. Ministry of Research and Information. Information Division. *Financial Assistance to the Cameroons.* Lagos: 1959.

————. National Archives Files. Item 357. Nigerian Constitutional Conference Report, May–June, 1957, p. 46.

————. ————. Item 358. Resumed Constitutional Conference, September–October 1958, p. 41.

————. ————. Item No. 382. J. Broyne Baker, Commission of Enquiry into Native Courts–Cameroons and Bamenda Provinces, 1952, p. 15.

————. ————. Item 605. "Statement of Policy of Encouragement of Foreign Capital," Southern Cameroons House of Assembly Sessional Paper No. 4, 1955.

————. ————. Item 735. Eastern House of Assembly, Debates, 1947–1960.

————. ————. Item 762. Estimates of Revenues and Expenditures, Southern Cameroons, 1954–1960.

————. *Population Census of the Northern Region of Nigeria, 1952.* Lagos: The Government Statistician, 1952.

————. *Population Census of the Eastern Region of Nigeria, 1953.* Bulletin No. 2 (Bamenda Province), No. 5 (Cameroons Province). Lagos: The Government Statistician, 1954.

————. Prime Minister, Broadcast on the Southern Cameroons Plebiscite, January 22, 1961.

————. *Report of the Native Courts (Cameroons, Bamenda Province)*

403

Commission of Inquiry. Lagos: Federal Government Printer, 1952.

———. *Second Progress Report on the Economic Programme, 1955–60*. Lagos: Federal Government Printer, 1958.

———. Southern Cameroons. Cameroons Development Corporation. *Annual Report*. Bota/Victoria, Southern Cameroon, from 1950.

———. ———. ———. Commissioner (Acting) Speech at opening of Budget Meeting Third Southern Cameroons House of Assembly, 1st session, March 19, 1959.

———. ———. ———. *Southern Cameroons Plebiscite, 1961, The Two Alternatives*. Buea: Printed by Authority of United Nations Plebiscite Commission, 1961.

———. ———. *Debates in the Southern Cameroons House of Assembly*.

Vol. I: First session, 26 Oct.–9 Nov. 1954. Buea: Southern Cameroon Government Press, 1955 (only to 2 Nov.).

Vol. II: First session, 26 Oct.–9 Nov. 1954, Calabar: St. Therese's Press, 1955 (only 3 to 9 Nov.).

Vol. III: First session, Fourth Meeting, 12 to 14 Dec., 1954. Calabar: St. Therese's Press, 1955.

———. Southern Cameroons Financial Secretary the Hon. A. D. A. Paterson, M.B.E. *Budget Speech,* March 23, 1961.

———. Southern Cameroons. Information Service. *Press Releases*. No. 1 in 1959.

———. ———. *Introducing the Southern Cameroons*. Lagos: Federal Information Service, 1958.

———. ———. *Report of the Accountant—General Buea, August 29, 1959*. Buea: Southern Cameroons Government Printer, 1959.

———. ———. Prime Minister's Office. *Report on the Financial, Economic and Administrative Consequences to Southern Cameroons of Separation from the Federation of Nigeria,* by Sir Sydney Philippson, K.B.E.

———. ———. *Report on the Mamfe Conference on the Plebiscite Question, August 10 and 11, 1959*. Buea: Southern Cameroons, Government Printer, undated.

———. ———. *Southern Cameroons Gazette*. 1957, 1958, 1959, 1960, 1961.

———. ———. Southern Cameroons Production Development Board. *First Annual Report 1956–57—Final Report. April–September, 1957*. Buea: Southern Cameroons, Government Printer, 1958.

———. ———. Southern Cameroons Development Agency (successor

to Southern Cameroons Production Development Board) *Reports*.
First Report: October 1957 to March 1958.
Second Report: March 1958 to March 1959.
Buea: Southern Cameroons Government Printer 1959–1960.
United Nations. *Industrial Development in Cameroon*. New York:
UNO, 1967.
————. Department of Economic and Social Affairs. *Economic Devel-
opments in Africa—1956–57*. Supplement to the World Economic
Survey, 1957. U.N. Doc. E/3117, St/ECA/56.
————. General Assembly. Fourth (Trusteeship) Committee. Petitions
concerning the Cameroons under French Administration, Observa-
tions of the French Government as Administering Authority. U.N.
Doc. T/OBS.5/7; (6 December 1955).
————. ————. ————. *Report*. (The Future of the Trust Territories
of the Cameroons under French Administration and the Cameroons
under United Kingdom Administration). March 13, 1959. U.N. Doc.
A/4096.
————. ————. Official Records. (by session).
————. ————. ————. Seventeenth Session, 146 Report of Standing
Committee on Petitions. Doc. L/637.
————. Plebiscite Commission. *The Two Alternatives*. Buea: Govern-
ment Printer, 1961.
————. Trusteeship Council. Records—by session.
————. ————. Official Records, Seventh Session, *Reports of United
Nations Visiting Mission to Trust Territories in West Africa*. 1949
Mission. Supple. 2, T/798.
————. ————. ————. Thirteenth Session. United Nations Visiting
Mission to Trust Territories in West Africa, 1952. *Report on the Ca-
meroons under United Kingdom Administration*. Suppl. 4. N.Y.:
1954 (T/1119). *Report on the Cameroons under French Adminis-
tration*. Supple. 5. New York: 1954 T/1110.
————. ————. ————. Seventeenth Session. United Nations Visiting
Mission to the Trust Territories of the Cameroons under British Ad-
ministration and the Cameroons under French Administration, 1955.
Report on the Cameroons under British Administration, New York:
1956), U.N. Doc. T/1239. *Report on the Cameroons under French
Administration,* New York: 1956, U.N. Doc. T/1240.
————. ————. ————. Twenty-third Session, United Nations Visiting Missions to Trust Territories in West Africa, 1958. *Report on
the Trust Territory of the Cameroons under British Administration*

New York: 1959, Suppl. 2, T/1426. *Report on the Trust Territory of the Cameroons under French Administration* New York: 1959 Suppl. 3, Doc. T/1427.

————. ————. Report of the United Nations Commissioner for the Supervision of the Plebiscite in the Cameroons under United Kingdom Administration. U.N. Docs. T/1491, 25 November 1959, T/1491 Corr. 1 T/1491 Add. 1, 1 December 1959.

————. ————. ————. February 1961, Doc. T/1546.

————. ————. Report of the Trusteeship Council, U.N. Doc. Suppl 4 A/3822, New York: 1959.

————. ————. Special Report on Administrative Unions Affecting Trust Territories and on Status of the Cameroons and Togoland Under French Administration Arising out of their Membership in the French union. New York: 1952, U.N. Doc. A/2151.

————. ————. Special Report of the Trusteeship Council. The Future of the Trust Territories of the Camerrons under French Administration and the Cameroons under United Kingdom Administration. New York: February 18, 1959. U.N. Doc. A/4094.

Index

Page references to maps and tables are in italics.

Abbia, 291, 296
Abendong, A. Z., 227n, 271n, 281n
Aberle, D. F., 27
Accord de Coopération Économique Monétaire et Financière, 110
Accra, 243-244, 351, 352
acetylene, *330*
Action Nationale, 139
Adamawa, 61
Adloff, R., 79n
Administering Authorities, 112, 117. *See also* League of Nations; United Nations
administration, federal, 207-226
Africa, 4-7; authoritarianism in, 196; charismatic leadership in, 69; colonialism in, 69; development in, 289; economic education in, 81; elite in, 288; integration in, 289; and language, 78-82, 296, 299n; and nationalism, 114, 287; religion in, 69; and single party system, 233, 280; violence in, 348; Westernization in, 68, 135-136
agriculture, 5, 70n, 95-97, 320-321
Ahidjo, Ahmadou, 175, 229, 236, 238, 314, 315; and appointments, 229-331; and Assalé, 247; and the Bamoun, 55; and Beybey Eyidi, 248; and *Bloc démocratique Camerounais,* 138; at Cairo conference, 289n; on Cameroon as model, 372; and centralization, 169n-170n, 183-198 *passim,* 370; on CNU, 285; and coalition government, 139; on Commonwealth of Nations, 326n; and constitutional proposals, 186-194, 205, 206n; creates Coordination Committee, 279; and cultural integration, 306; on customs barriers, 340-341; and Démocrates, 240; and East party system, 236-256 *passim;* on East-West federal equality, 312; and economic development, 217, 311, 343; and education, 300, 303; and Endeley, 266; and Foncha, 133, 212; and Foncha-Ahidjo agreements, 170n, 171, 171n, 176, 208n; and Fonlon, 308, 310; at Foum-

ban conference, 183-198; on French Union, 110n, 326n; and Islam, 139, 371; and Jua, 274-275; and KNDP, 272-275, 279-283, 309n; and *lamibé,* 236; and Mayi Matip, 243, 248; and Mbida, 139, 248; and mobilization, 161, 371; and Moumié, 129-130; and MANC, 247; on national goals, 288-290; on New African nations, 187; Nkrumah influence on, 370; on north-south cleavage in East, 63; on official language, 299-300; at Organization of African Unity, 289; and presidential system, 191-194; and reunification, 129-130, 139, 140, 143, 183-198; and single national party, 236-256 *passim,* 261; on socialism, 310, 311; and student discontent, 306; and tribalism, 158-162, 372; and UC, 55, 366; and UC-KNDP agreement, 263-265; and UPC, 236-256 *passim,* 358, 361; on world agriculture, 329. *See also Union Camerounaise*
A.I.D., 222-223, 319
aid, foreign, 185, 222, 320-321; to British Cameroons, 104; French, to Cameroun Republic, 109-110; French, to French Cameroun, 107-110, *108;* German, to Kamerun, 70; Nigerian, to British Cameroons, 103-104; from United States, 222-223, 298-299, 319, 320-321
Ajebe-Sone, F. N., 276
Ake, Claude, 372, 373
Akoa, Jean, 246n, 247, 254n, 255
Akpa-Yafe River, 45
Akwa clan, 121
Alexandre, Dr. Pierre, 296
Algeria, 124
Alldridge, T. J., 76-77
All-Party Conference on the Constitutional Future of Southern Cameroons, *see* Bamenda conference
Almond, G. B., 27, 33n
ALNK, *see Armée de Liberation Nationale du Kamerun*
aluminum, *96, 330,* 344

407

408

411

412

159, 241-244, 249-250, 255-256; in
British Cameroons, 130, 132, 144,
162, 164, 258, 259, 261; in East, 255-
256; federal, 254, 256, 267; in French
Cameroun, 154-155, 158-159, 237,
241, 243, 351, 355; in West, 258, 267,
271, 278
electoral law, 241-242
elite, 140-141, 200; in Africa, 288; in
Cameroon, 288; and cities, 214-217;
and conflict of values, 183; and consensus, 14; in East, 365, 372; in federal
government, 226-227; and independence; and modernization, 135; and reunification, 286; and single party system, 234; technical, 36-37; in West,
365, 372, 373
elite-mass gaps, 5, 12, 29, 33, 286, 323
emergency, *see* state of emergency
emirates, 214n, 371. *See also* Islam
Endangte, 252n
Endeley, Dr. E.M.L., and Bakweri, 163,
165; and Bamenda conference, 170n;
and centralization, 169n; and CPNC,
257-267, 276-277; and CYL, 117n;
and elections, 132, 267; and Foncha,
146-152; at Foumban conference, 188;
and French Cameroon, 92-93, 120-121;
and KNC, 127n, 132, 257; as leader of
government business, 104, 163, 277;
and Mbile, 122-123; and NCNC, 117n;
on Nigeria, 131, 169n; and plebiscite,
146-152; and reunification, 93, 119-
121, 127, 143, 146; and secession, 143,
146-152; and single national party,
257-267; and Southern Cameroons autonomy, 123; and tribalism, 162-163;
on UC-KNDP agreement; and UPC,
129
Endeley, Samuel M. L., 284-285
enfranchisement, 120-121
English language, 78-79, 123n, 162, 294-
300
Enugu, 117
Eseka, 125-126, 350, 354-355
ESOCAM, 124n
Etaki Mboumoua, 282n
Etame, Ebenezer, 242n
ethnic, affinities, 67; conflict, 59-60; factors, 40-41; groups, 5, 42-67
ethnicity, 367-368
Etoga, Bishop, 88

Eton area, *43;* people, *43,* 59
Etzioni, Amitai, 200, 226-227, 372-373
European Development Fund (EDF),
320-321
European Economic Community (EEC),
97, 107, 326-328, 331-332, 337
evolués, 5, 153
Ewondo, area, *43,* 229n; language, 297;
people, *43,* 59-60
exports, *96*-97, *328,* 331
Eyinga, Abel, 196-198
Eyumbi, John Sona, 227n

FAC, *see Fond d'Aide et de la Coopération*
Fang, language, 297; people, 60, 157,
229 (*See also* "Pahouin")
FCWU, *see* French Cameroun Welfare
Union
Federal Assembly, 227-229
Federal Court of Justice, 193
Federal Inspectors of Administration,
207-210, 212-213, 222, 342
federalization, 32n, 42, 168-198 *passim,*
200, 370
federal powers, 185-187, 190-191, 192,
201-232
federations, and integration, 28
FIDES, *see Fonds d'Investissements
pour le Développement Economique
et Social des Territories d'Outremer*
finance, federal policies of, 110, 218-
219, 223n, 224-225, 318-347. *See also*
budgets; revenue; tax
Five Year Development Plans, 62, 223n
FNU, *see* Front National Unifé
Foncha, John Ngu, 44-45, 132, 178, 210,
260, 274, 315; and Ahidjo, 212 (*See
also* Foncha-Ahidjo agreements); and
Bamileke, 263, 362n; on Commonwealth of Nations, 326n; on constitution, 170-172, 258, 316; on Coordination Committee; and CPNC, 260; on
customs barriers, 339n; and Douala
Yondo, 133; on East-West federal
equality, 312-317; on education, 300;
and education council, 303-305; and
Endeley, 146-152, 162-166; and federalization, 169n, 170-198, 370; on
federal powers,186;and Foncha-Ahidjo
agreements, 170n, 171, 176, 208n; on
Fonlon, 316; and forest areas, 270; at

413

415

416

417

migration, of Bamileke, 52, 54; of Foulbé,
65n
military, 95, 182, 208; bases, 110; and
conjunctivity, 22; and integration,
202-207; KNDP constitution proposals
for, 172n, 179
Minimum Common National Program,
246
Ministères de Conception, 218
Minister of Armed Forces, 231
Minister of Finance, 220, 247
Minister of Justice, 55
Minister of Labor and Social Welfare,
247
ministries, federal, 227, 229-232
Ministry for Overseas France, 114
ministry of education, state, 300
Ministry of Finance, 224
Ministry of Foreign Affairs, 230-231
Ministry of Health, 229n, 230, 231, 324
Ministry of Justice, 230
Ministry of Labor, 231
Ministry of National Economy, 224-225
Ministry of National Education, 248
Ministry of the Plan, 222, 225n
Ministry of Transport, 278
missionaries, 56, 59-60, 79, 83-88
mobilization, 21, 23-24, 35-37, 41, 160,
234, 286, 371
modernization, 4n, 37, 41, 214; in Africa,
4, 5; among Bamileke, 50; in East, 211;
and elite, 135; and integration, 233-
234; and reunification, 135; and UPC,
354
Modibo Adama, 65n
Mofor, Sam, 227n, 274n
Mofu people, 66
Mohammed Bello, 65
Mohammedan, *see* Islam
Mokolle people, 160n
Molongo society, 165-166
Momo Paul, 356-357
Mongo people, 56
Monte, Paul, 118n
Montesquieu, Charles, 73
Morocco, 124
Moslem, *see* Islam
Motomby Woleta, P., 165, 177, 180, 182,
259
Moumié, Dr. Roland Felix, 154; and
Endeley, 129; and Foncha, 129-130;
and *loi cadre,* 350; and Mbida, 240;

and UPC, 129-131, 238, 257, 354; and
UPC rebellion, 155, 349, 356
Moundame, 337n
Moundou, 343
Moussa Yaya, 282n; and CNU, 285; on
East-West equality, 315; on KNDP
constitutional proposals, 170n; on
KNDP-UC equality, 314; and *lamibé;*
160; as progressive, 159; and UC, 63n,
250, 309n
*Mouvement d'Action Nationale Came-
rounaise* (MANC) 250; and Assalé,
157; and Soppo Priso, 242n; support
of Ahidjo, 247; and UC, 157, 245n,
247, 249
Movement National du Congo, 16
Mua, Patrick, 309n
Mukete, Victor, 105, 150n, 309n
Mukong, 257
Muna, Solomon T., 227-228, 260; and
Coordination Committee, 283; and
CUC, 274; and Foncha, 269-276; and
forest areas, 269; and grassfields, 269,
270; and KNC, 259-260; and KNDP,
268-271, 274, 309n; as Minister of
Foreign Affairs, 230-231; on premier-
ship, 314n; as prime minister, 278,
283; and reunification, 143; rivalry with
Jua, 268-276; 308, 316; and tribalism
Mungo, area, 241, 349-350, 352; people,
42; Valley, 42
Municipal councils, 255-256

Naamdi Azikiwe, 117
Nachtigal, 57
Nagel, Ernest, 9, 26
Nangah, D. A., 95, 282n, 309n
Napoleon, 73n
National Council of Nigeria and the
Cameroons, 117
National Council of Nigerian Citizens, 17
nationalism, 33, 128, 139, 266, 287-288;
in Africa, 4, 287; and Britain, 71; and
reunification, 135
nation-building, 5, 374
Native Authority councils, 214-217, 259
Ncha, Simon, 227n, 228, 259n
Ndamukong, L. M., 84n
Ndoke, M. N., 274n
Ndounokong, 246n
Ndze, N. Y., 259n
Ndzendef clan, 48n

timber, *96,* 328
tobacco, *96,* 103, 335
Togo, *83,* 113, 125, 369n
Tomo Henri, 357
Tonpoba Youta, 246n
Tonye, Paul, 252n
Toscano, V., 13n
Totah, J., 309n
trade, 22, 318-347 *passim;* agreements,
 172n, 185; and Bamenda conference,
 179; and Bamileke, 50, 90, 95; in British colonies, 75, 78-79; in Douala, 57;
 and EFC, 224-225; and Five Year Development Plan, 223n; by grassfielders, 90; of Hausa people, 95; interstate,
 95-97, *329,* 330-344; in Kamerun, 70-
 71; and reunification, 89-91
Trade Union Congress, 342
trade unions, 16, 155, 342
transaction flows, 22
transaction tax, 221
Transcam Railway, 224, 320, 343-344,
 346, 347
transitional period, 204, 260, 312; and
 Bamenda conference, 173-183; and
 Federal Inspectors, 210; and Foumban
 conference, 189-190; vice president
 during, 210
transport, 223n
Travaillistes, 236
treasury, 220
tribalism, 266; and Ahidjo, 158-162, 372;
 among Bamileke, 49-54; among Bamoun, 54-56; among Bassa, 59-60;
 among Bulu, 59-60, 157; and chiefs,
 163-166, 214-217; and conflict, 59-60;
 among Douala, 56-59; and Endeley,
 163-166; among Ewondo, 59-60; and
 Fang, 157; and Foncha, 162-166, 182;
 among Foulbé, 61-62; and House of
 Chiefs, 163-164; and Jua, 164, 269;
 among Kirdi, 65-66; and KNDP, 162-
 166, 267-276; and Muna, 270; and
 "Pahouin," 157; and reunification, 367;
 in Southern Cameroons, 162-167; in
 Tanzania, 16; and UC, 158-162; and
 UPC, 153-157
Trusteeship Agreement, 114-116, 137,
 141, 145-146, 348
Trusteeship Council, *see* United Nations
Trust Territory, *see* French Cameroun;
 Northern British Cameroons; South-
 ern Cameroons

Tsalla Mekongo, 254n
Tsoungie Elie, 250n
TUC, *see* Trade Union Congress

UC, *see* Union Camerounaise
UDEFC, *see* Union Démocratique des
 Femmes Camerounaise
Uganda, 16
Um Nkoda Nton (Jông), 156
Um Nyobé, Reuben, 238, 247; and Bassa,
 155-156; on colonialism, 153n; and
 JC, 118n, killed, 351; and reunifica-
 tion, 124-126, 137-139; running for
 office, 126; and UPC, 59, 129, 154-
 156, 349-356. *See also* "What the People Want"
UNEK, *see* Union Nationale des Etudiants Kamerunaises
UNICAFRA, *see* Union Camerounaise
 Française
"unification plague," 325
Unilever, 332n
Union Camerounaise, 55, 61, 257, 307;
 and Ahidjo, 55, 366; and Assalé, 157;
 Bulu in, 247; and CNU, 284; and federal government, 212; and Coordination Committee, 265, 279-283; and
 CPNC, 262; and CUC, 275; and Démocrates, 139-140, 240-256; and East
 party system, 236-256; and East policy,
 314; and elections, 249, 255, 267; and
 electoral law, 241-242; and Federal Assembly, 228; and FNU, 252-254; and
 Foulbé, 67; on FPUP, 246-247, 249;
 and Islam, 162; and KNDP, 262, 283,
 313-314, 316; and Kaka peoples, 229;
 and Kirdi, 161-162; and Mimimum
 Common National Program, 246; and
 MANC, 157, 247, 249; national con-
 gresses of, 250, 251, 310, 311; and
 northern East Cameroun, 366; and OK,
 262; progressivism in, 160; and reunification, 365-366; and single national
 party, 250-256, 265; *Stage de Formation* of, 253; and tribalism, 158-162;
 and UC-KNDP agreement, 263-265;
 and UC-KNDP conference, 309; and
 UC-KNDP merger, 281, 282-285; and
 UPC, 254; in West, 262
Union Camerounaise Française
 (UNICAFRA), 118
*Union Démocratique des Femmes Ca-
 merounaises* (UDEFC), 349n, 350

424